RELIGION AND THE CONDUCT OF WAR
c. 300–1215

Warfare in History

General Editor: Matthew Bennett

ISSN 1358–779X

*Previously published volumes in this series
are listed at the back of this book*

RELIGION AND THE CONDUCT OF WAR
c. 300–1215

David S. Bachrach

THE BOYDELL PRESS

First published 2003
The Boydell Press, Woodbridge

ISBN 0 85115 944 3

The Boydell Press is an imprint of Boydell & Brewer Ltd
PO Box 9, Woodbridge, Suffolk IP12 3DF, UK
and of Boydell & Brewer Inc.
PO Box 41026, Rochester, NY 14604–4126, USA
website: www.boydell.co.uk

A catalogue record for this book is available
from the British Library

Library of Congress Cataloging-in-Publication Data
Bachrach, David Steward, 1921–
Religion and the conduct of war, c. 300–1215 / David Steward Bachrach.
    p. cm. – (Warfare in history)
Includes bibliographical references and index.
   ISBN 0–85115–944–3 (Hardback : alk. paper)
1. War – Religious aspects – Christianity – History of doctrines – Early
church, ca. 30–600.   2. War – Religious aspects – Christianity – History
of doctrines – Middle Ages, 600–1500.   I. Title.   II. Series.
BT736.2.B25 2003
261.8'73'09 – dc21   2002155172

This publication is printed on acid-free paper

Printed in Great Britain by
St Edmundsbury Press Ltd, Bury St Edmunds, Suffolk

Contents

General Editor's Preface

Few would doubt the role of religion in warfare. It has always been used to bolster morale and legitimise a cause; it allows individuals to deal with moral issues over the application of violence, and to face death itself with confidence. It might be thought that the 'medieval' centuries in particular were a period when such influences dominated, although the Christian 'Wars of Religion' are usually attributed to the sixteenth and seventeenth centuries. Of course, religion has always provided a motivation for warfare in Europe, the Mediterranean and the Middle East, from the time of the conversion of Constantine onwards. It is at this point that David Bachrach begins his examination of the development of religious observance in a military context, taking it up to another defining moment in the Latin Christian tradition in the early thirteenth century. He thus covers a broad sweep of time, from the collapse of the Roman Empire in the West, through its Carolingian revival, into the expansionist wars characterised by the crusades as an expression of religious motivation.

Inevitably, the evidence is slight prior to the intellectual and literary renaissance of the ninth century. Equally predictably, the Carolingian forms of expression of militant Christianity drew heavily upon the old Roman model. Yet Dr Bachrach discerns, within the justifications for 'public war', an increasing awareness of personal responsibility and a need to draw upon spiritual succour at an individual level. He is especially interested in the significance of chaplains who were able to provide this, and shows how they performed this role when attached to military units. His analysis of the 'priest hours' needed to hear a force's confessions prior to battle might lead to many fascinating calculations as to how this could be managed. Clearly there were large numbers of priests accompanying Latin Christian forces long before the concept of a holy war to liberate Jerusalem had been conceived.

The role of religion warfare does takes off on an exponential curve, not least due to the quantity of evidence, from around 1100 onwards. Bachrach focuses on the impact of late eleventh-century commentators, and especially Anselm of Lucca, in redefining what might be called the ethics of violence. But he is also careful to draw attention to developments in Ottonian practice prior to battle. The imperial thread remains strong in his argument, whatever the innovations of a reforming papacy. His final chapter emphasises how thoroughly the significance of religious experience in relation to warfare was expressed in Latin Christendom outside the context of the crusades. Aelred of Rievaulx's description of the Battle of the Standard against the Christian (if rather unpolished) Scots is suggestive of how imbued were clerical writers with religious imagery and ritual. This enabled communities, whether defined broadly as peoples or at the more intimate levels of community, such as urban militias, to express their motivation through observance of particular rites carried out under banners symbolising those self-identifying groups.

Dr Bachrach's research can be extended into the thirteenth century to offer an explanation as to how crusading ideology was turned upon internal dissenters in the Christian West. If killing had become an act of penance in itself then war was made into a form of religious observation. At a time when modern commentators are much concerned with the legitimacy, or otherwise, of the religious impulse leading to violence between communities, such analyses have a timeless relevance.

Matthew Bennett
Royal Military Academy Sandhurst

Preface and Acknowledgements

This project owes its origins to an article published in 1984 by Michael McCormick aptly entitled "The Liturgy of War in the Early Middle Ages."[1] As I read this piece in the mid-1990s, it suggested an exciting approach to both military and religious history by examining the dynamic interpenetration of these two areas of medieval life. McCormick's important contribution, which was developed from his major work on Roman and early medieval imperial ceremonial, was to see that religion played a crucial role in the conduct of medieval warfare long before the crusades and the putative creation of Christian knighthood. The soldiers of the Carolingian empire discussed by McCormick were not booty-crazed warriors inured to fear by blood lust and the innate desire for battle. Rather, they were complicated individuals who depended on a wide range of religious rites and ceremonies to assure them of divine support in battle, and to secure for them eternal salvation should they die in combat. In large part, the present study builds on this important insight by examining the impact of religious practice on the conduct of war over the course of nine centuries, from the elevation of Constantine I to the *imperium* of the late Roman Empire in 306 to the eve of the Fourth Lateran Council held at Rome in 1215. However, this study also considers the important development over time of religious rites and ceremonies pursued by soldiers, clerics, and their non-combatant supporters on the home front. *Religion and the Conduct of War* is therefore both a study in medieval military history and in the religious history of a broad cross section of medieval society.

No study of this type, which considers such a long period of time over much of western Europe and the Levant, can be written without the generous support and insights of a great many people. I owe an enormous debt of gratitude to many scholars who generously have read part or all of this manuscript, in some cases several times, offering friendly advice and careful criticism. I would like to thank John Van Engen, Remi Constable, Jonathan Boulton, Father Michael Driscoll, Thomas Noble, Doris Bergen, Patrick Geary, Michael McCormick, Bernard Bachrach, Deborah Bachrach, Christine Caldwell, Daniel Hobbins, and Michael Bailey. Of course, none of the above may be held responsible for whatever misguided ideas I may have propagated. Much of the research for this study was conducted while I was a Visiting Scholar at the Medieval Institute of Notre Dame, and I would like to offer a special thanks to its director, Thomas Noble, for his generous support, and to the library staff, particularly to David Jenkins. Finally, it is important to remember that scholars do not arrive fully formed from the university, but require a lifetime of help, guidance, and support. In this vein, I would like to thank my high-school Latin teacher David Sims whose patience and kindness I will always treasure.

[1]   Michael McCormick, *Viator* 15 (1984), pp. 1–24.

Abbreviations

Ble	*Bulletin de literature ecclésiastique*
CC	Corpus Christianorum
CCSL	Corpus Christianorum Series Latina
CHFB	Corpus Fontium Historiae Byzantinae
CSEL	Corpus Scriptorum Ecclesiasticarum Latinorum
HEF	*Historia de expeditione Friderici Imperatoris*
MGH	Monumenta Germaniae Historica
MGH AA	Auctorum Antiquissimorum
MGH SRG	Scriptores Rerum Germanicarum
MGH SRM	Scriptores Rerum Merovingicarum
MGH SS	Scriptores
MGH UKK	Urkunden deutscher Königen und Kaiser
MIÖG	*Mitteilungen des Instituts Für Österreichische Geschichts Forschung*
n.s.	new series
PL	Patrilogia Latina
SSCI	Settimani di Studio del Centro Italiano
ZRG	*Zeitschrift der Savigny-Stiftung für Rechts geschichte Kanonistische Abteilung*

Introduction

"Whoever takes a human life is to be excluded from the communion of the Church until cleansed through penance."[1]

Canon 1 of the Concilium Veneticum, c. 465

"If the Maccabees once earned great praise for their piety because they fought for their rites and the temple, it is fitting that you O soldiers of Christ defend in arms the freedom of your fatherland. Now we set before you the opportunity to participate in battles which offer the glorious prize of martyrdom and the renown of eternal glory."[2]

Guibert of Nogent's *God's Deeds through the Franks*, c. 1108–1112

In the first century A.D., the Roman army officer Onasander noted in his military handbook that soldiers who believed that they had the support of the gods fought more bravely than those who did not.[3] In making this observation, Onasander was simply recognizing a centuries-long phenomenon in which religious preparations by western armies and by the communities that supported them, that is the "home front," were intended to obtain divine aid in order to secure military victory. Thus, the story recounted in Joshua (6.3–4) of the Hebrews marching seven times around the city of Jericho served as a reminder to generations of Israelite warriors and their Judeo-Christian posterity that God could and would aid them in battle – if the people were worthy of this support.[4] Similarly, pre-battle sacrifices and the taking of omens confirmed for Greek soldiers the will of the Gods and encouraged them to fight bravely. In his *Anabasis*, Xenophon (born c. 430 B.C.) emphasized that before the battle of Cunaxa (401 B.C.), the Persian pretender Cyrus had the positive results of priests' auguries publicized in order to raise the morale of his Greek mercenary troops.[5] According to Livy, the Roman defeats at the hands of Hannibal during the Second Punic War (218–202 B.C.) were the result of the failure by public officials to fulfill their obligations to the Roman gods. As a consequence, massive games were held in honor of Jupiter and new temples were built at state

---

[1] *Concilium Veneticum*, ed. J.P. Mansi in *Sacrorum Conciliorum nova et amplissima collectio* 7 (Florence, 1762), col. 953.

[2] Guibert of Nogent, *Gesta Dei per Francos*, Recueil des Historiens des Croisades: Historiens Occidentaux, 5 vols. (Paris, 1844–95), IV: 138.

[3] Onasander, *Strategikos*, 10.25–27, ed. B.G. Teubner (Leipzig, 1860).

[4] The religious underpinnings of Israelite warfare have been discussed in detail by James A. Aho, *Religious Mythology and the Art of War: Comparative Religious Symbolisms of Military Violence* (Westport, 1981), pp. 165–81. See also, Robert Carroll, "War in the Hebrew Bible," in *War and Society in the Greek World*, ed. John Rich and Graham Shipley (London, 1993), pp. 25–44; and Doyne Dawson, *The Origins of Western Warfare: Militarism and Morality in the Ancient World* (Boulder, 1996).

[5] Xenophon, *Anabasis*, 1.8.15.

expense to worship Venus in order to rectify this problem.[6] For his part, Virgil stressed the eternal benefits to be earned by those who died in the service of the *res publica*, indicating that they would spend eternity in Elysium in the company of priests, prophets, and all those who made life better through their good works.[7]

But what of the Christian world? What role did religion play in the conduct of wars fought by those whose faith began as an ostentatiously pacifist cult opposed not only to all forms of bloodshed, but also to the apparatus of religious rites that undergirded the province of Mars? The early Christians were fully aware that religion played a crucial role in the conduct of pagan warfare. Indeed, it was the pagan religious practices of the Roman army, as much as the need for soldiers to commit homicide in the course of their duties, which offended the sensitivities of pacifist Christian writers such as Tertullian in the age before the accession of Emperor Constantine I.[8] This Christian apologist condemned his coreligionists for serving in the Roman army because, as he emphasized, "the camp religion of the Romans is all through a worship of the standards, a setting of the standards above all gods."[9]

Nevertheless, as the two quotations at the beginning of this Introduction suggest, Christian attitudes toward war changed dramatically over time. The followers of the Prince of Peace eventually developed doctrines that not only permitted but even encouraged and glorified Christian participants in holy wars fought in defense of the church and the faith. These questions have received extensive attention from scholars.[10] What is less well understood, however, is the place of Christian religion within the conduct of war. Did Christians see their God as a force on the battlefield? How did Christian soldiers reconcile their obligation to kill the enemy with the stain of mortal sin caused by the act of homicide? What relationship, if any, was there between the increasing participation of Christians in the army and developments in Christian doctrine and practice?

This study seeks to answer these and related questions through an investigation of the dynamic interpenetration between wartime religious practices among Christian soldiers, priests, and their non-combatant supporters on the one hand, and the general transformation of Christian doctrine and practices on the other that occurred during the period c. 300–1215. As a study in the religious and the

---

6 Livy, *Ab condita urbe*, 22.9.9–10.

7 Virgil, *Aeneid*, 6.660.

8 Concerning Tertullian's hostility to the religious practices of the Roman army, see John Helgeland, "Roman Army Religion," *Aufstieg und Niedergang der Römischen Welt II Principat 16.2* (Berlin, 1978), pp. 1470–1505, here p. 1476.

9 The Latin text is from Tertullian, *Apologeticum*, 16.8, *religio Romanorum tota castrensis signa veneratur . . . signa omnibus deis praeponit*. I have used here Helgeland's translation from "Roman Army Religion," p. 1476.

10 Christian just war theory and the related question of Christian pacifism have received extensive attention from scholars. See, for example, C.J. Cadoux, *The Early Christian Attitude to War: A Contribution to the History of Christian Ethics* (New York, 1982); Frederick H. Russell, *The Just War in the Middle Ages* (Cambridge, 1975); and Roland H. Bainton, *Christian Attitudes toward War and Peace* (New York, 1960).

military history of Late Antiquity and the Middle Ages, this work seeks both to identify developments in wartime religious thought and practice over time, and to understand the roles played by Christianity in the conduct of war, on the battlefield and on the home front.

This volume covers an enormous period of time, some nine centuries, beginning with the age of Emperor Constantine I and ending just before the Fourth Lateran Council (1215). Constantine's elevation as emperor in 306 by his troops in Britain, his issue of the Edict of Toleration in 313, and the subsequent promotion of Christianity as the state cult created formidable challenges for Christian leaders. They were now forced to reconcile Christianity's pacifist inheritance with the responsibilities of administering an empire founded and sustained in war. Thus, the early fourth century marks a crucial point of departure for a study of wartime Christian religious thought and practice. The Fourth Lateran Council, called together in 1215 by Pope Innocent III, was the most important religious assembly during the entire Middle Ages, and marks a watershed period in the history of the papacy, centralized control over religious practice, the development of national churches, and reform movements epitomized by the Franciscan and Dominican orders. Consequently, it provides a useful if not necessary concluding point for this study.

Because of the great sweep of time covered here, a long *durée* approach that I think is justified by the benefits obtained through the observation of incremental change over time, it has been necessary to highlight certain periods and regions over others. The decision to focus in this study on the core lands of Europe – modern France, Germany, Italy, the Low Countries, and England – has been determined by the greater survival from these regions of sources that bear on the questions of wartime religious behavior and thought. Thus, for example, it is possible to say a great deal more about the religious practices of Christian soldiers in the tenth-century kingdom of Germany than it is about their contemporaries in Scotland, Hungary, or Iberia. Similarly, in considering the religious behavior and beliefs of crusaders, this study benefits from a much wider corpus of sources for the First Crusade (1095–1099) than for any of the later crusade campaigns.

This work is further limited in scope to an examination of wartime religious behavior and thought that is considered through the prism of the experiences of lay soldiers and religious doctrines promulgated on their behalf. The foundation of the militant monastic orders, including the Templars, Hospitallers, and Teutonic Knights, over the course of the twelfth and thirteenth centuries, both reflected and furthered dramatic developments in contemporary Christian doctrine and wartime religious practice. However, the military orders are of such importance, and their history and historiography is so complex, that they would require an entire study of their own in order to do them justice.

Finally, I have intended this volume, primarily, to consider religious behavior, and the military and religious thought and expectations that undergirded this behavior within the context of late antique and medieval warfare. Nevertheless, the primary focus of this volume on lay people, their religious practices, developments in their practice, and the religious ideology that supported these developments, may permit this study to serve as a basis for further research into the more general problem of lay religiosity in the period before 1215. In this context, I suggest two general hermeneutic principles: first, the exigencies of war almost certainly called forth a higher intensity of religious devotion and practice among Christian soldiers, priests, and their supporters than might be expected during periods of peace. Secondly, wartime religious practice and the belief system that undergirded these practices overlapped consistently with ordinary lay religious practice and belief. To make this point somewhat differently, it would seem highly unlikely that soldiers who faced the possibility of being called on to kill or to die in battle would turn to new or fundamentally unfamiliar rites in this moment of exceptional stress.

The first chapter begins with a brief consideration of pagan military religious practice in the late Roman army before the Edict of Toleration (313). It then examines the impact of Constantine's promotion of Christianity and its eventual rise to the status of the state cult on the conduct of military-religious rites in the armies of the late Roman empire and the early medieval successor states in Anglo-Saxon Britain, Visigothic Spain, and the Merovingian *regna* in *Francia*. The final section of the chapter examines the development of Christian attitudes toward homicide and the reconciliation of pacifism with the spiritual needs of soldiers in an increasingly Christian army and society.

Chapter 2 deals with the question of wartime religion in the *regnum Francorum* c. 750–c. 900. The focus of the first and second sections is on the organization of the "liturgies of war" at the level of the kingdom and the army respectively. An effort is made first to identify the range of religious rites and ceremonies carried out by the soldiers and on their behalf, and then to determine the impact of these religious behaviors – and the belief system supporting them – on the actual conduct of war. The final section of Chapter 2 considers the introduction of individual religious preparations of Christian soldiers for battle, particularly the linked rites of confession and the acceptance of penance.

The third chapter addresses the problem of wartime religious behavior and belief in the post-Carolingian/pre-crusade world, c. 900–1095. As in Chapter 2, these religious rites and ceremonies are considered at three levels: the society as a whole, the army, and the individual soldier. This period witnessed considerable innovation at each of the three levels of wartime religious practice brought about, in part, by the new political conditions facing post-imperial Europe, and, in part, by developments in Christian doctrine and practice. Of particular significance in this context was the initial development during the second half of the twelfth century of a radical transformation in Christian attitudes toward homicide and war, dealt with in the final section of the chapter, which contributed ultimately to the Christian doctrine of crusade and holy war.

Chapter 4 develops the problem of wartime religion within the context of the Christian crusading movement during the period 1095–1215. The chapter begins with an examination of the First Crusade from its origins at Clermont in 1095 to the final conquest of Jerusalem in July 1099. The second half of the chapter considers four further crusade campaigns conducted over the course of the twelfth and early thirteenth centuries: the Lisbon expedition (1147–1148), the crusade of Emperor Frederick I (1189–1190), the Fourth Crusade (1203–1204), and the Albigensian Crusade (1213). The focus of this chapter is on identifying continuities and developments in the religious practices of crusaders as contrasted with soldiers in pre-crusade Europe, and on the continuing impact of religion on the conduct of what were ostensibly holy wars.

The fifth chapter serves as a companion to the fourth, and examines the religious practices of soldiers and their supporters within the context of non-crusading or secular wars fought in Europe during the period 1095–1215. Because of the greater density of surviving source material in this period, Chapter 5 focuses on individual campaigns and battles in an effort to identify both the impact of religion on the conduct of war, and the range of religious rites being celebrated in various regions of the West. The case-studies detailed in this chapter are drawn from the Anglo-Norman state, the kingdom of France, and the German Empire, including both northern Italy and the Low Countries.

1

The Religion of War in Late Antiquity c. 300–c. 750

Introduction

Late Antiquity, considered here as the period between the Roman civil wars of the early fourth century and the firm establishment of the Carolingian dynasty in Francia during the mid-eighth, witnessed the continuation of the millennia-long intersection of religion with the conduct of western warfare. Nevertheless, the gradual elevation of Christianity – an ostentatiously pacifist cult – to the status of the state religion of the Roman Empire required important shifts in the traditional Roman religion of war, leading eventually to the abolition of paganism in the armies as in the societies of the late empire and its successor states. The new status of Christianity in the fifth century as the imperial state religion and the integration of Christian rites into wartime religion also forced important changes in the ideology and practice of this faith, particularly Christian attitudes toward homicide. This chapter will trace the development of wartime religious rites practiced both by soldiers and by their civilian supporters in the period c. 300–c. 750, including such important practices as prayer, the celebration of mass, and the use of relics. The chapter will conclude with a consideration of the ways in which Christian teaching and practice changed over time to accommodate the new status of Christianity as the religion of the state and army.

Traditional Army Religion and the Constantinian Augmentation

In 306, when Constantine the Great was acclaimed Augustus by his father's troops in Britain, he inherited an army that was endowed with a centuries-long military-religious tradition. For hundreds of years, upon entering military service Roman soldiers had sworn sacred oaths of loyalty to the gods and to the emperor, and renewed these oaths on a daily and yearly schedule. They partici-pated in a regular round of cultic observances and sacrifices organized and led by their officers. The unit standards and eagles that led the army into battle were understood by the soldiers to be imbued with sacred power (*numen*) from which Roman fighting men drew strength and courage. At an even broader level, the Roman state held public religious celebrations intended to secure the support of the gods for Roman military victories in the field.[1]

---

[1]   Alfred Domaszewski, "Die Religion des römischen Heeres," *Westdeutsche Zeitschrift für*

Roman military officers understood that these religious practices served a variety of useful military functions. Perhaps most importantly, the morale of the Roman troops depended in part on their belief that the gods were on their side.[2] The men were encouraged to believe not only that they could obtain divine aid in securing victory but also that death in battle would bring honor to their families and benefits in the afterlife. As Virgil emphasized in the *Aeneid*, those soldiers who gave their lives for the fatherland found themselves in Elysium alongside the priests, prophets, and all of those who made life better through their good works.[3] The shared religious experiences and expectations of the Roman soldiers also served to shape their sense of themselves as part of a cohesive group.[4] Finally, army rites gave religious sanction to the maintenance of military discipline. One particularly important element of army religion that embodied the religious undergirding of discipline was the sacralization of the army camp, which soldiers were to defend with their lives.[5]

Constantine's reversal of the great Diocletian military purges of the late third century paved the way for the gradual reintegration of Christian soldiers into the imperial army but did not alter the critical role of religion in Roman military organization. Constantine and his Christian successors were fully aware of the exceptionally important role that religion had played and must continue to play in motivating soldiers to fight and die for the *res publica*. Nevertheless, Constantine's own adoption of Christian practices and the gradual elevation of Christianity over the course of the fourth century to the status of the state religion required a new *modus vivendi* between the formerly pacifist cult and the newly Christian empire.[6] Constantine and his successors, therefore, instituted

---

Geschichte und Kunst 14 (1895), pp. 1–128 [repr. in *Aufsätze zur römischen Heeresgeschichte* (Darmstadt, 1972)] remains a fundamental work in this area. Also see, Eric Birely, "Religion of the Roman Army: 1885–1977," in *Aufstieg und Niedergang der Römischen Welt II Principat* 16.2 (Berlin, 1978), pp. 1506–41; John Helgeland, "Roman Army Religion," in *ibid.*, pp. 1470–1505; Michael P. Speidel, *The Religion of Iuppiter Dolichenus in the Roman Army* (Leiden, 1978); Géza Alföldy, *Römische Heeresgeschichte Beiträge 1962–1985* (Amsterdam, 1987), pp. 262–8; and Brian Campbell, *The Roman Army, 31 BC–AD 337: A Sourcebook* (London, 1994), pp. 127–36.

2   On this point, see Helgeland, "Roman Army Religion," p. 1471; Campbell, *The Roman Army*, p. 127; and Graham Webster, *The Roman Imperial Army of the First and Second Centuries A.D.*, 3rd edn (Totowa, 1985), p. 275.

3   Virgil, *Aeneid*, 6.660.

4   Helgeland, "Roman Army Religion," p. 1472.

5   Ramsay Macmullen, *Soldier and Civilian in the Later Roman Empire* (Cambridge, 1967), pp. 174–5, notes that the development of fixed rituals for all manner of military activities – rituals that were often endowed with religious significance – served to alleviate anxiety among the soldiers. Concerning the religious nature of the army oaths and their value in reminding the soldiers of the essentially religious function of military service, see Birely, "Religion of the Roman Army," pp. 1509–16.

6   There was a concomitant accretion of Christian ideas and practices in other aspects of formal imperial ceremonial. In his exceptionally important study *Eternal Victory: Triumphal Rulership in Late Antiquity, Byzantium, and the Early Medieval West* (Cambridge, 1986), Michael McCormick draws attention to the gradual nature of Constantine's efforts at Christianization and the enduring role of traditional imperial symbolism.

reforms that took into account Christian sensitivities while at the same time maintaining the essential forms of traditional military religion.

In general, this meant that the imperial government adapted older religious practices to fit within a Christian paradigm, or simply gave a Christian overlay to long-standing religious traditions. For example, the imperial government modified the centuries-old oath of military service so that it would be understood as Christian. The basic elements of the military oath were established during the Roman republic and remained virtually unchanged up through the fourth century. Soldiers swore to be faithful to the emperor, never to desert from military service, and to be willing to die for the good of the Roman state. Constantine and his successors maintained the army oath of service according to its ancient form, only adding a clause in which soldiers swore to carry out their duties by God, Christ, and the Holy Spirit.[7]

In a similar manner, the traditional military standards of the Roman army, which had been compromised by their long association with pagan religious rites, were replaced gradually by the Chi-Rho symbol of the new faith. In his *Life of Constantine*, Bishop Eusebius of Caesarea repeatedly stressed that the first Christian emperor had introduced the Chi-Rho as the new insignia for battle standards because this was the sign that he had seen in heaven before his battle against Maxentius at the Milvian bridge.[8] Eusebius was, of course, a vigorous Christian apologist, and his claim that the new Chi-Rho banners were introduced wholesale to replace the "golden images" formerly used to lead the troops into battle must be read in this light.[9] Nevertheless, it is clear from surviving contemporary images on coins and other artifacts that at least some battle standards were distinguished by the Christian sign, as were shields used by soldiers in Roman army units.[10] Indeed, Bishop Ambrose of Milan (374–397) included a battlefield prayer in his work *De fide* that claimed, "there are no

---

[7] Vegetius, *Epitoma Rei Militari* 2.5, ed. Alf Önnerfors (Stuttgart, 1995), *Iurant autem per Deum et Christum et Sanctum Spiritum et per maiestam imperatoris . . . iurant autem milites omnia se strenue facturos quae praeceperit imperator, nunquam deserturos militiam nec mortem recusaturos pro Romana republica.* The development of the oath of service can be seen in a later fourth-century military manual *Epitoma Rei Militaris*, written by Publius Flavius Vegetius Renatus (c. 390), who served as an officer of the imperial court in the West. Concerning the dating of this work, see Walter Goffart, "The Date and Purpose of Vegetius' *De Re Militari*," in *Rome's Fall and After* (London, 1985), pp. 45–80, here pp. 49–67 [originally published in *Traditio* 33 (1977), pp. 65–100].

[8] *Über das Leben des Kaisers Konstantin*, 2nd edn, ed. Friedhelm Winkelmann (Berlin, 1991), bk 1.28–31, pp. 29–31.

[9] *Ibid.*, bk 4.20, p. 127.

[10] The value of Eusebius' reports concerning the introduction of Christian symbols, if not the complete replacement of older pagan iconography, is buttressed by the representation of the Chi-Rho on military banners and shields in a wide variety of media ranging from coins to tableware. For example, the reverse sides of a run of coins minted in 327–328 holds the image of a military banner (*vexillum*) bearing a Chi-Rho sign. On this point, see Wendelin Kellner, *Libertas und Christogram: Motivesgeschichtliche Untersuchungen zur Münzprägung des Kaisers Magnentius (350–353)* (Karlsruhe, 1968), p. 88. Similarly, a silver dish fashioned in the mid-fourth century bears the image of a triumphant Constantius II accompanied by a soldier bearing a shield marked with a very large Chi-Rho. For this image, see *Wealth of the Roman World AD 300–700*, ed. J.P.C. Kent and K.S. Painter (London, 1977), p. 25.

eagles here, nor do the flights of birds lead this army, rather it is you Lord Jesus, your name, and your cult."[11]

Perhaps the single most important change brought about by Constantine was the favor that he showed to Christians and Christianity in the army and the example that he provided by his own adoption of Christian practices, such as prayers to the Christian God, attendance at mass, and regular consultation with Christian bishops. In considering this first question, Eusebius stressed that Constantine not only gave Sunday as a day of rest to all Christian soldiers, but also required the non-Christian troops to participate in religious rites on this day. They were ordered to march out onto the parade ground and recite together a monotheistic prayer that called on the one universal God to support them, the emperor, and the emperor's sons just as He had in the past.[12] Eusebius also stressed that Constantine himself participated in teaching this prayer to the troops.[13] At a more personal level, the emperor outfitted a portable chapel and recruited bishops to accompany him so that he could pray and participate in other Christian rites while on campaign.[14]

It must be stressed, however, that alongside these important symbolic and even ritual additions to the traditional practices of the Roman army, the Christianization of the imperial military forces was neither uniform nor complete during the fourth, and even well into the fifth century.[15] Large numbers of pagan troops and officers, including Ammianus Marcellinus, the well-known military historian, defended the Roman state under Christian emperors.[16] In addition, significant numbers of heterodox Christians, particularly Arians, also served in imperial units or as *feoderati*, frequently ac-

---

[11] Ambrose, *De fide*, 2.41 lines 141–2, in CSEL 78 part 3, ed. Otto Faller (Vienna, 1962), pp. 106–7. This text had a wide circulation and traveled as far as England. See J.E. Cross, "The Ethic of War in Old English," in *England Before the Conquest: Studies in the Primary Sources Presented to Dorothy Whitelock*, ed. Peter Clemoes and Kathleen Hughes (Cambridge, 1971), pp. 269–82.

[12] *Leben des Kaisers Konstantin*, bk 4.20, p. 127. Averil Cameron and Stuart G. Hall make the important point that although Eusebius was happy to leave the impression that soldiers all over the empire regularly engaged in this type of prayer service, the requirement may only have been enforced among the troops serving in the garrison at Constantinople. See *Eusebius: Life of Constantine*, ed. Averil Cameron and Stuart G. Hall (Oxford, 1999), p. 318. However, even if this prayer was only said by Constantine's household troops, the emperor's own interest in furthering Christian practice would have been obvious to contemporary observers.

[13] *Leben des Kaisers Konstantin*, bk 4.18, p. 126.

[14] See the apparatus in *ibid.*, p. 144 .

[15] On this point, see Ramsay MacMullen, *Christianizing the Roman Empire A.D. 100–400* (Yale, 1984), who argues convincingly that non-Roman elements continued to be important in the Roman military throughout the fourth century.

[16] Concerning the number of high-ranking pagan officers in the Roman army of the fourth and fifth century, see Raban von Haehling, *Die Religionszugehörigkeit der hohen Amtsträger des Römischen Reiches seit Constantins I.: Alleinherrschaft bis zum Ende der Theodosianischen Dynastie* (Bonn, 1978), p. 511. One of the most famous examples of pagan troops in imperial service practicing their religion during the Late Empire comes from Prosper of Aquitaine's discussion of Litorius' Hunnic cavalry operation in 439. See Prosper of Aquitaine, *Chronicon*, ed. Theodor Mommsen, MGH AA 9 (Berlin, 1892), p. 476.

companied by their own chaplains.[17] Consequently, the religious traditions of the late imperial army must be understood as syncretic rather than purely orthodox Christian.

Religious Practice and Practical Implications for the Army of the Late Empire

The religion of war in Late Antiquity, whether pagan or Christian, heterodox or orthodox, can be understood to fall into two broad categories: the religious practices of the army carried out by soldiers and priests while in camp or on campaign, and the rites and ceremonies carried out by the general population on behalf of the emperor and soldiers in the field. Both spheres of religious practice had as their main focus bringing divine support to bear in order to obtain victory. As we will see below, these ceremonies could take a variety of forms. However, they all had in common an explicit request for divine support and an implicit understanding that divine support could be obtained.[18]

As had been true in the pre-Constantinian period, hope of divine aid of this type could have a profoundly positive effect on military morale. Concomitantly, religion, particularly as practiced by the soldiers themselves, served as an important tool in the hands of military leaders trying to maintain discipline by tying the likelihood of positive divine intervention to the proper behavior of the troops.[19] In contrast to the religious practices of the earlier period, however, the syncretism of the late imperial army mitigated against the use of religion as a means of establishing *esprit de corps* among the troops. Indeed, the heterogeneous religious backgrounds of imperial soldiers could occasion negative comment by observers or even dissension and rebellion in the ranks.[20]

Perhaps the single most common religious practice among soldiers was an intercessory prayer begging God or divine power to aid them on the battlefield. As we saw above, Eusebius described a prayer of this type that was to be said on

[17] The fullest account of the religious care available to Arian soldiers in the Roman army is Ralph W. Mathisen, "Barbarian Bishops and the Churches 'in barbaricis gentibus' during Late Antiquity," *Speculum* 72 (1997), pp. 664–97.

[18] McCormick, *Eternal Victory*, pp. 237–52, has identified the main lines of continuity and development in public ceremonies designed to seek divine favor. The following discussion differs from McCormick's work largely in its emphasis on the practical implications of religious practices on the conduct of war.

[19] For an overview of the penitential aspects of military religion in Late Antiquity, see *ibid.*, pp. 250–1 and 312.

[20] Prosper of Aquitaine disparaged the Roman officer Litorius for consulting with auguries before going into battle against the Visigoths. See *Chronicon*, p. 476. This event also was noted by Salvian of Marseilles who stressed that the Visigoths, even though they honored God through foreign priests, were superior to the Romans who spurned God through their own. See Salvian, *De gubernatione Dei*, 7.9.17–18, ed. F. Pauly, CSEL 8 (Vienna, 1883), p. 167, *illi etiam in alienis sacerdotibus deum honorarent nos etiam in nostris contemneremus.* As we will see below, Procopius emphasized the grievances of Arian soldiers in the Roman imperial army against their orthodox colleagues as one of the primary motivations behind their revolt in North Africa in 536.

a weekly basis by Constantine the Great's non-Christian troops while the Christian soldiers attended regular church services. The prayer explicitly called on the unique divine power to support them in the future as they had been supported in their previous victories. The language of the prayer permits the inference that soldiers who believed in the possibility of divine intervention in human affairs could have taken comfort in knowing that they had propitiated heaven in an appropriate manner.

The important positive effect on morale that prayers of this type could have is emphasized explicitly by Lactantius (240–329), in his description of the battle between Licinius and Maximinus on 30 April 313 near the city of Adrianople. According to Lactantius, on the night before the battle Licinius received a vision informing him that if he prayed to God along with his entire army he would have victory.[21] Licinius took this vision very seriously and summoned his secretary to copy down the words of the prayer just as he had heard them from the divine messenger. Then, as soon as the text was written down, a large number of copies were made and distributed among the army officers and tribunes so that they could teach the prayer to their men.[22] According to Lactantius, the distribution of the prayer had a profound effect on Licinius' outnumbered troops. The author claimed that as news of the vision and the prayer spread, the soldiers grew confident because they believed that their victory had been ordained by heaven.[23]

The prayer is reported to have had a further positive effect on morale the next day just before the battle began. After the two armies had taken up positions opposite each other, Licinius' men, following the example set by their officers and commander, set aside their helmets and shields and stretched their arms to heaven. They then recited the short, forty-four word prayer in which they commended themselves to the protection of the "highest God" who made their victories possible, and begged that this God listen to their prayer.[24] Lactantius emphasizes again at this point that after having recited the prayer three times, Licinius' troops were now full of courage.[25]

We can see the attribution of a similar positive effect on the morale of Roman troops in the description by Rufinus (345–410) of the battle at Cold River between Emperor Theodosius I (379–395) and the pagan usurper Eugenius. According to Rufinus, the battle initially went against Theodosius' troops as the emperor's auxiliaries wavered.[26] In response, the emperor lay prostrate on the ground and called on God, who is described as Theodosius' customary source of aid. The emperor is then reported to have cried out that he undertook this campaign in the name of Christ and of God in a just cause. Theodosius added

[21] Lactantius, *De Mortibus Persecutorum*, ed. J.L. Creed (Oxford, 1984), p. 66, *ut ocius surgeret atque oraret deum summum cum omni exercitu suo; illius fore victoriam, si fecisset.*
[22] *Ibid.*, *scribuntur haec in libellis pluribus et per praepositos tribunosque mittuntur, ut suos quisque milites doceat.*
[23] *Ibid.*, *crevit animus universis victoriam sibi credentibus de caelo nuntiatam.*
[24] *Ibid.*, p. 68.
[25] *Ibid.*, *virtute iam pleni.*
[26] Rufinus, *Historiae ecclesiasticae*, 11.33 in *Eusebius Werke* 2.2: *Die Kirchengeschichte*, ed. E. Schwartz and T. Mommsen (Leipzig, 1908), repr. in an unrevised form in *Eusebius Werke* 2.2: *Die Kirchengeschichte*, ed. Friedhelm Winkelmann (Berlin, 1999), p. 1037.

that if this were truly a just cause then he sought divine aid in order to confound those gentiles who would ask, "where is your God?"[27]

Rufinus emphasized that the imperial officers standing nearby drew fresh courage after observing Theodosius' prayer because they were certain that it had been accepted by God.[28] In this context, Rufinus singled out an officer named Bacurius, who is described as so outstanding in faith, piety, and strength of mind that he deserved to have a place on the emperor's staff.[29] The author stressed that it was Bacurius who captured and killed Eugenius after fighting his way through the usurper's bodyguard.[30]

The civil war between Theodosius and Eugenius was interpreted by contemporaries in the context of the ongoing struggle between paganism and the now dominant Christian faith. As a consequence, Christian writers, such as Rufinus, were eager to attribute Theodosius' victory at Cold River to divine intervention. It is, therefore, difficult to ascertain how much of the account reflects Theodosius' own religious practice or whether the emperor is being used by Rufinus as a synecdoche for religious practice among the Roman troops generally. What is certainly clear, however, is Rufinus' own view that soldiers viewed prayers to God as important for their success in battle with concomitantly important implications for their morale.

In his discussion of the battle of Cold River, the Christian historian Orosius (390–418) took the model of Theodosius as a synecdoche for the army even further than Rufinus while emphasizing the positive impact that prayer could have on a soldier's fighting spirit. In Orosius' account, rather than providing an example to his troops, Theodosius is described as standing alone and surrounded on all sides by enemy soldiers. As darkness fell, the emperor stretched himself out on the ground in order to pray to Christ and maintained his vigil all through the night.[31] When morning came, Theodosius took up his arms knowing, as Orosius emphasizes, that he was not alone. God was with him. Then, given courage by this divine aid, the emperor hurled himself into battle after making the sign of the cross knowing that he would be victorious even though there was no one to follow him.[32]

Prayers of the type described by Eusebius, Lactantius, Rufinus, and Orosius, were also associated with a wider range of religious rites. Orosius, for example, took care to describe the religious preparations undertaken by the Moorish-Roman officer Mascezel who was chosen in 398 by Stilicho, *magister militum* in the West, to crush a revolt in Africa led by Mascezel's brother Count Gildo.

---

[27] *Ibid.*, p. 1038.

[28] *Ibid.*, pp. 1038–9, *quam supplicationem pii principis certi a deo esse susceptam hi qui aderant duces animantur ad caedem.*

[29] *Ibid.*, p. 1039, *et praecipue Bacurius, vir fide, pietate, virtute animi et corporis insignis et qu comes esse et socius Theodosii mereretur. . . .*

[30] *Ibid.*

[31] *Orose: Histoires contre le païens*, 3 vols., ed. and trans. Marie-Pierre Arnoud-Lindet (Paris, 1991), III: 100, *Dominum Christum solus solum qui posset omnia, corpore humi fusus, mente caelo fixus, orabat.*

[32] *Ibid.*, *fiducialiter arma corripuit solus, sciens se esse non solum, signoque crucis signum proelio dedit ac se in bellum, etiam nemo sequetur, victor futurus, inmisit.*

Orosius drew an explicit connection between Mascezel's undertaking and Theodosius I's earlier campaign against Eugenius, emphasizing that like the emperor, Mascezel recognized that prayers to God could bring about divine help in desperate situations.[33] As a consequence, before he embarked for Africa, Mascezel went to the island of Capraria and sought out the "sanctos servos Dei," whom he convinced to come with him on campaign. Orosius emphasizes that Mascezel spent the following days and nights in continuous prayer, fasting, and psalmody. According to Orosius, it was these religious acts that brought about his subsequent victory.[34]

Orosius then moved from his description of the religious rites that prepared the way for the campaign to an account of the religious practices undertaken by the Roman commander in the field. After finally reaching Africa and making contact with the enemy forces, Mascezel is reported to have kept his men in camp for three days after receiving a visitation in his dreams from the recently deceased Bishop Ambrose of Milan. Then, after keeping a nighttime vigil spent in prayer, Mascezel prepared for battle on the third day by going to mass and receiving the host.[35] As had been the case earlier with Theodosius, the pious commander, though his troops were outnumbered, was then able to secure victory through God's aid.

Perhaps the most detailed surviving description of military prayers and associated rites is Corippus' panegyric in honor of John Troglyta's war against the rebellious tribes of North Africa during the mid-sixth century.[36] According to Corippus, after moving out of his fortified camp to pursue enemy tribesmen, John drew up his troops late in the afternoon to deliver a harangue about going into battle on the next day. John addressed his officers directly, calling on them to join him in serving Christ with joy, and begging Him with weeping eyes to protect the army. John added that he was sure God would come to their support and help them crush the enemy if the Romans did their part as soldiers.[37] John went on to add that before preparing dinner and settling in for the night, the army's priest would have to celebrate mass– lit. finish the holy rites and offer the heavenly gifts to the Lord – and the soldiers would have to participate in religious rites in an appropriate manner.[38]

---

[33] *Ibid.*, p. 104, *Igitur Mascezil iam inde a Theodosio sciens quantum in rebus desperatissimis oratio hominis per fidum Christi a clementia Dei impetraret.*

[34] *Ibid.*, *cum his orationibus ieiuniis psalmis dies noctesque continuans sine bello victoriam meruit. . . .*

[35] *Ibid.*, p. 105, *substitit ac tertio demum die post noctem orationibus hymnisque per vigilem ab ipsis caelestium sacramentorum mysteriis in hostem circumfusum processit.*

[36] In addition to the great quantity of detail provided by Corippus, the description of this program of religious rites may be atypical because the battle against the North African tribesmen was fought on a holy day. On this point, see *Flavii Cresconi Corippi Iohannidos seu de bellis Lybycis libri viii*, ed. Jacob Diggle and F.R.D. Goodyear (Cambridge, 1970), bk 8.213–14, p. 173; and McCormick, *Eternal Victory*, p. 246.

[37] Corippus, 8.216–23 in Diggle, p. 173, *praesidium lacrimis humiles oremus ab illo, et veniet, confido citum: gentesque malignas confringet virtute deus nostrosque labores respiciet nostrisque dabit nova gaudia rebus.*

[38] *Ibid.*, *At ubi perfectis caelestia munera sacris obtulerit domino venerandus rite sacerdos votaque Romanus persoluerit ordine miles, ponemus mensas.*

Demonstrating his appreciation of the important role that religion played generally in lives of soldiers, Corippus also dealt with the rites of the pagan North Africans against whom the Romans were fighting. The author describes them setting up altars the night before the battle on which they sacrificed cattle to a range of gods including Ammon and Sinifer, identified as the local version of the war god Mars. Corippus added that the North African tribal priests ripped the entrails from the bellies of the animals to find out about the fate of their army in the forthcoming battle.[39] As a Christian writer, however, Corippus had no sympathy for these rites. Consequently, after he described the great importance attached by the pagans to their sacrifices, the author emphasized that God was deaf to their entreaties so that the North African priests could provide no help to the soldiers.[40]

In fact, these pagan ceremonies are described in stark contrast to the efficacious Christian ceremonies celebrated by the Romans the next morning, which Corippus set out in great detail. As dawn broke over the Roman camp, the soldiers, led by their officers and unit standard bearers, marched into position. Corippus explains that they acted in the prescribed manner, "ordine certo," suggesting that processions of this type had a formal place in Roman military ritual.[41] The troops took their places around an altar that had been erected at the center of camp near the commander's own tent. As soon as the soldiers were in their places they formed up into "choirs" to sing hymns and psalms.[42] All attention then turned to the commander John. As the general stepped toward the altar, Corippus explains, everyone present burst into tears and offered up a penitential chant begging Christ to forgive them and their fathers for their sins. John then took on the role ascribed by Rufinus to Emperor Theodosius I, noted above, by praying to God on behalf of his army. The prayer, which divides neatly into two parts, first recognizes the power of the one God who holds absolute power over the entire earth. In the second portion of the prayer, the general begs God to use this power to crush the enemy and to preserve the Christians in battle.[43] After John completed his prayer, the general's staff, the officers, and then the units of the army poured forth their own prayers to God.[44] The final element of the ceremony was the celebration of mass under the leadership of the highest Roman cleric – lit. high priest (*summus sacerdos*).[45] Corippus concludes his discussion

---

[39] Corippus, 8.300–15 in Diggle, pp. 176–7.

[40] Corippus, 8.316–17 in Diggle, p. 177, *Presserat ista deus, surdumque ad carmina numen omne fuit: nulli retulit responsa sacerdos.*

[41] Formal religious processions of this type are described in the *Strategikon* ascribed to Emperor Maurice (582–610). See Mauricius, *Strategikon*, ed. G.T. Dennis, CFHB 17 (Vienna, 1981), bk 2.18, pp. 138–40.

[42] Corippus, 8.328–9 in Diggle, p. 177, *instituuntque choros et dulcia psallunt carmina deflentes humili cum voce ministri.*

[43] Corippus, 8.350–3, in Diggle, p. 178, *Dominumque potentem te solum agnoscant populi, dum conteris hostes et salvas per bella tuos.*

[44] Corippus, 8.360–3 in Diggle, p. 179, *magnanimique duces umecto pectore fletus ad caelum misere suos fortesque tribuni, atque omnes pariter lacrimosa voce cohortes ante deum fudere preces.*

[45] Corippus, 8.363 in Diggle, p. 179.

of the pre-battle religious rites of the Christian army by declaring that the gifts brought forward by the priest were acceptable to God who immediately blessed and cleansed the entire "Latin nation."[46]

Corippus' description of the religious rites carried out by John's troops is consistent with the practices detailed in the *Strategikon* attributed to Emperor Maurice (582–610). This text enumerates the regular order of religious ceremonies in which soldiers were to engage, including both routine rites and pre-battle preparations. The most common ceremonies were daily morning and evening prayers celebrated both in camp and on campaign.[47] When hostilities were expected, additional religious rites were required. Two to three days before the expected battle, the commanders (*merarchs*) of the units of 6,000–7,000 men had to ensure that the standards of all of the sub-units (*tagmata*) were blessed by priests.[48] On the day of battle itself, priests serving with the army along with the officers were required to lead the soldiers in the *Kyrie eleison*. Then each of the *meroi* was to shout "nobiscum Deus" three times as it marched out of camp in hope of having success in battle.[49] Interestingly, the manual urges against shouting "nobiscum" as a battle cry during rapid advances because it might disturb the ranks by causing the timid to hold back and the braver to break ahead.[50]

Much of the responsibility for ensuring proper religious behavior among the troops rested on the efforts of their officers and generals. Not only did commanders lead their men in prayers and organize religious rites, they also addressed the soldiers in order to instruct them in their religious duties. In Corippus' account, John spoke to his troops on the day before the battle in order to maintain their fighting spirit. Addresses of this type could also be used to help maintain discipline among the troops when fighting was not imminent. For example, in his account of the Vandal campaign (533–534), Procopius describes an address by Belisarius to his troops after he had two auxiliary troopers executed for murdering their comrade during a drunken brawl.[51] The general reminded the imperial troops that although they had frequently defeated larger and stronger military forces, it was God who chose the victor in every struggle. Belisarius added that for an army to have victory it was more important to have justice and all of the things that relate to God on one's side than it was to be physically strong in body and to have fine weapons. The general concluded by emphasizing the necessity of executing the two Massagetae in order to maintain justice within the army and thereby maintain the divine support that came from justice.[52]

---

[46] Corippus, 8.368–9 in Diggle, p. 179, *Munus erat summi domino acceptabile caeli, sanctificans mundansque simul genus omne Latinum.*

[47] *Strategikon*, 7B.17 in Dennis, p. 262.

[48] *Strategikon*, 7A.1 in Dennis, p. 232.

[49] *Strategikon*, 2.18 in Dennis, pp. 138–40.

[50] *Ibid.*

[51] Procopius, *De bello Vandalico*, 12. 13–16 in *Procopius Caesariensis Opera Omnia: De bellis libri I–IV*, 2 vols., ed. Jakob Haury (Leipzig, 2001), I: 367.

[52] Procopius describes a similar oration during the Gothic war, but on this occasion from the point of view of Totilla, the Gothic king. Procopius, *De bello Gothico*, 8. 12–25, in Haury, II:

Nevertheless, no matter how important a role generals and officers played in organizing and leading religious practices, the armies of the Late Empire still required the service of priests to carry out particular religious tasks, particularly in the field, that only those who were ordained as priests could perform. As was noted above, Constantine I required bishops to join him on campaign and ordered the preparation of a specially designed tent to serve as a portable chapel, which, of course, was equipped with a portable altar. Similarly, during his campaign against Count Gildo, Mascezal recruited priests to serve with his forces. These *ad hoc* approaches to recruiting priests for service in orthodox Christian units would appear to have given way to regular service by chaplains during the sixth century. The author of the *Strategikon* clearly envisioned a complement of priests regularly serving with large military units in the field in order to lead the soldiers in prayer and to bless their battle standards. Corippus indicates that by the time of John's campaign against rebellious North African tribes (547–551), soldiers were already being trained to follow a routine procedure when attending religious services in the field; this suggests that the organization outlined in the *Strategikon*, a handbook recounting normal behavior, was based on established military practice.

We can catch a glimpse of how priests were recruited to serve in the army during the sixth century, in a letter from Pope Pelagius I (555–560) to Bishop Lawrence of Civitavecchia.[53] Pelagius notes that the commander of the garrison at Civitavecchia had sought and received permission from the emperor to recruit a priest, a deacon, and a sub-deacon to serve with his forces.[54] The pope urged Bishop Lawrence to investigate these individuals to ascertain whether they were fit for service and then to assign them to their new positions. In discussing this text, A.H.M. Jones argues that the papal letter indicates that "military chaplains were not universal, but a privilege granted by special imperial order."[55] While Jones is correct that the garrison commander had received an imperial order, there is nothing in Pope Pelagius' letter to indicate that this was a rare occurrence. Given the fact that the garrison officer wanted to utilize the bishop's personnel, it does not seem unreasonable that he sought permission from higher up in the chain of command, that is, from the emperor and the pope.

As Mathisen has pointed out, however, whether *ad hoc* or normal procedure, recruiting priests for campaign service from among the largely orthodox populations of the empire would have been difficult for pagan and heterodox units in the Roman army.[56] It is therefore not surprising that it is among the empire's

330–3. Here the Gothic king is seen to defend his punishment of a rapist by stressing that the failure of the Goths to live justly during Theodatus' reign led God to abandon them and give victory to the Romans.

[53] PL 69: 416.

[54] *Ibid.*, *Principali devotissimorum militum, qui illic in civitate Centumcellensi consistunt, relatione ad nos directa sacram insinuant se clementissimi principis impetrasse, quae eis presbyterum, diaconum, et subdiaconum fieri debere praecepit.*

[55] A.H.M. Jones, "Military Chaplains in the Roman Army," *Harvard Theological Review* 46 (1953), p. 240.

[56] Mathisen, "Barbarian Bishops," pp. 680–1.

Arian soldiers that we find what appear to be regular army chaplains by the late fourth century.[57] We also catch glimpses of priests operating among pagan troops serving in the Roman army. Prosper of Aquitaine, for example, heartily condemned Litorius, Aetïus' sub-commander in Gaul, for permitting his Hunnic cavalry to place their trust in auguries and "signs from demons" during the 439 campaign against the Visigoths.[58] As we learn from the historian Jordanes, these types of rites were customarily carried out among the Huns by their native priests.[59]

The great importance of the non-orthodox and pagan priests for the proper functioning of imperial military operations is indicated by the problems caused when Emperor Justinian I (527–565) began to enforce religious orthodoxy in the army. According to Procopius, one of the major causes of the mutiny in North Africa that followed the conquest of the Vandal kingdom in 534 was the exclusion of Arian soldiers from the army's religious rites.[60] Justinian refused to permit non-orthodox soldiers or their families to receive baptism or to participate in any of the other rites of the church. The anger of the Arian troops at this mistreatment grew to a boiling point during the Lenten season of 536, and resulted in a plan to begin the mutiny on Easter day (23 March).[61]

The religious rites celebrated by soldiers and priests in the field in order to purify the army and to seek divine aid were mirrored by large-scale religious rites and ceremonies on the home front.[62] As was true of army religion, Constantine and his successors took a gradual approach in changing long-standing imperial military ceremonial.[63] Thus, in the early fifth century, the pagan historian Zosimus, although he complained that Constantine the Great refused to participate personally in the traditional army religious rites, makes clear that these ceremonies nevertheless took place.[64] The first surviving reference to an entirely Christian program of military-religious ceremonies organized by the emperor is Rufinus' discussion of Theodosius' preparations for the campaign that culminated in the battle of Cold River. According to Rufinus, the emperor began his program of rites with fasts, prayers, and all-night vigils. Theodosius then undertook a series of public penitential processions, marching from church to church at the head of a column of priests and lay people. At each place, he lay prostrate before reliquaries and begged the saints to intercede on his behalf in the forthcoming campaign.[65] Rufinus then contrasted the sacred

---

[57] *Ibid.*, pp. 670–81.

[58] Prosper, *Chronicon*, p. 476.

[59] Jordanes, *De origine actisbusque Getarum*, ed. Francesco Giunta and Antonino Grillone (Rome, 1991), p. 82, reports that since Attila was afraid to go into battle against Aetïus, he ordered the *aruspices* to inquire about future events. According to Jordanes, the *aruspices* worked in their customary manner (*more solito*) while inspecting the cattle and birds.

[60] Procopius, *De bello Vandalico* II. 14. 13–16 in Haury, I: 184.

[61] *Ibid.*

[62] For a valuable discussion of these ceremonies, see McCormick, *Eternal Victory*, pp. 237–44.

[63] *Ibid.*, p. 100.

[64] Zosimus, *Historia Nova*, 2.29, rev. edn, ed. François Paschoud (Paris, 2000), p. 101.

[65] Rufinus, *Historiae ecclesiasticae*, 11.33 in Winkelmann, p. 1037, *Igitur, praeparatur ad bellum non tam armorum telorumque quam ieiuniorum orationumque subsidiis, nec tam*

rites of the Christians with the polluting sacrifices carried out by the pagan Eugenius as he made his own preparations for war.[66] On both sides, the public rituals gave confidence to the leaders for success in the approaching conflict. Eugenius' prefect Flavianus oversaw the pagan rites at Rome and, according to Rufinus, the latter's great reputation for wisdom convinced the usurper's supporters that they would have victory.[67] Theodosius, for his part, is described forcing the Alpine passes against Eugenius' determined resistance because of his confidence in the assistance provided by true religion.[68]

Public ceremonies of the type described by Rufinus were also combined with the mobilization of the massed prayers and penitential offerings of the civilian population in order to invoke divine assistance on behalf of soldiers. For example, in a sermon delivered during the invasions of Italy in the early fifth century, Bishop Maximus of Turin repeatedly emphasized that because military victory was in the hands of God, the civilian population had a part to play in securing this victory through its own pious behavior.[69] In the first half of the sermon, Maximus echoes the portrayal of Emperor Theodosius in the works of Rufinus and Orosius by concentrating on the role that the ruler had to play in leading his people in a virtuous manner so that they would be worthy of divine support. Thus, the bishop stressed, "one who is more powerful than the rest must also be more devoted than everyone."[70] In the second half of the sermon, Maximus stresses that the current suffering of the people could only be overcome by devotion to God. In this vein, the bishop concluded his sermon by calling out, "let us fast, my brothers, without any break so that we will be able to overcome our enemies with our prayers and our restraint."[71]

Wartime Religion in the Roman Successor States of the West

The religious syncretism of the Late Roman army gradually gave way to a purely Christian, and then to purely orthodox Christian military-religious organization as the Roman successor states formally adopted Nicene dogma over heterodox positions. However, the military traditions of the Late Roman state, including the important part played by religion in the conduct of war, were taken

---

excubiarum vigiliis quam obsecrationum pernoctatione munitus, circumibat cum sacerdotibus et populo omnia orationum loca, ante martyrum et apostolorum thecas iacebat cilicio prostratus et auxilia sibi fida sanctorum intercessione poscebat.

[66] *Ibid., At pagani, qui errores suos novis semper erroribus animant, innovare sacrificia et Romam funestis victimis cruentare, inspicere exta pecudum et ex fibrarum praescientia securam Eugenio victoriam nuntiare. . . .*

[67] *Ibid., . . . magna enim erat eius in sapientia praerogativa, Eugenium victorem fore pro certo praesumpserant.*

[68] *Ibid., seb ubi verae religionis fretus auxilio Theodosius Alpium fauces coepit.*

[69] *Maximi episcopi Tavrinensis sermones*, ed. Almut Mutzenbecher, CCSL 23 (Turnholt, 1962), pp. 332–4.

[70] *Ibid.,* p. 333, *necesse enim erat, ut qui potentior cunctis fuerat, devotior fieret universis.*

[71] *Ibid.,* p. 334, *Ieiunemus, ergo, fratres, sine intermissione, ut hostes nostros orationibus et abstinentia superare possimus.* The bishop emphasized here that even the prople of Nineveh had been forgiven after a 3 day fast.

over by its successors. We can see an important example of wide-scale military religious rites in Constance of Lyon's *Life* of Germanus of Auxerre (418–446). Constance notes that while the saint was on a preaching mission to Britain, the local Romano-Celtic population became aware of a combined Saxon–Pictish invasion that it feared could not be checked by its own resources.[72] After hearing about the arrival of Germanus, the Britons hurried to him and his fellow bishops to beg for aid. According to Constance, the very presence of the holy bishops in camp was enough to give the beleaguered Britons new hope and faith such as they might obtain from the arrival of an entire army.[73] For, as Constance stressed, they believed that Christ was with the bishops in the army camp as he had been with the apostles.[74]

It happened that news of the impending Saxon–Pictish invasion reached the Britons during the Lenten season. Consequently, the local leaders and the bishops built on the initial improvement in the morale of the troops by engaging them in regular religious rites designed to bring them closer to God and thereby help bring divine aid to their cause. The bishops preached every day, and according to Constance, urged the men to accept baptism. The preaching had the desired effect because the majority of the men in the army are reported to have accepted baptism at this time.[75] Constance emphasized that as a result of their religious preparations the army, described as soaked in baptismal waters, had a fervent faith in its own side and had nothing but contempt for physical protection because of its expectation of divine grace.[76]

This account was repeated by Bede (672–735) in his *Ecclesiastical History*, and is of a piece with the author's own conception of the crucial part played by religion in war.[77] While discussing Æthelfrith's campaign to capture the fortress city of Chester, for example, Bede emphasizes the local practice of having priests come to the battlefield to pray to God on behalf of their troops.[78] In this case, Bede suggests the effect that prayers could have in bringing about divine aid, but does not emphasize the point too vigorously because these priests were

---

[72] Constance of Lyon, *Vie de Saint Germain d'Auxerre*, ed. René Borius (Paris, 1965), p. 154. Concerning the historical value of Constance of Lyon's account dealing with the Aleluja victory of the Britons over the Saxons and Picts, see Michael E. Jones, "The Historicity of the Alleluja Victory," *Albion* 18 (1986), pp. 363–73.

[73] *Ibid.*

[74] *Ibid.*, pp. 154–6, *itaque apostolicis ducibus Christus militabat in castris.*

[75] *Ibid.*, p. 156, *nam maxima devoti exercitus multitudo undam lavacri salutaris expetiit.*

[76] *Ibid.*

[77] *Bede's Ecclesiastical History of the English People*, ed. Bertram Colgrave and R.A.B. Mynors (Oxford, 1969), p. 62. It is possible and perhaps even likely that Bede, who was renowned even in his own day for his role in contemporary religious and political matters, discussed the religious behavior of fifth-century Britons with an eye toward the concerns of the late seventh and early eighth centuries. Concerning Bede's use of history for contemporary political purposes, see Walter A. Goffart, *The Narrators of Barbarian History (A.D. 550–800): Jordanes, Gregory of Tours, Bede, and Paul the Deacon* (Princeton, 1988). The basic argument concerning Bede's political and religious views is repeated by Goffart in "The *Historia Ecclesiastica*: Bede's Agenda and Ours," *Haskins Society Journal* 2 (1990), pp. 29–45.

[78] *Bede's Ecclesiastical History*, p. 140, *Cumque bellum acturus videret sacerdotes eorum qui ad exorandum Deum pro milite bellum agente convenerant.*

heretics and, moreover, were slaughtered by Æthelfrith's men. Nevertheless, Æthelfrith does give voice to the value of priests in war when declaring to his men, "if they call on their God against us, they are themselves fighting against us even if they do not bear arms, for they are attacking us with hostile prayers."[79]

Bede was more enthusiastic in his description of the positive effect that religious rites could have on the outcome of a battle when discussing the actions of orthodox Christians. After the death of his brother Eanfrith at the hands of the British king Cædwalla, Oswald led his outnumbered force of Bernicians against the British near the brook of Denise (modern Rowley Water), and won a victory because, Bede insists, they were strengthened by their faith in Christ.[80] In order to focus this faith in Christ and to stir up the spirits of his soldiers for battle, Oswald is reported first to have set up a cross in view of the entire army and then knelt down in prayer to God.[81] The king then called on all of his men to follow his example to kneel and pray that God protect them since they were fighting in a just cause and for the preservation of their people against an arrogant and ferocious foe.[82] Bede concludes by noting that Bernicians then launched a surprise dawn assault and obtained the victory merited by their faith in God.[83]

We can see a similarly important role for religion in the armies of Visigothic Spain. In his account of the invasion of the Visigothic kingdom by the Merovingian kings Childebert I (511–558) and Chlothar I (511–561), Gregory of Tours provides a vivid description of the religious rites undertaken by the population of Saragossa to ward off the Frankish army. The men of Saragossa dressed in hair shirts, fasted and marched in processions around the inner walls of the city singing psalms and carrying the tunic of Saint Vincent as a holy relic. The women marched behind them wearing black clothing.[84] Echoing the language of Maximus of Turin's sermon, noted above, Gregory adds that the prayers of the people of Saragossa were like those of the people of Nineveh, and that it would be unimaginable for God to fail to heed their prayers. According to Gregory, the Franks were at first unimpressed by the spectacle that they were watching. However, after a local peasant told them that the people of Saragossa were marching in procession behind the tunic of Saint Vincent, following as if it

---

[79] *Ibid., ergo si adversum nos ad Deum suum clamant, profecto et ipsi quamvis arma non ferant, contras nos pugnant, qui adversis nos inprecationibus persequuntur.*

[80] *Bede's Ecclesiastical History*, p. 214, *cum parvo exercitu, sed fide Christi munito.*

[81] *Ibid.*

[82] *Ibid., flectamus omnes genua, et Deum omnipotentem vivum ac verum in commune deprecemur, ut nos ab hoste superbo ac feroce sua miseratione defendat; scit enim ipse quia iusta pro salute gentis nostrae bella suscepimus.*

[83] *Ibid.*

[84] Gregory, *Historia Francorum*, 3.29, ed. Wilhelm Arndt and Bruno Krusch, MGH SRM 1 (Hanover, 1884), pp. 133–1, *At ille tanta humilitate ad Deum conversi sunt, ut induti ciliciis abstinentia cibis et poculis cum tonica beati Vincenti martiris muros civitatis psallendo circumirent. Mulieres quoque amictae nigris palleis, dissoluta caesariae superposito cinere, ut eas putares virorum funeribus deservire plangendo sequebantur.*

were a battle flag in order to implore God to aid them, the troops grew frightened and broke off the siege.[85]

Large-scale public religious celebrations of this type were complemented in the Spanish kingdom by an extensive series of wartime liturgies and prayers intended to invoke divine aid on behalf of Visigothic kings and their armies.[86] Much like the Roman army celebrations described by Rufinus, Orosius, and Corippus, Visigothic ceremony was centered on the military commander. He is represented in the liturgy entering the church, lying prostrate on the ground, and praying. Following the personal prayers of the king for victory, there followed blessings from the clergy for the success of the campaign as a whole, and subsequent blessings for the king's golden marching cross and battle standards.[87]

Like their Roman predecessors, the Visigothic armies in the field also augmented these pre-campaign rites with religious ceremonies carried out in preparation for battle itself. In his history of the reign of Wamba (672–680), Julian of Toledo recounts an effort to purify the royal army before the troops went into combat against the usurper Paul in 673.[88] After Wamba had divided his army into three columns the men under his direct command began to pillage the countryside, to burn down houses, and, Julian says, to fornicate, although from the context it would appear that the soldiers were in truth guilty of rape.[89] Wamba had the guilty men circumcised and explained this severe punishment in the following manner. He first asked rhetorically whether the men truly believed that *fornicatio* was acceptable when battle was imminent. Wamba then explained that if he did not proceed with the punishments after seeing the manifest guilt of his people, he himself would be judged guilty by God.[90] The king offered the example of the high priest Eli who, knowing the evil deeds of his own two sons, refused to punish them and therefore not only lost them in battle but himself suffered a broken neck when he heard the news.[91] He concluded by

---

[85] *Ibid.*, p. 134, *Tunc adpraehensum unum de civitate rusticum, ipse interrogant, quid hoc esset quod agerent. Qui ait: 'tonicam beati Vincenti deportant et cum ipsa, ut eis Dominus misereatur exorant.' Quod illi timentes, se ab ea civitate removerunt.*

[86] For a detailed discussion of these rites, see McCormick, *Eternal Victory*, pp. 305–14; and Bernard S. Bachrach, *Early Carolingian Warfare: Prelude to Empire* (Philadelphia, 2001), p. 147 for a summary of the recent literature on Visigothic military-religious ceremonies.

[87] For the blessings on cross and battle flags, see *Le liber ordinum en usage dans l'église wisigothique et mozarabe d'Espagne du cinquième siècle*, ed. Marius Férotin, *Monumenta ecclesiae liturgica* 5 (Paris, 1904), cols. 149–53, new edn, ed. Anthony Ward and Cuthbert Johnson (Rome, 1996). Concerning the use of the marching cross by the Visigoths, see Bachrach, *Early Carolingian Warfare*, p. 147.

[88] *Historia Wambae regis*, ed. B. Krusch and W. Levison, MGH SRM 5 (Hanover, 1910), p. 510.

[89] *Ibid.*, *Se quia insolens quorundam e nostris non solum praedae inhiabat, sed etiam cum incensione domorum adulterii facius perpetrabat.* Engaging in fornication while plundering the neighborhood and burning down houses has the sound of forcing women against their will.

[90] *Ibid.*, *ad hoc ergo vadam, ut iusto Dei iudicio capiar, si iniquitatem populi videns ipse non puniam.*

[91] *Ibid.*, *Exemplum mihi praebere debet Eli sacerdos ille in divinis litteris agnitus, qui pro*

insisting that if these crimes were punished, the royal army would be victorious.[92]

As we saw earlier in Gregory of Tours' description of the assault on Saragossa by Chlotar and Childebert, Frankish soldiers are depicted sharing the belief of their Visigothic opponents that divine forces could and would have an impact on the field of battle. According to Gregory, Frankish soldiers believed that their actions either could help to bring divine aid to their cause or conversely alienate heavenly powers. Clovis I (481–511), the first Merovingian king, was reportedly driven by the fear of alienating Saint Martin during his campaign in 507 against the Visigothic kingdom to institute very strict regulations regarding foraging in the territories near Tours.[93] While passing through this region, Clovis issued orders that no one should take anything from the neighborhood except for grass and water. When it was reported to Clovis that one of his men had seized some hay by force from a poor peasant, the Frankish king executed him on the spot, telling the onlookers that his army would have no hope of victory if it offended Saint Martin, the patron of the city of Tours.[94]

In a further effort to propitiate Martin, and to inspire his men for the approaching campaign, Clovis sent soldiers loaded with gifts to the saint's cathedral at Tours. According to Gregory, Clovis then prayed to God to give him some sign indicating divine support if the Frankish cause were just and if they were carrying out a virtuous task in attacking the heretical Visigothic Arians. When the soldiers entered the cathedral church, the precenter was just beginning to read from Psalm 18.39–40, "you have girded me with strength for battle: you have subdued those who have risen up against me."[95] Gregory reports that once the men heard this, they thanked God and happily went back to the army camp to report the good news to Clovis. The rest of the campaign, culminating in the overwhelming Frankish victory at Vouillé, is portrayed by Gregory as the fulfillment of the promise implied by the psalm.[96]

We see the same type of faith in the power of divine aid on the battlefield in the continuator of Fredegar's depiction of Pippin III's campaign against the Lombard king Aistulf in 754.[97] According to the chronicler, while passing over the Alps, Pippin was forced to leave the main body of his troops behind taking only a picked force into the valley of Susa. The Frankish forces were heavily outnumbered by the Lombards and realized that they would have no chance of

---

immanitate scelerum filios, quos increprare noluit, in bello concidisse audivit, ipse quoque filios sequens fractis cerbicibus expiravit.

[92] Ibid., Haec igitur nobis timenda sunt, et ideo, si purgati maneamus a crimine, non dubium erit, quod triumphum capiamus ex hoste.

[93] Gregory, Historia Francorum, 2.37 in Krusch, p. 99, Sed quoniam pars hostium per territorium transiebat, pro reverentia beati Martini dedit edictum, ut nullus de regione illa aliud quam herbarum alimenta aquamque praesumeret.

[94] Ibid., Et ubi erit spes victoriae sic beato Martino offendimus.

[95] Ibid., p. 100.

[96] Ibid.

[97] The Fourth Book of the Chronicle of Fredegar with its Continuations, ed. J.M. Wallace-Hadrill (London, 1960), ch. 37, p. 105.

victory if they relied on their own strength alone. The Franks therefore called on God and Peter the Apostle to aid them in the fighting, thereafter driving the Lombards from the field.[98]

Christianity and the Practice of War

One of the major religious difficulties that was peculiar to Christian soldiers serving in the armies of the Late Empire and its western successor states was the consistently hostile attitude of the church toward the taking of human life. It had always been one of the central tenets of early Christian doctrine that killing, even in self-defense, was a terrible sin that separated a perpetrator from the community.[99] The continuing and strong antipathy of the Christian leadership toward the taking of human life even after Constantine I's conversion and the gradual elevation of Christianity to the status of the state cult can be seen in the decisions of episcopal councils from the fifth, sixth, and seventh centuries. In many cases, bishops refused to distinguish between types of killing, and grouped together all forms of taking a human life, including killing in the course of war, under the rubric *homicidio*. Thus, for example, under the leadership of Pope Hillary IV, the *Concilium Veneticum* (465) ruled in its very first canon that those guilty of taking a human life were to be excluded from the communion of the church until they confessed their sins and successfully carried out the prescribed penance.[100]

Over time, however, conciliar canons begin to suggest that although bishops maintained an exceptionally rigid position concerning the sinfulness of taking a human life, they were also moving toward a more nuanced view of the nature of *homicidio*. For example, bishops attending the council of Arles in 541 drew attention to those cases in which someone might commit homicide *voluntarily*.[101] The bishops defined this act as daring to kill an innocent.[102] It would appear that in the view of the twenty-four bishops gathered at this council, *homicidio* still meant any taking of a human life. However, they also thought that it was necessary to distinguish, at least implicitly, between killing those who were innocent and killing those who were not innocent. A similar distinction

---

[98] *Ibid., haec cernentes Franci non suis auxiliis nec suis viribus liberare se putabant sed Deum invocant et beati Petri apostoli adiutorem rogant.*

[99] On the question of early Christian pacifism, see Roland H. Bainton, *Christian Attitudes toward War and Peace* (New York, 1960), pp. 66–84. Concerning early Christian hostility toward military service, see Frederick H. Russell, *The Just War in the Middle Ages* (Cambridge, 1975), pp. 10–12; Helgeland, "Roman Army Religion," pp. 1476–78; and Cecil John Cadoux, *The Early Christian Attitude to War: A Contribution to the History of Christian Ethics* (New York, 1982).

[100] *Concilium Veneticum*, ed. J.P. Mansi in *Sacrorum Conciliorum nova et amplissima collectio* 7 (Florence, 1762), col. 953, *a communione ecclesiastica submovendos, nisi poenitentia satisfactione crimina admissa diluerint.*

[101] *Concilium Aurelianense*, ed. F. Maassen, MGH Concilia Aevi Merovingici (Hanover, 1893), p. 93, *quisquis homicidium voluntate commiserit.*

[102] *Ibid., ita ut occidere audeat innocentem.*

between those who *homicidium sponte comiserit*, that is those who willingly took an innocent human life, and those who killed the guilty was drawn by the bishops at the council of Clichy (626–627).[103] Here, the prelates were concerned about the potential spiritual salvation of those guilty of having committed homicide "sponte." They concluded that if someone carried out a penance for this act then he should not be denied reception of the eucharist – described here as the "viaticum" – when he died.[104]

Given the continuing innately sinful nature of *homicidio* in official church doctrine, Christian soldiers were faced with the prospect that by engaging in the necessary defense of the *res publica* they were not only endangering their lives, they were endangering their souls as well. This problem was compounded by the fact that Christian soldiers did not have the opportunity to cleanse their souls of sin before going into battle or after returning home from war. The two rites in the early church that served to cleanse the soul of sin, baptism and sacramental penance, were unsatisfactory for soldiers because individuals could only undergo them once in a lifetime. Sacramental penance had the further disadvantage of committing an individual to a life of fasting, abstinence, and prayer, which largely excluded penitents from normal lay life for fear of falling back into irredeemable sin.[105] Clearly, soldiers, whose duties normally entailed the taking of human life, could not participate in the rite of sacramental penance and remain soldiers.

This inherent contradiction between Christian practice and military service was not lost on the leaders of the church. Nevertheless, during the period of the Late Empire, bishops refused to compromise on the status of penance as a once-in-a-lifetime rite. The church leaders gathered at Nicaea in 325 were adamant in their objection to the notion that someone who had been called by grace (*quicumque vocati per gratiam*) to leave the world could then return.[106] They insisted that if anyone who had quit military service (*deponentes militiae cingulum*) then went back – described as returning to his own vomit – he was required to undergo thirteen years of penance.[107] This canon was interpreted by later councils to mean that those who had undergone the rite of sacramental or public penance could not go back into military service. For example, the bishops gathered at Arles in 538 ruled that if anyone had accepted the blessing of penance and then returned to his secular life and military service, he was to be treated as an excommunicate until the end of his life.[108]

---

[103] *Concilium Clippiacense* in Concilia Aevi Merovingici, p. 198.

[104] This same canon was adopted by the bishops gathered in council at Rheims (627–630). See *Concilium sub sonnatio episcopo Remensi habitum* in Concilia Aevi Merovingici, p. 204.

[105] For an overview of early Christian teaching on baptism, see Peter Cramer, *Baptism and Change in the Early Middle Ages c. 200–c. 1400* (Cambridge, 1993). On the nature of sacramental penances, see Bernhard Poschmann, *Penance and the Annointing of the Sick*, trans. and rev. Francis Courtney (New York, 1964), pp. 81–116; Cyrille Vogel, *Le pécheur et la pénitence dans l'église ancienne* (Paris, 1966), pp. 27–54; and Philippe Rouillard, *Histoire de la pénitence des origines à nos jours* (Paris, 1996), pp. 27–33.

[106] *Conciliorum Oecumenicorum Decreta*, 3rd edn (Bologna, 1973), pp. 11–12.

[107] *Ibid.*

[108] *Concilium Aurelianense*, Concilia Aevi Merovingici, p. 81, *Si quis paenetentiae*

Other councils expressed the prohibition against relapsing from the penitential life in even broader terms. The bishops at the council of Tours in 461 would appear to have had the Nicene canon in mind when ruling on the question of relapsed penitents. Like their forebears, the bishops described those who returned to secular life after having accepted penance as being like dogs returning to their vomit who were to be excluded not only from the communion of the church but also from any association with the faithful.[109] The bishops at the council of Yenne (517) took the same position regarding lapsed penitents, ruling that anyone who accepted penance and then returned to the secular world was not to be permitted to participate further in the rites of the church.[110]

These stringent positions concerning both the sinfulness of homicide and the nature of penance as a once-in-a-lifetime act were to remain unchallenged at an ideological level until the seventh century. Nevertheless, by the mid-fifth century bishops and priests began to develop practical strategies to provide spiritual care to lay people, including soldiers, who were burdened by sin in the course of their daily lives.

Clearly, it must have been a difficult choice for many lay people to choose a life of penitence while still in the prime of life. This must have been particularly true of soldiers, who would have been faced with the difficult prospect of either ending their careers or risking death in battle in a state of sin. This problem was raised specifically by Bishop Rusticus of Narbonne (427–461) in a letter to Pope Leo I (440–461). Rusticus' letter is no longer extant. However, it is clear from Leo's response that among other matters the Gallic bishop was seeking guidance about how to deal with the spiritual difficulties of the soldiers under his care.[111] In the twelfth of his nineteen responses to the bishop's questions, Leo stated categorically that "it is completely contrary to all the rules of the church for a soldier to return to duty after receiving penance."[112] In stressing this point, the pope was merely reiterating the position that church leaders had taken since at least the First Council of Nicaea (325). However, the fact that Leo made this point in the context of a letter that was intended to respond to Rusticus' questions, that is, concerns, suggests that, at the very least, the bishop of Narbonne wanted some guidance about the participation by soldiers in the rite of penance.

---

benedictione suscepta ad saeculare habitum miliciamque reverti praesumserit, viatico concesso usque ad exitum excummunicatione plectatur.

[109] *Concilium Turonicum* in Mansi 7: 946, *Si quis vero post acceptam poenitentiam, sicut canis ad vomitum suum ita ad saeculares illecebras, derelicta quam professus est poenitentia, fuerit reversus, a communione ecclesiae, vel a convivio fidelium extraneus habeatur. . . .* Cf. the council of Venice (465) where the bishops took essentially the same position; Mansi 7: 953, *Poenitentes quoque, qui susceptam publice poenitentiam intermiserint, et ad prioris erroris consuetudinem revoluti, vitae se saeculari conversationique reddiderint, non solum a communione dominicorum sacramentorum, sed etiam a conviviis fidelium submovendos.*

[110] *Concilium Epaonense* in Concilia Aevi Merovingici, p. 24.

[111] In his response to Rusticus, Pope Leo noted that he had happily received the letter from the bishop, which dealt with a wide variety of matters but which was nevertheless not burdensome to the reader. See Pope Leo I, *Epistolae*, PL 54: 1199–1200.

[112] *Ibid.*, cols. 1206–7, *contrarium est omnino ecclesiasticis regulis, post poenitentiam actionem redire ad militiam saecularem.*

The vehemence with which Leo stated official doctrine on this point – emphasizing that it "contrarium est *omnino* ecclesiasticis regulis" to return to military service – suggests that Rusticus wanted permission for some modification in this practice.

Even if Bishop Rusticus of Narbonne simply wanted a clarification of church doctrine and was not interested in changing established teaching concerning the status of penance as a once-in-a-lifetime rite, some of his contemporaries were aware of practical changes in penitential practice that had already developed. We can see this in the letters of the fifth-century moralist Salvian of Marseilles (died c. 480). In his discussions of lay Christian life, Salvian was concerned largely with the failure of lay people to live up to their obligations as Christians. He was particularly incensed by their lackadaisical approach to the obligations imposed by a penitential life. However, Salvian also was aware of a less onerous means of spiritual renewal, which he addressed in a letter to his former student, Bishop Salonius of Geneva. Here, Salvian drew an explicit contrast between sacramental confession and satisfaction on the one hand and the easier gifts and works of mercy which were available to lay people ill-equipped to undergo the full rigor of the penitential life.[113]

Salvian's younger contemporary and famous preacher, Bishop Caesarius of Arles (502–542), also addressed the possibility of lay people engaging in a limited form of spiritual renewal that did not require the full obligation of sacramental penance. Well aware of how difficult it would be for many lay people to choose a penitential life while still young and hale, Caesarius made use of a sermon by Bishop Faustus of Riez (died c. 500) in order to address this problem.[114] The preacher considers how, when calling everyone to a penitential life, he should respond to the young married man who questions whether it is truly fitting for him to cut his hair and take on a religious habit.[115] The sermon addresses this concern obliquely by asking whether a married man would suffer if he were willing to undo the damage caused by his sins through such good deeds as almsgiving, fasting, and prayer.[116] Caesarius was unwilling to alter Bishop Faustus' sermon to say explicitly that these penitential acts could replace sacramental penance. Nevertheless, the suggestion is there that these repeatable rites offered an opportunity to obtain eternal life by living a life full of merit and avoiding sinful acts.[117]

---

[113] Salvian of Marseilles, *Oeuvres*, ed. Georges Lagarrigue, Sources Chrétiennes 176 (Paris, 1971), p. 124, *non modo ea quae admiserunt exomologes, ac satisfactione, sed ne hoc quidem, quod facillimum est, donis saltim ac misericordiis redimere dignantur*.

[114] Caesarius of Arles, *Sermones*, 2 vols., ed. D. Germani Morin, CCSL 103 (Turnholt, 1953), I: 250, *sed forte, quando generaliter omnes ad paenitentiam provocamus, aliquis infra se cogitet dicens, 'Ego iuvenis homo uxorem habens quomodo possum aut capillos minuere aut habitum religionis adsumere?'*

[115] *Ibid., Quid enim homini uxorem nocet, si mores perditos voluerit ad opera bona vel honesta convertere, si peccatorum suorum vulnera elemosyniis ieiuniis et orationibus ad sanitatem pristinam studeat revocare*.

[116] *Ibid., hic extinguamus mortem moriendo peccatis, hic vitam vitae mertis adquiramus*.

[117] Caesarius was clearly aware of the distinction between these repeatable good deeds and

Two generations later, Pope Gregory I (590–604) is reported to have made a much more explicit claim that repeatable penitential acts such as fasting, almsgiving, and prayer could bring about not only spiritual renewal but even temporal gain. In an address to the people of Rome, which was preserved by Gregory of Tours, Pope Gregory emphasized that the current danger posed to Rome by the Lombards could be overcome through reliance on God. Gregory began by listing the suffering of the Roman people and making reference to what appears to be a full confession of sin, but one that was to be combined with repeatable good works of the type noted by Caesarius and Salvian. Thus, the pope urged the crowd to consider all of their misdeeds and to weep over their transgressions. Then, quoting Jeremiah 3.41, Pope Gregory added that they should come before God with their confessions, lifting up their hands to God with their words. The pope stressed that this entailed enhancing the effort of their prayers with the merit of their good works.[118] Gregory emphasized the repeatable and transitory nature of this type of penance by proclaiming that not even the greatest sinners in the city needed to give up hope because the people of Nineveh had obtained mercy for their long-standing sins after a penance of just three days.[119]

The gradual development of a practical penitential *modus vivendi* that permitted lay people to engage in a process of spiritual renewal that did not require a commitment to lifetime of penitential obligations reached a culmination during the seventh century. First in Ireland and then in England monastic houses developed pastoral manuals that regularized the concept of short-term penitential acts that could be employed regularly over a lifetime in order to cleanse oneself of the stain of sin.[120] These penitential manuals were essentially schedules of sins with corresponding penances, and therefore have been labeled by scholars as "tariff books."[121] Once a penance had been completed successfully, the individual was understood to be fully reconciled with God and the

---

public penance. He describes the latter in great detail. See Caesarius of Arles, *Sermones*, pp. 284–6.

[118] Gregory, *Historia Francorum*, 10.1, *revocemus ante oculos mentis quidquid errando commisimus; et quod nequiter egimus flendo puniamus. Praevenimus faciem eius in confessionem . . . Et sicut propheta ammonet: 'levamus corda nostra cum manibus ad Deum: ad Deum quippe corde cum manibus levare est orationis nostrae studium cum merito bonae operationis eregere.'*

[119] *Ibid., Nullus autem de iniquitatem suarum immanitate disperet; veternosas namque Ninnivitarum culpas triduana paenitentia abstersit.* Clearly, Gregory the Great's reference to Nineveh here recalls both Gregory of Tours' earlier mention of this city's penance in his discussion of the siege of Saragossa and Maximus of Turin's sermon, noted above.

[120] On this point, see Oscar D. Watkins, *A History of Penance*, 2 vols. (London, 1920), II: 632–62; Bernard Poschmann, *Die abendländische Kirchenbuße im frühen Mittelalter* (Breslau, 1930), pp. 73–91; Rosamond Pierce (McKitterick), "The 'Frankish' Penitentials," *Studies in Church History* 11, ed. Derek Baker (Oxford, 1975), pp. 31–9, here pp. 34–6; and Rouillard, *Histoire de la pénitence*, pp. 43–8.

[121] See, for example, the discussion by Poschmann, *Penance and Annointing*, pp. 122–31; Cyrille Vogel, "Le rituels de la pénitence tarifée," in *Liturgia opera divina e umana, studi offerti à S.E. Mons A. Bugnini: Bibliotheca 'Ephemerides liturgicae' subsidia* 26 (Rome, 1982), pp. 419–27; and Rouillard, *Histoire de la pénitence*, pp. 43–8.

Christian community. This development in practice was of particular importance to soldiers as it meant that they could now reasonably hope to die in a state of grace after a recent confession. In addition, soldiers could continue to serve in the army however often they confessed.

At a practical level, the adoption of repeatable confession by church authorities meant that the long-standing Christian treatment of *homicidio* as a single sin rather than a rubric covering a wide variety of cases had to change. As we saw above, during the sixth century some bishops had already begun to differentiate between *homicidio* and *homicidio* that was committed *sponte*, the latter case having been defined as daring to kill an innocent person. The development of the penitential manuals gave much greater scope to religious authorities in defining and differentiating between types of *homicidio*. For example, a *poenitentiale* composed in England during the late seventh or early eighth century differentiated between a range of cases in which a penitent had taken a human life.[122] Killing a monk or another cleric was treated as an exceptionally serious crime requiring not only that the perpetrator undergo seven years of penance but also that he lay down his arms (*arma relinquat*) and dedicate his life to God's service (*Deo serviat*).[123] A penitent who killed a layman in a brawl was required by this same manual to undergo four years of penance.[124]

Of particular importance to soldiers was the inclusion of clauses in the penitential manuals dealing specifically with *homicidio* in the context of war, specifically publicly sanctioned warfare (*bellum publicum*) or warfare conducted by the king.[125] In contrast to the very heavy penances imposed on those who were guilty of committing homicide *sponte*, to use the vocabulary of earlier church councils, soldiers were required to undergo much less vigorous penances sometimes amounting to a mere forty days, or in some rare examples no penance at all.[126] The *poenitentiale Cummeani*, for example, required that anyone who

---

[122] F.H.W. Wasserschleben, *Die Bußordnungen der abendländischen Kirche* (1851, repr. Graz, 1958), pp. 224–5.

[123] *Ibid.*, p. 224.

[124] *Ibid.*, p. 225.

[125] The basic study of penances imposed on soldiers in the early Middle Ages is Raymond Kottje, "Die Tötung im Kriege: Ein moralisches und rechtliches Problem im frühen Mittelalter," *Beiträge zur Friedensethik* 11 (1991), pp. 1–21. Also see Bachrach, *Early Carolingian Warfare*, pp. 153–4.

[126] Carl Erdmann, *The Origin of the Idea of Crusade* [orig. *Die Entstehung des Kreuzzugsgedankens* Stuttgart, 1935], trans. Marshall W. Baldwin and Walter Goffart (Princeton, 1977), p. 17, n. 32, lists a large number of penitential manuals that required a forty-day penance for having killed an enemy soldier in battle. However, Erdmann asserts against this body of evidence that "a provision was in force that penitents should not bear arms and should never again participate in war after having completed their penance." No such provision was in force either in the eighth century or during later periods. As has been noted above, the purpose of repeatable penance was to permit penitents to undergo the rite as often as was necessary. Kottje, "Tötung im Kriege," pp. 3–4, arguing against Erdmann, emphasizes that not only were penances imposed on soldiers usually very light, in some cases no penances at all were imposed for killing an enemy soldier in battle. Thus, for example, the *Paenitentiale Oxoniense II*, c. 5, ed. Raymund Kottje in *Paenitentialia minor Franciae et Italiae saeculi VIII–IX*, CCSL 156 (Turnholt, 1994), p. 191, notes that if anyone kills in the course of an *expeditio* without cause (*sine causa*) he must do a penance for twenty-two

killed a man in battle while fighting under the command of his king "XL dies paeniteat."[127] The *poenitentiale Valicellanum II* listed a penance of forty days on bread and water for anyone who killed a man in battle while serving with the king, and assigned the same penance to anyone who killed someone at the order of his "dominus."[128] By the mid-eighth century, at the latest, penitential manuals of this type were also being produced not only in Ireland and England, but in large numbers in *Francia* and Italy as well.[129] As we will see in the next chapter, these developments in Christian penitential practice and in teaching about the sinfulness of killing had a profound impact on medieval wartime religion.

Conclusion

The rise of Christianity as the state cult of the Roman empire had profound implications for both wartime religious practices in Late Antiquity and for Christianity itself. As the population of the Roman empire was gradually Christianized, it became increasingly important first to augment and then to replace traditional religious rites of the army in order to accommodate the Christian soldiers filling its ranks and the Christian civilians it protected. As had been true in earlier periods, fighting men continued to depend on a wide range of religious practices carried out by the soldiers themselves and on their behalf by the wider society to give them the courage and motivation to risk injury and death in battle. Like their pagan forebears, Roman army officers in the Christian empire and their late antique successors made full use of contemporary religious ideals and beliefs to maintain discipline in the ranks. The syncretism of the Late Antique period mitigated against the traditional role of religion as a force for cohesion and *esprit de corps* in the ranks. However, the gradual elimination of paganism and heterodoxy from both the armies and societies of Rome's successor states opened a path for orthodox Christianity to serve this function as it had in the past. As we will see in the next chapter, this point was not lost on medieval military commanders.

The augmentation of traditional Roman army and wartime religion to accommodate Christian practices and the subsequent wholesale replacement of the former by the latter coincided with significant developments in Christian ideology and practice. Over time, the obvious and intolerable strain of forcing Christian soldiers to choose between damnation and military service gave way to compromises on the nature of penance and the sinfulness of homicide. The once-in-a-lifetime rite of sacramental penance was augmented through the

weeks. However, if he was defending himself or others then he is without fault. He may do a penance if he wishes, but is not required to do so because he was forced to carry out this deed (*si voluerit ieiunare, illius est potestatem, quia coactus hoc fecit*).
[127] *Poenitentiale Cummeani*, ch. 2, ed. Hermann Joseph Schmitz, *Die Bußbücher und die Bußdisciplin der Kirche*, 2 vols. (1898, repr. Graz, 1958), I: 655.
[128] *Poenitentiale Valicellanum II*, ch. 13, ed. Schmitz, *Bußbücher*, I: 356.
[129] See the edited collection of penitential manuals by Kottje in *Paenitentialia minor Franciae et Italiae saeculi VIII–IX*.

development and spread of repeatable penitential exercises culminating in the tariff books. Within the context of this new penitential regime, church leaders also relaxed official teaching about the nature of homicide, bringing nuance to the formally absolute prohibition against taking human life. As we will see in the following chapter, this development, traceable through the statutes of episcopal councils and the lists of sins and penances in tariff books, had a profound impact on military-religious practice throughout the following centuries.

2

Religion in the Armies of the Carolingian *Imperium* 742–c. 900

Introduction

This discussion of the military religion in Carolingian *Francia* deals with three basic areas: the support provided to the army by the wider society of the Carolingian *imperium* involving both lay people and clerics from all stations of life, the preparation of the army as a whole for combat through religious rites, and finally the individual preparations of soldiers to ready themselves for combat and the possibility of dying in battle. The participation of the Carolingian government in organizing large-scale public religious ceremonies can be seen as a continuation of imperial and late antique practices discussed in the previous chapter. The army-wide rites also owe a great deal to previous military religious practice. Nevertheless, observers in the Carolingian period were much more likely than their predecessors to turn their attention to the participation of ordinary soldiers in religious rites and ceremonies. Thus, while Carolingian kings and emperors remained at the center of wartime narratives, the religious behavior and beliefs of regular fighting men now also come into clearer focus. However, as we shall see below, the most striking development in military-religious practice during the Carolingian period was in the reconciliation of soldiers with God before and after battle at an individual level. As was noted in the previous chapter, the seventh and eighth centuries witnessed the culmination of a long period of development in religious practice and thought regarding the rite of penance resulting in the diffusion of penitential manuals or tariff books throughout most of western Europe. These new practices had an important impact on religious practice in the army as the leading clerical and lay figures in the Carolingian government launched a major effort to make individual soldiers responsible for their own relationships with God, particularly through the rites of confession and penance.[1]

---

[1] There is still great controversy among scholars concerning the participation of lay people in the rite of confession, particularly individual confession, during the early Middle Ages. Some scholars argue for an eleventh-century or even a twelfth-century introduction of individual confession while other historians suggest that this rite was common as early as the ninth century. It will be argued here that individual confession was common among soldiers by the end of the eighth century.

The poles of the debate are now represented by André Vauchez and Joseph Avril, two of the leading French scholars dealing with medieval Christian practice. Vauchez holds a minimalist

Royal and Imperial Rites of War

As was the case with their Roman and late antique predecessors, the Carolingian kings and emperors developed and sustained a matrix of public religious rites and ceremonies involving broad sections of the population in an effort to propitiate God and to obtain divine support in battle. Charlemagne, in particular, would appear to have established a program of fasts, alms, prayers, special intercessory masses, and public liturgical rites that were designed to galvanize public support for military actions and to gain God's aid for Carolingian arms.[2] In 780, Charlemagne issued a capitulary containing wide- ranging instructions for the bishops in the *regnum Francorum* to organize an entire program of Christian rituals on behalf of the army. Each bishop was to say three masses: one on behalf of the king, one on behalf of the army, and one to alleviate the present suffering in which the kingdom found itself. In addition, each priest in the kingdom was to celebrate a similar three masses, and each monk and nun and canon was to say three psalms. Finally, all of the bishops, monks, nuns, and canons were to maintain a two-day fast and to give alms according to their means. The capitulary ends with the injunction to finish all of these rituals, performed on behalf of the king and army, by the feast of St John.[3]

view that early medieval society was only superficially Christian and that lay people rarely if ever participated in the rite of confession. On this point, see André Vauchez, *Les laïcs au moyen âge: pratiques et expériences religieuses* (Paris, 1987), p. 49, and "Présentation," in *Faire croire, modalités de la diffusion et de la réception des messages religieux du XIIe au XVe siècle* (Paris, 1981), pp. 8–16, here p. 10. By contrast, Avril argues for a rather more positive view of early medieval Christianity in which regular confession by lay people was a standard element of Christian religious practice by the early ninth century and continued to be treated as such by lay Christians right up to the eve of the Fourth Lateran Council in 1215. See Joseph Avril, "Remarques sur un aspect de la vie religieuse paroissiale: la pratique de la confession et de la communion du Xe au XIVe siècle," in *L'Encadrement religieux des fidèles au moyen âge et jusqu'au concile de Trente* (Paris, 1985), pp. 345–63, here pp. 345–9. Sarah Hamilton, *The Practice of Penance 900–1050* (London, 2001), provides a new synthesis on the problems of private and public penance, and argues for the wider practice of confession among lay people during the early Middle Ages than has generally been accepted. For a further summary of the literature with a particular emphasis on confession by soldiers, see David S. Bachrach, "Confession in the 'Regnum Francorum' (742–900): The Sources Revisited," *Journal of Ecclesiastical History* (forthcoming).

2 On this point, see Michael McCormick, "The Liturgy of War in the Early Middle Ages: Crisis, Litanies, and the Carolingian Monarchy," *Viator* 15 (1984), pp. 1–24, here p. 8 and passim; and Christoph T. Maier, "Crisis, Liturgy and the Crusade in the Twelfth and Thirteenth Centuries," *Journal of Ecclesiastical History* 48 (1997), pp. 628–57, here pp. 629–30. Erdmann, *Idea of Crusade*, pp. 39 and 82, incorrectly argues that the Visigothic kingdom was the only early medieval kingdom to employ public religious rites in support of the army. For criticisms of Erdmann's views in this regard, see Bernard S. Bachrach, *Early Carolingian Warfare: Prelude to Empire* (Philadelphia, 2001), p. 345, n. 148. Concerning the actual celebration of intercessory masses on behalf of the Carolingian army in the field, see Michael McCormick, "A New Ninth-Century Witness to the Carolingian Mass Against the Pagans," *Revue bénédictine* 97 (1987), pp. 68–86; and *Eternal Victory*, pp. 348–52.

3 MGH Concilia 2.1, ed. A. Werminghoff (Hanover, 1906), pp. 108–9. For discussion of this text, see McCormick "Liturgy of War," pp. 9–10. Similar programs of religious ceremonies

Charlemagne's direct efforts to secure spiritual support of this type can be seen in a letter that he sent to his wife Fastrada in 791 from the banks of the Enns river where the Carolingian army was preparing to invade Avar territory. After informing Fastrada of the religious rites that were being celebrated in camp, Charlemagne indicated his wish, which in this context should be read as a command, that the *fideles* remaining at home participate in the same round of religious rites (*letaniae*) as those being celebrated by his troops.[4] The form that these litanies likely took is indicated by an early ninth-century set of *laudes* included in Cologne MS 138.[5] In this text, God and Christ are called on to give victory to the emperor and to the army of the Romans and the Franks.[6] Following the refrain "Christus vincit, Christus regnat, Christus imperat," the second portion of the litany includes a series of the intended beneficiaries of divine support. Within this section are included "arma nostra invictissima," "murus noster inexpugnabilis," and "defensio et exaltatio nostra."[7] Litanies of this sort were also complemented by even more extensive rites, as is indicated by a letter sent by Rabanus Maurus to the monks at Fulda. He ordered them to say 1,000 masses and an equal number of cycles of the psalms on behalf of Louis the German and his army, then campaigning against the Bulgars (828).[8]

Charlemagne's efforts to mobilize prayers, masses, almsgiving, fasts, and other rites on behalf of the troops may well help to explain the fifth canon of the council of Friuli, held either in 796 or 797 under the leadership of Patriarch Paulinus of Aquileia. The bishops wished to stress that they could not serve in war in a military capacity, which was a continuing difficulty facing prelates during Charlemagne's reign.[9] Typically, the prelates quoted 2 Timothy 2.4, "nemo militans Deo implicat se negotiis secularibus," to defend their stance against providing personal military service under arms.[10] However, the bishops added that for those who were pleased to be *milites regis* while fighting in the fortresses of the Lord (*in castris dominicis*) it was necessary to consider care-

---

were included within the corpus of texts gathered by Benedict the Levite in the mid-ninth century, indicating that Charlemagne's efforts made an impact upon both contemporaries and those in later generations. See *Capitularia Spuria*, MGH, Legum 2 pars altera, ed. G.H. Pertz (Hanover, 1837), pp. 91–2 and 110–11.

4 MGH Epistolae 4, ed. E. Dümmler (Berlin, 1895), p. 529, *Unde volumus, ut tu cum ill. et ill. vel ceteris fi[de]libus nostris considerare debeas, qualiter ipsas letanias ibidem factas fiant.*

5 For a discussion of these texts, see Ernst H. Kantorowicz, *Laudes Regiae: A Study in Liturgical Acclamations and Mediaeval Ruler Worship* (Berkeley, 1946), pp. 105–6.

6 *Ibid.*, p. 105, *Domino nostro N. augusto et a Deo coronato magno et pacifico imperatori vita et Victoria,* and *Exercitui Romanorum et Francorum vita et victoria.*

7 *Ibid.*, p. 106.

8 *Epistolarum Fuldensium Fragmenta*, ed. E. Dümmler, MGH Epistolae 5 (Berlin, 1899), p. 518, *Monachi Fuldenses pro rege Francorum, qui in Bulgariam susceperat expeditionem, et patre et exercitu eius in quadragesima mille missas et totidem psalteria se murmarasse iactitant in epistola ad eundam.*

9 Friedrich Prinz, *Klerus und Krieg im früheren Mittelalter* (Stuttgart, 1971), pp. 73–113, demonstrates that Charlemagne did require many of his bishops to participate in military campaigns, often against their will.

10 Concilia 2.1, p. 191.

fully what arms they might use to fight against their adversaries.[11] Admittedly, the canon as a whole would appear to have as its primary focus distinguishing a secure role for bishops and priests as non-combatant clerics rather than as soldiers. However, the wording used by the bishops does indicate that they were aware of their obligations to serve the military needs of the *regnum* in a spiritual if not in an armed capacity.

Alcuin, a senior advisor to Charlemagne, was certainly aware of the ongoing need to involve clergy in pre-war religious preparations. He made this clear in a letter to Archbishop Riculf of Mainz on the occasion of the latter's journey to join Charlemagne's campaign against the Saxons in 794.[12] In the course of wishing him well, Alcuin urged Riculf to prepare himself for the journey by confessing his sins, and to seek divine aid for the campaign by giving alms and seeking the prayers of the "servants of God."[13] In Alcuin's view, proper religious preparations of this type would bring the Lord's angel to accompany and protect the royal forces against all danger so that the archbishop could set out with security and return home with peace.[14]

In addition to suggesting the common nature of such pre-war religious rites, Alcuin's remarks would also seem to reflect a general view that proper religious preparations would in fact bring divine assistance to Carolingian military undertakings. As we saw in the context of Roman and late antique warfare, promises of heavenly aid played a crucial role in maintaining army morale. In addition, the fact that promises of such aid were contingent on proper behavior among the troops was a useful tool in the hands of officers attempting to enforce discipline among their men. We shall see below that military sermons preached to the troops made explicit this connection between proper behavior, divine aid, and personal salvation.

It is possible to gauge the essence of such prayers for the king and royal campaigns from the "missa pro rege in die belli contra paganos" that survives in the sacramentary of Angoulême, which likely was composed during the last quarter of the eighth century.[15] In the collect, the eternal trinitarian God is begged to provide help to his church and to free the Christian people from the oppression of the nations (*gentes*) just as the sons of Israel had been saved from

---

[11] *Ibid., Intueri quapropter subtilius libet, cuius nos esse regis milites gratulamur. Et quia in castris dominicis militamus, sollicite pensare constringimur, quibus armis muniti cum tanto adversario certaminis bella adgressi pugnare valeamus. . . .*

[12] Epistolae 4, p. 66.

[13] *Ibid., Tu vero iter tuum confessione confirmare, elemosinis roborare, orationibus servorum Dei undique munire memento. . . .*

[14] *Ibid., ut angelus Domini te inter omnia adversa tueatur et comitetur, quatinus cum securitate vadas et cum pace revertaris.* It would appear that Charles the Bald took a similar attitude to pre-battle preparations as he readied for a campaign against Lothar in 841. According to Nithard, *Historiae*, ed. Reinhold Rau (Darmstadt, 1968), bk 2.6, pp. 414 and 416, the West Frankish king stopped at the monasteries of St Denis and St Germain to praise God and to pray.

[15] *Liber sacramentorum Engolismensis*, ed. Patrick Saint-Roch, CCSL 159C (Turnholt, 1987), pp. xi–xii. McCormick, *Eternal Victory*, p. 348, suggests that this text may have been written in 800.

the Egyptians.[16] The secret contains a prayer for God to release the king and his entire army from the fear of tyrants and to order them to return to their own lands in exultation, presumably after securing victory over their enemies.[17] The preface again requests divine aid, specifically asking that God provide assistance to the king and his army, just as he had aided Abraham, so that the evil peoples would not triumph over the Christians. This aid was to be brought through the holy angel with whose help the Christians would merit returning home, not only in triumph but in faith as well.[18]

As McCormick has indicated in his study of Carolingian liturgies of war, Charlemagne's efforts to mobilize public religious celebrations on behalf of the army met with considerable success. Thus, for example, a document contained in a late eighth-century formulary contains a *fragmentum* of a royal *mandatum* for a three-day fast to be carried out, for special masses to be celebrated, and for cycles of psalms to be sung, on account of "the sword which hangs over us."[19] In addition, the text of the document indicates that every cleric who knew them was to sing sixty psalms and abstain from fatty foods.[20] All of the lay people in the kingdom, who were not prevented by their youth or extreme age, were to go to church for each of the three days during these public religious celebrations, to fast, and to give alms.[21] The royal *mandatum* concluded by insisting that everyone remember that God was powerful enough to save them from their present difficulties, which was why a recent assembly had decided to impose these religious obligations, namely "in order that God save us from many troubles."[22] It should be noted that this document was not included in the formulary because it

---

[16] *Liber sacramentorum Engolismensis*, p. 358, n. 2307, *Sempiterna Trinitas Deus . . . deprecamur, ut omni ecclesiae tuae praestas auxilium; et sicut liberasti filios Israel de manibus aegyptiorum, ita libera populum tuum christianum de oppressione gentium.*

[17] *Ibid.*, n. 2308, *ita dignare famulo tuo illo cum omni exercitu suo liberare de tirannorum terrore et iube eos cum exultatione ad propria remeare.*

[18] *Ibid.*, n. 2309, *ut sicut fuisti auxiliator Abraham servo tuo . . ., ita praestare digneris auxilium famulo tuo illo cum omni exercitu suo contra gentes perfidas quod contra nos cognoscimus prevalare . . . ut non valeant contra populum christianum generare dispendia, sed mitte angelum tuum sanctum protectorem, ut triumphantes de victoria mereantur cum fidelitate remeare ad propria.*

[19] *Formulae Merkelianae Salicae*, ed. K. Zeumer, MGH Formulae (Hanover, 1882), n. 63, "Indiculum regalem admonitio," p. 262, *Congnoscat sanctitas vestra, quia domnus rex ille nobis dedit sua epistola, et in ipsa epistola habet insertum: 'Ut triduanum ieiunium faciatis pro istum gladium, quae super nos est; tam pro civitate quam pro monasteria virorum feminarumque seu per cunctos vicos generaliter factiatis missa et psalmodia. Unusquisque presbiter missa specialiter decantare faciat propter istam tribulationem.* . . . Concerning the value of this text for showing the effectiveness of Charlemagne's legislation, see McCormick, "Liturgy of War," p. 14.

[20] *Formulae Merkelianae Salicae*, n. 63, p. 262, *et unusquisque clericus, qui psalmus tenet, 60 cantet, et abstineant se adiperiis cibiis;* . . . .

[21] *Ibid., et alii homines hoc faciunt, nisi seni et parvuli, qui hoc implere non possunt, et illis tres diebus ad ecclesiam veniunt cum Dei adiutorium. Unusquisque elemonisa faciat;* . . . .

[22] *Ibid., consideret unusquisque, quia potens est Dominus, eripere nos de omni tribulatione. Et hoc sciatis, quia in nostrum placitum consideratum habemus ea facere, ut pius Dominus a multis tribulationes* (sic) *nos eripuit.*

was unique, but rather because, like all of the other documents included, it provided a model for a common type of royal edict.[23]

The continuing success of Carolingian efforts in the ninth century to utilize public prayers, masses, almsgiving, processions, and fasting to obtain divine aid for soldiers in the field is indicated by a collection of authentic and forged documents gathered during the mid-ninth century. Around 850 a deacon, called Benedict the Levite by modern scholars, compiled a corpus of royal and imperial edicts, some of which were genuine and some of which were forgeries, for the purpose of creating a dossier of arguments against the improper exploitation of church resources and personnel by secular authorities.[24] Consequently, when the author included materials listing the obligations of priests and bishops it is very likely that these represented common rather than extraordinary tasks. It is in this context that we should understand these ninth-century sources detailing not only the duties of priests serving at home on behalf of the army, but also the explanations given for these duties.[25]

For example, after noting the obligations of those priests and bishops selected to serve the pastoral needs of soldiers on campaign, Benedict included a discussion of the duties required of those clerics remaining in their own parishes.[26] After having mobilized the military contingents required from their districts, these priests and bishops were ordered to celebrate special masses on behalf of the ruler and his army (*pro nobis et cuncto exercitu nostro missas*), to carry out litanies (*letaniae*), and to give gifts (*oblationes*) and alms (*elymosinas*).[27] In addition, they were to offer prayers to God so that the troops would have a successful campaign and obtain divine aid in achieving victory over their enemies.[28]

This document, which was clearly intended to serve as a warning against requiring priests to bear arms, then compares the military failures of those nations that employed priests in battle as compared with the success of those that utilized the spiritual weapons available to clerics. The Gauls, Spanish, and

---

[23] On this point, see McCormick, "Liturgies of War," p. 14.

[24] Concerning the authorship of the pseudo-capitularies, see F.L. Ganshof, *Recherches sur les capitulaires* (Paris, 1958), pp. 8–9 and 71; Eugen Ewig, *Handbook of Church History III*, trans. Anselm Biggs (New York, 1969), pp. 167–9; and Hubert Mordek, *Bibliotheca Capitularium regum Francorum manuscripta: Überlieferung und Traditionszusammenhang der fränkischen Herrschererlasse* (Munich, 1995), pp. 1032–5. Concerning Pseudo-Benedict's use of sources, see Gerhard Schmitz, "Die Waffe der Fälschung zum Schutz der Bedrängten? Bemerkungen zu gefälschten Konzils-und Kaptilarientexten," in *Fälschungen im Mittelalter: Internationaler Kongress der Monumenta Germaniae Historica*, 5 vols. (Hanover, 1988), II: 79–110. Schmitz argues specifically (p. 92) that Pseudo-Benedict created his collection from previously existing materials.

[25] According to Ganshof, *Recherches sur les capitulaires*, pp. 67–8, the collections of capitularies made during the ninth century were intended to serve the practical needs of the bishops, abbots, and counts who comissioned them.

[26] *Capitularia Spuria*, p. 110, no. 141. Benedict's efforts in this regard are discussed by McCormick, "Liturgy of War," p. 15.

[27] *Capitularia Spuria*, p. 110, no. 141.

[28] *Ibid., orantes Deum coeli, ut proficiamus in itinere quo pergimus, victoresque Deo amminiculante existamus.*

Lombards are singled out by the author as being among those peoples who permitted their priests to fight and subsequently lost in battle.[29] By contrast, victory was granted when priests celebrated mass and offered the Lord's body to Christians for the redemption of their souls.[30]

One final type of public rite suggested by the surviving evidence was the organization of public prayers for soldiers on the anniversaries of the battles in which they died. McCormick has argued convincingly that additions to liturgical calendars of battle dates, such as the one included in a sacramentary from Lorsch commemorating Louis the Younger's victory over Charles the Bald at Andernach in 876, may have been intended to recall those who fell so that prayers could be made on behalf of their souls on the anniversary of their sacrifice.[31] The requirement that similar types of prayers be said can be found in endowment grants such as Charles the Bald's bequest to St Denis in which he asked for annual prayers on a number of anniversaries including a military victory.[32] The public nature of these prayers for the battle-dead may well have helped to ease the fears of soldiers about their own salvation should they fall in battle as well as giving to their families and friends the solace that their loved ones were being cared for in a spiritual sense.

Public Rites of the Carolingian Army

Much like their Roman and late antique predecessors, the armies of the Frankish kingdom and empire participated in a broad range of religious rites and ceremonies that were intended to purify the fighting force, to propitiate God, and to beg for divine assistance in battle. As we saw in the previous chapter, contemporary representations of these rites in the empire and Late Antiquity frequently focused attention on the actions of the general or king. John Troglyta, for example, is shown by Corippus both instructing his men in their religious obligations and leading them in their prayers. Similar representations mark the accounts of Julian of Toledo and Bede with respect to King Wamba and King Oswald respectively. As the mass for the king in the Angoulême sacramentary, noted above, makes clear, Carolingian army rites still emphasized the role played by the king. Nevertheless, we can also see more attention being paid in this period to the religious behavior of the simple soldiers themselves. This phenomenon in turn suggests a concomitant effort at an ideological level to

---

[29] *Ibid., Gentes enim et reges earum qui sacerdotes secum pugnare permiserunt, nec praevalebant in bello. . . . Haec vero Galliarum, Hispaniarum, Langobardum nonnullasque alias gentes et reges fecisse cognovimus.*

[30] *Ibid., Qualis enim victoria datur, ubi sacerdotes una hora dominica pertractant mysteria, et christianis dominicum porrigunt corpus pro suarum animarum redemptione. . . .*

[31] McCormick, *Eternal Victory*, pp. 360–2.

[32] *Recueil des actes de Charles II le Chauve, roi de France*, vol. 2, ed. A. Giry, M. Prou, and G. Tessier (Paris, 1963), n. 246, pp. 54–6. Stuart Airlie, "True Teachers and Pious Kings: Salzburg, Louis the German, and Christian Order," in *Belief and Culture in the Middle Ages*, ed. Richard Gameson and Henrietta Leyser (Oxford, 2001), pp. 89–105, here p. 100, notes that prayer clauses of this type were a standard feature of many royal charters.

create a sense of corporate identity or *esprit de corps* among the troops by tying the behavior of individual soldiers to the success of the army as a whole, an effort made simpler by the uniformly orthodox allegiance of the troops.

In one famous case, we have evidence directly from Charlemagne for the religious preparations made by his army before battle in 791. In the letter to Fastrada, noted above, Charlemagne detailed the religious ceremonies and rites celebrated by his soldiers and priests as they prepared to invade Avar territory. He explained that the men performed three days of litanies from the fifth through the seventh of September. These celebrations may well have featured relics of the type discussed by the bishops at the *Concilium Germanicum* in 742 who required that bishops and their attendant chaplains serve on campaign in part to guard the sacred relics (*patrocinia*) that were being brought to war.[33] Indeed, Notker the Stammerer reported that it was common for Frankish kings to bring St Martin's *cappa* to war in order to secure the safety of their troops and to defeat the enemy.[34] During the ceremonies everyone in camp begged that God in his mercy act as their support, their councilor, and their defender. They specifically asked that God grant them victory in the approaching battle and keep them safe and free from danger.[35] Charlemagne further informed his wife that those who could do so abstained from meat and wine, and that everyone gave alms according to his means. Furthermore, every cleric familiar with the text sang fifty psalms and each priest celebrated a votive mass unless he was prevented by some infirmity.[36]

In his letter to Fastrada, Charlemagne did not refer to the specific intercessory masses celebrated by priests in his camp, and it is therefore impossible to know which particular prayers that were said on behalf of the troops and the army. However, a mass from the well-known Sacramentary of Gellone that was specifically intended for those going to war against the enemy "in profectium hostium eontibus in prohelium" does survive from the late eighth century.[37] The

---

[33] *Concilium Germanicum*, ed. Albertus Werminghoff, MGH Concilia 2: Concilia Aevi Karolini 1.1 (Hanover, 1906), canon 2, p. 3.

[34] Notker the Stammerer, *Gesta Karoli Magni Imperatorism*, MGH SRG n.s. 12 (Munich, 1980), p. 5, *Quo nomine reges Francorum propter cappam Sancti Martini, quam secum ob sui tuitionem et hostium appressionem iugiter ad bella portabant, sancta sua appellare solebant.*

[35] Epistolae 4, p. 528, *nos autem, Domino adiuvante, tribus diebus letania fecimus, . . . Dei misericordiam deprecantes, ut nobis pacem et sanitatem atque victorium et prosperum iter tribuere dignetur, et ut in sua misericordia et pietate nobis adiutor et consiliator atque defensor in omnibus angustiis nostris exsistat.* McCormick, *Eternal Victory*, p. 352, suggests that the liturgical rites deployed by the Carolingian forces at the Enns river in 791 were the fruit of Charlemagne's promotion of a new series of services that directly involved the army and which were meant to obtain divine aid in battle. At least one element of this religious ensemble, however, would appear to have had its roots at an earlier date. As was noted above, the *Concilium Germanicum* ruled in 742 that each military commander should have one or two bishops on his staff along with their chaplain priests who were to celebrate mass and carry relics on campaign. See Concilia 2.1, canon 2, p. 3.

[36] Epistolae 4, p. 529, *Et sacerdos unusquisque missam specialem fecisset, nisi infirmitas inpedisset. Et clerici, qui psalmos sciebant, unusquisque quinquaginta cantasset . . . .*

[37] The text of this intercessory mass was first discovered by Gerd Tellenbach and published in "Römischer und christlicher Reichsgedanke in der Liturgie des frühen Mittelalters," in *Sitzungsberichte der heidelberger Akademie der Wissenschaften* 24 (1934), pp. 67–70. The

opening prayer of this mass calls upon God to offer light to his army as it goes into the shadows in order to increase the motivation of those setting out, just as He had offered his protection to the Israelites fleeing from Egypt by providing them with signs and guidance during their journey. The prayer continues by asking God to ensure that those setting forth to battle be protected without difficulties being interposed and that they be highly motivated to fight without being held back by fear. The prayer concludes by promising that victory under these conditions would be attributed to God, who acted as a fighting man in battle on behalf of his faithful supporters.[38]

The prayers in this mass corresponded closely to supplications of the Carolingian troops recorded by Charlemagne in his letter to Fastrada when they asked God as their support, their councilor, and their defender to grant them victory and free them from danger. Eric Goldberg has identified another heretofore unknown prayer from the late 820s, which was also intended to be said by Carolingian soldiers before they went into battle.[39] The Blessing of the Cross (*Benedictio Crucis*) was written for Louis the German by Bishop Baturich of Regensburg. The prayer called upon God to bless the standard of the cross so that it would aid His faithful followers and help to defend them against their enemies. The prayer envisioned a cleric holding up the cross on a banner of some sort before which the king and his men were to kneel and beg God to aid them. Bishop Baturich's use of the *vexillum crucis* as the focus of his prayer echoes Theodulf of Orléans' remarks in the *Opus Caroli regis* where he drew a distinction between the ineffective Byzantine worship of mere pictures and the Carolingian veneration of the true cross. Theodulf claimed that images of the cross were commonly used as a flag or rallying sign (*vexillum*) by Charlemagne's troops in the field so that they could follow it into battle and fight more

best current edition is *Sacramentarium Gellonense*, ed. A. Dumas, Corpus Christianorum 159 (Turnholt, 1981) 430: 2750 (p. 431). See also Bernard Moreton, *The Eighth-Century Gelasian Sacramentary: A Study in Tradition* (Oxford, 1976), pp. 187–91. McCormick, *Eternal Victory*, pp. 347–8, has identified the army rather than the commander as the object of this mass. Concerning the value of the mass for the morale of Carolingian soldiers, see Bachrach, *Early Carolingian Warfare*, p. 149. This prayer is repeated in *Le sacramentaire gélasien d'Angoulême*, ed. P. Cagin (Angoulême, n.d. [1919]), fol. 167v, no. 2310. Concerning this text, see Moreton, *Eighth Century*, pp. 192–3; and McCormick, *Eternal Victory*, p. 349.

[38] *Sacramentarium Gellonense*, p. 431, *Prebe domine exercitui tuo eunti in tenebris claritatem, proficiendi augeas voluntatem, et sicut israheli properanti ex egypto securitatis prebuisti munimen, ita tuo predistinato eunti in prelio populo lucis auctor[m] adicias angelum, ut diem adque noctem qui nubis ignisque claritatis tue columne non deserat. Sit eis it[in]erandi[s] sine labore protectus, ubique providus eventus, meditatus sine fortitudine, conversatio sine fastidio, sine terrore copia proeliandi voluntas, ut cum tuum duce angelum victur exteterit, non suis tribuat viribus, sed victori domino gratias referat de triumpho qui fuit belliger fidelibus in conflictu. Per dominum.*

[39] Concerning the employment of prayers on behalf of Louis the German and the general use of religious rites in support of the army in Louis the German's realm, see Eric J. Goldberg, " 'More Devoted to the Equipment of Battle than the Splendor of Banquets': Frontier Kingship, Martial Ritual, and Early Knighthood at the Court of Louis the German," *Viator* 30 (1999), pp. 41–78, here pp. 60–72. The discussion of this prayer is found on p. 67. The text of this prayer is to be found in Munich Clm 14510, fols. 71v–72v.

bravely.[40] We get yet another glimpse of pre-battle prayers from the *Ludwigslied* whose author affirmed that the Frankish troops prepared to attack the Northmen in 881 by singing the *Kyrie eleison*, much like Byzantine soldiers are supposed to have done.[41]

These types of pre-combat rites were mirrored, on occasion, by post-battle ceremonies that focused on attributing ultimate credit for victory to God, thereby justifying Carolingian successes within the penumbra of divine support. In victories against non-Christian enemies, these celebrations could take on truly triumphalist tones. Louis the Pious, for example, delayed entering the conquered city of Barcelona in 801 until he could consecrate his victory in a manner befitting the grace shown to the Frankish forces by God.[42] After all of the arrangements had been settled, the Carolingian army staged a grand procession led by the army's priests with the soldiers marching behind. As they passed the city gates the men sang psalms and *laudes*. They then proceeded up to the Church of the Holy and Victorious Cross where they gave thanks to God for the divine victory.[43] We can see a similarly joyous post-battle celebration following Arnulf's victory over the Northmen at the batthle of the Dyle in 891. Here, the Frankish king ordered litanies to be celebrated. Then, along with his entire army, Arnulf marched in a victory procession singing God's praises since, as the chronicler recalled, it was by divine grace that victory had fallen to the Christians.[44]

However, in wars among Christians, the post-battle rites could have penitential rather than triumphant overtones. Thus, for example, in the aftermath of the battle of Fontenoy in 841 among Louis the Pious' three sons, the victorious Charles the Bald and Louis the German had their own dead as well as Lothar's

---

[40] Theodulf of Orléans, *Opus Caroli regis contra synodum (Libri Carolini)* 2.28, ed. Ann Freeman, MGH Concilia 2, suppl. 1 (Hanover, 1998), pp. 296–7, *Non igitur quaedam materialis imago, sed Dominicae crucis mysterium est vexillum, quod in campo duelli, ut fortius confligamus, sequi debemus; arma, quibus libertatem tueri valeamus; munitio, qua infestantium hostium incursus evitemus*. On this point, see Goldberg, " 'More Devoted to the Equipment of Battle than the Splendor of Banquets,' " p. 64.

[41] *Ludwigslied*, in *Die kleinen althochdeutschen Sprachdenkmäler*, ed. E. von Steinmeyer (Berlin, 1916), p. 86. Concerning contemporary use by Byzantines and the eastern origin of this Frankish practice, see McCormick, *Eternal Victory*, p. 354.

[42] Astronomer, *Vita Hludowici imperatoris*, ed. Ernst Tremp, MGH SRG separatim editi 64 (Hanover, 1995), c. 13, p. 318, *ipse autem ab eius ingressu abstinuit, donec ordinaret, qualiter cum digna Deo gratiarum actione cupitam atque susceptam victoriam eius nomini consecraret*.

[43] *Ibid.*, pp. 318–20, *Antecedentibus ergo eum in crastinum et exercitum eius sacerdotibus et clero, cum sollempni apparatu et laudibus hymnidicis portam civitatis ingressus et ad ecclesiam sanctae et victoriosissime crucis pro victoria sibi divinitus conlata gratiarum actiones Deo acturus est progressus*.

[44] *Annales Fuldenses*, ed. F. Kurze, MGH SRG 7 (Hanover, 1891), p. 121, *Eodem in loco . . . letanias rex celebrare praecepit; ipse cum omni exercitu laudes Deo canendo processit, qui talem victoriam tribuit . . .*; and p. 120, *subveniente gratia Dei victoria ad Christianos concessit*. Cf. *Chronicon Laurissense breve*, ed. H. Schnorr von Carolsfeld, in *Neues Archiv* 36 (1911), pp. 15–39, here p. 31, and *Annales regni Francorum*, ed. G.H. Pertz and F. Kurze, MGH SRG 6 (Hanover, 1895), p. 40, for Charlemagne's triumphant entry into Pavia in 774, which was celebrated *cum hymnis et laudibus*. For a discussion of this event, see Bachrach, *Early Carolingian Warfare*, p. 148; and McCormick, *Eternal Victory*, pp. 374–5.

fallen troops buried after a solemn mass.[45] Then the bishops from the two victorious armies held a public council in which they declared that the victory was a clear divine judgment for their side.[46] Yet rather than hymns and victory processions, the victorious troops underwent a three-day fast to mourn for the fallen Christians on both sides.[47]

The impact of both pre- and post-battle rites for raising morale, building a sense of *esprit de corps* among the troops, and giving religious sanction to military discipline was a function of contemporary belief that God's support was obtainable, inherently good in itself, and necessary for victory.[48] We can see this view propagated in a wide range of royally supported narrative accounts in which victory is attributed to the aid of God. Thus, for example, the author of the *Annales regni Francorum* routinely emphasized that Frankish victories came about *auxiliante Domino, Deo volente, Domino volente,* and *Domino protegente.*[49]

But it was not simply enough that God could be the guarantor of victory, soldiers also had the obligation to ask for this aid and to be worthy of receiving it. Thus, the author of the *Annales regni Francorum* insisted that the rites carried out by Charlemagne's troops in the Avar campaign of 791 were performed for the safety of the army and in order to obtain Christ's help in achieving victory over the Avars.[50] In his letter to Archbishop Riculf of Mainz, noted above, Alcuin stressed that whoever had justice on his side and fought for God could rest assured that divine aid would be forthcoming.[51] Arnulf of Carinthia used God's name and the promise of divine aid to inspire his men in 891 before engaging the Northmen at the battle of the Dyle. Thus, before the fighting began, he harangued his troops, reminding them that they had always been invincible when they kept God in their thoughts and protected their fatherland (*patria*) under God's grace.[52] Perhaps of equal importance to maintaining high morale was the notion that when men fought in a just cause and on behalf of God, they could be assured of salvation if they died in battle. In 853, Pope Leo IV promised that this was the case in a letter to Emperor Lothar I when requesting aid in case of future Muslim attacks in Italy. The pope emphasized that God knew that each Frankish soldier who died in battle would have done so

---

[45] Nithard, *Historia*, bk 3.1, p. 428.

[46] *Ibid., hoc Dei iuditio manifestum effectum sit.*

[47] *Ibid.*, p. 430.

[48] Bachrach, *Early Carolingian Warfare*, p. 148, makes this point with regard to the early Carolingians, noting the frequency with which royal writers use the phrases *Deo auxiliante* and *Christo auxiliante* when describing Frankish victories in the field.

[49] *Annales regni Francorum,* pp. 36, 42, 44, 54, 68, and 82.

[50] *Ibid.*, p. 88, *Ad Anisam vero fluvium properantes ibi constituerunt laetanias faciendi per triduo missarumque sollemnia celebrandi; Dei solatium postulaverunt pro salute exercitus et adiutorio domini nostri Iesu Christi et pro victoria et vindicta super Avaros.*

[51] Epistolae 4, p. 66, *Tamen, qui iustitiam habet eundi et pro Deo decertandi, fiduciam potest habere de auxilio illius . . .*

[52] *Annales Fuldenses*, p. 120, *Viri, Deum recolentes et semper sub Dei gratia patriam tuendo fuistis invincibiles.*

for the true faith (*pro veritate fidei*), for the safety of his fatherland (*salvatio patriae*), and for the defense of Christians (*defensio Christianorum*). Consequently, none of these men would be denied the kingdom of heaven.[53]

Personal Religious Preparations for War

The mobilization of religious resources at a kingdom-wide and army-wide level had a crucial impact on the morale, *esprit de corps*, and discipline of Carolingian troops, much as it had on their Roman and late antique predecessors. These ends were certainly helped by offering the promise of divine aid in battle, tying this aid to proper behavior, and reminding the men through participation in common rites of their ties to each other and to the army as a whole. However, the development of repeatable confession and the control this gave to individual soldiers over their own personal salvation opened an entirely new area of military-religious practice. Fighting men now had to be given an opportunity to confess their sins before battle in order to propitiate God for the sake of divine aid in battle, and for the sake of their eternal souls.

The earliest surviving evidence for the provision of private confession by soldiers in the *regnum Francorum* comes from canon two of the *Concilium Germanicum* held in 742 under the direction of Carloman, Carolingian Mayor of the Palace, and the English missionary Boniface.[54] It has been suggested that

---

[53] PL 115: 657, *quisquis . . . in hoc belli certamine fideliter mortuus fuit, regna illi coelestia minime negabuntur. Novit enim Omnipotens si quilibet vestrum morietur, quod pro veritate fidei, et salvatione patriae, ac defensione Christianorum mortuus est; ideo ab eo praetitulatum praemium consequetur.*

[54] Canon two of the *Concilium Germanicum* has been discussed by Albert Michael Koeniger, *Die Militärseelsorge der Karolingerzeit: Ihr Recht und ihre Praxis* (Munich, 1918), pp. 12–17; Erdmann, *The Origin of the Idea of Crusade*, p. 16; Prinz, *Klerus und Krieg*, pp. 8–9; and Wilfried Hartmann, *Die Synoden der Karolingerzeit im Frankreich und in Italien* (Paderborn, 1989), pp. 50–3. Jean Chélini, *L'Aube du moyen âge: naissance de la chrétienté occidentale* (Picard, 1991), pp. 372–3, emphasizes that the portion of canon two dealing with the provision of confessors for soldiers was an element of the general Carolingian effort to reform the penitential practices of the Frankish church. The most recent discussion of the council and its relevance to Carolingian warfare is now Bachrach, *Early Carolingian Warfare*, pp. 49–50.

For a tour of the horizon concerning the historiographical tradition dealing with Boniface's role in organizing the *Concilium Germanicum* in 742 and two subsequent councils in 745 and 747, see the introduction to *The Letters of Saint Boniface* by Thomas F.X. Noble (New York, 2000), pp. vii–xxxv, esp. pp. xx–xxi. Boniface's role as the organizer of these councils had earlier been stressed by Timothy Reuter, "Saint Boniface and Europe," in *The Greatest Englishman: Essays on St. Boniface and the Church at Crediton*, ed. Timothy Reuter (Exeter, 1980), pp. 69–94, here p. 79. More recently, Reuter, " 'Kirchenreform' und 'Kirchenpolitik' im Zeitalter Karl Martells: Begriffe und Wirklichkeit," in *Karl Martell in seiner Zeit*, ed. Jörg Jarnut, Ulrich Nonn, and Michael Richter (Sigmaringen, 1994), pp. 35–9, has argued that there was no plan of church reform at an institutional level, but rather an effort to require clerics to carry out their pastoral duties in a proper manner. Joseph Semmler, "Bonifatius, die Karolinger, und die Franken," in *Mönchtum-Kirche-Herrschaft, 750–1000*, ed. Dieter R. Bauer, Rudolf Hiestand, Brigitte Kasten, and Sönke Lorenz (Sigmaringen, 1998), pp. 3–49,

Boniface, who had traveled widely in Italy, may have been encouraged by his knowledge of Byzantine military-religious practice to encourage the introduction of legislation dealing with the pastoral care of soldiers, including the recruitment of priests capable of hearing their confessions.[55] Alternately, Boniface may have been drawing on his own experiences in England, where he was educated.[56] As was noted in the previous chapter, the earliest tariff books with their schedules of sins and penances, including penances for killing in war, appeared in Ireland and England, subsequently making their way to *Francia* by the end of the seventh century.[57] There is no direct evidence, however, that Boniface dealt with the provision of pastoral care to soldiers, or more specifically with soldiers' confession and penances prior to or after the *Concilium Germanicum*. Consequently, the inclusion of clauses dealing specifically with this question in canon two of the council may also be understood to have come about as a result of Carolingian interest rather than Boniface's own overriding concern for the reform of the church. Carloman's unprecedented act of reissuing the decrees of the *Concilium Germanicum* as a capitulary in 742 underscores the Mayor of the Palace's own deep concern with pushing the religious reforms enunciated by the council.[58] Of course, inspiration for the introduction of military-pastoral legislation may have come from all three sources and there is no need to preclude the possibility that information and ideas were transmitted among England, Italy, and *Francia*.

Whatever the origins of the council's effort to apply reform efforts in the area of military pastoral care, it is clear that the participants in the *Concilium Germanicum* were concerned with the problems of confession and penance in

here pp. 21–3, emphasizes Carloman's proactive role in seeking out Boniface and pushing for the *Concilium Germanicum*.

[55] Koeniger, *Militärseelsorge*, pp. 22–3. Boniface would appear to have had ample opportunity to see and hear about Byzantine soldiers and military organization during his trips to Rome in 718–19 and 722. Byzantine forces stationed in the exarchate of Ravenna were engaged in substantial military operations against both the Lombards and the papal state in the period from 718 to 725. In particular, the Lombards first captured and were then forced to give up the port of Classe in 719, and Exarch Paul invaded papal territories in 725 in response to a tax revolt. Concerning these Byzantine military actions and Boniface's journey south from Bavaria through northern Italy down to Rome, see Thomas F.X. Noble, *The Republic of St. Peter: The Birth of the Papal State, 680–825* (Philadelphia, 1984), pp. 25–9. Concerning the pastoral care available to Byzantine soldiers, see A. Heisenberg, "Kriegsgottesdienst in Byzanz," *Aufsätze zur Kultur-und Sprachgeschichte vornehmlich des Orients* (Munich, 1916), pp. 244–57; J.R. Vieillefond, "Les pratiques religieuses dans l'armée byzantine d'après les traités militaires," *Revue des études anciennes* 37 (1933), pp. 322–30; and Paul Goubert, "Religion et superstitions dans l'armée byzantine à la fin du VIe siècle," in *Orientalia christiana periodica: miscellanea Guillaume de Jerphanion* 13 (1947), pp. 495–500.

[56] Concerning Boniface's education, see Wilhelm Levison, *England and the Continent in the Eighth Century* (Oxford, 1946), pp. 70–2; and Noble, *Introduction*, pp. viii–xi. Concerning Boniface's contacts with England, see Dorothy Whitelock, "After Bede: Jarrow Lecture 1960" (Jarrow, 1960), pp. 6–8; and Levison, *England and the Continent*, p. 70.

[57] Pierce (McKitterick), "The 'Frankish' Penitentials"; Kottje, "Die Tötung im Kriege"; and Bachrach, *Early Carolingian Warfare*, pp. 153–4.

[58] For the unprecedented nature of Carloman's subsequent capitulary, see Noble, *Introduction*, p. xxi.

the army, as well as with assuring the proper celebration of mass and the utiliza-
tion of sacred relics within the wider context of improving the general quality of
lay religious life. Thus, for example, the third canon issued by the council
includes an injunction that parish priests be able to demonstrate an ability to
perform baptisms, discuss the tenets of the faith, and be familiar with Christian
prayers as well as the order of the mass.[59] Similarly, bishops were required by
the fifth canon to be defenders of the church, and to keep their parishioners from
succumbing to pagan rites, particularly those that parodied or incorporated
elements of Christian liturgy.[60]

It was in the second canon, however, that the council dealt specifically with
the pastoral care to be provided to soldiers in the field. The commander of the
army was required to have on his staff one or two bishops with their attending
chaplains who were responsible for celebrating mass and bringing relics on military campaign, practices that would appear to have had their origins in the
pre-Carolingian period.[61] What was now new was the requirement that the
commander (*praefectus*) of every military unit in the Carolingian army have on
his staff a priest capable of hearing confessions (*peccata confitentibus iudicare*)
and assigning penances (*indicare poenitentiam possint*) to the soldiers under his
care.[62] It would appear that a distinction should be drawn here between the great
mass of priests, who were to serve on the staff of individual unit commanders,
and the one or two bishops who served on the staff of the army commander
(*praefectus*). The latter, along with their *capellani*, were responsible for celebrating mass for the whole army, and were entrusted with the relics that the
army brought into the field, tasks that had been fulfilled by bishops and priests
since the days of Constantine the Great more than four centuries earlier. The
new participants in the military campaign were simple priests who were
assigned the time-consuming and labor-intensive task of hearing the soldiers'
confessions and assigning them appropriate penances according to the models
set out in the "tariff books."

The wording of canon two of the *Concilium Germanicum* makes clear that
each priest had to be capable of assigning penances (*indicare poenitentiam*).
This indicates that the responsible authorities in the Frankish leadership
intended soldiers to have an opportunity to make individual confessions while

---

[59] Concilia 2.1, p. 3, . . . *de babtismo sive de fide catholica sive de precibus et ordine
missarum, episcopo reddat et ostendat.*
[60] *Ibid.*, p. 3.
[61] *Ibid.*
[62] *Ibid., et unusquisque praefectus* [habeat] *unum presbiterum, qui hominibus peccata
confitentibus iudicare et indicare poenitentiam possint.* I read the *habeat* in this canon as a
jussive. One of the major purposes of this council was to formalize the religious obligations
of priests with respect to the laymen under their care. This canon was clearly intended to
ensure that Carolingian soldiers also had access to pastoral care while on campaign. On this
point, see Koeniger, *Militärseelsorge*, pp. 18–24; Erdmann, *Idea of Crusade*, p. 16; and
Bachrach, *Early Carolingian Warfare*, p. 150. The text of the canons issued by the council
was quickly reissued by Carloman as a capitulary in 742. On this point, see *Capitularia regum
Francorum* 1, ed. Alfred Boretius, MGH (Hanover, 1883), pp. 24–6, where the entire collection of canons from the council was reissued as a capitulary.

serving in the field away from their home parishes and priests. The very nature of the tariff-type penance required that the penance fit the sin, a circumstance that could only occur when the priest responsible for assigning penances had heard a list of sins from the individual penitent, in this case the individual penitent soldier.[63] In situations where soldiers gathered together and offered a common admission of guilt in a general form, priests were not in a position to assign penances. The bishops who composed this canon undoubtedly were fully aware of the necessary connection between individual private confession and penance by tariff.

Although there is no direct evidence for how many priests served with Carolingian forces in the field or what kind of ratio of priests to soldiers, if any, Frankish military and religious planners had in mind, it is useful to consider, at least for heuristic purposes, what kinds of participation would have been required in order to have priests hear the individual confessions of soldiers.[64] If we take a force of 5,000 fighting men and then figure that the average confession of individual sins required three minutes, we arrive at 15,000 minutes or 250 "priest hours."[65] If each chaplain serving with the army worked for ten hours before battle without taking a break, the entire army could be confessed by twenty-five priests. However, if the average confession took five minutes, the number of priest hours jumps to over 400, with the concomitant need for more priests or longer periods of service. Of course, if the priests worked for fewer

---

[63] I would like to thank Father Michael Driscoll for focusing my attention on this crucial aspect of the rite of confession and thus assuring us that these rituals were not a form of mass public confession.

[64] Ferdinand Lot's assertion that Carolingian armies had a maximum size of about 5,000 men has generally been rejected by medieval military historians. For the minimalist figures on Carolingian military demography, see Ferdinand Lot, *L'Art militaire et les armées au moyen âge en Europe dans le proche orient*, 2 vols. (Paris, 1946), I: 94–103. On the new state of the question, see Bernard S. Bachrach, "Early Medieval Military Demography: Some Observations on the Methods of Hans Delbrück," in *The Circle of War in the Middle Ages: Essays on Medieval Military and Naval History*, ed. Donald J. Kagay and L.J. Andrew Villalon (Woodbridge, 1999), pp. 3–20. For the large size of Carolingian field forces and the capability of mobilizing some 100,000 effectives, see Karl Ferdinand Werner, "Heeresorganization und Kriegsführung im deutschen Königreich des 10. und 11. Jahrhunderts," *Ordinamenti Militari in Occidente nell'Alto Mediaevo: Settimane di Studio del Centro Italiano di Studi sull'Alto Medioevo* 15 (Spoleto, 1968), pp. 791–843, here pp. 814–16; and Philippe Contamine, *La guerre au moyen âge*, 4th edn (Paris, 1994), trans. into English by Michael Jones under the title *War in the Middle Ages* (Oxford, 1984), p. 24. For a review of the litterature on the question of early medieval military demography including the rejection of the small army thesis, see Bachrach, "Early Medieval Military Demography."

[65] This figure may in fact be low considering the normal form confession was supposed to take. First, the penitent had to approach the priest and admit that he was sinful. The priest was then to question the penitent about his social and marital status, and manner in which he earned his living. He was then to lead him through the appropriate list of sins asking whether he was guilty of any of them. Afer ascertaining what sins had been committed, the priest was to urge the penitent to search deeply for any further sins. Only then was the priest supposed to assign an appropriate penance. For a detailed model of this procedure, see See Dhuoda, *Manuel pour mon fils*, ed. Pierre Riché, Sources Chrétiennes 225 (Paris, 1975), pp. 194–6.

than ten hours before battle, there would also have been a need for a greater number of priests.

The impact of Carloman's legislation concerning confession by soldiers in the army can be gauged by subsequent measures intended to help priests perform the necessary religious duties on campaign. Thus, for example, the perceived frequency with which priests served as military chaplains is indicated by the statutes issued in 800 at Charlemagne's order by the councils of Riesbach, Freising, and Salzburg. In the fifth canon issued by the bishops at Riesbach, which was reiterated by the later councils mentioned here, priests were enjoined to abstain from eating meat and drinking wine on every Thursday and Saturday with the exception of the period from Christmas to Epiphany, and from Easter to Pentecost. They were also permitted to abstain from this fast on the feast days of Mary, John the Baptist, the Twelve Apostles, Archangel Michael, St Martin, and interestingly, the feast of the particular saint venerated in their parishes.[66] Of particular importance in the present context, the bishops also added certain other occasions when priests could avoid fasting. These were when giving charity, when a fellow priest arrived, when a priest was ill, when he was on a journey, when he was at the royal court, or when he was serving with the host (*in hoste*).[67] The addition of the last clause suggests that priests served in war frequently enough to merit attention to this practice at the conciliar level. The reference to the patron saints of the individual parishes, noted above, would seem to indicate that parish priests had a role to play in military campaigns.

The text of this canon concerning clerical abstinence also survives in a shortened form in an epitome of a now lost collection of conciliar *acta*.[68] Here, the priests are given permission to eat meat and drink wine on Thursdays and Saturdays when these fell on feast days, in the period between Easter and Pentecost, or when a friend arrived. The text adds that they were not required to fast if they were on a journey, at the palace or in court, when sick, or when serving in a military campaign (*in bello*).[69] The survival of this epitomized version of the statute issued in 800 indicates both that conciliar decisions were transmitted to the local level and that the service of priests on campaign seemed pertinent to the author of the epitome, who did not hesitate to alter other elements of the original canon.

It is likely that by including the clause granting a temporary indulgence to priests serving on military campaign, the bishops at Riesbach, and subsequently at Freising and Salzburg, were reacting to an already established need rather than to a hypothetical future concern. As we saw above, Charlemagne's army had a substantial number of priests in service as it camped along the Enns river in 791. Similarly, a letter sent to Charlemagne by Pope Hadrian I sometime between 784 and 791 indicates that latter was both aware of and approved the

---

[66] *Concilia Rispancense, Frisingense, Salisburgense*, in Concilia 2.1, p. 208.
[67] *Ibid., vel etiam caritatis officium implendum, in adventu fratrum supervenientum, et his, qui in hoste vel in itinere constituti vel ad palatium domni regis veniunt vel infirmitate etiam detenti, indulgentiam concedimus.*
[68] *Notitia concilii Rispacense*, in *ibid.*, p. 214.
[69] *Ibid., item non tenentur ieiunare qui in bello, in itinere, in palatio, aut in curia principis, infirmi. . . .*

regular service of priests on campaign in a religious capacity. In the course of his letter, the pope rehearsed several of the main points of an earlier conversation that he had with Duke Garamannus, who was the Frankish king's *missus* to the court of St Peter. This colloquy between the pope and Charlemagne's representative concerned a certain monk named John, who had been in Charlemagne's service but seems to have earned papal opprobrium for discussing certain of his theologically questionable visions in public.[70] Thus, at Charlemagne's request, Garamannus conveyed the king's petition to the pope so that the latter would grant John his grace and thus absolve the monk from the consequences of his misbehavior.[71]

It is clear from the nature of Hadrian's letter that he and/or his functionaries debriefed John in order to obtain the full details of his misadventure. In the course of this interrogation, it became obvious that John had information regarding Charlemagne's plans to use bishops actively on military campaign, probably, in light of their status, in a command function.[72] Thus, perhaps in an effort to demonstrate his own adherence to church teaching, John answered the questions of his papal interrogators by emphasizing that he had told the Frankish king that bishops were only permitted to use spiritual weapons, and were prohibited from using physical weapons. This point was obviously consistent with both general church teaching, and with the specific requirements of the canons issued by synods such as the *Concilium Germanicum* in 742 and the council of Friuli in 796.[73]

The pope utilized the opportunity provided by this mention of John's conversation with Charlemagne about the military service of bishops to encourage the Frankish king to avoid involving his bishops in improper actions.[74] However, Hadrian then contrasted this improper use of bishops with Charlemagne's practice of bringing bishops and priests to war for the sake of providing pastoral care to Frankish soldiers serving in the field. According to Hadrian, it was proper for the king to bring clerics with him to any place that he wished (*in quolibet deferri cupit loco*) in order for them to hear the confessions of the soldiers (*eorumque confessionem suscipientes*).[75]

The pope added the important point that it was proper for bishops and priests serving with the army to secure the spiritual well-being of the soldiers under

---

[70] MGH Epistolae 3, ed. E. Dümmler (Berlin, 1892), p. 625, *Porro de revelatione eiusdem Iohannis monachi, sicut eius referebat locutio, vere fantasma esse existimatur.*

[71] John had earned Charlemagne's gratitude by bringing to his attention the capture of certain individuals and other crimes comitted by "depraved men." On this point, see Epistolae 3, p. 624.

[72] Prinz, *Klerus und Krieg,* pp. 73–113.

[73] Epistolae 3, p. 625, *Fatus quippe est nobis Iohannes monachus, quia dixisset vobis* [Charlemagne], *ut omnis episcopus spiritalem teneret arma et non terrenam.* The pope indicates here that he knew John because of the latter's remonstrance to Charlemagne concerning the service of bishops on military campaign. It is difficult to see how the pope could have acquired this information without having interrogated John either directly or through papal agents.

[74] *Ibid., Quatenus, si ita est, quia militaris induunt arma, hortantes vestrae notescimus a Deo protectam regalem excellentiam, ut nullo modo sic fieri permittat.*

[75] *Ibid.*

their care by preaching to them about "attaining eternal life."[76] Hadrian's letter clearly indicates that he saw nothing innovative or problematic in the practice of having priests serve in the army for the purpose of hearing confessions and preaching. In fact, he saw this as an important part of their priestly duties.[77]

It should be noted here that just as had been the case at the *Concilium Germanicum*, Pope Hadrian dealt with the question of pastoral care for soldiers within a broader context that included the religious care available to all lay people living in the *regnum Francorum*. Thus, the pope emphasized in his letter to Charlemagne that the other bishops and priests (*ceteri vero episcopi atque presbiteri*), that is, the priests who remained at home during military campaigns (*in eorum degentes ecclesiis*), had a responsibility to serve the people under their care in a canonical manner (*canonice*) at the direction of the king himself.[78] Hadrian made clear that it was up to Charlemagne to ensure that all of his people, including both soldiers and civilians, received proper religious care on a regular basis.[79]

Hadrian's view that both confession and preaching played an important role in the conduct of Carolingian military operations is supported by the texts of a number of military sermons dating from the late eighth and early ninth century. For example, a sermon, probably delivered to Carolingian troops sometime during the last three decades of the eighth century – perhaps during the Avar campaigns of 791–799 – explicitly stated that the rite of confession was an essential and integral part of military life.[80] The sermon in question was composed in simple Latin and seems to have been intended to be understood by

---

[76] *Ibid., ut cuncto populo ea quae pro salute animae sunt sue aeternam vitam adipisci praedicantes.*

[77] *Ibid., inreprehensibileter sacerdotalem gerant officium.*

[78] *Ibid., ceteri vero episcopi atque presbiteri in eorum degentes ecclesiis, canonice unusquisque per vestrum regale robustissimum presidium suum valeant regere populum a Deo sibi commissum.*

[79] See in this regard F.L. Ganshof, "L'église et le pouvoir royal dans la monarchie franque sous Pépin III et Charlemagne," SSCI 7 (Spoleto, 1960), pp. 95–141, trans. as "The Church and Royal Power under Pippin III and Charlemagne," in *The Carolingians and the Frankish Monarchy*, trans. Janet Sondheimer (London, 1971), pp. 205–39.

[80] Joseph Michael Heer, *Ein karolingischer Missionskatechismus* (Freiburg, 1911), pp. 60–2, argues that the sermon was preached during the Avar wars of 791–799. Joseph Schmidlin reviewed Heer's book in *Zeitschrift für Missionswissenschaft* 2 (1912), pp. 257–8, and concluded that the Avars were the likely opponents considered by the author of the sermon. These arguments are summarized by Koeniger, *Militärseelsorge*, p. 51, n. 1, who accepts a late eighth-century date for the preaching of this sermon. Bachrach, *Early Carolingian Warfare*, pp. 348–9, n. 184 and n. 190, reviews the treatment of this text by scholars after the appearence of Koeniger's *Militärseelsorge* in 1918, and concludes that Erdman, *The Idea of Crusade*, p. 16, is unsuccessful in his effort to discredit this text and a second military sermon identified by Koeniger, discussed below, as actual sermons. In particular, Bachrach points out that Erdmann's effort to classify as a letter the second military sermon, identified by Koeniger, *Militärseelsorge*, pp. 72–4, is "tendentious on two counts." Bachrach notes that the original text of the sermon does not survive, and the word "epistola" upon which Erdmann based his conclusions is only present in a shorthand copy of the sermon. Secondly, the use of the word "epistola" does not in itself disqualify a text from having been preached as a sermon.

the common soldiers to whom it was addressed.[81] It began with a short seventy-word exhortation for the soldiers to remember that they were Christians with Christian obligations. The preacher emphasized this identity by reminding the men of the sacred bond that they shared with Christ through the rite of baptism.[82] Thus, from the very start of his exhortation the preacher stressed that the religious obligations of the soldiers were not unique to their current situation but were rather incumbent upon all those who had joined Christ's church, the vast majority of whom were civilian or non-combatant contemporaries of the fighting men.

In the next section of the sermon, the preacher called upon the men to stand bravely and fight with vigor in "the battle line of Christ," so that they might be crowned auspiciously [with the glory of heaven].[83] The preacher then drew together the idea of fighting bravely for Christ with the need for the soldiers to confess their sins before battle was joined. He insisted that the thing most to be feared by soldiers was to put themselves into physical danger without the remedy of confession (*confessionis remedio*) and thereby make themselves vulnerable to the spears of the devil.[84]

It should be noted that in the sermon up to this point, the preacher dealt with themes that were important for military discipline, for the cohesion of the force, and for the morale of the troops. First, he gave religious sanction to fighting bravely and maintaining position in the battle line – two elements of combat for which discipline is of great importance. Secondly, the preacher identified the fighting men as being unified by their common ties to Christ, thereby enhancing the bonds among soldiers already tied to one another by their common duty in the battle line. Finally, the preacher assured the soldiers that by confessing their sins they would be able to avoid the snares of the devil. By offering hope of redemption even if they fell in battle the preacher was attempting to limit their fears and thereby raise their morale before the fighting began.

In the next phase of the sermon, the preacher enunciated the reasons why soldiers, even more so than their civilian contemporaries, had an immediate need to participate in the rite of confession. He argued that no person could predict how long he would live, and that it was therefore necessary for each

---

[81] For an overview of recent work on the question of early medieval Latinity and its relationship to vernacular speech, see Michel Banniard, *Viva voce: communication ècrite et communication orale du IVe au IXe siècle en occident latin* (Paris, 1992), and a review of this work by Roger Wright, *The Journal of Medieval Latin* 3 (1993), pp. 78–94. On the ability of Carolingian soldiers to understand simple Latin of the type included in this sermon, see Bachrach, *Early Carolingian Warfare*, p, 348, n. 190. Bachrach accepts Banniard's view that Latin was the vernacular in *Francia* until at least the end of the eighth century and concludes that these sermons would have been intelligible to the Carolingian troops who heard them.

[82] Koeniger, *Militärseelsorge*, pp. 68–70, *A Christo enim nomen christianum sumpsit exordium et quia Christo nos* (H s. vos) *domino nostro in baptismo spondimus . . . ideo maxime nobis oportet, ut, quod Christo promisimus, omni studio ac devotione reddamus. . . .*

[83] *Ibid.*, p. 69, *stemus viriliter in acie Christi, pugnemus fortiter, ut vincamus efficaciter et coronemur feliciter.*

[84] *Ibid., formidandum est, ne venenatis diaboli telis vulnerati in laqueum incidentes peccati absque confessionis remedio pereamus.*

Christian to confess while time still remained. The preacher then emphasized that confession was necessary for everyone, but that it was even more important for soldiers to confess their sins because they were risking their lives immediately by going into battle.[85] Then, after reminding the soldiers of the stark realities of the battlefield, the preacher once again encouraged them to take advantage of the opportunity to confess their sins to God. He pointed out that priests were standing by who could help them. Indeed, the preacher emphasized that these priests were the specialists who held the "spiritual antidote" that could cure their souls from the wounds of sin.[86]

The content of this sermon sheds light on three important aspects of the rite of confession. First, the preacher did not treat the fact that the soldiers had all been baptized and were Christians as a sufficient guarantee of their salvation in the event of their deaths in battle despite the fact that he describes them as fighting in the battle line of Christ (*in acie Christi*). Instead, the preacher emphasized the obligations of all Christians to participate in the rite of confession and warned against waiting until the moment of death, since this cannot be known in advance.[87] This would appear to be a clear indication that the religious

---

[85] *Ibid., confessionem igitur peccatorum iugiter exhibere necesse est, quia incerta sunt unicuique huius vitae spatia et quia nemo scit horam vel tempus vocationis suae. Unde nos dominus ammonet dicens 'vigilate itaque quia nescitis diem neque horam.' Cum ergo omnibus est confessio necessaria, quanto magis his, qui cotidie visibiliter contra inimicos suos dimicant.* The preacher's comments here indicate that soldiers participated in religious rites that were common to the laity as a whole. Indeed, it is clear that Carolingian bishops serving in the late eighth and early ninth century expended considerable effort to create an obligation for lay people to confess their sins at least once a year and in some cases three times yearly.

In this context, in 800 Theodulf of Orléans (798–821), one of Charlemagne's most prominent reforming bishops, emphasized the importance of confession as a central act of Christian religious observance in a set of statutes issued to the priests serving in his diocese. He required that every Christian in his diocese confess at least once a year, specifically in the week before the beginning of Lent. See Theodulf of Orléans, *Capitula ad presbyteros parochiae suae*, PL 105: 218, *prima autem hebdomada ante initium quadragesimae confessio danda de omnibus peccatis quae sive opere sive locutione perpetrantur.* In addition, Theodulf insisted that everyone should confess to God each day as a form of piety. While practicing this rite the penitent was to say Psalm 50, 44, or 31, which pertained to the questions of confession and penitence. Theodulf's injunctions were, of course, an outline for a best-case scenario, and should not be seen as evidence for wide-scale daily confessions by laymen or even by priests. However, the bishop's plan does demonstrate an ideological commitment to the proposition that confession should constitute a central element of Christian worship. Concerning the efforts by Theodulf and other Carolingian bishops to encourage lay people to participate in the right of confession, see Avril, "Remarques sur un aspect de la vie religieuse paroissiale," pp. 345–63.

[86] Koeniger, *Militärseelsorge*, p. 69, *ideo ammonemus dilectionem vestram, ut confiteamini domino peccata vestra; quaerite testes confessionis vestrae, sanctos sacerdotes domini, qui antidoto spiritali vestrorum curare praevaleant vulnera peccatorum.*

[87] This argument is also made by Patriarch Paulinus of Aquileia and Alcuin of York in treatises that they wrote for two of Charlemagne's officers, Duke Eric of Friuli and Wido, count of the Breton march. Paulinus of Aquileia, *Liber exhortationis*, PL 99: 197–282, here cols. 242–3, emphasized that *Ne quaeso taliter cogitemus, quia summa stultitia est haec cogitare . . . Ideo, inquam, ne talia cogitemus, cum nesciamus qua die morituri sumus. Nemo enim hominum novit diem exitus sui. Non omnes in senectute moriuntur, sed in diversis aetatibus de hoc mundo migrant: et in quibus actibus unusquisque homo inventus fuerit, in eisdem*

behavior of soldiers was understood by contemporaries within the context of general lay religiosity, and that the latter might still have included a tendency toward once-in-a-lifetime confession. Secondly, the form of the sermon suggests that the preacher thought his audience already understood the rite of confession and what it was meant to accomplish. This interpretation of the sermon is indicated by the fact that the preacher's rhetoric was hortatory rather than explanatory. Simply put, he urged his audience to do what they knew they were supposed to do rather than introducing them to a new religious practice. Finally, the numerous priests serving with the army were ready to hear the individual confessions of the soldiers. The preacher made this point explicitly when he told the men to seek out the *sacerdotes domini* who could cure the wounds of their sins with a "spiritual antidote." This emphasis on seeking out a priest in order to confess would seem to conform to the normal pattern of the repeatable rite.[88]

The preacher's language here also suggests that the men were to receive penances through which they could purge themselves of sin, consequently indicating that they were to confess their sins individually to priests serving with the army. In fact, the medical imagery used in the military sermon finds important echoes in the works of more widely known writers who definitely had individual confession in mind. Alcuin, for example, used a similar image when he argued that one cannot be healed without summoning the doctor, and that in the same manner confession was the surest medicine for wounds and the guarantee for salvation.[89]

A similar military sermon, perhaps dating from the reign of Louis the Pious (814–840), likewise emphasized the crucial idea of confession in reconciling soldiers to God, and urged the men to confess their sins individually to priests serving with the troops.[90] The soldiers were told that it is necessary to prepare

judicabitur, quando anima exierit de corpore. For his part, Alcuin, *De virtutibus et vitiis liber,* PL 101: 613–38, here col. 223, argued *Nonne homines subito moriuntur?* and *Si subito intrat dies extremus, perit dilatio et restat damnatio.*

[88] See Vogel, "Les rituels de la pénitence tarifée," pp. 419–20, and Dhuoda, *Manuel,* pp. 194–6.

[89] Michael S. Driscoll, "*Ad Pueros Sancti Martini*: A Critical Edition, English Translation, and Study of the Manuscript Transmission," *Traditio* 53 (1998), pp. 37–61, here p. 52, *Opinor enim, nisi interpellatur medicus, non curatur aegrotus. Confessio tua medicina est vulnerum tuorum, et salutis tuae certissimum subsidium.*

[90] The text was originally published by Wilhelm Schmitz, "Tironische Miszellen," *Neues Archiv* 15 (1890), pp. 605–7, and then reprinted with some alterations in *Miscellanea Tironiana* (Leipzig, 1896), pp. 26–8. The sermon may have begun as letter of consolation intended for a recipient about to go to war but this has not been proved. On this point, see Bachrach, *Early Carolingian Warfare,* pp. 348–9, n. 190. Koeniger, *Militärseelsorge,* reprints this sermon, pp. 72–4 and suggests (pp. 52–3) that even if this sermon began as a letter, it is still representative of contemporary military sermons. Michael McCormick described this sermon as a part of a *vade mecum,* composed during the 830s as part of a collection of texts intended for a military chaplains in the field. His comments came in the course of a paper that he delivered at the University of Notre Dame during a symposium on military chaplains (18–19 March 2000) entitled "Military Chaplains in their Contexts," organized by David S. Bachrach and Doris L. Bergen. McCormick's essay will appear in a forthcoming volume from this conference to be published by the University of Notre Dame Press.

their consciences and remember each of the sins they committed. Every man is urged to confess his sins to a priest (*confiteatur sacerdoti*) in a devoted manner with God as a witness in order to free himself from the wounds of sin. We note here that the author of this sermon utilized the same metaphor that we saw in the earlier preaching text. Finally, each soldier was "to propitiate" God in order to wash himself clean before going into battle so that he could stand in battle without any sin and without any doubts – clearly an important matter when considering military morale.[91]

As was true of the earlier military sermon, this text would appear to be dealing with individual confessions by soldiers to priests. First, each man was instructed to search his own conscience and remember his own sins – a prerequisite for making a full and individual confession. Secondly, the soldiers were told to confess these sins to a priest. The language here is not ambiguous. There is no suggestion in the sermon that the soldiers were to confess as a group that they were guilty of some unspecified failings. Each man was told to remember his own sins and then confess them to a priest. Finally, the soldiers were told to satisfy God after having confessed their sins, which would appear to be a clear reference to accepting penance.

In addition to dealing with the personal religious preparations necessary to reconcile soldiers with God before battle, the author of the sermon also emphasized a number of matters that pertained directly to the cohesion, morale, and discipline of the soldiers. As was true of the earlier sermon, noted above, the preacher emphasized that the fighting men shared a common bond to Christ. The sermon begins with the following summons: "men, brothers and fathers, you who bear the Christian name and carry the banner of the cross on your brows, listen and hear."[92] This reference to the *vexillum crucis* echoes the prayer composed by Bishop Baturic for Louis the German as well as Theodulf of Orléans' emphasis on banners of this type leading Carolingian troops to victory.

The preacher then stressed that the soldiers had a common obligation, that is, to defend the name of Christ because of the sacrifice that he had made for them.[93] As we saw above with respect to intercessory masses celebrated in camp, Carolingian leaders were eager to emphasize the common bonds among the Frankish troops and their status as Christians unified under God. Thus, it seems likely that the common religious ties and obligations noted by the preacher were also intended to play a role in creating a sense of unity between Frankish fighting men. This stands in marked contrast to the difficulties experi-

---

[91] Koeniger, *Militärseelsorge*, p. 74, *praeparet sibi unusquisque contra conscientiam suam, rememoret peccata sua, quae prius fecit; non portet ea apud se in praelium Christi, sed antea confiteatur sacerdoti et coram deo devote peccata sua, et liberi de ipsis tantis vulneribus securi de praeteritis, propitiante deo, sine ulla dubitatione et sine ullo peccato positis stare in praelio in die domini. . . .*

[92] *Ibid.*, p. 72, *Viri, fratres, et patres, qui christianum nomen habetis et vexillum crucis in fronte portatis, attendite et audite.*

[93] *Ibid., Considerate diligenter, quale pretio redempti estis . . . quia vos Christus sacro sanguine redemit . . . Considerate hoc diligenter, ubi pergitis contra inimicos vestros ad decertandum ambuletis, ut christianum nomen, deo adiuvante, defendatis.*

enced by the religiously heterogeneous armies of the later Roman empire noted in the previous chapter.

The preacher also reminded the soldiers about the regulations governing their behavior both on the march and during battle. In the first instance, the sermon notes that the men were to refrain from sexual activity (*abstinete vos a concupiscentia karnale*), and to refrain from looting along the line of march (*ubi enim ambulatis nolite rapinas facere*).[94] The preacher added injunctions for the soldiers to be brave in combat. He stressed that if the men wished to maintain their faith and fulfill God's will they could have no fear of their enemies and had to be prepared to defend their Christian name with all of the bravery and strength with which they were endowed by God.[95] Of course, following orders along the line of march and being brave and doing one's duty during battle were fundamental to sound discipline among the Carolingian troops as they had been in the Roman army or in the armies of the Merovingian and Visigothic kings.

In addition to stressing the soldiers' obligations to God, the preacher also emphasized that if the Frankish fighting men fulfilled their religious duty, they would receive divine support. He stressed that if the men fought for God, meaning that they acted in accordance with divine law, then God would send His angels to support them, to defend their camp, and to protect them against their enemies.[96] The author of the sermon added that if the men went into battle with fear and reverence asking God for aid, the Lord would be with them against their enemies just as he had helped Joshua against the Amalekites (Ex. 17.9).[97] Promises of divine support in battle, of the kind noted here, may have played a role in raising the spirits of soldiers as they went into combat, giving them confidence both that God supported their efforts and that God would look upon their souls with favor if they died during the fighting. Indeed, as was noted above, the Carolingians knew well that He could and would give victory to those who honored Him. But the injunction to follow divine law also reminded the men that proper behavior along the line of march and in battle was necessary to obtain this divine aid.

Both of these sermons offer valuable evidence for the expectations of priests serving with Carolingian soldiers in the field. Of particular importance is their view concerning the role that religious rites, including confession and prayers, could play in reconciling soldiers to God before battle and in ensuring divine support for the army as a whole. However, these sermons may also offer insight into the views of the Carolingian soldiers themselves. Alexander Murray has shown that sermons can shed light on the expectations and beliefs of audiences

---

[94] *Ibid.*, p. 73.

[95] *Ibid.*, pp. 73–4, *Propterea si vos firmiter vultis fidem vestram servare et dei voluntatem implere, nolite timere adversarios vestros sed omni audacia et cum omni fortitudine brachii dei sitis parati ad defendendum nomen christianitatis vestrae.*

[96] *Ibid.*, p. 73, *Si . . . certare pro deo vultis, ut in lege dei permaneatis et taliter agite, ut Christo delectet apud vos angelum suum dirigere, qui vos in fortitudine defendat et kastra* (sic) *vestra auxilio pietatis suae protegat, ut contra inimicos vestros ipse sit armatura.*

[97] *Ibid.*, p. 74, *Sciatis, si cum timore et reverentia vultis pergere et deo in auxilium invocare, erit dominus vobiscum contra inimicos vestros, sicut cum Josue quando certavit contra Amalech.*

that heard them. He argues that preachers familiar with their audiences addressed them in a manner that the people could understand and appreciate. Otherwise, the preachers would fail in their task to motivate people to behave in a proper manner.[98] The same understanding of the relationship between preacher and audience can be postulated for the Carolingian soldiers who formed the audiences for the sermons discussed above. Consequently, even if these particular sermons were never preached – and there is evidence to suggest that they were in fact preached to soldiers – they nevertheless can be understood to represent the views of priests familiar with the men for whose spiritual well-being they were responsible.[99]

The views expressed in these sermons concerning the important role played by religious rites, including confession, in preparing common soldiers for battle can also be found in late eighth-century treatises written for Charlemagne's high-ranking military officers.[100] For example, Patriarch Paulinus of Aquileia composed in the late 790s a treatise for Duke Eric of Friuli, the commander of the march of Friuli, entitled *Liber exhortationis*, in which the bishop set forth a series of moral lessons appropriate for a career military officer.[101] Throughout the work Paulinus addressed standard religious questions of sin, virtue, and the celebration of appropriate rites but added elements to the text that took into account the duke's primary secular responsibilities. Indeed, Paulinus dedicated a chapter to the question of how the duke must live as both a *miles spiritualis* and a *miles terrenus*. Drawing a series of parallels between earthly warfare and spiritual combat, the patriarch compared the physical preparations required by the duke as a soldier in the service of the Frankish realm with the religious obliga-

---

[98] Alexander Murray, "Religion Among the Poor in Thirteenth-Century France: The Testimony of Humbert de Romans," *Traditio* 30 (1974), pp. 285–324, here esp. pp. 286–8.

[99] Concerning the actual use of these sermons on the battlefield, see Bachrach, *Early Carolingian Warfare*, pp. 348–9, n. 184 and n. 190.

[100] The importance of literacy to high-ranking Carolingian army officers has been considered by Rosamond McKitterick, *The Carolingians and the Written Word* (Cambridge, 1989), pp. 244–50.

[101] Paulinus of Aquileia, *Liber exhortationis*, PL 99: 197–282. Concerning Eric of Friuli's service under Charlemagne, see James Bruce Ross, "Two Neglected Paladins of Charlemagne: Eric of Friuli and Gerold of Bavaria," *Speculum* 20 (1945), pp. 212–35; and Katherine Fischer Drew, "The Carolingian Military Frontier in Italy," *Traditio* 20 (1964), pp. 437–47.

Similar efforts were made by ecclesiastical reformers to emphasize the importance of confession within the context of monastic life. Thus, for example, Alcuin of York (735–804), who served as one of Charlemagne's leading advisors concerning educational and religious reform, sent a treatise to the monastery of St Martin of Tours in which he addressed the role of confession in religious life and how it ought to be considered by the brothers and particularly by the novices. After listing the normal monastic virtues of sobriety, chastity, modesty, humility, and obedience, Alcuin insisted that the most important element for living a religious life was to confess one's sins. On this point, see Michael S. Driscoll, "Penance in Transition: Popular Piety and Practice," in *Medieval Liturgy: A Book of Essays*, ed. Lizette Larson-Miller (New York, 1997), pp. 121–63, here p. 143; and Driscoll, "*Ad Pueros*," p. 48, *exhortamini illos sobrie, caste, pudice, cum omni humilitate et oboedientia Deo servire in bonis moribus et sancta conversatione et relegiosa castitate, et maxime de confessione peccatorum suorum. . . .*

tions he had as a soldier in the service of Christ. In the course of the text Paulinus makes clear that the soldier's first responsibility should be to his Savior.[102]

The general theme of Paulinus' chapter on military life was that a soldier must never forget his obligation to God even while he fought in temporal battles. Thus, the patriarch argued that while the earthly soldier protects himself with a hauberk, the soldier of God is strengthened through charity. Similarly, the earthly soldier fights against his enemies with spears and arrows, while one who is loyal to Christ struggles against his enemies with humility. In concluding this line of thought, Paulinus stressed that, while the physical battle might end, the struggle to control oneself and live a spiritual life never ended as long as one lived.[103]

Paulinus took up the theme of the danger of temporal life when he emphasized for Duke Eric the vital importance of confessing one's sins without delay. He pointed out to the duke that although it was possible to put off confessing one's sins until old age, this plan was the height of foolishness. Paulinus stressed that no one can know when he will die, and that putting off confession was simply too great a risk.[104] Although he did not specifically refer to the dangers of death in battle, the patriarch's message to Duke Eric, whose military obligations he had already addressed, was very clear. Many soldiers die suddenly, and confession was the surest means of attaining salvation.

Alcuin delivered this same message in 799 to Count Wido, Charlemagne's march-commander in Brittany. In the preface of *De virtutibus et vitiis liber*, Alcuin noted that he was writing in response to Wido's request for a manual detailing how he should organize his daily life while engaged in *bellicis rebus*.[105] The treatise, divided into thirty-five chapters, deals with important religious behaviors, a catalogue of sins, and finally the four virtues of prudence, justice, courage, and temperance. In the first part of the work, in a section dealing with confession, Alcuin utilized medical imagery common to discussions of penance, noting that scripture urges one to hurry to this rite in the same manner that one would take a necessary medication. Alcuin then insisted that

---

102 Paulinus, *Liber exhortationis*, cols. 212–13, *Miles terrenus quocumque loco mittitur paratus ac promptus est . . . multo magis miles Christi sine impedimento hujus saeculi imperatori suo Domino Jesu Christo debet obedire, qui ipsum pretioso sanguine suo redemit.*

103 *Ibid.*, col. 213, *Tu ne vulnereris, lorica indutus es, sed ille pro lorica Christi charitate est vestitus. Tu contra inimicum tuum lanceas et sagittas emittis; ille contra inimicum suum humilitatem et salubria verba dirigere studet. . . . Tuus hostis ad tempus dimicat; illius vero hostis, quamdiu in corpore consistit, cum illo vero hostis non cessat.* The *tu* and *ille* of these sentences refer to the terrestrial and spiritual soldier.

104 *Ibid.*, cols. 242–3, *Ne quaeso taliter cogitemus, quia summa stultitia est haec cogitare . . . Ideo, inquam, ne talia cogitemus, cum nesciamus qua die morituri sumus. Nemo enim hominum novit diem exitus sui. Non omnes in senectute moriuntur, sed in diversis aetatibus de hoc mundo migrant: et in quibus actibus unusquisque homo inventus fuerit, in eisdem judicabitur, quando anima exierit de corpore.*

105 Alcuin, *De virtutibus et vitiis liber*, PL 101: 613–38, here col. 613. Luitpold Wallach, "Alcuin on Virtues and Vices: A Manual for a Carolingian Soldier," *The Harvard Theological Review* 48 (1955), pp. 75–95, has treated this text in great detail and concludes that Alcuin relied heavily upon Caesarius of Arles for his material.

without the remedy of confession it is impossible to attain salvation.[106] Somewhat later, in a chapter entitled *De non tardendo converti ad Deum*, Alcuin emphasized that it was entirely possible for a man to die unexpectedly and to be damned because of his failure to accept the path to salvation offered by confession.[107] Alcuin reiterated this theme throughout the chapter and concluded by urging again that everyone make his way to God as quickly as possible out of fear that not wishing to do so when he is able, he is unable to do so when he finally tries.[108] As was true of Duke Eric of Friuli, an experienced officer such as Count Wido would have been fully aware of the dangers that he, and his men, faced every time they went into battle, and thus could appreciate the importance of taking advantage of the rite of confession while time still remained.

This emphasis upon the importance of confession can also be seen in the manual written by Dhuoda, a Carolingian noblewoman, for her son William as he prepared to enter royal service with Charles the Bald in 843. In the course of his training as an administrator and military officer, Dhuoda thought that William should make sure that he made private confession a regular part of his religious routine. She cautioned her son to pay attention to the priests and to heed their counsel. She added that William should confess his sins privately to the priests and that during the rite he should both weep and sigh.[109]

References to confession by soldiers in both sermons and in manuals discussing the religious duties of fighting men thus help to illuminate contemporary understanding of the important part played by confession and penance in the religious preparation of Carolingian troops. Similar clarity is also provided by a passage in an epic poem known as the *Waltharius*, likely composed at the Carolingian court during the reign of Charlemagne.[110] According to the story,

---

[106] Alcuin, *De virtutibus*, col. 621, *Hortatur nos saepius Scriptura ad medicamentum fugere confessionis . . . nos aliter salvi fieri non possumus, nisi confiteamur poenitentes quod inique gessimus negligentes.*

[107] *Ibid.*, col. 223, *Nonne homines subito moriuntur?* and *Si subito intrat dies extremus, perit dilatio et restat damnatio.*

[108] *Ibid.*, col. 224, *Festinare debet ad Deum convertendo unusquisque, dum potest, ne si, dum potest, noluerit, omnino cum tarde voluerit, non possit.*

[109] See Dhuoda, *Manuel pour mon fils*, p. 196, *Da illis, ut melius nosti, tuam occulte cum suspiro et lachrymis veram confessionem.* Later in the text Dhuoda told her son to pay close attention to the psalms because it was here that William could find a model for the intimate confession of his sins and a full prayer for divine mercy. See *ibid.*, p. 362, *In psalmis invenes intimam confessionem peccatorum tuorum, et integram deprecationem divinae atque dominicae misericordiae.* Still later Dhuoda told William that if he ever felt abandoned by God he should chant the psalms with contrition in his heart. See *ibid.*, p. 364, *Si te tribulationis a Deo derelictum intelligas compuncto corde hos psalmos decanta.* In particular she suggested that he chant Psalm 51, which begins *miserere me*.

[110] Alf Önnerfors, *Die Verfasserschaft des Waltharius – Epos aus sprachlicher Sicht* (Düsseldorf, 1978), pp. 42–6, argues for an early ninth rather than a late ninth-century or early tenth-century date for the *Waltharius* poem, as had been widely accepted by scholars up to the publication of his work. Karl Ferdinand Werner, "Hludovicus Augustus: gouverner l'empire chrétien – idées et réaltités," in *Charlemagne's Heir: New Perspectives on the Reign of Louis the Pious (814–840)*, ed. Peter Godman and Roger Collins (Oxford, 1990), pp. 3–123, here pp. 104–5 and 121, argues for an early ninth rather than a late ninth-century date. For the most up-to-date review of the literature, see Bachrach, *Early Carolingian*

Walter, an Aquitanian once held as a hostage at Attila's court who subsequently rose to be commander of the Hunnic army, was conscious both of his relationship to God and the need to express this relationship through participation in formal religious rites. This religious feeling was made manifest when Walter was forced into battle against a group of Frankish soldiers whom he defeated one after the other in single combat. According to the story, as night fell Walter sought solace in prayer. Then addressing God directly, Walter thanked his savior for protecting him from the spears of the enemy and for keeping him from disgrace.[111] He then confessed his sins to God with a contrite mind (*contrita mens*), wishing to turn from sin and to rid himself of the guilt that burdened him.[112] It was only after completing his confession that Walter again felt able to commit himself to battle.[113]

Of course, the *Waltharius* epic was a work of fiction and its representations of soldiers' religious expectations must be read in this light. Furthermore, it should be noted that Walter confessed his sins directly to God rather than to a priest, as would appear to have been the normal expectation for soldiers in the Carolingian period.[114] However, these observations should not obscure the important role played by this soldier's act of confession, described as having been carried out with a contrite mind, in reconciling himself to God before returning to battle. Furthermore, the incidental nature of the detail concerning Walter's religious behavior within the context of the poem, including references to pre-battle prayers, suggests that the poet was utilizing easily recognized elements of soldiers' ritual practice to add an air of realism to his narrative. Finally, the views attributed to Walter concerning God's role in warfare and the need to reconcile oneself with God before going into combat are fully consonant with other non-fictional texts, including Pope Hadrian's letter to Charlemagne, the military sermons, and the treatises written for military officers, noted above, from roughly the same period.

The successful incorporation of confession, penance, and even preaching as normal elements of military religion over the course of the eighth and ninth centuries, which is suggested by the evidence adduced thus far, is further indicated by the inclusion of documents dealing with these duties in the collection of pseudo-capitularies ascribed to Benedict the Levite, noted above. Indeed, the compiler included texts in his dossier that dealt specifically with the question of a priest's duties when he served with military forces on campaign. The most detailed of these documents, ostensibly drafted to prohibit the armed service of

---

Warfare, pp. 74 and 192. Bachrach argues for a late eighth-century date for the composition of *Waltharius*. He suggests that lines 764–7 of the *Waltharius*, ed. K. Strecker, with a German translation by P. Vossen (Berlin, 1947), are an an attack on Saxon pedantry that may be taken as a jab at Alcuin and his Saxon origins. The English advisor to Charlemagne left the royal court in 796 after being named abbot of St Martin at Tours where he died in 804.

111 See *Waltharius*, lines 1160–4. For a valuable discussion of this text's religious imagery, see Bachrach, *Early Carolingian Warfare*, p. 56.

112 *Waltharius*, lines 1165–6, *Deprecor at dominum contrita mente benignum,/ Ut qui peccantes non vult sed perdere culpas.*

113 *Ibid.*, line 1168, *qui postquam orandi finem dedit, ilico surgens.*

114 Concerning the propriety of confession to God, see Vogel, *Le pécheur*, p. 161.

bishops and priests on campaign, not only provides a list of the cleric's duties but also describes in detail the reasons why they were so essential to war efforts.[115]

The text begins with an injunction against priests serving in an armed capacity in the army that was drawn from prohibitions against such behavior issued by the papal see and by numerous episcopal synods, including the *Concilium Germanicum* of 742.[116] However, the author then added the clause that two or three bishops, chosen by their fellow prelates, along with a picked group of priests could serve with the army in order to provide pastoral care to the troops.[117] This specially selected cadre of priests was required to have a thorough knowledge of a variety of religious duties, including the assignment of penances to the men, blessing the soldiers and preaching to them, celebrating mass, and anointing the sick and wounded with holy chrism and saying the proper prayers for them. Furthermore, the priests were specifically instructed that they should not permit any soldier to die without first receiving the eucharist.[118]

The range of duties assigned to priests clearly is more detailed than that required by the *Concilium Germanicum* in 742 and includes duties of the sort carried out by priests serving in Charlemagne's armies. Indeed, it would appear that the officials of the *regnum Francorum* had successfully popularized their proposals, at least at the administrative level, to provide pastoral care, including access to confession, to Carolingian troops in the field, and perhaps even augmented the range of spiritual support available to soldiers. In this context, it should be emphasized again that the dossier of documents in Benedict's collection was intended to limit priests' obligations to those permitted by the law – priests whose time and resources might otherwise have been abused by over-zealous secular authorities. Consequently, those duties specifically mentioned in these documents are likely to have been the accepted norm rather than extraordinary.

Despite the evidence from sources such as Benedict the Levite's collection, it would be unreasonable to conclude that all Carolingian soldiers participated in

---

115 *Capitularia Spuria*, p. 110, nr. 141.

116 *Ibid., Secunda vice propter ampliorem observantiam apostolica auctoritate et multa sanctorum episcoporum ammonitione instructi sanctorumque canonum regulis edocti . . . volumus ut nullus sacerdos in hostem pergat.* The council of Quierzy, held in November 858, reiterated the ban on priests participating on campaign in a military capacity. Regarding this point, see *Die Konzilen der karolingischen Teilreiche 843–859*, ed. Wilfried Hartmann, MGH Concilia (Hanover, 1984), p. 426, *Nos et quidem pacem et quietem, non rixas et bella optamus et quaerimus, quia sicut dicit apostolus, non sunt nobis carnalia arma, sed spiritualia. . . .*

117 *Capitularia Spuria*, p. 110, nr. 141, *duo vel tres tantum episcopi electione ceterorum . . . et cum illis electi sacerdotes.* The selection of the bishops by their fellow prelates rather than by the king was in keeping with the author's overall effort to limit royal power.

118 *Ibid., nisi duo vel tres tantum episcopi electione ceterorum propter benedictionem et praedicationem populique reconciliationem, et cum illis electi sacerdotes qui bene sciant populis poenitentias dare, missas celebrare, de infirmis curam habere, sacratique olei cum sacris precibus unctionem impendere, et hoc maxime praevidere, ne sine viatico quis de seculo recedat.*

all of the appropriate rites all of the time or even that religious care always was available to them. Thus, for example, it would appear that under some circumstances it was expected that soldiers would not be able to complete their penances before they went into battle. That this view was widely accepted is indicated by Benedict's inclusion of a text in his dossier stressing that it was the act of accepting the penance rather than carrying it out immediately that made the penitent worthy of salvation. In fact, the text clearly states that when individuals facing the possibility of death accept penances imposed upon them by priests, they are not to be understood as condemned if they die before satisfying their penance. However, if the penitent survived, he was still responsible for carrying out his penance.[119]

The same point was made by Pope John VIII in 879 in a letter that he sent to a group of Frankish bishops who had asked whether soldiers who fell fighting in defense of the church (*pro defensione sanctae Dei Ecclesiae*), for the Christian religion (*pro statu Christianae religionis*), and for the realm (*res publica*) could have forgiveness (*indulgentia*) for their sins (*delicti*).[120] John emphasized in his reply that if the soldiers at issue died fighting against pagans (*pagani*) and infidels (*infideles*), "with the piety of the Catholic Religion (*cum pietate catholicae religionis*)," they would attain eternal life (*requies eos aeternae vitae suscipiet*).[121] In justifying this position, the pope quoted from Ezekiel 18 and Luke 27 to argue that God accepted even those who came to Him at the final moment, indicating that dying for the church and the Christian faith was itself a demonstration of this reconciliation with God. John concluded his letter by absolving (*absolvimus*) the soldiers of their sins and commending them to God in his prayers (*precibusque illos Domino commendamus*) based upon the authority invested in him by Saint Peter (*intercessio beati Petri*) into whose hands God placed the power to bind and loose (*cujus potestas ligandi atque solvendi est in caelo et in terra*).[122]

Confession and the acceptance of penance before battle helped to prepare men for combat. But in the Carolingian period, killing enemy soldiers was still sinful and required expiation. As we saw in the previous chapter, tariff books composed in *Francia* took account of this need by including penances for killing enemy soldiers in battle, penances that were invariably much lighter than those

---

[119] *Ibid.*, p. 52, n. 125, *placuit his, qui accepta poenitentia ante reconciliationem migrant ad Dominum, communicari pro eo quod honoraverunt poenitentia . . . Qui si supervixerunt, stent in ordine paenitentum.* However, in some cases, soldiers would appear to have feared for their comrades who fell in battle without completing their penances. This point will be discussed further below.

[120] The recipients of the letter are described as *omnibus reverendissimis et sanctissimis venerabilibus episcopis per totum regnum charissimi filii mei Ludovici.* See MGH Epistolae 7, ed. P. Kehr (Berlin, 1928), p. 126. Concerning the value of this text for understanding contemporary religious understanding of killing in warfare, see James A. Brundage, *Medieval Canon Law and the Crusader* (Madison, 1969), pp. 22–3, who emphasizes that the word *indulgentia* does not refer to an indulgence, because there is no mention in the text of a remission of sins for the soldiers. He argues instead that dying in the course of fighting against the infidel had salvific value for those who died.

[121] Epistolae 7, pp. 126–7.

[122] *Ibid.*

imposed for other forms of homicide.[123] We are not well informed about actual post-battle practice among Frankish troops when they fought against non-Christian enemies such as the Spanish Muslims, the Avars, and the Northmen. However, Nithard's account of the battle of Fontenoy makes clear that killing fellow Christians was seen as a sinful act, even when the battle was judged to be just and the victory a sign of divine favor. According to Nithard, although the bishops concluded that while the victory was a manifestation of God's will in favor of Charles and Louis, any soldier who was conscious (*quicumque consciens*) of the fact that he had fought out of anger, hatred, or vainglory was responsible for confessing his sins privately (*vere confessus secrete*) to a priest and then being judged according to the nature of his guilt.[124] Nithard added that at least some soldiers felt so strongly about the importance of confessing their sins in order to obtain divine mercy, that they even carried out additional penances on behalf of their dead comrades. They hoped that by praying and holding fasts, the soldiers who had died without having had an opportunity to confess, or who had carried out their penances in an imperfect manner, would be granted mercy by God.[125]

But even as Frankish soldiers eagerly confessed their sins and sought extra penances to ease the path of their fallen comrades, a struggle was taking shape in the Carolingian church about the sinfulness of killing in a just war and the need to confess and accept penance for this act. In an effort to bring some clarity to the rite of confession generally and to the problem of homicide more specifically, Archbishop Otgar of Mainz requested that Rabanus Maurus, abbot of Fulda, produce a teaching text to deal with problems then current in the penitential system.[126]

Within the context of his reply to the archbishop, Rabanus noted that some supporters of Louis and Charles, who had been victorious at Fontenoy, were arguing that it was not necessary for soldiers from the winning side to confess and do penance for their actions during the campaign.[127] As Nithard noted in his

---

123 Kottje, "Tötung im Kriege," and Bachrach, *Early Carolingian Warfare*, pp. 153–4.

124 Nithard, *Historia*, 3.1, pp. 428–30, *at quicumque consciens sibi aut ira aut odio aut vana gloria aut certe quolibet vitio quiddam in hac expeditione suasit vel gessit, esset vere confessus secrete secreti delicti et secundum modum culpe iudicaretur.* Hamilton, *Practice of Penance*, pp. 191–2, suggests that the imposition of penances on the victorious soldiers after the battle of Fontenoy fell out of the mainstream of traditional penitential practice because the bishops assembled there had declared the victory a *iudium Dei*, and only required soldiers who had been motivated by anger, hatred, or pride to confess their sins. One might ask how many soldiers were not motivated, at least in part, by one of these three. As Nithard points out, many soldiers did, in fact, confess and even undertook heavier than necessary penances because of the guilt and fear that they felt.

125 Nithard, *Historia*, 3.1, p. 430, *verumtamen in veneratione ac laude tantae declarationis iusticiae pro remissione delictis mortuorum fratrum suorum – in eo, quod inperfectis peccatis interventibus se noverant, ut in multis volentes nolentesque delinquebant – ut suo adiutorio ab his exuti liberarentur . . . proque his omnibus triduanum ieiunium inventum immoque libenter ac celebre celebratum est.*

126 Epistolae 5, p. 462. Rabanus' role in the penitential controversy is noted by Kottje, "Die Tötung im Kriege," pp. 6–7.

127 Epistolae 5, p. 464, *quod autem quidam homicidium, quod nuper in seditione et proelio*

account, despite defining the victory as a divine judgment, the bishops at Fontenoy had urged each soldier to consider his own motives when fighting, specifically naming anger, hatred, and vainglory as sinful reasons for killing, even in a divinely sanctioned war. Rabanus took this same position, asking rhetorically whether those in favor of doing away with penances for killing in battle could excuse those who had fought out of greed, or for the favor of their temporal lords all the while spurning their eternal Lord.[128] This debate remained far from settled throughout the Carolingian period. As we shall see in the next chapter, the debate over the sinfulness of killing in just and then holy wars was to continue up to and through the First Crusade.

Conclusion

In the preceding discussion, we have seen that both ecclesiastical and secular authorities in the *regnum Francorum* during the period of Carolingian rule (742–c. 900) initiated a significant program of religious reform in order to incorporate both repeatable confession and penance into the religious practices of the army, apparently within the wider context of the general reformation of lay religiosity. Moreover, in addition to adapting to the new religious environment inspired by the rapid spread and adoption of repeatable confession, Frankish authorities also can be seen to have expended considerable resources to maintain forms of military religion traditional in Christian armies of the West in both the later empire and in the Romano-German successor states. While on military campaign, soldiers were encouraged to participate in intercessory prayers, processions, almsgiving, and fasting. For their part, priests accompanying the army also said prayers, led the troops in public litanies, maintained sacred relics, and celebrated intercessory masses. Finally, Frankish officials mobilized the "home front" to provide religious support to fighting men in the field through large-scale public prayers, almsgiving, fasting, and processions among both lay and religious populations, as well through specifically clerical responses such as intercessory masses.

These religious rites and ceremonies at every level had a tremendous role in Carolingian military operations through their impact on morale, army cohesion, and discipline. The prevailing consensus that God could and would help His faithful supporters gave soldiers the promise of divine aid on the battlefield provided that they were serving in a just cause, that they had merited aid through their own good behavior, and finally that they sought this aid through the proper matrix of religious rites and ceremonies. This promise had an obvious and con-

---

principum nostorum perpetratum est, excusant, quasi non necesse sit pro hoc cuilibet agere paenitentiam.

[128] *Ibid., unde oportet eos considerare, qui hanc necem nefariam defendere cupiunt, utrum illos coram oculis Dei quasi innoxios excusare possint, qui propter avaritiam, quae omnium malorum radix est . . . atque favorem dominorum suorum temporalium aeternum Dominum contempserunt, et mandata illius spernentes, non casu, sed per industriam homicidium perfecerunt.*

tinuing positive effect on morale. But the fundamental emphasis on meriting divine support provided an equally important tool in the hands of officers striving to maintain discipline. Finally, the public and large-scale nature of intercessory rites carried out at the level of the army and the kingdom as a whole provided a regular reminder to the individual soldiers of their own place within a larger Christian community bound together by common obligations not only to each other but to God as well.

3

Religion of War in the West c. 900–1095

Introduction

Wartime religion during the period c. 900–1095 was characterized by broad continuities with Carolingian practice within which, however, we can see important new emphases and developments. At the broadest level, tenth- and eleventh-century Christians shared with their predecessors a belief in God and the saints as active agents on earth whose aid was important both in securing military victory and in assuring the eternal salvation of individual souls. As a consequence, intercessory prayers, votive masses, penitential rites, sermons, consecrated battle flags, and relics continued to play a prominent role on the home front and on the battlefield in raising morale, forging *esprit de corps* among the troops, and strengthening military discipline.

The collapse of the Carolingian empire and the fragmentation of the West into competing Christian states created new contexts for the conduct of wars, which in turn required new responses from both secular and religious authorities. At the public level, it became increasingly important to assure soldiers fighting against fellow Christians about the justness of their cause and about the evil nature and intent of their opponents. Rulers concomitantly expended considerable resources to secure intercessory prayers and masses on behalf of the souls of fallen soldiers who had been forced to shed Christian blood in battle. At the level of individual soldiers, the Carolingian practice of pre-battle confession was augmented gradually during the course of the tenth century by an emphasis on the reception of the eucharist, which was understood by many contemporaries to strengthen both the bodies and the souls of fighting men. The most radical development in the religion of war during this entire period came during the second half of the eleventh century as leading churchmen attempted to redefine the nature of the sinfulness engendered by homicide committed in battle. This process would culminate in the development of a doctrine of holy war and crusade. This chapter, therefore, will be divided into four parts dealing in turn with the public religion of war, army rites, individual religious preparations for battle, and the problem of homicide in a just war.

Public Religion of War

As had been true of their predecessors, the rulers of the Carolingian successor states attributed great importance to public wartime religious rites as a crucial means of obtaining divine assistance in battle, and more generally for assuring the protection of their people and territories. At the level of human interaction, state-supported religious rites had a variety of other purposes, particularly in the area of propaganda, but also in assuaging the grief and fears of the families and friends of soldiers lost in war. As we will see below, the fragmentation of the Carolingian empire and the greater number of wars waged among Christian armies required that increasing attention be paid both to establishing a just *casus belli*, and to assuring the spiritual support provided to soldiers who found it necessary to kill other Christians in battle.

In the foundation charter for the monastery of St Peter and St Marculf, issued in 906, King Charles III of France (893–923) emphasized that the current wave of attacks by the Northmen (*paganorum infestatio*), which had resulted in the displacement of many monks, was the result of the sins weighing down society.[1] Therefore, in order to imitate the good rulership of his predecessors and for the salvation of his own soul (*ob anime nostre remedium*), Charles agreed to provide lands for the establishment of a new monastery whose members were to pray incessantly both for the well-being of the church and for the stability of the entire kingdom (*totius regni stabilitas*).[2] In 918, within the context of the ongoing struggle against the Northmen, King Charles also granted the monastery and lands of Croix-Saint-Ouen to the monks of Saint-Germain-des-Près. As was true of his earlier grant, Charles emphasized that this donation was intended both for his own spiritual well-being and to ensure the safety of his entire kingdom from enemy attack.[3]

Donations of land and immunities to monasteries and churches that were intended to obtain divine support in military affairs remained quite common in *Francia* over the course of the tenth and eleventh centuries. Following in the tradition of his predecessors, the government of King Philip I (1059–1108) regularly invoked the safety of his kingdom as the reason for supporting monastic foundations, agreeing to the transfer of property, and granting ecclesiastical immunities. In 1060, King Philip confirmed an act previously issued by his father Henry I permitting the donation of several properties to the monastery of St Peter of Chartres. In the context of this charter, Philip noted that he considered it of importance to give his consent both for the sake of his own salvation, and for maintaining the integrity of his kingdom (*pro integritate regni*).[4]

In the royal view, the very act of supporting the church meant that the king was helping to protect his kingdom. However, the French ruler also sought more explicit aid from churchmen in return for royal largesse. Thus, in 1075, in return for confirming the rights and possessions of the monastery of St Philbert at

---

[1] *Recueil des actes de Charles III le Simple, roi de France (893–923)*, ed. Philippe Lauer (Paris, 1940), p. 115.

[2] *Ibid.*, *quique pro statu ecclesie nostraque incolumitate totius regni stabilitate incessanter exorent instituere curavimus.* Cf. *ibid.*, pp. 175–6, where Charles grants perpetual possession of property to the monastery of St Aignon in Orléans under the condition that the monks never cease to pray to God on behalf of the entire kingdom.

[3] *Ibid.*, p. 211, *pro nostra totiusque salute regni.*

[4] *Recueil des actes de Philippe Ier roi de France (1059–1108)*, ed. M. Prou (Paris, 1908), p. 5, *pro nostra salute et integritate regni.* For similar statements concerning the benefits to the kingdom from supporting the church, see *ibid.*, pp. 147, 223, and 284.

Tornus, Philip demanded that the monks pray both for the royal *familia* and for all of the king's supporters.[5] When confirming a donation to the monastery of St Benedict sur-Loire in 1077, Philip similarly emphasized that the beneficiaries were to pray to God without fail for the state of the realm (*pro statu regni*).[6]

These generalized invocations of divine support for the safety of the realm were complemented in *Francia* by requests for aid in specific military campaigns. Thus, Rodulfus Glaber emphasized the importance of invoking heavenly assistance in his discussion of the struggle between Geoffrey Martel, count of Anjou (1040–1060), and forces of the count of Blois led by Theobold and Stephen, sons of the dead count Odo II, for control over the strategic city of Tours in 1044.[7] When Geoffrey, who was besieging the city, heard that relief forces were approaching, he not only prayed to Martin, the patron saint of Tours, he also promised to restore any property that he had stolen from his patrimony. Indeed, Geoffrey went even further and promised to return any property that he had stolen from any saint.[8] Rodulfus compared the promise of the victorious Geoffrey with actions of Theobold and Stephen who had stolen from the monks of St Martin in order to pay their troops.[9]

When preparing for his invasion of England in 1066, Duke William II of Normandy sought and received papal support and prayers on behalf of the campaign, and publicly received a banner (*vexillum*) from the see of Saint Peter.[10] Pope Alexander II's gift of the *vexillum* was a public demonstration of his support for Duke William's undertaking and, according to contemporary observers, made it possible for the Norman duke to invade England with greater

---

5   *Ibid.*, p. 197, *quo fideles cuncti assidue orant, non modo pro regibus verum etiam pro omnibus in sublimitate constitutis.*
6   *Ibid.*, p. 225, *Ipsi namque pro statu regni nostri sine intermissione Deum exorant. . . .*
7   Rodulfus Glaber, *Historiarum libri quinque*, ed. Neithard Bulst, trans. John France and Paul Reynolds (Oxford, 1989), 5.19, p. 242.
8   *Ibid.*, *Quod Gozfredus comperiens expetivit auxilium beati Martini, promisit et humiliter emendatorum possessionibus raptu abstraxerat.*
9   *Ibid.*, pp. 242–4, *Nam ex rapina pauperum eiusdem confessoris ferebant supplementum suis filii Odonis.*
10   For the tradition of papal grants of banners for military campaigns, Carl Erdmann, "Kaiserliche und päpstliche Fahnen im hohen Mittelalter," *Quellen und Forschungen aus italienischen Archiven und Bibliotheken* 25 (1933), pp. 1–48, remains an important and valuable study. Concerning William's negotiations with Pope Alexander II and his subsequent use of the papal banner, see Erdmann, *Idea of Crusade*, p. 154; and H.E.J. Cowdrey, "Pope Gregory VII and the Anglo-Norman Church and Kingdom," *Studi Gregoriani* 9 (1972), pp. 78–114, here pp. 84–5. Elisabeth van Houts, "The Norman Conquest Through European Eyes," *English Historical Review* 110 (1995), pp. 832–53, here pp. 852–3, argues that the invasion, as well as papal support for it, were well known across Europe, although both were subject to negative comment in contemporary European historical literature. Orderic Vitalis, *The Ecclesiastical History*, 6 vols., ed. Marjorie Chibnall (Oxford, 1969–80), II: 58, notes that William of Montreuil had a papal banner (*vexillum Sancti Petri*) when he served in Campania as one of Alexander II's mercenary commanders. Similarly, Erlembald of Milan received a *vexillum Sancti Petri* from Pope Alexander II during his conflict against Godfrey, King Henry IV's choice for archbishop of Milan. See Arnulf of Milan, *Gesta archiepiscoporum Mediolanensium*, ed. L.C. Bethmann and W. Wattenbach, MGH SS 8 (Hanover, 1848), p. 22.

confidence and with greater safety.[11] Indeed, the importance attributed by William to divine support for military operations was echoed in 1084 by another Norman, Robert Guisgard, when he emphasized that he was giving property to the archbishopric of Bari in order that God might give him victory in battle.[12]

We can see very similar efforts to enlist divine support for military campaigns in the East. In 999, for example, Emperor Otto III (983–1002) granted control over the city and district of the northern Italian bishopric of Vercelli to its prelate Leo in order that "this church of God might freely, securely, and permanently support our empire, so that the crown of military strength might triumph, that the power of the Roman people might grow, and that the *res publica* might be restored."[13] Henry II of Germany (1002–1025), Otto's cousin and successor, made explicit in his donation charter to the monastery of Nienburg that God aided those both in this world and in the next who supported the saints.[14] As a consequence, during the preparations for his campaign against the Slavs in August 1004, Henry made clear that he was making his donation of lands to the monastery so that he would have a "more certain grace of victory" in his forthcoming *expeditio*.[15]

In the eyes of the German kings and their supporters, these donations to monasteries and churches were not only beneficial in themselves, they also encouraged priests and monks to pray for the king, army, and kingdom. Thus, for example, during Conrad II of Germany's campaign against the Ljutici in 1035, all of the clergy and people of his kingdom are reported to have under-

---

[11] *The Gesta Guillelmi of William of Poitiers*, ed. R.C.H. Davis and Marjorie Chibnall (Oxford, 1998), p. 104, *Huius apostolici favorem petens dux, intimato negotio quod agitabat, vexillum accepit eius benignitate velut suffragium sancti Petri, quo primo confidentius ac tutius invaderet adversarium.* The value of William's work as a historical source is emphasized by Roger D. Ray, "Orderic Vitalis and William of Poitiers: A Monastic Reinterpretation of William the Conqueror," *Revue belge de philologie et d'histoire* 50 (1972), pp. 1116–27, here pp. 1116–17.

[12] *Recueil des actes des ducs Normands d'Italie (1046–1127)*, ed. Léon-Robert Ménager (Bari, 1980), p. 143, *ut Deus det mihi victoriam in bello....*

[13] *Die Urkunden der deutschen Könige und Kaiser*, vol. 2, ed. T. Sickel, MGH (Hanover, 1898), p. 753, *ut libere et secure permanente dei ecclesia prosperetur nostrum imperium, triumphet corona nostre militie, propagatur potentia populi Romani et restituatur res publica.* ... This charter was renewed in 1054 by Emperor Henry III, who repeated the earlier formula emphasizing the connection between the gift to the bishop and the future success of the empire. See *Die Urkunden der deutschen Könige und Kaiser*, vol. 5, ed. H. Bresslau and P. Kehr (Berlin, 1931), pp. 448–9.

[14] *Die Urkunden der deutschen Könige und Kaiser*, vol. 3, ed. H. Bresslau, MGH (Hanover, 1903), p. 104, *Si loco sanctorum munificentiae regalis largitate sublimamus, hoc nobis tam in praesentis vitae decursu quam in futurae gloriae statu prodesse liquido profitemur.*

[15] *Ibid.*, *et quia ea tempestate proxima nobis in Sclavoniam instabat expeditio, pro certiori gratia triumphi....* In 1005, the next year, Henry prepared for a campaign against the Poles by first celebrating the assumption of the Virgin Mary. The contemproary chronicler Bishop Thietmar of Merseburg emphasized that King Henry II did not set out until he had fufilled his religious obligations. Thietmar of Merseburg, *Chronicon*, ed. Werner Trillmich based on the original edition by R. Holtzmann (Darmstadt, 1985), p. 262, *Et rex sanctae Dei genitricis assumptionem Magadaburch celebrans, in ipso die post missam et caritatem expletam comitante regina transnavigans Albiam proficiscitur.*

gone penitential rites and to have prayed to the Lord for vengeance and victory.[16] The form taken by specific requests for prayers on behalf of the king and army is indicated by a letter sent in 1075 by King Henry IV of Germany to the monks and abbot of St Maximin at Trier. In his missive, Henry informed the brothers that he would soon be waging a campaign against the Saxon rebels, which he hoped to bring to a conclusion by early June. Henry requested that the monks begin to pray immediately for the army and continue to pray until the expedition ended. The king explained that these prayers to God were necessary so that the army would not fail in its task.[17]

Prayers on behalf of soldiers and the army survive in several pontificals from the tenth and eleventh centuries, and these probably represent the types of religious aid sought by German kings. Thus, for example, the Romano-German pontifical of Mainz includes the prayer *praebe domine*, which was discussed in detail in the previous chapter and can be traced to the Gellone sacramentary of the eighth century.[18] As was noted above, this prayer calls on God to support the efforts of the army (*opus exercitui*) and to give aid to the soldiers just as He had aided the Israelites fleeing from Egypt.[19] However, the late tenth-century version of this prayer does differ in some respects from its progenitor. In particular, rather than giving credit for victory to God (*victori domino gratias referat*), as had been the case in the Gellone sacramentary, the later version assigns the victory to Christ who triumphed on the cross because of his humility and his death.[20] This prayer continued to be in wide use in the post-Carolingian period and was included by Bishop Gondekar II of Eichstätt (1057–1075) in his pontifical composed between 1071 and 1073, just two years before King Henry IV sent his letter to the monks at St Maximin.[21] A contemporary *missa in tempore belli* was utilized by the Norman bishop, Robert of Jumièges, in his missal.[22] However, rather than specifically seeking divine support in battle, the votive mass in Robert's missal sought protection from the enemy.[23]

The invocation of divine aid on behalf of the army was important for the morale of the soldiers because it helped to assure them that every possible means of support was being pursued on their behalf. However, war rites also

---

[16] Rodulfus Glaber, *Historiarum*, 4.23, p. 208, *ob quam rem totius ecclesie clerus ac plebs regni sui, semet affligens, Dominum rogaverunt, ut ultionis vindictam de tanta barbarorum vesania illi concederet, ut ad sui nominis honorem Christianis foret ex illis victoria.*

[17] *Quellen zur Geschichte Kaiser Heinrichs IV*, ed. Franz-Josef Schmale and Irene Schmale-Ott (Darmstadt, 1968), pp. 57–8, *vestra nos prosequatur oratio. Pro illo vero iugitur orate, et ne in proposito suo deficiat, precibus deum exorate.*

[18] For the text of the eighth-century prayer, see *Sacramentarium Gellonense*, p. 431. The late tenth-century version can be found in the *Le pontifical Romano-Germanique du dixième siècle*, ed. Cyrille Vogel and Reinhard Elze (Vatican, 1963), p. 380.

[19] *Pontifical Romano-Germanique*, p. 380.

[20] *Ibid.*, *sed ipsi victori Christo filio tuo gratias referat de triumpho, qui humilitate suae passionis de morte mortisque principe in cruce triumphavit.*

[21] See Michel Andrieu, *Les ordines Romani du haut moyen âge: les manuscrits* (Louvain, 1931), pp. 117–18, for the reference to the pontifical of Bishop Gondekar II of Eichstätt, fol. 112r.

[22] *The Missal of Robert of Jumièges*, ed. H.A. Wilson (London, 1846), p. 267.

[23] *Ibid.*, *ut ab omni nos exuat bellorum nequitia et in tuae protectionis securitate constitutat.*

served as a public means of reminding soldiers, their families, and the community as a whole that God was on their side. Within this context, therefore, it was exceptionally important for rulers to demonstrate that they were worthy of heavenly assistance. When King Otto II of Germany (973–983) invaded the West Frankish kingdom in 978, he took great care to be seen as a protector of the church even as he ravaged the territory around Rheims and then Paris. The contemporary chronicler Richer, who completed his history less than two decades after the invasion, emphasized that when advanced elements of Otto's army destroyed the monastery of St Baltild de Chelles, this was done without the king's knowledge.[24] Indeed, the chronicler affirmed that the destruction of the religious house not only made Otto very upset, he even made large donations in order to have it restored.[25] Otto's generosity to the churches in West *Francia* would appear to have made such a great impression on contemporaries that two generations later the author of the *Gesta pontificum Cameracensium* also took pains to emphasize this aspect of the German campaign.[26] The chronicler stressed that Otto had been well instructed in the customs of his ancestors so that rather than robbing the churches he decided instead to give them rich gifts.[27]

The author of the Cambrai account added the further information that in addition to making donations to churches, even in territories that he was attacking, the German king ordered his own staff to hold public religious celebrations in order to draw attention to his recent victories over the West Frankish forces and to demonstrate his superiority over Hugh Capet who was ensconced within the walls of Paris. According to the chronicler, these rites were so magnificent that when Otto ordered the priests serving with his army to sing the "Alleluia te martirum," the volume of their singing astounded Hugh and the entire population of Paris.[28] King Otto's actions, including his donations to the local churches and his orchestration of an enormous public religious celebration outside of Paris, would appear to have succeeded, at least in the eyes of the chronicler, in demonstrating to his own troops and to his enemies that the German army was favored by God.

The consequences of being perceived to be pursuing unjust objectives could prove to be sufficiently negative that rulers would humiliate themselves in order

---

[24] Richer, *Histoire de France (888–995)*, 2nd edn, ed. and trans. R. Latouche, 2 vols. (Paris, 1967), II: 92, *Nec minus centuriones praevii, eo ignorante, Sanctae Baltildis monasterium apud Chelas penitus subruerunt atque combusserunt.*

[25] *Ibid., Quod non mediocriter dolens, multa in ejus restaurationem delegavit.*

[26] The *Gesta pontificum Cameracensium*, ed. L.C. Bethmann, MG SS 7 (Hanover, 1846), was written by a canon at Cambrai between 1041 and 1043 at the order of Bishop Gerard II (1013–1048).

[27] *Gesta pontificum Cameracensium*, p. 441, *Paternis tamen moribus instructus, aecclesias observavit, immo etiam oppulentis muneribus ditare potius estimavit.*

[28] *Ibid., Deinde vero ad pompandam victoriae suae gloriam Hugoni, qui Parisius residebat, per legationem denuncians, quod in tantam sublimitatem Alleluia faceret ei decantari, in quanta non audieret, accitis quam pluribus clericis Alleluia te martirum in loco qui dicitur Mons Martirum, in tantum elatis vocibus decantari precepit, ut attonitis auribus ipse Hugo et omnis Parisiorum plebs miraretur.*

to reestablish their reputations. In 996, for example, Count Fulk Nerra of Anjou (987–1040) damaged property belonging to the monastery of St Martin while besieging the city of Tours. In response, the monks denied entry to Fulk and his troops to the tomb of Saint Martin and to the church. In addition, the monks ritually humiliated the saint's relics by placing them on the floor of the church and piling thorns over them.[29] In the end, Fulk was forced to appease the monks.

The importance of being on the just side in battle and, moreover, being seen to be on the side of heaven is also emphasized by Rodulfus Glaber in his description of the efforts by King Robert II of France (996–1031) to capture Auxerre and the nearby monastery of St Germain in Burgundy.[30] According to Rodulfus, the Burgundians were rebels against their legitimate ruler. However, when Odilo, the great abbot of the monastery of Cluny, came to mediate between the king and the rebels, King Robert refused to be reconciled and insisted on undertaking the siege of the fortified monastery of St Germain. As a consequence, Odilo exhorted the eight monks who remained in the monastery along with the garrison to pray assiduously so that God would show them compassion and lift the siege.[31]

Rodulfus contrasted the holy man Odilo with King Robert, who by the sixth day of the siege is described as being beside himself with rage (*nimio rex arreptus furore*).[32] When the abbot approached Robert and his officers for the second time to criticize them for assaulting the property of Saint Germanus, he was ignored and the assault went forward. Rodulfus emphasized that the king's impious attack was spoiled by a huge black fog that covered the monastery and allowed the defenders to look out while keeping the royal troops from seeing in – a situation that led to great losses among Robert's men. According to the chronicler, the descent of the fog corresponded in time with the celebration of mass by brother Gilbert, a devout monk, a circumstance that was appropriate given the divine sanction for the victory by the monastery's defenders.[33] Thus, in Rodulfus' account, the rebels had divine support because the king had failed, and failed publicly, to behave in a manner befitting one seeking God's aid.

As Rodulfus Glaber's narrative suggests, the corollary to demonstrating the justness of one's own cause was to establish publicly that the enemy had forfeited any right to divine support. When fighting against non-Christian enemies this was a relatively easy task. As we saw above in the case of the battle of Fontenoy (841), however, fighting against Christian enemies could pose

---

[29] The charter dealing with this episode has been published by Louis Halphen, *Le Comté d'Anjou au XIe siècle* (repr. Geneva, 1974), pp. 318–19. This episode is discussed by Patrick Geary, "Humiliation of Saints," in *Saints and Their Cults: Studies in Religious Sociology, Folklore and History*, ed. Stephen Wilson (Cambridge, 1983), pp. 123–40, here pp. 130–2. Also see Lester K. Little, *Benedictine Maledictions: Liturgical Cursing in Romanesque France* (Ithaca, 1993), p. 43.

[30] Rodulfus Glaber, *Historiarum*, 2.15, p. 78.

[31] *Ibid.*, *hortabatur fratres octo tantum numero qui ad confessoris custodiam relicti fuerant . . . ut orationi instarent assidue, si forte Domini pietas eos pariter et locum a tanta obsidione dignaretur eripere.*

[32] *Ibid.*, p. 80.

[33] *Ibid.*, *quod scilicet factum satis celitus prestite congruit victorie.*

morale problems for soldiers, for who was to know which side God would support, and whether the souls of the dead soldiers would be accepted into heaven? In such cases, it was important to give soldiers a clear sign that the enemy had been abandoned by God. In 948, for example, a combined force under the command of King Louis IV of West *Francia* and Duke Conrad of Lotharingia assaulted the fortress of Montaigu held by Count Theobold of Blois, a supporter of Hugh the Great.[34] According to Flodoard, the bishops serving under Louis and Conrad gathered at the monastic church of Saint-Vincent de Laon and there excommunicated Theobold.[35] In addition, they sent letters to Hugh, both on their own behalf and on behalf of the papal legate, insisting that he give compensation for his misdeeds against both the king and the bishops.[36] Because Hugh refused to satisfy the claims, the next year at a council held at Cluny, Pope Agapitus II (946–955) excommunicated him and refused to remove the ban until he became reconciled with King Louis.[37] As a consequence, Louis' troops could feel confident that they were fighting for a just cause, while Hugh's men had to worry about the ability of their side to win divine aid.

We can see a similar use of excommunication in 1014, when Pope Benedict VIII took action against some of the vassals of Count William of Provence. In a letter to William, Pope Benedict asserted that wicked injuries (*nefanda injuria*) were being committed against the monastery of St Gilles by individuals seeking to control its property.[38] In response, Benedict imposed on them an exceptionally florid sentence of excommunication in which he not only condemned the wrongdoers in all four corners of the world, but also expressed the hope that their wives would go with them into perdition and that their children would die by the sword.[39]

In a much more famous case of excommunication being used as a weapon of war, Pope Gregory VII banned King Henry IV of Germany in 1076, in response to the latter's refusal to accept papal jurisdiction in imperial episcopal affairs.[40]

---

[34] *Les Annales de Flodoard*, ed. P. Lauer (Paris, 1906), p. 116.

[35] *Ibid.*

[36] *Ibid.*, *Hugonem vero principem vocant litteris ex parte Marini legati apostolicae sedis et sua venire ad emendationem pro malis quae contra regem et episcopos egerat.*

[37] *Ibid.*, p. 125

[38] PL 139: 1630–2. This text is discussed in some detail by Little, *Benedictine Maledictions*, p. 43.

[39] PL 139: 1631.

[40] The importance of this episode for the development of excommunication as a tool against German emperors is dealt with by Rudolf Schieffer, *Die Entstehung des päpstlichen Investiturverbots für den deutschen König* (Stuttgart, 1981), pp. 132–52. The valuable study by Elisabeth Vodola, "Sovereignty and Tabu: Evolution of the Sanction against Communication with Excommunicates. Part 1: Gregory VII," in *The Church and Sovereignty c. 590–1918: Essays in Honour of Michael Wilks*, ed. Diana Wood (London, 1991), pp. 35–55, examines the canonical and political realities underlying Pope Gregory's excommunication of King Henry IV in 1076, with a particular emphasis on the problems incurred by an excommunicate in dealing with his supporters. See also, Uta-Renate Blumenthal, *The Investiture Controversy: Church and Monarchy from the Ninth to the Twelfth Century* (Philadelphia, 1988), pp. 121–7.

The anonymous author of the *Vita Heinrici iv imperatoris* emphasized that as a result of the pope's action, many of the bishops who had been supporting King Henry in his ongoing civil war against Saxons rebels abandoned him out of fear of losing their offices. This significant diminution of the king's military strength was compounded by the defection of many of the secular nobles.[41] As a consequence, King Henry was forced to go to Canossa and beg Pope Gregory VII's forgiveness in order to reclaim the support of the German episcopate and nobility.

King Henry had his revenge, however. After he crushed the Saxon revolt, the German king redistributed the territories of his enemies to churches that had remained loyal to the crown during the civil war. In 1086, for example, Henry seized the property of Markgraf Ekbert and transferred it to the control of the episcopal church of Utrecht.[42] According to the donation charter, even after Saxony and Thuringia had been reconciled to the king, Ekbert violated the norms of piety, good faith, legality, and his oath, by taking up arms against his king without any justice or reason. Indeed, King Henry went further, denouncing the markgraf not only for attacking his right to rule (*dignitas*), but also for trying to kill him in time of war – lit. when the banners were unfurled "erecto vexillo."[43] In these terms, Henry was able to portray Ekbert as a rebel not only against the king, but also as a rebel against God who broke his sacred oaths and attacked the Lord's anointed. This public image was further reinforced by the grant of the traitor's lands to the church.[44]

In addition to its value in wars among princes, excommunication also proved to be the most effective tool used by bishops attempting to enforce the codes of conduct arising from the movements known as the Peace of God and the Truce of God.[45] The author of the *Gesta episcoporum Cameracensium* emphasized that the bishops of the kingdom of France issued a decree (*decretum*) that

---

[41] *Vita Heinrici iv imperatoris*, in *Quellen zur Geschichte Kaiser Heinrichs IV.*, ed. Irene Schale-Ott (Darmstadt, 1968), p. 420, *Mox episcopi, tam illi quos amor quam quos timor in partem regis traxerat, metuentes ordini suo, ab eius auxilio plerique se retrahebant.*

[42] *Die Urkunden der deutschen Könige und Kaiser*, vol. 6, 2nd edn, ed. D. v. Gladiss, MGH (Weimar, 1959), p. 513.

[43] *Ibid.*, pp. 513–14, *Ekbertus quasi ex ipso dilectionis nostre sinu prosiliens arma corripuit pietate * fide legibus et * sacramentis suis promiscue violatis Saxones et Turingos, quoscumque potuit, in societatem furoris ac sceleria attrahens absque omni iusta vel probabili causa non solum exinanire dignitatem nostram, set et vitam nostram erecto vexillo moliebatur extinguere.*

[44] King Henry reauthorized the transfer of this property in 1089, emphasizing again that Ekbert had dared to attack him in time of war. *Die Urkunden der deutschen Könige und Kaiser*, vol. 6, p. 532, *ausus contra nos levare gladium et erecto vexillo nos impugando. . . .*

[45] Richard Landes, "Popular Participation in the Limousin Peace of God," in *The Peace of God: Social Violence and Religious Response in France around the Year 1000*, ed. Thomas Head and Richard Landes (Ithaca, 1992), pp. 184–219, here p. 210; and Daniel F. Callahan, "The Cult of the Saints in Aquitaine," in *ibid.*, pp. 165–83, here pp. 172–8. Some scholars have argued that excommunication was an ineffective method of cooercion in comparison with secular legal penalties. See, for example, Pierre Bonnassie, *La Catalogne du milieu du Xe à la fin du XIe siècle: Croissance et mutations d'une société*, 2 vols. (Toulouse, 1975–6), pp. 652–3; and Elisabeth Magnou-Nortier, *La société laïque dans la province ecclésiastique de Narbonne* (Toulouse, 1974), p. 309. For an opposing view, see the detailed study by Jeffrey

whoever failed to keep the peace and refused to accept penance was to be deprived of contact with other Christians and to be denied burial when he died, that is the penalties normally imposed on excommunicates.[46] Similarly, a council under the leadership of Archbishop Raginbald of Arles, held between 1037 and 1041, decreed the establishment of a Truce of God (*treuga Dei*) for his archdiocese that limited the periods in which fighting could take place and imposed severe sanctions on those who broke the regulations.[47] The bishops at the council emphasized that by the authority granted to them by God through the apostles, they gave a blessing to all those who followed the Truce ordinance and, excommunicated, cursed, and anathematized those who violated them.[48]

The excommunication of secular nobles who refused to support peace councils was clearly a problem for leaders seeking prayers to God on behalf of their military operations. Furthermore, excommunicated nobles and their soldiers faced the additional problem that they could not be buried in consecrated ground, so that fighting men who violated peace statutes ran the risk of never finding eternal rest.[49] Ademar of Chabannes described the fate of just such a viscount who had been excommunicated as a violator of the peace. After the man had been killed in battle, the bishop of Cahors forbid his burial in consecrated ground so his troops were forced to carry him off and bury him in secret, without the sacred office and without any cleric present. When the priests at the church where he was buried discovered what had happened, they ordered his body removed.[50]

As was true of their Carolingian predecessors, the rulers of tenth- and eleventh-century Europe complemented pre-campaign war rites with extensive post-campaign liturgies and religious foundations. As we saw in the previous chapter, conflicts between Christians, particularly the battle of Fontenoy in 841, raised concerns among both soldiers and their leaders about the justness of war and the sinfulness of killing in battle. The fragmentation of the Carolingian empire led inexorably to an increase in wars between Christians as smaller Christian states vied for power. As a consequence, Christian rulers found it necessary to expand on earlier Carolingian practice by investing heavily in reli-

---

A. Bowman, "Do Neo-Romans Curse?: Law, Land, and Ritual in the Midi (900–1100)," *Viator* 28 (1997), pp. 1 32.

[46] *Gesta episcoporum Cameracensium*, p. 485, *Et haec sacramento se servare firmarent; quod qui nollet, christianitate privaretur, et exeuntem de saeculo nullus visitaret nec sepulturae traderet.*

[47] On this point, see *Constitutiones et Acta Imperatorum et Regum* I, ed. Ludwig Weiland, MGH (Hanover, 1893), p. 597.

[48] *Ibid., secundem auctoritatem a Deo collatam et ab apostolis traditam omnes qui hanc pacem et Dei treuvam amaverint benedicimus et absolvimus, sicut superius dictum est; illos autem qui contradicunt excommunicamus, maledicimus et anathematizimus et a liminibus sanctae matris ecclesie eliminamus.*

[49] Callahan, "Cult of the Saints," p. 178.

[50] Concerning this account, see *ibid.* The text is found in Mansi 19: 541, *quia ille vicecomes excommunicatus . . . me ignorante a militibus suis ad monasterium nostrum deportatus est: cuius corpus neque suscepimus, neque sepelivimus, sed sine officio sacro retro ultra aquam revehi jussimus, ubi milites ipsi, nullo clericorum adstante, sepelierunt illud.*

gious rites and institutions that not only made manifest God's support for their causes, but also brought comfort to those who participated in these struggles. This religious support was, of course, also available to the families of the men who had died in battle.

One of the ways in which rulers helped to alleviate the fears of soldiers and their families about the eternal consequences of dying in battle before having the opportunity to expiate their sins through the rites of confession and penance was by subsidizing regular prayers on behalf of the fallen troops. As we saw above, Carolingian rulers arranged for prayer services on the anniversaries of great battles. In the post-Carolingian period, rulers undertook to expand this effort by subsidizing prayers that were intended to benefit directly the souls of the soldiers who had died in their service. One of the earliest surviving examples of a memorial donation on behalf of a fallen soldier came about at the instigation of Count Conrad, an officer serving in Emperor Otto II's army at the battle of Cap Callone in 982. According to the emperor's donation charter to the monastery of St Gorgonius at Gorze, Conrad had requested publicly that if he were to die fighting against the Saracens, all of his property be given to Gorze.[51] Otto, of course, acceded to this request noting that it was in his own interest to aid the efforts of his *fideles* to support the church for the benefit of their souls.[52]

In some cases, families of soldiers took on the obligation of securing prayers for their dead relatives. Thus, for example, in 1095, the relatives of Geoffrey Fetu, who had been killed serving with the Angevin comital army at Passavant, came to the cathedral chapter at Angers and asked that the canons there bury him in return for a donation of property. The family also sought to have prayers said for Geoffrey, alms given in his name, and to have him inscribed in the cathedral's *martirologium*.[53] The canons agreed to these requests after the family made a formal transfer of the property by placing a small knife on the cathedral altar.[54]

This concern for the ultimate fate of the souls of soldiers killed in combat is addressed explicitly by Bishop Thietmar of Merseburg (1009–1018). In his *Chronicon*, Thietmar begins by describing the ambush and destruction in 1015

---

[51] *Die Urkunden der deutschen Könige und Kaiser*, vol. 2, p. 326, *Cunradus filius Ruodolfi quondam comitis in die belli quod fuit inter nos et Sarracenos, sub fanone nostro, hoc est imperiali vexillo, legali ritu tradendum nobis commendavit omne predium suum quod habuit in regno Lothariensi, rogavitque in conspectu totius exercitus nostram dominationem humiliter, ut hoc totum parvum cum magno ad monasterium sancti Gorgonii martyris in loco Gorzia vocato constructum nostra perceptione, si ea die moreretur, sicut fecit, traderemus.*

[52] *Ibid.*, pp. 325–6, *Si peticiones fidelium nostrorum quas pro usu et statu ecclesiarum ac remedio animarum suarum in conspectu imperii nostri fundunt, pia devotione compleverimus, id procul dubio ad presentis vite statum et eterne beatitudine premia capessenda nobis proficere confidimus.*

[53] *Cartulaire noire de la cathédrale d'Angers*, ed. Ch. Urseau (Paris, 1908), p. 118, *Haimo Guischardus et Bota, uxor eius, et filius uxoris et filia et Renaldus Grossa Barba venerunt in capitulum nostrum, supplicantes et petentes ut Gosfridum cognomento Festucam, qui interfectus erat in exercitu Passavantum, super gradus ecclesiae nostrae sepeliremus et ut ei benefium elemosinarum et orationum, sicut caeteris fratribus nostris, impertiremus ad remedium animae suae et in martirologio nostro inscriberemus.*

[54] *Ibid.*

by Duke Boleslav Chrobry of Poland (992–1025) of a German force under the command of Archbishop Gero of Magdeburg.[55] After recalling the deaths of two counts named Gero and Folkmar, and 200 soldiers, Thietmar stepped out of his role as narrator and called directly on God in prayer to have mercy when considering their souls. In addition, Thietmar asked God to have mercy on the souls of those still living for having caused this disaster through the sinfulness of their lives, and to protect them from ever suffering such a tragedy again.[56] What makes this case even more striking is the fact that Boleslav Chrobry was seen by Thietmar as a manifestly evil ruler and thus a man against whom it was not only licit but even good to fight.[57] Thus, the men for whose souls Thietmar was praying had died in a manifestly just cause.

Care for the souls of battle-dead was seen as a high priority by all of the leading figures in the contemporary German military-religious establishment. When King Henry II received reports about the ambush, he wanted to go himself and retrieve the bodies for burial. The king was dissuaded from doing so out of fear for his safety. However, Bishop Eid of Meißen did obtain permission from Duke Boleslav Chrobry to return to the site of the battle where the prelate and his men prayed for the dead soldiers and buried them.[58] The soldiers who fell in the battle were subsequently included in the *Liber memorialis* of Merseburg so that their souls could receive the benefit of an annual remembrance and prayers.[59]

King Henry IV, whose wars were fought almost exclusively against fellow Christians, played an exceptionally active role in securing prayers for his fallen troops. Thus, in a donation charter issued to the monastery of St Ulrich and St Afra in Augsburg on 12 June 1074, Henry requested that an intercessory mass be said every Thursday by the brothers on behalf of his fallen supporters.[60] Henry made a similar request in 1097 of the monks residing at the monastery of St George near Innsbruck, whom he asked to celebrate regular rites on behalf of all of the *fideles* who had been killed in his service.[61] Every Wednesday, the brothers were to sing mass for his dead soldiers, and every Saturday they were to sing a mass on behalf of those who were still living.[62] The frequency with which King Henry asked for prayers on behalf of his fallen troops is indicated by the

---

[55] Thietmar, *Chronicon*, 7.21, p. 374.

[56] *Ibid.*, *Gero ac Folcemarus comites cum CC militibus optimis occisi spoliati sunt, quorum nomina et animas Deus omnipotens misericorditer respiciat; et nos quorum culpa hii tunc oppetiere, sibi per Christum reconciliet et, ne quid tale ulterius paciamur, clemens custodiat.*

[57] Concerning Thietmar's intense dislike of Boleslav Chrobry, see *ibid.*, 4.28, p. 144.

[58] *Ibid.*, *ut miserabilem aspexit stragem, flebiliter ingemuit et supplicter pro hiis oravit.*

[59] *Die Totenbücher von Merseburg, Magdeburg, und Lüneburg*, ed. G. Althoff and J. Wollasch, MGH Libri Memoriales et Necrologia n.s. 2 (Hanover, 1983), fol. 5r, p. 11, *Gero et Vuolcmar comites cum sociis.*

[60] *Die Urkunden der deutschen Könige und Kaiser*, vol. 6, p. 351, . . . *ut deinceps omnibus seculis a fratribus ibidem deo servientibus missa pro defunctis fidelibus cunctis et specialiter nostris parentibus omni IIII feria cantetur et noster anniversarius non minus celebretur.* Henry IV clearly saw no need to limit his requests, and therefore also asked for votive masses to be sung on behalf of his relatives and for his birthday.

[61] *Ibid.*, p. 613, *aliorum fidelium nostrorum in nostro servicio vel occisorum.*

[62] *Ibid.*, p. 614, *specialiter in omni septimana semper in tertia feria missa pro fidelibus defunctis et in sexta feria missa pro salute vivorum ibi celebretur.* Cf. in *ibid.*, p. 638, n. 470 b,

inclusion of a request of this type in a formulary book assembled at Bamberg during the mid-twelfth century. Here, Henry asks that monks celebrate a daily intercessory mass for the souls of those who died in a public war (*bellum publicum*) for the honor and defense of the kingdom. The text adds that every Thursday the monks should gather in a choir and sing once through all of the psalms normally included in the celebration of the hours.[63]

These types of prayers on behalf of the souls of dead fighting men served as a reminder to living soldiers that their spiritual well-being was a matter of concern to their leaders. In addition, however, the regular, weekly celebration of mass on behalf of the dead also served as a public reminder to the community at large, including the families of the fallen, that the soldiers had died fighting for a just cause and on the side of heaven. And while Christian rulers saw that this statement could be made very effectively through the support of memorial liturgies, some leaders concluded that an even more enduring statement about divine support could made by the grant of lands or the actual foundation of new churches and monasteries in memory of military victories.

This was certainly the intention of King Henry III of Germany in 1051 when he granted property to the monastery of St Mary in Hainburg. The donation was made in the context of a recent German military victory over the Hungarians in lands that would become the duchy of Austria. Thus, while noting that his donation was meant to assure the spiritual salvation of his family and "pro pace etiam et stabilitate regni nostri," Henry emphasized that all of the property that was being granted came from areas recently conquered (lit. taken by the sword) from the enemy.[64] Indeed, it would appear that Henry's grant to the monastery of lands just seized from the enemy was meant to show that the German victory was divinely sanctioned.

While following the same reasoning, Count Robert I of Flanders (1070–1093) chose to endow new churches rather than supporting existing religious foundations in order to commemorate his victory over Countess Richilde and his final conquest of Flanders in 1072. According to Lambert of Ardres, Robert founded the canonry of Watten in honor of St Mary with places for thirty canons as a memorial to his military successes.[65] Robert then established a

where Henry asks that the monks of St Jacob at Lüttich to celebrate mass every Tuesday on behalf of his dead supporters.

63 *Ibid.*, p. 415, *Hoc quoque statutum est, ut pro animabus eorum qui in bello publico pro nostri regni honore et defensione corruerunt gladio, cottidie missa una specialis, omni quarta feria in choro a fratribus missa communis, ad omnes horas psalmus unus decantetur.* Similar requests for prayers on behalf of Henry IV's soldiers who died fighting in a *bello publio*, with the specific mention of the king's faithful supporter Siegfried, are included in two forgeries composed during the twelfth century. See *ibid.*, pp. 406 and 414.

64 *Die Urkunden der deutschen Könige und Kaiser*, vol. 5, ed. H. Bresslau and P. Kehr, MGH (Berlin, 1931), p. 378, *decimum mansum rectamque fructuum decimationem totius regionis in finibus Ungarorum gladio ab hostibus adquisitae.*

65 Lambert of Ardres, *Historia comitatum Ghisnensium*, ed. J. Heller, MGH SS 24 (Hanover, 1879), p. 575, *Ob cuius facti mentoriam et memoriam comes Robertus, adepto tocius Flandrie principatu, in honorem beatissime semperque virginis Marie Watiniensem fabrecit ecclesiam et triginta regulariter viventium canonicorum deserviri instituit obsequio.* Lambert wrote during the third quarter of the twelfth century. However, he used sources reaching back

second church in honor of St Peter. The chronicler emphasized that the battle against Richilde's forces had taken place on the apostle Peter's feast day, and that Count Robert and his men not only commended themselves to the saint but won their victory through his intercession.[66] The foundation of the second church therefore served as a continuing and physical reminder to the entire community that Robert's victory was the result of heavenly intervention and was in accord with the will of God as expressed through the actions of Saint Peter.

The triumphalist impulse indicated by Count Robert's foundation of two churches in memory of his conquest of Flanders could also coexist, however, with feelings of remorse and penitence for having killed fellow Christians in battle. Feelings such as these were almost certainly the inspiration for Count Fulk Nerra of Anjou's (986–1040) own foundation of a 'battle abbey.' By his own admission, Fulk was wracked with guilt following his crushing victory over Count Conan of Rennes at the battle of Conquereuil on 27 June 992.[67] As a result of his remorse, Fulk first made a pilgrimage to Jerusalem to expiate his sins.[68] He then founded a monastery at Loches, which was to be called *Belli Locus*.[69] According to the foundation charter, Fulk gave property to the house for the salvation of his soul and as a penance for the great slaughter of Christians that had taken place at the plain of Conquereuil.[70]

Perhaps the most famous foundation in commemoration of military victory in this period – the monastery dedicated in 1094 on the site of William the Conqueror's triumph over Harold Godwinson – may also have been intended as a penitential act. Eleanor Searle argues convincingly that the decision to build Battle Abbey, as it was called by the Normans, came about a result of King William's consultation with papal legates in 1070 and their subsequent imposition of heavy penances on the Conqueror's soldiers for their participation in the battle of Hastings.[71] It was certainly the case that the monks living at Battle Abbey thought of their house as penitential foundation. During the mid- to late twelfth century the monastery produced several forged charters and supported

---

to the tenth century, and his discussion of the establishment of the two churches should be seen as the culmination of a long written tradition. On this point, see Leah Shopkow, *The History of the Counts of Guines and Lords of Ardres* (Philadelphia, 2001), pp. 4–8.

[66] Lambert, *Historia*, p. 575, *Nec contentus eo, quoniam quidem in die, qua sancti Petri apostolorum principis solemnis habetur cathedra, meritis et intercessione eiusdem apostolorum principis, cui se et suos ipso die conflictus et belli commendaverat, divina semper preeunte gratia, de Richilde victoriosum diem exultaverat . . . in honorem apostolorum principis sancti Petri fabricavit et fundavit ecclesiam. . . .*

[67] On the battle and Fulk's reaction, see Bernard S. Bachrach, "The Combat Sculptures at Fulk Nerra's 'Battle Abbey,' " *Haskins Society Journal* 3 (1991), pp. 63–80.

[68] Radulfus Glaber, *Historia*, 2.4, p. 60.

[69] See *ibid*. On the name of the monastery and its development over time, see Bernard S. Bachrach, "Pope Sergius IV and the Foundation of the Monastery at Beaulieu-lès-Loches," *Revue bénédictine*, 95 (1985), pp. 240–65.

[70] *Cartulaire noire*, pp. 60–1, *ego Fulco, in Dei nomine, Andecavorum comes, hoc facio dinotari litteris propter remedium animae meae et pro poenitentia de tam magna strage christianorum quae acta est in planicie Conquareth.*

[71] *The Chronicle of Battle Abbey*, ed. Eleanor Searle (Oxford, 1980), pp. 20–1. The imposition of penances on William's troops will be discussed in greater detail below.

the composition of the *Chronicle of Battle Abbey* in which the view was propagated that William had sworn before the battle of Hastings to build a religious house on the site of the fighting in order to assure the salvation of those who had died in combat.[72]

Army Rites

In order to complement the intercessory rites carried out on behalf of the army on the home front, military commanders and their religious advisors routinely organized and led a wide variety of religious celebrations among their troops. Of primary importance was the invocation of heavenly support for soldiers on the field through intercessory prayers and masses. As was the case among their Carolingian predecessors, these rites were intended primarily to beg God and the saints to protect the soldiers in combat and to help the army as a whole to achieve victory. The perceived supernatural benefits that resulted from these religious rites had a concomitant impact on soldiers' morale as they saw the extensive efforts being undertaken to assure divine support on their behalf. They could now be more confident both of temporal military victory and of the state of their eternal souls should they fall during the fighting.

The importance of battlefield prayers for raising the spirits of the troops should not be underestimated. It was hardly coincidental that after King Charles III of *Francia* delivered a rousing oration to his troops on the eve of the battle of Soissons in June 923, the bishops and other clerics serving with his forces ostentatiously withdrew to the nearby high ground where a basilica dedicated to Saint Genvieve was located. Richer emphasized that they went there to help prepare for the battle, almost certainly by praying to God to intercede on behalf of their soldiers.[73] The fact that these prayers could not be heard by Charles' men was less important than their almost certain knowledge of what the clerics were doing.[74]

The great importance that these intercessory rites could have for the morale of soldiers on the battlefield can be seen even more clearly in the context of the Hungarian siege of Augsburg in August 955.[75] According to his biographer

---

[72] *Ibid.*, p. 66; and *Regesta Regum Anglo-Normannorum: The Acta of William I (1066–1087)*, ed. David Bates (Oxford, 1998), pp. 147–9 and 161–4. The importance of these texts for twelfth-century military-religious ideology will be discussed in detail in chapter five.

[73] Richer, *Historia*, II: 88, *Et post haec cum episcopis virisque religiosis qui aderant montem loco oppositum conscendit, ubi est basilica beatae Genovefae virginis dedicata, eventum belli inde experturus.*

[74] *Ibid.*, pp. 200–2, where Charles of Lorraine, the son of King Louis IV of France, and his men pray to God to support their small army against the large force under the command of Hugh Capet. Richer adds that Archbishop Arnoul of Rheims accompanied the soldiers and assured them that if they kept their faith in God, they would be victorious in battle.

[75] Gerhard of Augsburg, *Vita Sancti Uodalrici*, ed. Walter Berschin and Angelika Häse (Heidelberg, 1993). Gerhard was likely an eyewitness to the events discussed here. See *ibid.*, pp. 9–12. The siege of Augsburg took place within the overall Hungarian invasion of Germany that was defeated by King Otto I at the battle of the Lech.

Gerhard, Bishop Ulrich of Augsburg galvanized the defenders of his city through a series of intercessory religious rites that continued throughout the siege. On the first day of the Hungarian assault, Ulrich joined the episcopal bodyguards at the main gate of the city where they were fighting a desperate battle against the onrushing enemy troops. While his men fought, Ulrich calmly looked on as he sat astride his horse without the protection of a shield, hauberk, or helmet. He was guarded, his biographer emphasized, by his stole alone, which marked him out as a priest and as an intercessor with God. As the battle raged on, Ulrich remained unharmed despite the spears and stones that fell around him.[76]

It is clear from author's description that Ulrich's presence served as a sign to his troops that God was with them on that day. Indeed, the biographer made clear that Ulrich's appearance at the gate was essential to the victory of the defenders over the first wave of pagan Hungarians. Gerhard emphasized that it was in that hour when the bishop was astride his horse that the enemy leader was killed and the remainder of the attackers fled in disarray.[77]

As dusk fell, Ulrich ordered that the walls be repaired and strengthened, work that Gerhard said went on all night long. Then, after assuring as best he could the soundness of the physical defenses of his city, the bishop turned his attention to its spiritual defenses, and specifically to Augsburg's female inhabitants. Ulrich divided the women into two groups. The first group of women took up crosses and marched in processions around the city praying devotedly to God. According to Gerhard, the other group of women cast themselves to the ground, flailing themselves and begging for mercy from the mother of God. The prayers of all of the women were intended to assure the defense of the people of Augsburg and the liberation of their city.[78] For his part, Bishop Ulrich also spent the entire night in prayer.[79]

The following morning, Bishop Ulrich first celebrated a public mass and then had each of the soldiers receive communion. The author described this ceremony in a very particular manner, insisting that the bishop had brought all of his men back to life through the sacred *viaticum*.[80] Gerhard's terminology is important here because by the tenth century the word *viaticum* had taken on two very specific meanings in the liturgy celebrated in the eastern portions of the old Carolingian empire. It could either signify a health-bringing rite designed for those who were ill, or it could be used to describe the consecrated bread and wine that was taken when an individual was about to die and after he had made

---

[76] *Ibid.*, p. 194, *episcopus super cavallum suum sedens stola indutus, non clipeo, non lorica, aut galea munitus, iaculis et lapidibus undique circa eum discurrentibus intactus et inlesus subsistebat.*

[77] *Ibid.*

[78] *Ibid.*, p. 196, *religiosas mulieres in civitate congregatas concitabat, ut una pars earum cum crucibus ad dominum devote clamando circumirent, et altera pars clementiam sanctae dei genetricis mariae pro defensione populi et pro liberatione civitatis sutdiosissime pavimento prostrata flagitaret.*

[79] *Ibid.*, *ille autem totum spatium noctis in oratione pernoctens.*

[80] *Ibid.* p. 196, *Ministerio sacro peracto, viatico sacro omnes recreavit. . . .*

his last confession.[81] In either case, the potential value of receiving communion for the morale of soldiers going into battle is clear. Indeed, Gerhard himself commented that following the reception of communion the men were prepared both "*interius*" and "*exterius*" for battle.[82]

While the defenders of Augsburg were fending off the Hungarian assault, King Otto I of Germany was preparing his troops for a final battle against the invaders in the fields along the banks of the nearby Lech river. According to Widukind of Corvey (died c. 973), Otto ordered all of his soldiers to fast on the evening of 9 August 955 in order to prepare themselves for battle.[83] Ruotger, the biographer of Otto's younger brother Archbishop Brun of Cologne, also noted that Otto ordered a fast to be held before the battle, stressing that this was the vigil of the feast of Saint Lawrence whom the German king begged to intervene with the Lord on behalf of himself and his army.[84] Bishop Thietmar of Merseburg (1009–1018) emphasized that on 10 August, the feast of Saint Lawrence, Otto prostrated himself on the ground, confessed his sins directly to God, and then received the host from his chaplain. Otto then swore that if he had victory that day, he would establish a bishopric in Merseburg whose special patron was Saint Lawrence.[85]

We can see a further example of the important role that battlefield rites played in preparing men for combat in the context of King Henry IV of Germany's struggle against a force of rebellious Saxons on the Elster river in

---

[81] See Frederick S. Paxton, *Christianizing Death: The Creation of a Ritual Process in Early Medieval Europe* (Ithaca, 1990), pp. 192–5. Gerhard's use of the term *viaticum* would also seem to reflect Benedict the Levite's usage of this word (*Capitularia Spuria*, p. 110, n. 41) to describe the reception of the eucharist by wounded or very ill soldiers in his text dealing with the pastoral care of Carolingian troops.

[82] Gerhard, *Vita S. Oudalrici Episcopi Augustani*, p. 196.

[83] Widukind of Corvey, *Rerum Gestarum Saxonicum*, ed. P. Hirsch, MGH SRG 60 (Hanover, 1935). p. 124, *Ieiunio in castris predicato, iussum est omnes in crastino paratos esse ad bellum*. Concerning Widukind's high status within the Ottonian *familia* and the historical value of his observations, see Gerd Althoff, "Widukind von Corvey, Kronzeuge und Herausforderung," *Frühmittelalterliche Studien* 27 (1993), pp. 253–72; and Hagen Keller, "Widukind's Bericht über die Aachener Wahl und Krönung Ottos I.," *Frühmittelalterliche Studien* 29 (1995), pp. 390–453, esp. pp. 403–10. With respect to Widukind's efforts to lionize the Saxon people, see Ernst Karpf, "Von Widukind's *Sachsengeschichte* bis zu Thietmars *Chronicon*: Zu den literarischen Folgen des politischen Aufschwungs im ottonischen Sachsen," *Angli e sassoni al di quà e al di là del mare: Settimane di Studio del Centro Italiano di Studi sull'Alto Medioevo*, 2 vols. (Spoleto, 1986), pp. 547–80, here pp. 549–53.

[84] Ruotger, *Vita Brunonis archiepiscopi Coloniensis*, ed. Irene Ott, MGH SRG n.s. 10 (Weimar, 1951), c. 35, p. 36, *Imperator indici sanxit ieiunium ipsa, que tunc erat, in vigilia sancti Laurentii martyris, per cuius interventum sibi populoque suo ipsum Deum poposcit esse refugium*. The importance of the feast of Saint Lawrence in the tenth-century German church is discussed by L. Weinrich, "Laurentius-Verehrung in ottonischer Zeit," *Jahrbuch für die Geschichte Mittel-und Ostdeutschlands* 21 (1972), pp. 45–66.

[85] Thietmar of Merseburg, *Chronicon*, 2.10, p. 44, *Postea die, id est in festivitate Christi martyris Laurentii, rex solum se pre caeteris culpabilem Deo professus atque prostratus, hoc fecit lacrimis votum profusis: si Christus dignaretur sibi eo die tanti intercessione preconis dare victoriam et vitam, ut in Merseburgiensi episcopatum in honore victoris ignium construere domumque suimet magnam noviter inceptam sibi ad aecclesiam vellet edificare.*

1080. In his account of this battle, Bruno, the author of the *Saxon War* and a firm partisan of the rebels, described in some detail the efforts of the clerics on both sides to invoke divine aid.[86] Before the fighting began, priests serving in Henry IV's army sang the *Te Deum laudamus*, almost certainly in an effort to enlist the support of God for their cause and to lift the spirits of the royal soldiers who were fighting at the fords to forestall a Saxon crossing.[87] But, at the same time as Henry's bishops were praying on his behalf, prelates supporting the Saxon rebels ordered all of the priests serving with them to sing Psalm 82 with great devotion.[88] The text of this psalm was particularly appropriate for the battlefield in that it calls on God to destroy the enemies of His people. Indeed, from the Saxon perspective, King Henry and his supporters were manifestly the enemies of God and the church after having been excommunicated a second time by Pope Gregory VII. It was therefore with evident satisfaction that Bruno emphasized that the intercessory efforts of the royalist prelates had gone for naught. Henry IV's bishops were forced to flee their camp and abandon their heavily laden baggage train. Saxon soldiers captured their costly tents as well as all of the sacred vestments and vessels that they had brought on campaign to celebrate mass and perform the other religious rituals in support of the king's army.[89]

The service of priests and bishops on both sides of the battle of the Elster river was thoroughly consistent with contemporary theological views about the military-pastoral obligations of the clergy. Burchard, bishop of Worms (1000–1025) and a close advisor to King Otto III and King Henry II of

---

[86] Bruno, *Saxonicum Bellum* in *Quellen zur Geschichte Kaiser Heinrichs IV.*, ed. Franz Josef Schmale (Berlin, 1963), pp. 388–90. Concerning the historical value of Bruno's text, see Gerd Althoff and Stephanie Coué, "Pragmatische Geschichtsschreibung und Krisen. I. Zur Funktion von Brunos Buch vom Sachsenkrieg. II. Der Mord an Karl dem Guten (1127) und die Werke Galberts von Brügge und Walters von Thérouanne," in *Pragmatische Schriftlichkeit im Mittelalter: Erscheinungsformen und Entwicklungsstufen*, ed. Hagen Keller, Klaus Grubmüller, and Nikolaus Staubach (Munich, 1992), pp. 95–129.

[87] Bruno, *Saxonicum Bellum*, p. 390. In other cases, it is reported that soldiers themselves broke into prayer in praise of God. Thietmar of Merseburg recorded that when King Otto III came to the relief of the German garrison at Brandenburg in October 995 and drove off an army of Liutizi, the defenders sang out the *Kyrie eleison*, a prayer which was then answered in kind by Otto's troops. Thietmar, *Chronicon*, 4.22, p. 138, *nostri autem in ereptione interius gaudentes kirieleison canunt, et advenientes unanimiter respondent*. In another case, Thietmar reports that the *Kyrie eleison* was used by King Henry II of Germany's troops as a watchword as they prepared for an attack on the camp of a rebel margrave named Henry. In *ibid.*, 5.34, p. 230, *alte voce per kirieleison sotios convocantes*.

[88] Bruno, *Saxonicum Bellum*, p. 388, *episcopi vero clericos omnes, qui aderant ut psalmum LXXXII multa devotione cantarent ammonebant*.

[89] *Ibid.*, p. 388, *multa episcoporum scrinia sacris indumentis et vasis plena*. Also see Karl Leyser, "Early Medieval Warfare," in *Communications and Power in Medieval Europe: The Carolingian and Ottonian Centuries*, ed. Timothy Reuter (London, 1994), pp. 29–50, here p. 34, who discusses the cultural advantages which Henry IV's bishops garnered by bringing treasures on a military campaign. Ludwig Arnst, "Der Feldalter in Vergangenheit und Gegenwart," *Zeitschrift für christliche Kunst* 28 (1915), pp. 89–105, here pp. 95–6, notes that the portable altars frequently used in field chapels were often decorated with the images of soldier-saints including George, Maurice, and Martin.

Germany, wrote an episcopal handbook (c. 1006–12) in which he dealt with the duties and obligations of the contemporary German episcopate. In his role both as a royal advisor and as an imperial bishop, Burchard was thoroughly familiar with the religious needs of soldiers on campaign and with the duties that could be expected of contemporary clerics.[90] It is therefore significant that Burchard chose to include in his collection documents assembled by Benedict the Levite, noted above, which specifically dealt with the question of military religious care. These texts emphasized that two or three bishops along with their attendant priests could serve with the army in order to carry out a wide variety of religious duties. These included offering blessings to the troops, preaching, reconciling the men with God, hearing confessions, assigning penances, celebrating mass, and giving last rites to the troops. The eucharist is described here as the *viaticum*, which, as we saw above in Gerhard's discussion of the siege of Augsburg, was meant for soldiers who were *in extremis*.[91]

A similar text written in France a few decades later illustrates that western bishops had the same expectations as their eastern brethren concerning the duties of clerics on military campaign.[92] In this text, bishops and priests are assigned the duty of going on campaign to celebrate mass and carry sacred relics. They were also given the task of hearing confessions and assigning penances.[93] The author of this document was fully aware of the Carolingian origin of the service of priests and bishops in military campaigns. He cites as his authority a capitulary, which he thought had been issued by Charlemagne.[94] In

---

[90] Burchard of Worms, *Decretum Libri XX*, 1.119, PL 140: 612–13. For the sources of Burchard's *Decretum*, see *Das Dekret des Bischofs Burchard von Worms: Textstufen, frühe Verbreitung, Vorlagen*, ed. Hartmut Hoffmann and Rudolf Pokorny (Munich, 1991), pp. 165–276. Burchard's purpose in writing the *Decretum* is discussed by Paul Fournier, "Études critiques sur le décret de Burchard de Worms," *Nouvelle revue historique de droit français et étranger* 34 (1910), pp. 41–112, 213–21, 289–331, and 564–84 [repr. *Mélanges de droit canonique I* (Darmstadt, 1983)]. There are over eighty surviving manuscripts of Burchard's *Decretum*. Concerning the manuscript tradition, see Otto Meyer, "Überlieferung und Verbreitung des Dekrets des Bischofs Burchard von Worms," *ZRG kan.* 24 (1935), pp. 141–83; and Hubert Mordek, "Handschriftenforschungen in Italien: Zur Überlieferung des Dekrets Bischof Burchards von Worms," *Quellen und Forschungen aus italienischen Archiven und Bibliotechen* 51 (1971), pp. 626–51.

[91] Burchard, *Decretum*, PL 140: 612–13, *volumus ut nullus sacerdos in hostem pergat, nisi duo vel tres tantum episcopi, electione caeterorum propter benedictionem, praedicationem populique reconciliationem, et cum illis electi sacerdotes, qui bene sciant populis poenitentiam dare, missas celebrare, de infirmis curam habere, sacratique olei cum sacris precibus unctionem impendere, et hoc maxime praevidere ne sine viatico quis de saeculo recedat.*

[92] This text was once attributed to Bishop Fulbert of Chartres (1006–1028) but has now been ascribed to an anonymous younger contemporary who is thought to have been attempting to promote church reforms in the mid-eleventh century. Concerning textual problems with this document and the purposes of its author, see *The Letters and Poems of Fulbert of Chartres*, ed. Frederick Behrends (Oxford, 1976), p. lxi.

[93] PL 141: 258–9, *nisi illis tantummodo qui propter divinum ministerium missarum scilicet solemnia adimplenda et SS. patrocinia portanda ad hoc electi sunt, id est unus vel duo episcopi cum capellanis presbyteris; et unusquisque princeps unum presbyterum secum habeat, qui peccata confitentibus indicare et indicere poenitentiam possit.*

[94] PL 141: 258, *proinde sciant sibi omnino inhibitum ad bella procedere, nisi quibusdam ex*

fact, however, the text, as quoted by the author, almost certainly came from the group of documents collected by the ninth-century Carolingian compiler Benedict the Levite who identified the original decision by the *Concilium Germanicum*, discussed in the previous chapter, to recruit priests for campaign duty as one of Charlemagne's capitularies.[95]

Of course, intercessory prayers by clerics as well as by lay soldiers were an ordinary part of warfare elsewhere in the West. In describing an early eleventh-century battle against Muslims in Sardinia involving contingents from Pisa and Genoa, Rodulfus Glaber emphasized that the Christian soldiers prepared themselves by praying to the saints.[96] The chronicler contrasted the behavior of the Muslims who trusted in their own ferocity and the size of their army, with that of the Christians who invoked God's aid by asking Saint Mary, Saint Peter, and all of the rest of the saints to intercede on their behalf. These prayers appear to have had a significant impact on the Christians' morale by giving them confidence in their own victory despite the fact that they were heavily outnumbered.[97] Indeed, the Christian soldiers were emboldened even further by the fact that they had vowed to dedicate all of the booty they won in battle to Saint Peter, and to give all of the spoils to his church at Cluny if God were to give them victory.[98] In this manner, the Christian soldiers reinforced the just nature of their conflict against a non-Christian foe by establishing a permanent memorial to the divine assistance they received on the field of battle.[99]

Perhaps the most detailed surviving descriptions of battlefield rites during this entire period deal with the preparations made by the Norman army before the battle of Hastings in 1066. According to William of Poitiers, who served as the Conqueror's chaplain in the years after the battle, as the Norman army and fleet waited at St Valery for a favorable wind to take them to England, Duke

---

causis quae in subsequenti Caroli regis edicto patebunt. Concerning the wide circulation of Benedict the Levite's collection of capitularies, see Hubert Mordek, *Bibliotheca Capitularum regum Franconum manuscripta: Überlieferung und Traditionszusammenhang der fränkischen Herrschererlasse* (Munich, 1995), pp. 1032–5.

[95] Schmitz, "Waffe der Fälschung," pp. 82–6.

[96] Rodulfus Glaber, *Historiarum*, 4.22, p. 206.

[97] *Ibid., Illi presumentes confidebant in rabida feritate immense sue multitudinis, victores sese fore existimabant, nostri vero, licet admodum pauci numero, Dei omnipotentis auxilium invocantes, per interventum genitricis ipsius Marie sanctique apostolorum principis Petri omniumque sanctorum sperabant de illis fiducialiter obtinere triumphum.*

[98] *Ibid., percipue quoque in voto quod in ipsius procinctu belli voventes sese obstrinxerunt, ut, si videlicet manus Domini valdia gentem illam perfidissimam in manus illorum concluderet, potito de illis triumpho, quicquid auri, argentique seu cetere suppllectilis ex eisdem capere contigisset, totum omnino ad locum Cluniaci apostolorum principi Petro destinarent.* We saw above that before Count Robert of Flanders went into battle against the followers of Countess Richilde, he and his men commended themselves to Saint Peter. Moreover, the count founded a church in the apostle's honor because, as the chronicler emphasized, it was through Saint Peter's intercession and merit that God gave his grace to Robert's men in battle. Lambert, *Historia*, p. 575.

[99] Cf. Thietmar of Merseburg, *Chronicon*, 7.45, p. 402, where the prayers of soldiers serving Pope Benedict VIII in 1016 against Saracen raiders in Lombardy are reported to have resulted in divine aid for the Christian army.

William never lost faith in God's support for his cause.[100] According to his chaplain, neither the contrary winds, nor the shipwreck of a part of his fleet as it passed from Dives-sur-Mer to St Valery, nor the desertion of some troops held any terrors for William because he had committed himself to heaven to the utmost of his abilities through prayers, vows, and gifts.[101]

In order to obtain favorable winds for the channel crossing, Duke William organized an impressive set of religious rites involving the entire army in order to beg for divine intervention and to embolden his remaining troops, who were described by the chronicler as frightened (*paventes*).[102] The invasion force first participated in a massive prayer service. Then, the duke had the relics of Saint Valery of Luxeuil taken from their resting place in the basilica and carried out in a solemn procession.[103] When favorable winds arose soon after, they were understood by the troops to be a sign from heaven, with the result that the men gave their thanks to God and raised a huge shout to encourage each other for the approaching battle.[104]

In his report of the battle of Hastings itself, William of Poitiers emphasized that Bishops Odo of Bayeux and Geoffrey of Coutances along with a multitude of other priests and many monks prepared to aid the Norman army by fighting with their prayers.[105] Orderic Vitalis similarly stressed the presence of numerous clerics and religious, including monks, who were serving with Duke William's forces. He concluded that William had brought these bishops, priests, and monks to England in order that they might fight with their prayers (*pugnare precibus*).[106] Wace emphasized that while Duke William's troops slept, the priests remained in vigil all night long praying, chanting litanies, and singing

---

100　William of Poitiers, *Gesta Guillelmi*, p. 108.

101　*Ibid., Ibid quoque precibus, donis, votis, caelesti suffragio se commisit optime confidens princeps, quem neque mora sive contrarietas venti, neque terribilia naufragia, neque pavida fuga multorum, qui fidem sponponderant, frangere praevalent.*

102　*Ibid.*, p. 110.

103　*Ibid., Sacris supplicationibus adeo decertavit, ut corpus etiam acceptissimi Deo confessoris Gualerici contra praepedientem et pro secundo vento, extra basilicam defferet, concurrente in eadem humilitatis arma concione profecturorum cum ipso.*

104　*Ibid., Spirante dein aura expectata, voces cum manibus in caelum gratificantes, ac simul tumultus invicem incitans tollitur.*

105　*Ibid.*, p. 124, *Aderant comitati e Normannia duo pontifices, Odo Baoicensis et Goisfredus Constantinus, una multus clerus et monachi nonnulli. Id collegium precibus pugnare disponitur.*

106　Orderic Vitalis, *Ecclesiastical History*, II: 172, *religiosi quoque viri pugnaturis e Normannia comitati fuerant. Nam duo pontifices Odo Baiocensis et Goisfridus Constantius aderant cum monachis et clericis multis quorum officium erat pugnare precibus.* Orderic Vitalis is generally considered by scholars to have been the best informed and most careful of the Anglo-Norman historians writing in the first half of the twelfth century. See Marjorie Chibnall, *The World of Orderic Vitalis* (Oxford, 1984); and Antonia Gransden, *Historical Writing in England c. 550 to c. 1307*, 2 vols. (Ithaca, 1974), I: 151–65. Orderic Vitalis' reliance on and trust of William of Poitiers' text is discussed by Ray, "Orderic Vitalis and William of Poitiers," pp. 1116–27; and Pierre Bouët, "Orderic Vital lecteur critique de Guillaume de Potiers," in *Mediaevalia christiana, XIe–XIIIe siècles: homage à Raymonde Foreville de ses amis, ses collègues et ses anciens élèves*, ed. Coloman Etienne Viola (Paris, 1989), pp. 25–50.

psalms and kyries.[107] Then, according to Wace, during the battle itself these same priests were called upon to continue to pray for victory. In Wace's description of the events, much of the liturgical effort carried out by the priests serving in William's army was performed in portable chapels, which the Norman Duke had shipped over from the continent.[108]

The content of the actual prayers said by the priests serving with Duke William's army at Hastings is suggested by a prayer composed by Bishop Fulbert of Chartres entitled "A prayer of one who is on the attack."[109] It begins by emphasizing God's awesome and awe-inspiring power compared with which human existence is only a momentary event.[110] After establishing this severe dichotomy between man and God, the second verse begs the Lord to stand with his soldiers and to motivate them to fight.[111] The content of this prayer, its brief length (only fifty-two words), and the use of *nos* to designate those benefiting from the Lord's aid all suggest that Fulbert intended it to be used by soldiers as they went into battle, as well as by the priests who served with them.

Intercessory prayers and masses helped to assure soldiers that divine aid would be forthcoming. However, military commanders and religious leaders also found it useful to address their troops in order to reinforce this confidence in the availability of heavenly *auxilium*. These orations served the further purpose of reminding soldiers about the need to have faith in God and to behave properly in order to be worthy of God's aid both as individual Christians and as an army. As a corollary to this emphasis on the opportunity to gain heavenly support for their side, speakers also frequently affirmed the evil nature of the enemy forces.

We can see an example of just such an oration by Charles the Simple as he prepared his men for the battle of Soissons in June 923.[112] The king began his address by urging his troops to beg God for aid. He then assured the soldiers that they had nothing to fear in battle and no reason to doubt that they would be victorious.[113] Charles described the enemy commander, Robert of Paris, as an invader (*pervasor*) in the kingdom and claimed that such a person was abhorred by God, who would give no support to the arrogant. The Carolingian claimant to the West Frankish throne then asked rhetorically how such a person could hope

---

[107] Wace, *Le Roman de Rou*, 2 vols., ed. A.J. Holden (Paris, 1971), II: 157, *lor privees oreisons, salmes dient e misereles, letanies e kirieles*. Wace wrote in the late twelfth century but would appear to have had access to a wide variety of oral traditions concerning the battle of Hastings that were passed down among the descendents of the combatants. Concerning his value as a source for the eleventh century and the battle, see Elisabeth van Houts, "The Memory of 1066 in Written and Oral Traditions," *Anglo-Norman Studies* 19 (1996), pp. 167–80; and Matthew Bennett, "The *Roman de Rou* of Wace as a Source for the Norman Conquest," *Anglo-Norman Studies* 5 (1982), pp. 21–39.

[108] *Le Roman de Rou*, II: 158, *li proveires par lor chapeles qui esteient par l'ost noveles*.

[109] Behrends, *Letters and Poems of Fulbert of Chartres*, p. 246.

[110] *Ibid., Tu qui de nichilo mundum finxisse probaris, nam tibi materies nulla coeva fuit.*

[111] *Ibid., regem militibus propriis te semper adesse ad bene certandum nos vegetando proba.*

[112] Richer, *Historiarum*. II: 88.

[113] *Ibid., Hortatur vero plurimum ut Dei tantum auxilium implorent; nihil eis metuendum, nihil de victoria diffidendum memorans.*

to succeed without divine protection, or how he could prevail when he has already been rejected by God.[114]

By contrast, Bishop Ulrich of Augsburg had no need to belabor the evil nature of his opponents as he addressed the defenders of his city on the second day of the Hungarian siege, and concentrated instead on the divine support available to God's *fideles*.[115] According to his biographer, the basic premise of Ulrich's sermon was that the soldiers should maintain their faith and place their trust in God. The bishop quoted from Psalm 23, saying that "though I walk in the valley of the shadow of death I will fear no evil because you are with me."[116] This psalm would appear to be of particular value for soldiers going into battle because it claimed for them the support of God who, the psalmist wrote, would lead them over the roads of justice for the sake of His name and protect them with His staff and rod.[117] By focusing on this text, Bishop Ulrich let the soldiers know that respect for Christ would secure them protection in battle. In addition, the psalm offered God's mercy for all the days of one's life and eternal rest in the home of the Lord.[118] This theme would seem to have particular importance for men who faced the imminent possibility of death in combat. Indeed, in Gerhard's view, the bishop's sermon along with the reception of the eucharist by the soldiers were successful in convincing them to stand and fight, as is clear from his observation, noted above, that the troops were prepared to go into battle both *interius* and *exterius*.

King Otto I of Germany, whose victory at the Lechfeld served to break the Hungarian siege of Augsburg, also sought to provide his men assurances of both their temporal and divine superiority over their enemies.[119] The king began his address by calling out to the German soldiers that their task was now upon them and that they should take it up in good spirit, that is, with high morale. He reminded them that they had a glorious tradition of victory and scoffed at the notion of retreating from his own lands.[120] Otto then conceded that the Hungarians were more numerous than the imperial forces but emphasized that they were inferior both in armament and in spiritual strength (*virtus*). As a consequence, they lacked not only physical protection, but even more importantly, they lacked that which was the greatest consolation to the Germans – the aid of God (*auxilium Dei*). Indeed, Otto affirmed, the enemy placed their hope in their

---

114 *Ibid., Cum inquiens, Deus hujusmodi abomnetur et apud eum nullus superbiae locus sit, quomodo stabit quem ipse non munit? Quomodo resurget, quem ipse praecipitat?*

115 Gerhard, *Vita S. Oudalrici*, p. 196.

116 *Ibid., si ambulavero in medio umbrae mortis, non timebo mala, quoniam tu mecum es.*

117 Ps. 23.4. In the vulgate this is Ps. 22.4. *Biblia Sacra iuxta Vulgatam Versionem*, ed. Boniface Fischer (Stuttgart, 1994), p. 794, *deduxit me super semitas iustitiae propter nomen suum . . . virga tua et baculus tuus ipsa me consolata sunt.*

118 *Ibid., et misericordia tua subsequitur me omnibus diebus vitae meae et ut inhabitem in domo Domini in longitudinem dierum.*

119 Widukind, *Rerum gestarum Saxonicum*, p. 127.

120 *Ibid., Opus esse nobis bonorum animorum in hac tanta necessitate, milites mei, vos ipsi videtis, qui hostem non longe, sed coram positum toleratis. Hactenus enim impigris manibus vestris ac armis semper invictis gloriose usus extra solum et imperium meum ubique vici, et nunc in terra mea et regno terta vertam?*

own ferocity, while his troops had faith in divine protection (*protectio divina*).[121] Then, in order to give his men a physical symbol of this divine aid, Otto brandished the Holy Lance and ordered the advance.[122]

Widukind described a similar oration in his account of the battlefield preparations made by Otto's father King Henry I of Germany (919–936) before his victory over the Hungarians at the battle of Riade (15 March 933).[123] King Henry called on his troops to place their hope in divine mercy, and not to doubt that they would receive divine aid in this battle just as they had in others.[124] Henry stressed that the Hungarians were the common enemy of everybody and that the soldiers should bend all of their efforts to protecting their fatherland and their families. He then assured his troops that if they fought bravely, they would have victory.[125] Indeed, from the perspective of the Christian soldiers, defending their homes against a pagan enemy was necessarily a just cause deserving of divine aid and victory.

Several very detailed *reportationes* of battlefield orations have also survived from the period of Christian reconquest in the central Mediterranean in the decades before the First Crusade. One particularly valuable account was composed c. 1080 by Amatus of Montecassino at the request of his abbot Desiderius and of Robert Guiscard, noted above for his donation to the cathedral of Bari in return for divine aid in battle.[126] According to Amatus, Robert

---

[121] *Ibid., Superamur, scio, multitudine, sed non virtute, sed non armis. Maxima enim ex parte nudos illos armis omnibus penitus cognovimus et, quod maximi est nobis solatii auxilio Dei. Illis est sola pro muro audatia, nobis spes et protectio divina.*

[122] *Ibid.*, pp. 127–8, *Et his dictis, arrepto clipeo ac sacra lancea, ipse primus equum in hostes vertit.*

[123] *Ibid.*, p. 57.

[124] *Ibid., Rex vero postera die producens exercitum exhortatus est, ut spem suam divinae clementiae committerent divinum sibi auxilium quemadmodum in aliis preliis adesse non dubitarent. . . .*

[125] *Ibid., communes omnium hostes esse Ungarios; ad vindictam patriae parentumque solummodo cogitarent: hostes cito terga vertere vidissent, si viriliter certando persisterent.*

[126] The standard edition of Amatus' work is *Storia de Normanni*, ed. Vincenzo de Bartholomaeis (Rome, 1935). The most recent study of Amatus' text is Kenneth Baxter Wolf, *Making History: The Normans and their Historians in Eleventh-Century Italy* (Philadelphia, 1995). The original Latin text has been lost and Amatus' history is only available in a thirteenth-century French translation. However, there are only minor variations in the French text from the Latin original, as is clear from fragments of the Latin text utilized by contemporary authors. On this point, see Einar Joranson, "The Inception and the Career of the Normans in Italy – Legend and History," *Speculum* 23 (1948), pp. 353–96, here pp. 356–60. Concerning the date of Amatus' work, see William of Apulia, *La geste de Robert Guiscard par Guillaume de Pouille*, ed. Marguerite Mathieu (Palermo, 1961), pp. 17–24; and *Storia de Normanni*, pp. lxvii–lxxiv. John France, "The Occasion of the Coming of the Normans to Southern Italy," *Journal of Medieval History* 17 (1991), pp. 185–205, here pp. 193–4, argues that Amatus' history is exceptionally important for understanding the Norman conquest of southern Italy. Joranson, "Normans in Sicily," p. 364, takes a rather more negative view of Amatus' reliability, arguing that he naively accepted information provided to him about the Normans' entrance into Southern Italy. However, even if this judgment of Amatus' work is correct, it is nevertheless the case that he can be understood as a reliable informant of contemporary expectations for battlefield addresses, particularly given his close association with Robert Guiscard.

Guiscard addressed his troops before the battle of Enna (1061) in Sicily with the apparent intention of reminding them both of the value of God's grace to fighting men and of their own duties as Christian soldiers.

The Norman commander began his oration by insisting that it was not the size of the forces involved that mattered but rather God's favor.[127] Robert urged his men to put aside their fears because God could and would save them. Citing Matthew 17:19, "if you have faith as a grain of mustard seed, you shall say to this mountain, remove from here, and it shall move," Robert is reported to have insisted that Jesus stood with the army because the Christian troops were carrying out a holy task in purifying Sicily of its accumulated dungheap of heresy and perversion (*l'ordure de heresie et perversité*).[128] This particular verse was appropriate in the current circumstance, both for its call for the soldiers to have faith in God and for the reminder that even mountains can be moved by faith. The latter point was certainly significant given the task facing the Christian troops of driving the Muslims from their mountain redoubts. The Norman leader then concluded by insisting that the holiness of the Normans' task was not enough by itself to earn God's grace and support. The soldiers also had to be worthy as individuals of receiving divine aid. To this end, Robert ordered his men to cleanse themselves through the rites of confession and penance, and then to receive both the body and blood of Christ so that they would be worthy of a divine victory.[129]

When considered from the point of view of Robert's soldiers, the commander's battlefield address would seem to have important implications both for their morale and their *esprit de corps*. According to Amatus, Robert drew an explicit connection between confession, penance, and the reception of Christ's body and blood on the one hand and obtaining God's favor on the other. It is in this context that the soldiers are reported to have been told that if they carried out the proper religious rites they would have the favor of God, who, Robert emphasized, had the power to give them victory in battle over their numerically superior but non-Christian foe. This understanding of God's power could only have raised the spirits of the soldiers. In addition, Robert's emphasis upon the common bond of his soldiers as Christians, who had an obligation to fight against heresy and perversity (*heresie et perversité*) would appear to have been intended to increase their sense of group cohesion.[130] Indeed, Robert even

---

[127] *Storia de Normanni*, p. 241, *L'esperance nostre est fermée plus en Dieu que en grant multitude de combateors.*

[128] *Ibid., La fermeté de la Foi nostre a la calor de lo saint Esperit, quar, en lo nom de la sainte Trinité, chacerons ceste montainge, non de pierres né de terre, mès d l'ordure de heresie et perversité accolta.*

[129] *Ibid., Purgame adonc nos pechiés par confession et par penitence, et recevons lo cors et lo sanc de Crist, et rappareillons les armes nostres. Quar Dieu es potent à nouz, petite gent et fidel, de donner victoire de la multitude de li non fidel.*

[130] As was noted in the previous chapter with respect to the content of military sermons, it is likely that these messages appealed to Robert Guiscard's men, or at least that he thought they would. Murray, "Religion Among the Poor," pp. 286–8, emphasizes that speakers had an interest in being believed, and those speakers familiar with their audiences were in a position to know which message worked and which did not.

provided his men with a common watchword, namely the faith of the mustard seed.

Robert Guiscard's oration at Enna shared many elements in common with a battlefield sermon delivered by Bishop Benedict of Modena during the 1087 campaign against Mahdia conducted by contingents from Pisa, Genoa, Rome, and Amalfi.[131] According to the narrator, Bishop Benedict addressed the Christian army just before the soldiers went into battle against the Muslim forces defending the town of Mahdia on the North African coast in what is today Tunisia. Benedict began his sermon by calling the troops "bravest soldiers" and ordering them to prepare to fight and to forget all of the things of this world for Christ.[132] Following this introduction, the bishop preached a sermon that divided neatly into two distinct sections and explained in turn why the Christians would win, and offered examples of others who had won victories in the past through God's grace.

Benedict began the first section of the sermon by reminding the Italian troops that they had nowhere to go and that the only way home was first to defeat the enemy before them.[133] But, according to the text, he assured the Christian soldiers that they had nothing to fear from the enemy because the latter had already suffered heavy losses. The bishop then alluded to the Israelite invasion of Canaan when adding that the troops should not fear the tall buildings in Mahdia because even Jericho with its high walls had fallen down. In the end of this section of his sermon, Benedict gave additional encouragement to the Christian soldiers by emphasizing the just nature of their campaign. The bishop stressed that their enemies were also the enemies of the Lord because they had taken Christian captives for the sake of gaining worthless glory.[134] In this manner, Benedict made clear that the Christians were fighting in a just cause against an evil foe.

The second section of Benedict's sermon concentrated on three biblical stories that were chosen in an effort to show the benefits of trusting in God and the penalties to be paid for opposing him. For his first example, the bishop called out "remember the death of Goliath the Giant whom David, as a small lad, laid low with one stone."[135] Benedict's second model was Judah Maccabee who trusted in the Lord and did not fear to attack when outnumbered by the enemy. For the bishop of Modena, the most important fact for the soldiers to recall about Judah would appear to be that he trusted in God's power rather than

---

131 The events of this campaign were recorded in the *Carmen in victoriam Pisanorum*, whose author remains anonymous, although scholars have identified him as a Pisan churchman who composed his text shortly after the Christian victory. See H.E.J. Cowdrey, "The Mahdia Campaign of 1087," *English Historical Review* 92 (1977), pp. 1–29, here pp. 2–3.

132 *Ibid.*, p. 25, *Preparate vos ad pugnam milites fortissimi, et pro Christo omnis mundi vos obliviscimini.*

133 *Ibid., maris iter restat longum non potestis fugere; terram tenent quos debetis vos hostes confundere.*

134 *Ibid., Inimici sunt factoris qui creavit omnia, et captivant Christianos pro inani gloria.*

135 *Ibid.*, p. 25, *mementote vos Golie gigantis eximii, quem prostravit unus lapis David parvi pueri.*

any strength of his own.[136] For his final example, Benedict chose to close the temporal gap between the Christian soldiers and the Bible by linking together their present situation with that faced by the ancient Israelites. He argued that because of the intervention of the Lord on their behalf, the Pisans and their fellow Italians did not suffer under the yoke of persecution that Pharaoh in his arrogance had imposed upon God's people.[137] The narrator ended his report of Benedict's sermon at this point, but not before adding that the troops were so moved by these and other inspirations that they were motivated to offer penance to God with devoted hearts and then to receive the eucharist.[138]

As was true of Robert Guiscard's oration before the battle of Enna, Benedict's sermon would appear to have been important both for the morale of the Italian soldiers and for the *esprit de corps* of the entire force. Benedict stressed to the soldiers not only that they were fighting in a just cause, but also that God would indeed support them in battle. As a consequence, the soldiers could expect not only to have victory in the temporal battle, they could also have confidence about the state of their souls if they died during the fighting. Moreover, Benedict consistently portrayed the soldiers as a Christian force motivated by a single purpose. In this manner, the bishop was able to subsume the local identities of the Pisans, Genoese, and others within the greater category of Christian with the result that the men could concentrate on what unified them rather than on the petty differences of local loyalties.

Clearly, sermons and battlefield orations served several crucial military-religious functions. In particular, they reminded soldiers of their obligations toward God so as to make the army worthy of divine aid, and reinforced the perception among the troops that such aid was forthcoming. As we have seen already, however, the words of military and religious leaders were themselves frequently reinforced by the presence of sacred and consecrated objects on the battlefield. These relics and banners served both as a continuing physical reminder of the support provided by God and the saints to soldiers, and as *loci* of heavenly power on the battlefield.

At the Lechfeld, King Otto I's brandishing of the Holy Lance gave even greater force to his claims that the German host benefited from divine power (*virtus*) and that their greatest solace was the expectation of God's aid (*auxilium Dei*).[139] Even before the epic struggle against the Hungarians, however, the Holy Lance had played a prominent role in Otto's efforts to secure the royal title. Before attacking the rebel forces led by his brother Henry at the battle of Birten in March 939, Otto and all of his men dismounted from their horses and prostrated themselves before the Holy Lance, which had been fixed in the ground. In

---

[136] *Ibid., nec confidens in virtute cuiusquam fortissimi, sed in maiestate sola Dei potentissimi.*

[137] *Ibid., Vos videtis Pharaonis fastum et superbiam, qui contempnit Deum celi regnantem in secula; Dei populum affligit et tenet in carcere; vos coniuro propter Deum iam nolite parcere.*

[138] *Ibid., Hinc incitamentis claris multis similibus, inardescunt omnes corde irritantur viribus; offerunt corde devote Deo penitentiam, et communicant vicissim Cristi eucharistiam.*

[139] Widukind of Corvey, *Rerum gestarum Saxonicum*, p. 127.

this position they then prayed to God and, according to Otto's aide and confident Bishop Liudprand of Cremona, placed their fate in the hands of Christ.[140] In fact, the Holy Lance was understood by the German king and his followers to have such power that Liudprand described this relic as an invincible weapon against both visible and invisible enemies.[141]

William the Conqueror, as was noted above, was similarly convinced of the power of relics to affect military operations and made full use of the sacred remains of Saint Valery of Luxueil in an effort to obtain favorable winds for the channel crossing. William also made use of relics at the battle of Hastings itself. In the early morning, as he prepared to lead his troops against the Anglo-Saxon army, William heard mass, received communion, and then adorned himself with a chain of relics, which he hung around his neck. According to both William of Poitiers and Orderic Vitalis, these were the same relics on which Harold Godwinson had sworn to respect Duke William's claim to the English crown.[142]

Thus, in addition to establishing his own body as a locus of divine power on the field of battle, William's decision to wear the relics into battle would appear to have been part of his well-established message that he was the legitimate king of England acting against a usurper and a perjurer.[143] Wace, for example, reported that after mass had been celebrated on the morning of the battle, William harangued his troops, emphasizing time and again that the entire campaign was designed to punish the crimes and treason of the English who had defied the law and denied him his legitimate crown.[144] By assuming the role of the legitimate successor of King Edward the Confessor, a position approved by Pope Alexander II, William could hope to even assure his most apprehensive men that they were fighting in a just war and that God was on their side.[145]

---

[140] Liudprand of Cremona, *Antapodosis*, ed. P. Chiesa, Corpus Christianorum 156 (Turnholt, 1998), 4.25, p. 111, *protinus de equo descendit seseque cum omni populo lacrimas fundens ante victoriferos clavos, manibus domini et salvatoris nostri Iesu Christi adfixos suaeque lanceae interpositos, in orationem dedit.*

[141] *Ibid.*, p. 112, *adversus visibiles atque invisibiles hostes arma invictissima.* Concerning the use of the Holy Lance as a religious totem by the Ottonian kings in battle, see Karl Leyser, "Ritual, Ceremony, and Gesture: Ottonian Germany," in *Communications and Power in Medieval Europe: The Carolingian and Ottonian Centuries*, ed. Timothy Reuter (London, 1994), pp. 189–213, here p. 206. Also see Howard L. Adelson, "The Holy Lance and the Hereditary German Monarchy," *The Art Bulletin* 48 (1966), pp. 177–91, esp. pp. 180–2.

[142] William of Poitiers, *Gesta Guillelmi*, p. 124, *Appendit etiam humili collo suo reliquias quarum favorem Heraldus abalienaverat sibi, violata fide quam super eas iurando sanxerat.* Orderic Vitalis, *Ecclesiastical History*, II: 172, *ipse missam audivit, et dominicis sacramentis corpus et animam munivit reliquiasque sanctas super quas Heraldus iuraverat collo suo humiliter appendit.*

[143] On this point, see Matthew Strickland, *War and Chivalry: The Conduct and Perception of War in England and Normandy 1066–1217* (Cambridge, 1996) p. 34.

[144] Wace, *Le Roman de Rou*, pp. 159–60.

[145] Concerning the Augustinian principle that only legitimate rulers could authorize just wars, see Russell, *Just War in the Middle Ages*, p. 18. By claiming that Harold Godwinson had sworn a false oath and had "stolen" the kingdom of England, Duke William was able to point out the wrongs that his invasion would correct and thereby satisfy the Isidorian prerequisite of righting a wrong. The basic enunciation of this position by Isidore of Seville is *Etymologies* 18:1.2, *iustum bellum est quod ex praedicto geritur de rebus repetitis aut*

Relics continued to be of considerable importance on the battlefield through the end of the eleventh century. Indeed, the great canonist Bishop Ivo of Chartres (1090–1115) considered it worthwhile to discuss the deployment of these sacred objects in battle.[146] In his *Decretum* or handbook of episcopal duties, Ivo reiterated the position taken by Burchard of Worms, noted above, that bishops and priests should serve in the field with military forces and that those clerics selected for service had to be able to perform a wide variety of functions, including the bearing of relics (*patrocinia portanda*).[147] It should be emphasized that Ivo, like Burchard, was deeply involved in the military organization of his own kingdom and not only at the local level. As a result, he was in a position not only to be well informed about the duties of priests serving with the army, but also to enforce his own views concerning the proper conduct of the priests serving under his command, which included the bearing of relics.

In particular, Ivo was one of a cadre of French bishops who reinvigorated the institution of the rural militia on behalf of King Philip I. Ivo and his fellow bishops issued legislation requiring that these troops march to aid the king while he was engaged in sieges or preparing to fight a battle.[148] In this context, it is important to note that the French bishops also insisted that each of these village militia units be accompanied on campaign by its parish priest who was to bring a *vexillum*, that is a holy banner, to war.[149]

As this requirement suggests, the sacred and evocative power of relics could be supplemented and replicated through the deployment of consecrated banners on the battlefield. William the Conqueror expended considerable effort to obtain a *vexillum* of Saint Peter from the pope for his invasion of England in 1066 because, as William of Poitiers emphasized, this banner permitted the duke's soldiers to fight more bravely and with more confidence.[150] In addition to the papal banner, however, the Norman troops also seem to have had available the militarily appropriate banner of Saint Michael on the field of battle. In a grant to the monastery of Mont Saint-Michel, Robert, count of Mortain, noted that he

---

propulsandorum hostium causa, in *Isidore Hispalensis episcopi etymologiorum sive originum,* 2 vols., ed. W.M. Lindsay (Oxford, 1990). Concerning the use of this text by Ivo of Chartres and Gratian, see Brundage, *Medieval Canon Law and the Crusader,* p. 20; and Russell, *Just War in the Middle Ages,* p. 27.

[146] Ivo of Chartres, *Decretum,* 5.332, PL 161: 424. The basic work on Ivo as a scholar is Rolf Sprandel, *Ivo von Chartres und seine Stellung in der Kirchengeschichte* (Stuttgart, 1962).

[147] Ivo of Chartres, *Decretum,* 5.332, PL 161: 424.

[148] On this point, see Orderic Vitalis, *Ecclesiastical History,* VI: 156. Some scholars have tended to see these militia forces as an outgrowth of the peace movement. See Hartmut Hoffmann, *Gottesfriede und Treuga Dei* (Stuttgart, 1964), particularly p. 209; and *The Deeds of Louis the Fat,* trans. Richard Cusimano and John Moorhead (Washington, D.C., 1992), p. 190, n. 10. Susan Reynolds, *Kingdoms and Communities in Western Europe, 900–1300* (Oxford, 1984), p. 98, treats these military units as part of the overall development of parish institutions.

[149] On this point, see Orderic Vitalis, *Ecclesiastical History,* VI: 156, *tunc ergo communitas in Francia popularis statuta est a presulibus, ut presbiteri comitarentur regi ad obsidionem vel pugnam cum vexillis et parrochianis omnibus.*

[150] William of Poitiers, *Gesta Guillelmi,* p. 104.

had a banner (*vexillum*) of Saint Michael with him at the battle of Hastings. He subsequently gave the banner as well as some property to the monastery for the sake of his soul as well as that of his wife.[151]

The use of consecrated banners on the battlefield was undergirded by liturgical rites that were not directly related to actual fighting, but were nevertheless very important for the preparation of the army. As we saw above, the Visigothic kings of Spain supported the celebration of special liturgies during which their battle flags (*vexilla*) were blessed and endowed with spiritual power (*virtus*).[152] The Carolingians appear to have had similar rites for sanctifying their battle flags.[153] Liturgies of this type can also be found in pontifical manuals from the tenth and eleventh centuries that include prayers for the consecration of war banners. For example, the late tenth-century Romano-German pontifical from Mainz includes a *benedictio vexilli bellici*. This blessing calls upon God to respond to the humble prayers of his supplicants and to sanctify with the holy blessings of heaven (*coelesti benedictione sanctifica*) a *vexillum*, which has been prepared for use in war (*quo bellico usui preparatum est*).[154] According to the prayer, this banner would then be a strong force against enemies and rebels, and a terrible [force] against the enemies of the Christian people. Moreover, it would give confidence to those trusting in God (*in te confidentibus solidamentum*) as well as a firm promise of victory (*victoriae certa fiducia*).[155] This prayer is also found in a number of other tenth- and eleventh-century pontificals, indicating the widely recognized importance of consecrated banners for the conduct of war in this period.[156]

It is, therefore, hardly surprising to see regular mention of the appearance of sacred banners on the battlefield. During the summer of 992, Saxon soldiers, mobilized in response to an invasion by a major Slavic force, received religious support in the field from clerics who accompanied the troops on campaign carrying banners.[157] In both of the major battles against the Slavs that year,

---

151 Bates, *Acta of William*, p. 668. There are three versions of this charter, and considerable dispute about their authenticity as eleventh-century documents. For a detailed discussion of the matter, see *ibid.*, pp. 664–8.

152 *Le liber ordinum en usage dans l'église wisigothique et mozarabe d'Espagne du cinquième siècle*, cols. 149–53.

153 Goldberg, "More Devoted to the Equipment of Battle," pp. 64–8.

154 *Le pontifical romano-germanique du dixième siècle*, ed. Cyrille Vogel and Reinhard Elze (Vatican, 1963), p. 378.

155 *Ibid.*, *ut contra adversarios et rebelles nationes sit validum tuoque munimeque circumseptum, sitque inimicis christiani populi terribile atque in te confidentibus solidamentum et victoriae certa fiducia.*

156 Blessings for battle flags can be found in numerous manuscripts, including Bamberg öffentliche Bibliothek, cod. Lit. 53, fol. 137v; Bamberg öffentliche Bibliothek, cod. Lit. 54, fol. 3v; Episcopal archives of Eichstätt, the pontifical of Bishop Gondekar II of Eichstätt, fol. 139v; Munich Staatsbibliothek, Cod. lat. 6425 (Cod. Frising. 225), fol. 259v; Bibliothèque nationale, Cod. lat. 1817 (Vienne, 1817), fol. 134r; and Wolfenbüttel 4099, Landesbibliothek, Cod. lat. 4099 (Weissenburg. 15), fol. 39r. See the summary of these texts in Andrieu, *Les ordines Romani du haut moyen âge: les manuscrits*, p. 57.

157 *Annalista Saxo*, ed. D.G. Waitz, MG SS 6 (Hanover, 1844), p. 638. Concerning this incident, see Leopold Auer, "Der Kriegsdienst des Klerus unter den sächsischen Kaisern: 1.

clerics were killed carrying out their duties. In the first action, a deacon named Thiethard from the church of Verden, who is described as a *signifer*, was killed. In the second battle, Halegred, a priest also described as a *signifer*, was killed while serving in a military contingent drawn from the town of Bremen.[158]

The willingness of clerics, such as these two men, to go into battle, even at the risk of their own lives, underlines the understanding by priests of the important role they played in maintaining the fighting spirit of soldiers. Indeed, it was hardly unusual for priests and bishops to risk their own lives in battle in order to support the troops under their care. Rodulfus Glaber, a western writer, expressed no surprise that several bishops and many priests marched unarmed into battle with King Henry III of Germany's army while the latter was campaigning against the Hungarians in 1044.[159] The chronicler stressed that these brave clerics participated because of their great piety.[160]

Sacred banners also played an important role in the southern reaches of the erstwhile Carolingian empire. A battle flag that appears to have been commissioned by the eleventh-century Italian Count Ragenardus displayed both images of the saints and biblical text appropriate to war.[161] The portraits on the *vexillum* are of the archangels Michael and Gabriel, Saint Larius and Saint Raso, the sun and moon, as well as an image of Count Ragenardus. The words stitched along the outside of the banner are from Psalm 143.1, "blessed is the Lord who instructs my hands in war and teaches my fingers to do battle."[162]

An important regional variation on the use of consecrated battle flags in the field can be seen in the employment of a banner wagon or *carroccio* in northern Italy. In 1039, Archbishop Aribert II of Milan took the city militia into battle against an alliance of Italian cities supporting King Conrad II of Germany. The author of the *Gesta archiepiscopum Mediolanensium* explained that in order to give a sign (*signum*) to the people, the archbishop ordered that a tall mast-like pole be fixed onto a stout wagon.[163] Aribert is then reported to have ordered that

---

Teil," in *MIÖG* 79 (1971), pp. 316–407, here p. 401. Carl Erdmann, *Idea of Crusade*, p. 44, suggests that there was a transition from profane to sacred battle flags in the East Frankish realm at the turn of the millennium. However, Goldberg's identification of sacred battle flags in Carolingian sources, "'More Devoted to the Equipment of Battle," pp. 64–8, indicates that Erdmann was incorrect on this point.

158 *Annalista Saxo*, p. 638.

159 Rodulfus Glaber, *Historiarum*, 5.24, p. 248, *Erant etiam cum rege quamplures episcopi cum clericis multis qui pietatis gratia inermes cum eo in certamen introierunt.*

160 *Ibid.*

161 A reproduction of the image of this battle flag, formerly located in the cathedral of Cologne, can be seen in Ludwig Arnst, "Mittelalterliche Feldzeichen: Eine kunstgeschichtliche Studie," *Zeitschrift für christliche Kunst* 28 (1915), pp. 164–80, here p. 175.

162 *Ibid., Benedictus Dominus meus qui docet manus meas ad prelium et digitos meos ad bellum.*

163 *Gesta archiepiscopum Mediolanensium*, ed. L.C. Bethmann and W. Wattenbach, MG SS 8 (Hanover, 1848), p. 16. The author of this text wrote about a half-century after the events he described and his account may have more importance for the history of late eleventh-century Milan than for the behavior of Archbishop Aribert II's men. Concerning Archbishop Aribert's role in the development of the *carroccio*, see H.E.J. Cowdrey, "Archbishop Aribert of Milan," *History* 51 (1966), pp. 1–15, here pp. 12–13.

a crucifix bearing an image of Christ with outstretched arms be attached high on the pole so that it would be clearly visible to everyone in the line of battle (*agmen*).[164] According to the chronicler, not only was this image intended to be an object of veneration for the Milanese troops as the *carroccio* preceded them into battle, but it was also to serve as a comforting sign to them throughout the fight.[165] Thus, in addition to its role as a source of divine strength on the battle-field, the *carroccio* was exceptionally important in maintaining the morale of the Milanese troops.[166]

Personal Religion

Under the Carolingians, confession and the acceptance of penance became essential pre-battle rites for soldiers as they prepared themselves for combat. In the post- Carolingian world, confession remained exceptionally important for soldiers as it permitted them to reconcile themselves with God and to prepare for the possibility of dying in battle with a pure soul and a clean conscience. As we have seen, the need for soldiers to have the opportunity to confess their sins before battle was recognized both at an administrative level by figures such as Burchard of Worms and Ivo of Chartres, and by commanders in the field, such as Robert Guisgard, who urged their men to confess so as to be worthy of God's grace. Indeed, confession and the acceptance of penance remained such stan-dard and expected pre-battle rites that the failure to undertake them became a mark of illegitimacy. We can see an example of this in William of Malmesbury's account of the battle of Hastings where he contrasts the preparations made by the Anglo-Saxon and Norman armies.[167] The historian stressed that on the eve of the battle, while Harold Godwinson's troops spent the night engaged in drunken revelry, William the Conqueror's men spent the entire night confessing their sins.[168] And so, in this aspect of personal battlefield religion, there would appear to have been significant continuity from the Carolingian period up to the end of the eleventh century.

By contrast, the importance of communion as a battlefield rite seems to have increased significantly over the same period. The reception of the eucharist by individual fighting men in the armies of Carolingian *Francia* would appear to have been limited to those who were either very ill or gravely wounded. Thus,

---

[164] *Gesta archiepiscopum Mediolanensium: ad medium veneranda crux depicta Salvatoris ymagine extensis late brachiis superspectabat circumfusa agmina.*

[165] *Ibid., hoc signo confortarentur inspecto.*

[166] The importance of the banner wagon as means of building the morale of civic troops has been discussed by Diana M. Webb, "The Cities of God: The Italian Communes at War," *Studies in Church History 20: The Church and War*, ed. W.J. Sheils (1983), pp. 111–27, here pp. 115–18.

[167] William of Malmesbury, *Gesta regum Anglorum*, 2 vols., ed. R.A.B. Mynors, R.M. Thomson, and M. Winterbottom (Oxford, 1998), I: 454.

[168] *Ibid., contra Normanni nocte tota confessione peccatorum vacantes.* William had a strong *parti pris* in favor of the Norman cause, and his description of the Anglo-Saxon forces must be read in this light.

for example, the text included in Benedict the Levite's collection includes an admonition for priests serving with the army that fighting men not be allowed to die without first having received the *viaticum*, that is, the eucharist associated with last rites for the severely wounded.[169] As we saw above, this text was subsequently adopted by Burchard of Worms and Ivo of Chartres, indicating the continuing importance of the eucharist to the very sick and gravely wounded in the eleventh century.[170] However, it would appear that over the course of the tenth century the reception of the eucharist also became an important element of the religious preparations of individual soldiers before they went into battle.

From his perspective as an eyewitness to the Hungarian assault on his city in 955, Gerhard of Augsburg was convinced that the reception of the eucharist helped to prepare the German defenders both *interius* and *exterius* for battle.[171] According to Widukind of Corvey, when Saxon troops besieging the town of Lenzen in 929 were informed that a Slavic relief army was on its way, they made sure to receive the host in order to prepare for battle.[172] Widukind used the same language to describe the preparations made by the German forces just before the battle of the Lechfeld against the Hungarians. As was noted above, on the eve of the feast of Saint Lawrence, King Otto I ordered all of his troops to fast in order to prepare themselves for combat.[173] Of course, fasting was also a prerequisite for receiving the host. The next morning, at first light, the soldiers gave each other the sign of peace, promised to carry out their duties, and received the eucharist (*sacramentum*) before heading into battle under their banners.[174] In his account of the same battle, Thietmar of Merseburg chose to focus on the actions of Otto I himself. The chronicler emphasized that Otto confessed his sins and then received the eucharist from his personal chaplain before leading his men into battle.[175]

Writing about a battle that took place against a Slavic invasion force in 982, Thietmar offers further evidence that soldiers understood the reception of communion to be beneficial in preparing themselves for combat. According to Thietmar, whose father took part in this battle, the German commander ordered his troops to undergo a complete regimen of religious preparation before going into combat. First, because it was the sabbath, mass was celebrated in view of

---

169 *Capitularia Spuria*, p. 110, nr. 141.

170 Burchard, *Decretum*, PL 140: 612–13; and Ivo, *Decretum*, PL 161: 424.

171 Gerhard, *Vita S. Oudalrici*, p. 196.

172 Widukind, *Rerum gestarum Saxonicum*, pp. 52–3, . . . *et primo diluculo dato signo sacramento accepto, primum ducibus, deinde unusquisque alteri operam suam sub iuramento promittebat ad presens bellum.*

173 *Ibid.*, p. 124, *Ieiunio in castris predicato, iussum est omnes in crastino paratos esse ad bellum.* Cf. Ruotger, *Vita Brunonis*, c. 35, p. 36.

174 Widukind, *Rerum gestarum Saxonicum*, p. 124, *Primo diluculo surgentes, pace data et accepta operaque sua primum duci, deinde unusquisque alteri cum sacramento promissa erectis signis procedunt castris.* . . . In his earlier description of the siege of Lenzen in 929 (*ibid.*, p. 52), Widukind clearly distinguished between an oath (*iuramentum*) under which promises were made and the eucharist (*sacramentum*) that was accepted by each of the soldiers.

175 Thietmar, *Chronicon*, 2.10, p. 44, *post missae celebrationem sacramque communionem ab egregio porrectam Othelrico confessore suo.*

the entire Saxon force, very likely by Archbishop Gisilher of Magdeburg (981–1004) and Bishop Hilward of Halberstadt (968–996), whom Thietmar identified among the leading figures in the army.[176] Following the celebration of mass, Theoderic ordered that every soldier fortify (*munire*) himself with the sacrament (*sacramentum*).[177] In Thietmar's view, the men did so in order to strengthen both their bodies and their souls (*corpus animaque*).[178]

These examples of the piety of German soldiers before facing the enemy in battle can be compared with accounts dealing with soldiers serving in the southern and western regions of the erstwhile Carolingian *imperium*. As we saw above, before the battle of Enna, Robert Guisgard called on his men to purge themselves of their sins through confession, and then to receive the body and blood of Christ.[179] Similarly, before the battle of Mahdia, the Italians troops are reported to have accepted penance, offering this with a devoted heart to God, and then to have each received the eucharist.[180]

Dudo of St Quentin, a contemporary of Thietmar of Merseburg, also stressed the importance to soldiers of receiving the eucharist before battle in his history of the rulers of Normandy, written at the request of Duke Richard I (942–996). In the course of describing a battle between the Franks and the Norse ancestors of the Normans, Dudo emphasized that the former prepared to fight by going to the church of St Germanus where they heard mass and received both the body and blood of Christ.[181] It is well known that Dudo's text has long been seen by scholars as a poor factual account of historical events with very little value for tracing the political history of Normandy or the Norman leaders of the ninth to the mid-tenth centuries.[182] However, in providing this incidental detail concerning the religious preparations of the Frankish troops going into battle against the pagan Norsemen, Dudo should be understood to have been fulfilling the expectations of his late tenth and early eleventh-century Norman audience regarding the proper behavior of soldiers.[183]

---

[176] *Ibid.*, 3.19, p. 106.

[177] *Ibid.*, *Qui, ut dies sabbati primo illuxit, corpus animamque celesti sacramento muniunt.*

[178] *Ibid.*

[179] Amatus, *Storia de Normanni*, p. 241, *Purgame adonc nos pechiès par confession et par penitence, et recevons lo cors et lo sanc de Crist.*

[180] Cowdrey, "The Mahdia Campaign," p. 25, *offerunt corde devote Deo penitentiam, et communicant vicissim Christi eucharistiam.*

[181] Dudo of St Quentin, *De moribus et actis primorum normannie ducum*, ed. Jules Lair (Caen, 1865), pp. 155–6, *Franci vero diluculo venerunt ad ecclesiam S. Germani ibique missam audientes participantur corpore et sanguine Christi.* Concerning the date of Dudo's text, see Eric Christiansen, *Dudo of St. Quentin: History of the Normans* (Woodbridge, 1998), xiii.

[182] See, for example, Emily Albu [Hanawalt], "Dudo of Saint-Quentin: The Heroic Past Imagined," *The Haskins Society Journal* 6 (1994), pp. 111–18, here p. 113, who argues that it was Dudo's access both to the records of the ducal court as well as to the person of the duke and his advisors that annoys scholars who have found many historical inaccuracies in his text.

[183] Concerning the historical rhetoric tradition and its importance to late tenth- and early eleventh-century writers, see Richard W. Southern, "Aspects of the European Tradition of Historical Writing: 1. The Classical Tradition from Einhard to Geoffrey of Monmouth," *Transactions of the Royal Historical Society*, 5th ser. 20 (1970), pp. 173–96; Geoffrey

Indeed, William of Poitiers recorded that Duke William II of Normandy heard mass with the greatest devotion and then strengthened both his body and his soul with the body and blood of the Lord before going into battle at Hastings.[184] Orderic Vitalis found this report to be sufficiently convincing that in his own account of the battle of Hastings, he emphasized Duke William's participation in mass and his subsequent reception of Christ's body and blood. In describing the latter rites, Orderic insisted that William strengthened (*munire*) his body and soul (*corpus et anima*) with the divine sacraments.[185] William of Malmesbury recorded that the great majority of Norman soldiers followed a regimen similar to that of their commander when they prepared for battle by receiving the Lord's body (*mane Dominico corpore communicarunt*).[186]

In considering these accounts of soldiers receiving communion before battle, it would appear that this rite served a significantly different function than did confession and penance. The latter were crucial in preparing soldiers both to be worthy of divine aid in this world and in cleansing their souls in face of the possibility of dying in battle. Reception of the host, by contrast, would appear to have been understood as a strengthening rather than as a purifying rite. Observers stressed that the eucharist fortified (*munire*) the bodies and the souls of the combatants both inside and outside. Soldiers who now had the Lord within them could therefore expect to fight with greater strength. Consequently, the joining of communion to confession and penance as battlefield rites would seem to have had great importance for the confidence, and therefore the morale of soldiers going into combat.

The Problem of Homicide

The problem of homicide as a sinful act continued to disturb combatants in post-Carolingian Europe right up to the end of the eleventh century. As was seen above, when fighting on the plain of Conquereuil in 992, Count Fulk Nerra of Anjou could have had no doubt that he was engaged in a just effort to defend his *patria*. Nevertheless, he was so overcome with remorse for the slaughter of Christian soldiers that he went on pilgrimage to Jerusalem and built the monastery of *Belli Locus* to expiate his sins. Similarly, when rulers such as King Henry IV of Germany sought prayers on behalf of their dead *fideles* who were

---

Koziol, *Begging Pardon and Favor: Ritual and Political Order in Early Medieval France* (Ithaca, 1992), pp. 139–55; and Leah Shopkow, *History and Community: Norman Historical Writing in the Eleventh and Twelfth Centuries* (Washington, D.C., 1997), p. 130.

[184] William of Poitiers, *Gesta Guillelmi*, p. 124, *Ipse mysterio missae quam maxima cum devotione assistens, corporis ac sanguinis Domini communicatione suum et corpus et animam munivit.*

[185] Orderic Vitalis, *The Ecclesiastical History*, II: 172, *ipse missam audivit, et dominicis sacramentis corpus et animam munivit. . . .*

[186] William of Malmesbury, *Gesta regum Anglorum*, I: 454. Concerning William of Malmesbury's career as an historian and the substantial value of his work for the history of the Norman conquest, see Antonia Gransden, *Historical Writing in England*, I: 166–85.

killed in a *bellum publicum*, they were seeking to assure the salvation of men who had died in a just cause on behalf of the *res publica*. These were men who had the opportunity to confess their sins and accept penances before battle, but who had died before atoning for the enemy soldiers whom they themselves had killed.

The practical efforts of rulers and families of fallen soldiers to seek spiritual relief for these men came about within the context of a society that continued to treat all homicide as sinful. As was noted in the previous chapter, when the bishops from the armies of Charles the Bald and Louis the German gathered on the field of Fontenoy to consider the slaughter of Christian soldiers that had just taken place, they affirmed that the battle had been a *iudicium Dei* and that the soldiers had fought in a just cause. Nevertheless, the prelates added that anyone fighting out of anger, hatred, or for the sake of vainglory was guilty of a sinful act and had to expiate these sins through confession and the acceptance of penance.[187] In the view of these bishops, a soldier completely pure of heart could exist, but as a matter of practical policy, they believed that this was unlikely. When addressing the problem of homicide in a just war, Rabanus Maurus similarly left open the theoretical possibility that soldiers could have virtuous motives for fighting. However, in his view, this was very unlikely given the general tendency of man toward avarice, the root of all evil.[188]

Regino of Prüm, abbot of the monastery of St Martin in Trier, chose in his *Libri duo de synodalibus causis et disciplinis ecclesiasticis*, compiled c. 906, to follow very closely the tradition espoused by Rabanus Maurus more than two generations earlier.[189] In chapter fifty of the second book of his collection, Regino reiterated Rabanus' strongly worded view that anyone who wished to support the notion that soldiers were not required to carry out penances for having killed the enemy in a just war should consider whether these soldiers were truly innocent in the eyes of God.[190] Regino added that it was well known that many soldiers fought because of their greed (*propter avaritiam*) and in order to obtain the favor of their temporal lords (*propter favorem dominorum suorum temporalium*), and consequently spurned their eternal Lord (*aeternum Dominum contemserunt*) by killing.[191] Then, perhaps to emphasize his point, in the very next chapter of his collection Regino included a text from an earlier penitential manual that required forty days of penance for anyone who killed a man in the course of an officially sanctioned war (*bellum publicum*).[192]

The practical implications of Regino's text are made clear by the actions of Archbishop Seulf II of Rheims in the wake of the battle of Soissons in 923.

---

187 Nithard, *Historia*, 3.1, p. 428.
188 Rabanus Maurus, MGH Epistolae 5, p. 464.
189 Regino of Prüm, *De synodalibus causis et disciplinis ecclesiasticis*, ed. F.G.A. Wasserschleben (repr. Graz, 1964), pp. 233–4.
190 *Ibid., Scimus enim, quod Dei iudicium semper iustum est, et nulla reprehensione dignum, sed tamen opportet eos considerare, qui hanc necem nefariam defendere cupiunt, utrum illos quasi coram oculis Dei innoxios excusare possint. . . .*
191 *Ibid.*, p. 234.
192 *Ibid., Si quis hominem in bello publico occiderit, XL dies poeniteat.*

Seulf had been a strong supporter of Robert of Paris and continued to oppose Charles III even after the death of Robert at Soissons.[193] Nevertheless, at an episcopal council held at Rheims later that year, Seulf and his fellow bishops imposed penances on the soldiers who had fought on both sides in the conflict.[194] In fact, the penances imposed by the council of Rheims were far higher than the forty days of fasting generally found in tariff books. During the first year after the battle, the soldiers were excluded from attending church during Lent. During Lent in this year and in the two following, the men were required to subsist on bread, salt, and water on Tuesdays, Thursdays, and Saturdays, unless they redeemed this obligation through a payment (*redimere*). In addition, the soldiers were required to maintain the same penitential regime for fifteen days prior to the nativity of Saint John the Baptist, and the fifteen-day period before Nativity, as well as every Saturday over the course of this entire three-year period, unless these happened to fall on feast days. These conditions were to hold unless the soldiers were sick or were detained in military service (*sive militia detentum esse*).[195] By imposing penances on both Charles' and Robert's men, Seulf demonstrated his view that killing in battle was a sinful act requiring reconciliation with God no matter what the circumstances of the conflict.

This was certainly the view propagated by Abbot Odo of Cluny (926–944) in his *vita* of Gerald of Aurillac composed c. 930.[196] Odo stresses throughout the life that the protagonist Gerald was a just and pious man because he never shed blood despite the demands placed on him in his office as count. Whenever it became necessary to fight, Gerald ordered his men to reverse their weapons and to strike the enemy with the flats of their swords.[197] Odo addresses the apparent contradiction between military obligation and living a holy life by arguing that Gerald was no different than Abraham and King David who took up arms only when it was necessary to defend the poor and the defenseless. However, Gerald

---

[193] *Les Annales de Flodoard*, pp. 16–18.

[194] *Concilium Remense*, Mansi 18A, cols. 345–6.

[195] *Ibid.*, videlicet, ut tribus quadragesimis per tres annos agant poenitentiam: ita ut prima quadragesima sint extra ecclesiam, et coena Domini reconcilientur. Omnibus vero his tribus quadragesimis, secunda quarta, et sexta feria, in pane sale, et aqua abstineant, aut redimant. Similiter quindecim diebus ante nativitaem S. Joannis Baptistae et quindecim diebus ante nativitatem Domini Salvatoris, omni quoque sexta feria per totum annum, nisi redemerint, aut festivitas celebris ipsa die acciderit, vel eum infirmitate sive militia detentum esse contigerit. The penance as a whole is remarkably similar to the normal fasting required of priests in the Carolingian period by the councils of Riesbach, Freising, and Salzburg noted in the previous chapter. See Concilia 2.1, p. 208.

[196] Odo of Cluny, *De vita Sancti Geraldi*, PL 133: 709–52. On the dating of the life, see Barbara H. Rosenwein, *Rhinoceros Bound: Cluny in the Tenth Century* (Philadelphia, 1982), p. 57.

[197] *De vita Sancti Geraldi*, 1.8, cols. 646–7, Aliquoties autem cum inevitabilis ei praeliandi necessitas incumberet, suis imperiosa voce praecepit, mucronibus gladiorum retroactis, hastas inantea dirigentes pugnarent. Erdmann, *Origin of the Idea of Crusade*, pp. 87–9, identifies the *vita* of Gerald as clear evidence of the continuing Christian effort to come to an accommodation with the violence inherent in secular military life. On this point, also see Rosenwein, *Rhinoceros Bound*, pp. 73–83.

was superior to these biblical heroes because, as Odo reiterates, he never shed blood but rather relied on God's aid alone to win victories.[198] Whether the report made by Odo is accurate is not relevant in the present context.

As was true of his predecessors, Bishop Burchard of Worms strongly advocated the position that any type of homicide, including killing in the course of a just war or a publicly sanctioned war (*bellum publicum*), was sinful.[199] Thus, in book six of the *Decretum*, which deals largely with the problem of penances for various types of homicide, Burchard considered how to deal with soldiers who had killed while in the service of their prince. The bishop of Worms echoed the traditional admonition that it was necessary to warn those who argued against the need to carry out penances for homicides committed at the order of one's prince.[200] Following the argument made by Rabanus Maurus and reiterated by Regino of Prüm, Burchard emphasized that it was necessary to consider the reasons why someone killed in battle when judging whether or not he had committed a sin. He reiterated the view that soldiers had many reasons for fighting that were incompatible with Christian ethics, including fighting because of greed and fighting in order to obtain the favor of their lords.[201]

Burchard returned to the problem of homicide committed in a just war in book nine of his *Decretum*, where he drew a distinction between service under a legitimate prince (*legitimus princeps*) and fighting without the authority of this prince.[202] In the first case, Burchard asserts that if a soldier kills at the order of a legitimate prince, who is attempting to establish peace (*pro pace fieri jusserat*), or if this same soldier were to kill a tyrant (*tyrranus*), who was attempting to undermine peace (*pacem pervertere*), he would have to carry out a penance for three Lenten periods.[203] However, if the soldier killed someone in a battle not authorized by a legitimate prince, Burchard's text requires him to carry out the same seven-year penance imposed upon anyone who killed willingly and with no justification.[204] Thus, as he made clear in book six of the *Decretum*, Burchard held a nuanced view of wartime killing, but nevertheless saw the act as innately sinful.

This same attitude toward the sinfulness of homicide is in evidence in the penitential ordinance issued (c. 1067) by the bishops of Normandy dealing with

---

[198] *De vita Sancti Geraldi*, 1.8, col. 647, *gladium suum, sicut supra diximus, numquam humano sanguine cruentaverit.*

[199] Burchard, *Decretum*, 6.23, PL 140: 770.

[200] *Ibid.*, *Oportet autem diligentius eos admonere, qui homicidia in bello perpetrate pro nihilo ducunt, excusantes non ideo necesse habere de singulis facere poenitentiam, eo quod jussu principium peractum sit, et Dei judicio ita finitum.*

[201] *Ibid.* Burchard quotes the original text from Rabanus Maurus' penitential manual that was sent to Bishop Heribald of Auxerre. PL 110: 471–2. This text is also found in Rabanus' letter to Archbishop Otger of Mainz. MGH Epistolae 5, p. 464.

[202] Burchard, *Decretum*, 9.5, PL 140: 952.

[203] *Ibid.*, *Fecisti homicidium in bello, jussu legitimi principis, qui pro pace hoc fieri jusserat, et interfecisti tyrannum qui pacem pervertere studuit? tres quadragesimas per legitimas ferias poeniteas.*

[204] *Ibid.*, *Si autem aliter fuerit, id est, sine jussu legitimi principis, ut homicidium sponte commissum poenitas, id est carinam unam cum septem sequentibus annis.*

William the Conqueror's troops and their actions at the battle of Hastings. The ordinance itself is highly nuanced and contains thirteen clauses, including sections dealing with soldiers who killed the enemy in battle (*qui in magno praelio scit se hominem occidisse*), with those who simply struck the enemy in battle without killing him (*pro unoquoque quem percussit*), with those who did not know whether they had killed the enemy in battle (*percussorum vel occisorum ignorat*), and with those who did not kill the enemy but had wanted to do so (*percutere voluerat*).[205] There were even special penances imposed upon archers who had participated in the battle.[206] In the first instance, the soldiers were required to carry out penances for one year for each man they killed (*secundem numerum hominum pro unoquoque uno anno poeniteat*), no matter how many this might be.[207] This penitential requirement was clearly an innovation when compared with the penances imposed by earlier authorities, noted above, where soldiers received a single standard penance for having killed in battle. The imposition of a forty-day penance for each of the enemy soldiers whom they struck during the fighting (*pro unoquoque quadraginta diebus poenitat*) and an additional three-day penance (*triduo poenitat*) simply for wishing to kill the enemy would also appear to be innovations in that the bishops expanded the traditional penitential regime to include non-lethal participation in warfare.[208] Indeed, the very intensity of the penitential discipline imposed by the Norman bishops would seem to indicate their clear adherence to the view that all homicide, and even violence against a fellow man, was sinful whether committed in the course of a just war or otherwise.

In 1070, Pope Alexander II sent Bishop Ermenfrid of Sion and two other legates to England where they oversaw a series of ecclesiastical reforms that were being undertaken by King William I and his advisors. In the course of his duties as papal legate, Ermenfrid confirmed the penitential ordinance, discussed above, that had been issued by the Norman bishops and was to be imposed upon all the soldiers who had fought at the battle of Hastings.[209] In so doing, Ermenfrid sanctioned the view that even soldiers who had fought under a papal

---

[205] *Councils and Synods with Other Documents Relating to the English Church I A.D. 871–1204*, 2 vols., ed. D. Whitelock, M. Brett, and C.N.L. Brooke (Oxford, 1981), II: 583–4. This text is discussed in detail by H.E.J. Cowdrey, "Bishop Ermenfrid of Sion and the Penitential Ordinance following the Battle of Hastings," *Journal of Ecclesiastical History* 20 (1969), pp. 225–42.

[206] *Councils and Synods* (1981), II: 584, *De sagittariis, qui ignoranter aliquos occiderunt, vel absque homicidio vulneraverunt, tribus quadragesimis poeniteant.* The decision to include a specific provision referring to archers may be the result of the important part played by these soldiers at the battle of Hastings.

[207] *Ibid.*, p. 583, *Qui in magno praelio scit se hominem occidisse, secundum numerum hominum pro unoquoque uno anno poeniteat.*

[208] *Ibid.*, *Pro unoquoque quadraginta diebus poeniteat, sive continue, sive per intervalla,* and *Qui autem neminem percusserit, si percutere voluerat, triduo poeniteat.*

[209] Cowdrey, "Bishop Ermenfrid of Sion," p. 233, argues for an early date for this ordinance, perhaps as early as 1066. He notes that the only evidence adduced for a later date is the presence of Ermenfrid in Normandy in 1070. Cowdrey plausibly suggests that Ermenfrid might have confirmed a document that had already existed for some time.

banner in a manifestly just cause were required to carry out penances for killing the enemy in battle.[210]

Given this long tradition and the support it received from all levels of society, it is particularly striking that first Pope Alexander II (1061–1073) and then agents of his successor Pope Gregory VII (1073–1085) attempted to bring about a radical transformation in church teaching on the matter of homicide and its sinfulness in the context of a just war. The first surviving evidence for this rethinking of the nature of homicide can be found in a letter sent by Pope Alexander to the clergy of the city of Volturno in 1063.[211] Here, Alexander addressed the question of volunteers going to Spain to help fight against the Saracens. The pope began by enunciating the traditional military-religious view that it was crucial for soldiers to prepare themselves for the campaign by confessing their sins and accepting a penance. Alexander noted that by doing so, the soldiers could avoid the accusation from the devil that they were inpenitent.[212] This was another way of saying that by confessing their sins, the soldiers helped to make themselves worthy of divine aid.

What was new and striking in this letter was Pope Alexander's subsequent claim that by the authority vested in him by the apostles Peter and Paul, he could lift the obligation of these soldiers to carry out the penances which they had accepted; that, in fact, he could grant them what he called a remission of their sins (*remission peccatorum*) for going on campaign.[213] What this meant was that serving in war with all that entailed, including killing enemy soldiers, now became a means of expiating sins rather than a situation in which a soldier would incur sins that would have to be expiated through penance. Simply put, Alexander was asserting *de facto* that killing could be understood as a means of reconciling oneself with God and thereby obtaining eternal salvation.[214]

That Alexander was, in fact, making this very claim is indicated by a letter that he sent to Archbishop Wilfrid of Narbonne in the spring of 1063.[215] The pope noted in his missive that all law, both ecclesiastical and secular, prohibited

---

[210] Catherine Morton, "Pope Alexander and the Norman Conquest," *Latomus* 34 (1975), pp. 362–82, argues that Pope Alexander did not, in fact, either support William's invasion or provide the conqueror with a papal banner. In making this argument, Morton suggests (*ibid.*, p. 378) that it would be implausible for the papal legate to have imposed penances on soldiers who had fought with ecclesiastical approval. However, as many churchmen made clear over the course of the tenth and eleventh century, this was not only plausible, it was necessary given the inherently sinful nature of any type of homicide.

[211] The text of this letter is in *Epistolae pontificum Romanorum ineditae*, ed. S. Löwenfeld (repr. Graz, 1959), p. 43.

[212] *Ibid., qui iuxta qualitatem peccaminum suorum unusquisque suo episcopo vel spirituali patri confiteantur, eique, ne diabolus accusare de inpenitentia, modus penitentie imponatur.*

[213] *Ibid., Nos vero auctoritate sanctorum apostolorum Petri et Pauli et penitentiam eis levamus et remissionem peccatorum facimus, oratione prosequentes.*

[214] This text has long been understood to represent a crucial development in papal thinking leading toward the idea of crusade. See Brundage, *Medieval Canon Law and the Crusader*, p. 24, n. 90 and the literature cited there. However, the importance of this text for the question of homicide does not appear to have been broached by scholars.

[215] *Regesta Pontificum Romanorum*, 2nd rev. edn, ed. S. Löwenfeld, F. Kaltenbrunner, and P. Ewald (Leipzig, 1885), #4533, p. 573.

the shedding of blood. But Alexander singled out two exceptions to this general rule. The first was in the case of punishing crime. The second was the need to fight against the Saracens.[216] In this latter case, Pope Alexander emphasized that the shedding of blood was to be seen as praiseworthy.[217]

This praise for killing was a far cry from the understanding of homicide committed in the course of a just war as a necessary and yet still sinful act that required penance as a means of attaining reconciliation with God. Indeed, Alexander's position regarding the nature of homicide in wars against the Saracens in Spain stood in stark contrast to his own legate's action seven years later in England when Bishop Ermenfrid confirmed the penances imposed on William the Conqueror's men for their service at the battle of Hastings. The pope's mixed message concerning the nature of homicide committed in battle would seem to suggest that he still saw a clear distinction between wars fought against Christians and those fought against Muslims. The first could be construed as just, but the second were something more. These latter wars were sufficiently holy that the intentions of the participants ceased to be relevant in determining the sinfulness of their actions.

Alexander II's efforts to eliminate the sinfulness from homicide committed in wars against Muslims was taken a further step by Bishop Anselm II of Lucca (1073–1086). In book thirteen of his *Collectio canonum*, Anselm assembled twenty-nine *capitula* in which he drew on ideas from Augustine and Gregory the Great to explore the idea of fighting without sin. These chapters, which included "opposing the enemies of the church with all the strength of one's mind and body," "that it is necessary to pray for one going into battle," and "that Moses did nothing wrong when he killed at the Lord's command," were intended to show that wars against schismatics and heretics were virtuous.[218] However, Bishop Anselm went a step further in 1084 when he actually put this theory into practice. According to Bardo, who served under Anselm as primacarius of the cathedral church, as the soldiers of Lucca were preparing to go into battle against imperial forces at Sorbaria, the bishop promised them a *remissio peccatorum* in return for their military service.[219] Thus, as Alexander had done

---

216 *Ibid., Omnes leges, tam ecclesiasticas, quam saeculares, effusionem humani sanguinis prohibere, nisi forte commissa crimina aliquem iudicio puniant vel forte, ut de Sarracenis, hostilis exacerbatio incumbat.*

217 *Ibid., Laudat eum.*

218 These texts can be found in Edith Pásztor, "Lotta per le investiture e 'ius belli': La posizione di Anselmo di Lucca," in *Sant'Anselmo, Mantova e la lotta per le investiture*, ed. Paolo Golinelli (Bologna, 1987), pp. 375–421. The texts from book 13 of the *Collectio Canonum* are on pp. 405–21, and the specific titles mentioned here are on pp. 420, 408, and 405. Anselm's views on the sinfulness of war are discussed by H.E.J. Cowdrey, *Pope Gregory VII 1073–1085* (Oxford, 1998), p. 653. The collection of canons completed by Anselm c. 1083 does not refer to penances to be imposed upon soldiers for having killed in a just war. On this point, see Friedrich Thaner, *Anselmi episcopi Lucensis collectio canonum* (Vienna, 1906–15, repr. 1965), in particular pp. 507–10, which list the chapters of book eleven of the collection, which specifically deals with penances. Anselm was a leading supporter of Gregory VII.

219 *Vita Anselmi episcopi Lucensis*, ed. Roger Wilmans, MG SS 12 (Hanover, 1856), p. 20, *instruentes eos, quo pacto quave intentione deberent pugnare, sicque in remissionem omnium*

in 1063, Anselm promised that his men could reconcile themselves to God by killing enemy soldiers. Only now, the enemy was Christian rather than Muslim.

We will see in the next chapter that the radical reinterpretation of the nature of homicide as a sinful act, promulgated by Alexander II and adapted by Anselm of Lucca for use against Christians, would prove to be a foundational element in crusading ideology throughout the twelfth century. However, by the late eleventh century, the new interpretation of homicide had already achieved a prominent place in canon law, a process that is evident in the work of Bishop Ivo of Chartres.

In book ten of his *Decretum*, which deals with various types of homicide, Ivo included Burchard of Worms' objection to those who did not see the need for soldiers to carry out penances for having killed in the course of fighting a just war.[220] However, in addition to this single enunciation of the traditional view concerning post-battle penances for homicide, Ivo included more than thirty texts that justified fighting in one or another manner, the vast majority of which were taken from the church fathers, especially Augustine.[221] Thus, for example, Ivo quoted Augustine's view that it was possible for a soldier or a judge to kill an enemy or a criminal without committing a sin.[222] In another case, Ivo quoted Augustine's sermon on Matthew 19 in which he argued that it was not sinful to serve as soldier so long as one did not fight for booty.[223] Moreover, among the more recent authorities he cited on this issue, Ivo quoted a fragment of Alexander II's letter to Archbishop Wilfrid of Narbonne, noted above, in which the pope expressed support for campaigns against the Muslims in Spain and explicitly denied the sinfulness of killing Saracens in battle.[224]

If we briefly look beyond the scope of this chapter to c. 1140 and consider Gratian's *Decretum*, the single most important and influential canon law text of the twelfth century, it is clear that Ivo's treatment of the question of killing in a just war represented a final transitional stage in the history of the doctrine on the subject, which culminated in the complete disappearance of post-battle penances for homicide.[225] Like Ivo, and perhaps following his model, Gratian

---

peccatorum eorum instantis belli committeremus periculum. Cowdrey, *Gregory VII*, does not address Anselm's promise of a *remissio peccatorum*.

[220] Ivo of Chartres, *Decretum*, 10.151, PL 161: 736.

[221] *Ibid.*, 10.88–130, PL 161: 720–30. One of the few cases in which Ivo relies on more recent precedent is Pope Hadrian's request that Charlemagne take military action against the Lombards thereby giving the Carolingian military action the patina of papal authority. See *Decretum*, 10.91, col. 720.

[222] *Decretum*, 10.101, cols. 722–3: *Si homicidium est hominem occidere, potest occidere aliquando sine peccato. Nam et miles hostem, et judex vel minister ejus nocentem . . . non mihi videntur peccare cum hominem occidunt.*

[223] *Decretum*, 10.125, col. 728, *Militare non est delictum sed propter praedam militare peccatum est.*

[224] Concerning Ivo's use of this text, see Brundage, *Canon Law and the Crusader*, p. 24.

[225] Concerning the importance of Gratian's *Decretum* for later canonists and theologians, see Alain Boureau, "Droit et théologie au XIIIe siècle," *Annales: histoire, sciences sociales* 46: 6 (1992), pp. 1113–25, here pp. 1113–16; James A. Brundage, "The Rise of Professional Canonists and the Development of the *ius commune*," *ZRG kan.* 112: 125 (1995), pp. 26–63, who emphasizes the crucial role played by the *Decretum* in helping to establish canon law as

included many texts in *Causa* 23 of his *Decretum* that justified the use of violence and denied the sinfulness of killing in a just war, most of which came from Augustine.[226] However, unlike the great French canonist, Gratian failed to include a single text in his collection that required soldiers to do penances for having killed in the course of a just war.

Admittedly, Gratian began *questio* 5 of *causa* 23, which deals with the question of licit violence, with seven texts that denied the licitness of killing.[227] However, in the eighth canon, Gratian cited a passage from Augustine's *City of God*, where the bishop of Hippo argued that it was not sinful to kill if one does so in the course of one's public duty (*ex officio non est peccatum hominem occidere*).[228] The remaining forty-one canons of *quaestio* 5 all justify to one degree or another the use of deadly force.

Indeed, Gratian himself strongly denied that any sinfulness attached to a soldier who killed an enemy in the course of his authorized duties. He emphasized that since holy men (*viri sancti*) and public authorities (*publicae potestates*) who wage war (*bella gerentes*) do not transgress the commandment against murder (*non fuerunt transgressores illius mandati*) and since a soldier (*miles*) who obeys his orders (*suae potestati obediens*) is not guilty of murder (*non est reus homicidii*), it is clear (*patet*) that it is permitted not only to beat the wicked, but to kill them as well (*sed etiam interfici licet*).[229] By the middle of the twelfth century, the problem of sinfulness for killing in the course of just war had become a moot point.[230]

Conclusion

The tenth and eleventh centuries witnessed several important developments in the religion of war. At the level of the individual soldiers, reception of the eucharist was transformed from its original Carolingian status as the *viaticum* for dying and wounded soldiers into a pre-battle rite intended to strengthen men in both body and soul for combat. When combined with confession and the accep-

---

an area of professional specialization; and Charles Duggan, "Papal Judges Delegate and the Making of the 'New Law' in the Twelfth Century," in *Cultures of Power: Lordship, Status, and Process in Twelfth-Century Europe*, ed. Thomas N. Bisson (Philadelphia, 1995), pp. 172–99. Concerning the authority attributed to Gratian's text to the north as well as to the south of the Alps, see Winfried Stelzer, "Die Rezeption des gelehrten Rechts nördlich der Alpen," in *Kommunikation und Mobilität im Mittelalter: Begegnungen zwischen dem Süden und der Mitte Europas (11.–14. Jahrhundert)*, ed. Siegfried de Rachewiltz and Josef Riedmann (Sigmaringen, 1995), pp. 231–47.

226 On this point, see James A. Brundage, "The Hierarchy of Violence in Twelfth- and Thirteenth Century Canonists," *The Internationl History Review* 17 (1995), pp. 671–92, here pp. 673–81.

227 Gratian, *Corpus iuris canonici*, ed. Aemilius Friedberg (Leipzig, 1879), C. 23 q. 5 c. 1–7, pp. 928–32.

228 Gratian, C. 23 q. 5. c. 8, p. 932.

229 Gratian, C. 23 q. 5. c. 48, p. 945.

230 On this point, see Brundage, "Hierarchy of Violence," p. 679.

tance of confession, the eucharist became a crucial element in maintaining high morale among the troops.

At the level of public religion, rulers in post-Carolingian Europe also used a wide variety of means to identify their causes as just, particularly when fighting against Christian opponents, so as to assure their supporters that God was on their side. As a corollary to these efforts, rulers in the tenth and eleventh centuries appear to have expended considerably greater resources than their Carolingian predecessors to assure the provision of intercessory masses and prayers for fallen soldiers, even to the extent of dedicating new monastic houses in commemoration of and in atonement for battles. Much of this effort can be traced to ongoing concerns about the sinfulness of homicide, even in just wars, and the need to look after the souls of soldiers who could not themselves undertake penances for having shed Christian blood. Against this backdrop of penitential concern, the most striking development in the religion of war during the entire period was the effort at the highest levels of the church to redefine homicide as an act that could be meritorious rather than sinful. As will be seen in the next chapter, this new understanding of homicide would come to play an extraordinarily important role in motivating soldiers during the crusades.

These new developments and emphases occurred, however, within a framework of wartime religion that demonstrated remarkable continuities with Carolingian, and even Late Antique practices. At the broadest level, the overwhelming majority of the surviving evidence points to a society that believed in the power and the willingness of God and the saints to intervene in human affairs. As a consequence, secular and ecclesiastical leaders continued to devote great resources both on the home front and on campaign to seeking divine aid through a wide variety of religious rites, prayers, masses, and penitential acts, including fasting and giving alms and gifts to churches and monasteries. As was true of their Carolingian predecessors, commanders and religious leaders regularly emphasized the availability of divine aid to their troops through sermons and orations in which they stressed the need for the fighting men to be worthy of this heavenly assistance. Moreover, these promises of divine aid were frequently given greater force through the provision to fighting forces of consecrated battle flags and relics that were themselves widely understood to hold *virtus* or heavenly power. All of these invocations of divine support, whether through objects or prayer, were intended to give soldiers greater confidence as they went into battle, to convince them and their families of the justness of their cause, to caution them to behave in a manner worthy of God's aid, and to trust that they would find either victory or eternal rest in heaven. In the view of many contemporary observers, these efforts were frequently successful.

4

Military Religion among the Crusaders 1095–1215

Introduction

In contrast to what might be called "ordinary" or "conventional" warfare of the type discussed in the previous chapter, historians of the crusades have seen these campaigns either as a turning point *in* or as the culmination *of* the sanctification of war, particularly against non-Christians.[1] In the view of many scholars, the most salient aspect of this new kind of warfare was the union and subsequent transformation of the concepts of pilgrimage, penance, and just war theory to create the notion of a holy war fought by soldiers of Christ in return for personal salvation.[2] The efforts of Pope Alexander II and Bishop Anselm II of Lucca in the generation before the First Crusade to deny the sinfulness of homicide committed in just wars were crucial to the development of crusading ideology.[3] Nevertheless, they were not immediately successful in transforming public opinion concerning *merely* just wars. For it is clear that many observers from the late eleventh through the early thirteenth century thought of the crusades as a new kind of war characterized, in large part, by the spiritual benefits that accrued to the combatants including those who killed the enemy in battle.

Fulcher of Chartres, an eyewitness to Pope Urban II's sermon at Clermont and a participant in the First Crusade, emphasized the novel nature of this campaign. Fulcher recorded that the pope addressed his sermon to soldiers of Christ (*Christi milites*) "who once fought against their brothers and relatives but can now fight licitly against barbarians."[4] The fact that Christians had been

---

[1] The crucial figure in developing this model is Carl Erdmann, *The Origin of the Idea of Crusade*, whose work remains influential to the present. Also see Étienne Delaruelle, *L'Idée de croisade au moyen âge* (Turin, 1980), originally published as a series of articles, "Essai sur la formation de l'idée de croisade," *Bulletin de littérature ecclésiastique* (= Ble) 42 (1942), pp. 24–45 and 86–103; Ble 45 (1944), pp. 13–46 and 73–90; Ble 54 (1953), pp. 226–39; and Ble 55 (1954), pp. 50–63. Delaruelle emphasized the importance of earlier campaigns against the Muslims as well as Pope Gregory VII's plans for an eastern campaign in preparing Europe for the First Crusade. The legal transformation of just war into holy war has been studied in great detail by Brundage, *Medieval Canon Law and the Crusader*.
[2] The exceptional importance accorded by contemporaries to the crusade's penitential nature is emphasized by Jonathan Riley-Smith, *The First Crusaders, 1095–1131* (Cambridge, 1997), pp. 68–70. Marcus Bull, *Knightly Piety and the Lay Response to the First Crusade: The Limousin and Gascony, c. 970–c.1130* (Oxford, 1993), likewise emphasizes the great importance of religious feeling among the crusaders, arguing that piety was the motivating factor for almost all those who chose to go on crusade.
[3] On this point, see Cowdrey, *Gregory VII*, pp. 652–6.
[4] Fulcher of Chartres, *Historia Iherosolimitana*, Recueil des Historiens des Croisades:

campaigning against Muslims in Spain, North Africa, and Sicily at this time for more than two generations does not appear to have affected Fulcher's judgment concerning the innovative nature of the campaign to Jerusalem.[5]

A similar emphasis on novelty is apparent in the historical account written by Guibert of Nogent, who, utilizing eyewitness accounts of the assembly at Clermont, insisted that the pope had promised that soldiers could earn as much praise for defending the Holy Land as did the Maccabees for defending the Temple.[6] Indeed, Guibert's emphasis on Urban's promise of the status of martyrdom to all those who fell in battle would seem to indicate that the remission of sins offered by the pope meant something different from Bishop Anselm of Lucca's promise of a "spiritual benefit" to his soldiers ten years earlier. In Anselm's sermon, martyrdom was never mentioned.[7]

This chapter, therefore, will examine the religious behavior and beliefs of both the combatants and their supporters during the first long century of crusading warfare from Pope Urban's call to arms in 1095 up to the eve of the Fourth Lateran Council (1215). The particular focus will be on identifying

---

Historiens Occidentaux, 5 vols. (Paris, 1844–95), III: 324, *nunc jure contra barbaros pugnent, qui olim adversus fratres et consanguineos dimicabant.*

5 Concerning the ideology of crusade historians and the effect of the success of the First Crusade upon their works, see James M. Powell, "Myth, Legend, Propaganda, History: The First Crusade, 1140–ca. 1300," in *Autour de la première croisade: actes du colloque de la Society for the Study of the Crusade and the Latin East*, ed. Michel Balard (Paris, 1996), pp. 127–41.

6 Guibert of Nogent, *Gesta Dei per Francos*, Recueil des Historiens des Croisades: Historiens Occidentaux, 5 vols. (Paris, 1844–95), IV: 138, *Si machabaeis olim ad maximam profuit pietatis laudem, quia pro cerimoniis et templo pugnarent: et vobis, o milites christiani, legitime conceditur, ut armorum studio libertatem patriae defendatis.*

7 *Ibid.*, *Nunc vobis bella proponimus quae in se habent gloriosum martyrii munus quibus restat praesentis et aeternae laudis titulus.* The idea of martyrdom is also emphasized by Robert of Rheims, who completed his account of the crusade about two decades after the capture of Jerusalem in 1099. In a *reportatio* of an exhortation delivered by Bohemond to his troops before setting out for Constantinople, Robert had the Apulian nobleman and crusade commander emphasize the penitential nature of the campaign. Bohemond is reported to have promised that soldiers who prepared themselves with confession and penance were fighting for their place in paradise because they were fighting for God. On this point, see Robert of Rheims, *Historia Iherosolymitana*, Recueil des Historiens des Croisades: Historiens Occidentaux, 5 vols. (Paris, 1844–95), III: 747–8, *nunc iterum secundo regenerati estis, per confessionem scilicet et poenitentiam, quam quotidie duris laboribus exhibetis. O felices qui in tali opere deficient; qui ante visuri sunt Paradisum quam patriam suam . . . Quapropter, invicti milites, quia nunc primum incepimus Deo militare, non gloriemur in armis sive in viribus nostris, sed in Deo potentiore omnium, quoniam ipsius est bellum nostrum, et ipse dominabitur gentium.* Robert's *Historia* was largely a reworking of the anonymous *Gesta Francorum* and is therefore useful as a measure of attitudes at Rheims about the First Crusade, particularly in those places where Robert alters the text provided by his model. Concering Robert's use of sources, see James E. Cronin, "And the Reapers are Angels: A Study of Crusade Motivation as Described in the *Historia Iherosolimitana* of Robert of Rheims," unpublished dissertation (New York University, 1973), pp. 5–13. The role of martyrdom as an element in the ideology of Christian fighting men in the period before the First Crusade has been addressed by H.E.J. Cowdrey, "Martyrdom and the First Crusade," in *Crusade and Settlement*, ed. P.W. Edbury (Cardiff, 1985), pp. 46–56; repr. with the same pagination in *The Crusades and Latin Monasticism, 11th and 12th Centuries* (Brookfield, 1999).

continuities and developments in religious practice, and on the effect of religion on the conduct of military operations in crusade campaigns. The chapter is divided into two sections. The first considers the practices of military religion within the context of the First Crusade. The second half of the chapter deals with the religious behavior of soldiers and their supporters in the context of specific crusading campaigns carried out during the twelfth and early thirteenth centuries for which sufficient evidence survives to indicate the particular practices and functions of military religion.

The First Crusade 1095–1099

The crusades engendered an enormous narrative literature of "histories" composed both by participants in the actual campaigns and by later chroniclers recording the stories told by many thousands of returning veterans. We are fortunate to have a wide variety of accounts of the First Crusade, in particular, including chronicles written by both clerical and secular military participants, as well as letters from lay officers and ecclesiastical figures that deal with the religious behavior of the crusaders and their supporters. Within this wide range of accounts, one of the single most striking episodes, and one of the most revealing of the new forms of behavior associated with the new type of war, is the discovery of an object that was reputed to be the "Holy Lance" in the church of St Peter at Antioch following the capture of this city by the crusader army on 2 June 1098.

One particularly important eye-witness report dealing with the events surrounding the discovery of the weapon that was believed by Christians to have killed Jesus comes from the anonymous author of the *Gesta Francorum et aliorum Hierosolomitanorum*. He served with Bohemond of Apulia throughout most of the First Crusade, and his experiences were those of a middle ranking officer who understood the physical and psychological demands placed upon the men under his command.[8] Throughout his work, the Anonymous treated the religious behavior of soldiers and priests during the campaign in a frank and straightforward manner. He consistently tied success in battle to the proper observance of religious rites and ceremonies, including confession and communion. However, in addition to noting these elements of religious practice that were common in ordinary military campaigns, the chronicler also recorded his views concerning the extraordinary religious nature of the crusade itself. In particular, he was convinced that men who died fighting to regain Jerusalem would go directly to heaven as martyrs.[9] In his description of the casualties suffered during the siege of Nicaea (April 1097), the chronicler concluded that many of the crusaders had endured martyrdom and that their souls had returned

---

[8] *Gesta Francorum et aliorum Hierosolomitanorum*, ed. Rosalind Hill (London, 1962). Concerning the author's service with Bohemond, see *ibid.*, pp. xi–xii.
[9] Concerning the prehistory of the conception of martyrdom for Christian soldiers, see Cowdrey, "Martyrdom and the First Crusade," pp. 49–51.

to God "wearing the robe of martyrdom into heaven."[10] The chronicler's testimony is therefore a valuable entry-point into the dual nature of the crusade campaign combining elements of both ordinary and extraordinary warfare.

The basic story of the discovery of the Holy Lance is too well known to rehearse here in detail. Briefly, when the crusader army finally captured the city of Antioch on 2 June 1098, the soldiers were exhausted, starving, and threatened imminently by a siege of the city by a powerful Muslim army under the command of Kherboga, the governor of Mosul. It was under these circumstances that one of the crusaders, a man named Peter Bartholomew, claimed that he had received a vision regarding the location of this sacred relic.[11] He insisted that Saint Andrew the Apostle revealed to him the resting place of the Holy Lance in the church of St Peter. According to the vision, God would send a sign within five days that would make the troops confident and joyful (*laeti et gavisi*) and would lead them to victory over their enemies (*omnes inimici eorum vincentur*).[12] When news of this vision was spread among the rank and file of the soldiers, there was great rejoicing and the men began to encourage each other saying that they would have victory because God was with them.[13] A few days after the first vision of Saint Andrew was made public, Peter Bartholomew again reported a vision and went with twelve other men to the church of St. Peter where they dug up an item that the Anonymous reported they claimed was the Holy Lance.[14] The author of the *Gesta Francorum* concluded that after it became known that the lance had been found, the crusaders again rejoiced, and from that moment on were prepared to fight against the enemy despite all of the disadvantages the Christians faced.[15] His report is consistent both with the other

[10] *Gesta Francorum*, p. 17, *multi ex nostris illic receperunt martyrium . . . Qui in caelum triumphantes portarunt stolam recepti martyrii. . . .*

[11] *Ibid.*, pp. 59–60. Colin Morris, "Policy and Visions. The Case of the Holy Lance at Antioch," in *War and Government: Essays in Honour of J.O. Prestwich*, ed. John Gillingham and J.C. Holt (Woodbridge, 1984), pp. 33–45, provides a valuable survey of the sources and literature dealing with the Holy Lance in Antioch. It should be emphasized that the object discovered by Peter Bartholomew at Antioch was not the same weapon employed by the Ottonian emperors of Germany to lead their forces into battle.

[12] *Gesta Francorum*, p. 60.

[13] *Ibid.*, *audientes itaque quod inimici eorum ab eis omnino essent vicendi, protinus coeperunt sese vivificare, et confortabant se adinvicem dicentes: 'expergiscimini, et estote ubique fortes ac prudentes, quoniam in proximo erit nobis Deus in adiutorium, et erit maximum refugium populo suo quem respicit in merore manentem.'* The importance of this vision and subsequent discovery of the Holy Lance for the morale of the crusading army was reported by many other participants including Raymond d'Aguilers, *Liber*, ed. John Hugh and Laurita L. Hill (Paris, 1969), p. 75; Bohemond, Raymond of Toulouse, Duke Godfried of Lotharingia, Duke Robert of Normandy, Count Robert of Flanders, and Count Eustace of Boulogne in their letter to Pope Urban II in Heinrich Hagenmeyer, *Die Kreuzzugsbriefe aus den Jahren 1088–1100* (repr. Hildesheim, 1973), p. 163, and Anselm of Ribemont, in Hagenmeyer, *Die Kreuzzugsbriefe*, p. 159.

[14] *Gesta Francorum*, p. 65. Concerning the Byzantine tradition of the True Cross, see A. Frolow, *Les reliquaires de la vraie croix* (Paris, 1965).

[15] *Gesta Francorum*, p. 65, *Et acceperunt illam cum magno gaudio et timore, fuitque orta immensa laetitia in tota urbe. Ab illa hora accepimus inter nos consilium belli.*

eyewitness accounts and with the reports of later chroniclers, who themselves depended, in part, on oral reports from returning veterans.[16]

However, despite the general rejoicing, not all of the crusaders were equally convinced of the authenticity of the relic found at St Peter's church. Fulcher of Chartres, who served in Baldwin of Boulogne's military household, reported that his lord was suspicious of the object.[17] Scholars generally are agreed that Baldwin's concerns were based in large part on the prestige garnered by Count Raymond of Toulouse, his competitor for dominance among the crusader commanders and Peter Bartholomew's patron. Furthermore, Bishop Adhemar of le Puy, the papal legate, is reported to have been concerned about the relic's status because he had seen at Constantinople an object that was claimed to be the Holy Lance.[18] Nevertheless, in the end no one immediately raised public objections because, as even Fulcher had to admit, most of the crusaders rejoiced to have the relic and treated its discovery as a sign from God.[19]

Indeed, it would be difficult to overstate the importance of the discovery of the Holy Lance for rebuilding the morale of the Christian soldiers battered by fatigue, hunger, and despair. The discovery of this relic, so intimately connected with Jesus' death, was widely interpreted as a manifestation of God's grace upon the army. All of our accounts, both eyewitness and second-hand, are in agreement that the Christian soldiers, who had endured a lengthy siege, were convinced rapidly by the discovery of the Holy Lance that they would triumph

---

[16] Raymond of Aguilers, *Liber*, p. 75, insisted, *quantum gaudium et exultatio civitatem replevit, non possum dicere*. Anselm of Ribemont, a soldier serving in the crusader army, wrote in a letter to Archbishop Manasses of Rheims that, "when this precious gem was found it revived all of our spirits." See *Kreuzzugsbriefe*, p. 159, *ergo ista pretiosa margarita, cor omnium nostrorum revixit*. The commanders of the crusade also emphasized the crucial importance for the morale of the soldiers of the discovery of the Holy Lance and its use in battle. In a letter to Pope Urban II, they stressed that the soldiers were comforted (*confortati*) and strengthened (*corroborati*) by the discovery of the lance so that it was possible for the commanders to urge the men to go into battle in a bold manner (*ad proeliandum audacissimi promptissimique alii alios hortabamur*). On this point, see *Kreuzzugsbriefe*, p. 163. John France, *Victory in the East: A Military History of the First Crusade* (Cambridge, 1994), pp. 278–80, provides a useful review of the main sources treating the Holy Lance.

[17] For a useful survey of the contemporary sources dealing with the Holy Lance as a fake, see Wolfgang Giese, "Die *Lancea Domini* von Antiochia (1098/99)," in *Fälschungen im Mittelalter: Internationaler Kongress der Monumenta Germaniae Historica*, 5 vols. (Hanover, 1988), V: 485–504.

[18] Concerning Bishop Adhemar's private skepticism on this point, see Steven Runciman, "The Holy Lance Found at Antioch," *Analecta Bollandiana* 68 (1950), pp. 197–209; and Morris, "Policy and Visions," pp. 44–5. Adhemar's failure to make public his concerns may have resulted form his close relationship with Raymond of Toulouse with whom he had marched from southern France to Antioch.

[19] Fulcher of Chartres, *Historia Iherosolymitana*, p. 344, *Accidit autem, postquam civitas capta est, a quodam homine lanceam unam inveniri, quam in ecclesia beati Petri apostoli fossa humo repertam, asseverebat esse illam de qua Longinus in latere dextro Christum secundum Scriptores pupugit. Aiebat enim hoc a sancto Andrea apostolo revelatum fuisse. Et quum sic inventa fuisset, et episcopo Podiensi* (Le Puy) *atque Raymundo comiti hoc ipse intimasset, id episcopus falsum esse putavit, comes vero verum speravit. Sed quum omnis populus, hoc audito exsultans, Deum proinde glorificasset, et per centum fere dies ab omnibus in veneratione magna haberetur* . . . (my emphasis).

over a superior enemy force. In addition, the contemporary chroniclers would appear to have wanted their readers to believe that the manner of the Holy Lance's discovery, through the intervention of a saint, indicated that participants in the crusade were particularly conscious of the divine support accorded to their efforts. It would also appear that the writers wanted their readers to believe that the soldiers' morale was so raised up that they could find no other way to describe the event.

Unless we discount entirely the reports of both eyewitnesses and other contemporaries, the discovery of the Holy Lance, and more particularly the inference drawn from it of God's direct intervention in the campaign, played a crucial role in reestablishing the fighting spirit of the crusaders. However, as we will see below, this purported sign from God does not appear to have replaced the practices of military religion common in ordinary wars during the second half of the eleventh century. Following the discovery of the sacred relic by Peter Bartholomew, both the religious and military commanders of the army instituted a program of religious observances in order to prepare the army for combat. Following the practices observed in contemporary secular wars, discussed above, the leaders included some elements that were intended to facilitate the salvation of individual soldiers and others that required a common effort among the men that were intended to earn God's grace for the entire crusading force.

According to the anonymous author of the *Gesta Francorum*, for three days prior to the battle against Kherboga, soldiers, priests, and other non-combatants engaged in religious processions from church to church through Antioch. The lay people, likely including both the soldiers and civilians, were also asked to fast and give alms. The Anonymous noted that after they had completed these penitential rites, the troops confessed and then received absolution for their sins. They then "faithfully received the body and blood of Christ."[20] The efforts of the soldiers were reportedly complemented by special intercessory gifts of alms and masses sung by the priests then serving with the army.[21]

This description of the events at Antioch was considered sufficiently trust-worthy by Robert of Rheims, who worked from both written sources, including the *Gesta*, and various eyewitness accounts, that he described the religious behavior of the soldiers at Antioch in very similar terms.[22] According to this French chronicler, it was Bishop Adhemar of le Puy, with the consent of every-body (*nutu et assensu omnium*), who assigned a three-day fast to all of the crusaders. Robert added that after each man had confessed his sins with a pure heart, all of the soldiers participated in a three-day round of processions, begging for God's mercy.[23] Then, on the third and last day of the processions,

---

[20] *Gesta Francorum*, pp. 67–8, *tandem triduanis expletis ieiuniis, et processionibus celebratis, ab una ecclesia in aliam, de peccatis suis confessi et absoluti, fideliterque corpori et sanguini Christi communicaverunt. . . .*
[21] *Ibid.*, p. 68.
[22] Robert of Rheims, *Historia Iherosolymitana*, p. 827.
[23] *Ibid.*

masses were celebrated in churches throughout the city, and everyone received the body of Christ.[24]

According to the author of the *Gesta Francorum*, the program of religious ceremonies, which had been organized by the leaders of the crusade, continued right up to the moment when the troops went into combat. As the battle lines were formed, bishops, priests, monks, and other clerics, dressed in their sacred vestments (*sacris vestibus induti*), moved among the troops. They carried crosses and prayed to God to protect his soldiers from danger during the battle. Other priests stood on the walls above the gates when the crusaders marched out of the city. They similarly were holding crosses and blessing the troops as they marched below.[25] In the view of the author of the *Gesta*, the prayers and religious symbols carried by the priests and other religious were intended to obtain God's protection for the men as they went into battle.[26] Spurred on by these prayers and protected by the sign of the cross, the men then marched out to fight against the Muslims.[27]

Robert of Rheims recorded that the papal legate Bishop Adhemar preached a sermon to the crusaders just before they attacked the Muslim army. According to the chronicler, Adhemar emphasized three major points, namely that the troops were reconciled to God, that God would aid them in battle, and finally that they should fight bravely in battle. Adhemar began his sermon by identifying himself with the soldiers, calling out "all of us who are baptized in Christ, we are the sons of God and brothers to each other."[28] He then reminded the crusaders of the great suffering they had endured during the course of the siege for their previous sins, and of how this contrasted with their present pure state and reconciliation with God.[29] According to Robert, the papal legate concluded this section of his sermon by emphasizing that no negative result was possible for the crusaders. In fact, he denied the possibility of defeat, insisting that those who died in battle would live forever at Christ's side while the remainder would enjoy the fruits of victory, including glory and spoils from their enemies.[30]

---

24 *Ibid.*, . . . *omnesque sancta Dominici corporis communione communicati sunt.*
25 *Gesta Francorum*, p. 68, *Episcopi nostri et presbyteri et clerici ac monachi, sacris vestibus induti, nobiscum exierunt cum crucibus, orantes et deprecantes Dominum, ut nos salvos faceret et custodiret et ab omnibus malis eriperet. Alii stabant super murum portae, tenentes sacras cruces in manibus suis signando et benedicendo nos.*
26 *Ibid.*, . . . *orantes et deprecantes Dominum, ut nos salvos faceret et custodiret et ab omnibus malis eriperet.* Robert of Rheims, *Historia Iherosolymitana*, p. 847, likewise recorded that priests prayed for victory at the battle before the walls of Antioch chanting psalms.
27 *Gesta Francorum*, p. 68, *Ita nos ordinati et signo crucis protecti, exivimus per portam quae est ante machomariam.*
28 Robert of Rheims, *Historia Iherosolimitana*, p. 829, *omnes qui in Christo baptismati sumus, filii Dei et fratres invicem sumus.*
29 *Ibid.*, *Mementote quantas tribulationes passi estis pro peccatis vestris: sicut nunc vobis innotescere dignatus est in visionibus suis Dominus Deus noster. Nunc vero purgati estis, Deoque per omnia reconciliati. Et quid timeretis.*
30 *Ibid.*, pp. 829–30, *Qui hic morietur, vivente felicior erit quia, pro temporali vita, gaudia adipiscetur aeterna, Qui vero remanserit superstes, super inimicorum suorum triumphabit victoria, divitiis illorum ditabitur et nulla augustiabitur inopia.*

Adhemar is reported to have devoted the second portion of his sermon to a promise of divine aid. First, he paraphrased Joshua 10.25, and told the troops "be comforted and be brave," because the Lord would send legions of angels to avenge them upon their enemies.[31] The papal legate then promised that the Christian troops would see the angels on that day, and warned them not to fear the unaccustomed sight because these angels had come to their aid in the past.[32]

In the final section of his sermon, Adhemar is reported to have encouraged the crusaders to fight bravely. According to Robert, the papal legate called upon the Christian troops to consider how the enemy, "with their necks extended in the manner of frightened deer," would see the approach of a foe better suited to battle than they.[33] He added that the crusaders knew well the ploys of the enemy more accustomed to running than to fighting once they had fired their bows. The sermon concludes with a command for the men to go forth against the enemy in the name of the Lord and of Jesus Christ while calling upon God to be with them in battle.[34]

This *reportatio* of Adhemar's sermon can be understood to indicate a crucial connection between the religious preparation of the crusaders and the availability of divine support. Adhemar stressed that the soldiers had already suffered for their previous sins (*passi estis pro peccatis vestris*) and were reconciled to God (*Deoque per omnia reconciliati*), presumably because of their participation in confession, penitential rites, and communion in the days before the battle. As a consequence, the crusaders could not lose because death would bring eternal salvation and life would bring victory in battle.

This same interconnection between religious preparation and divine aid can be seen in the letters of Anselm of Ribemont, a soldier who prior to the crusade had been in the service of Archbishop Manasses of Rheims. Anselm joined many thousands of his contemporaries in volunteering for the First Crusade, and subsequently fought all the way from Nicaea to Jerusalem. In a letter to Manasses, sent from Antioch, Anselm reported the circumstances surrounding the great victory won by the crusader army over Kherboga, including the important fact that his fellow soldiers prepared themselves for the fight by confessing their sins and receiving communion. He added that the men felt as if they were strongly armored after receiving the body and blood of Christ (*perceptione corporis et sanguinis Christi firmiter armati*), and consequently were prepared to go into battle (*parati ad bellum*).[35] In addition to his emphasis upon the

---

31 *Ibid.*, p. 830, *Confortamini, et estote viri robusti, quoniam jam mittet Dominus legiones sanctorum suorum, qui ulciscentur vos de inimicis vestris.*

32 *Ibid.*, *Non enim debet esse vobis inassueta visio illorum, quoniam vice altera venerunt vobis in auxilium.* It is not clear what event is being mentioned here.

33 *Ibid.*, p. 830, *Considerate quomodo adverarii vestri extento collo, sicut cervi aut damulae pavescentes, adventum vestrum aspiciunt.*

34 *Ibid.*, *Ite igitur contra eos in nomine Domini Jesu Christi ad bellum; et Dominus Deus noster omnipotens sit vobiscum.*

35 Hagenmeyer, *Kreuzzugsbriefe*, p. 160, *Christiani confessione mundati, perceptione corporis et sanguinis Christi firmiter armati, parati ad bellum.* Raymond d'Aguilers, *Liber,* pp. 108–9, described the death scene of Anselm of Ribemont during which the soldier called out to the priests to hear his final confession and then begged God to show him mercy upon

personal preparations of the soldiers, Anselm also stressed the role of the Holy Lance in raising the morale of his fellow crusaders. He pointed out that when the Holy Lance and a piece of the true cross were kept in the front rank of the army, the troops went into battle with the greatest trust (*cum fiducia maxima coeperunt proeliari*).[36] He credited these preparations for obtaining God's aid in driving the Muslims from the field.[37]

In their letter to Pope Urban II, the crusade commanders, including Bohemond, Count Raymond of Toulouse, and Duke Godfried of Lotharingia, likewise emphasized the importance of religious rites in preparing Christian troops for battle against Kherboga. They specifically noted both the participation of the troops in the rite of confession and the presence of the Holy Lance, which made them bold in the face of the enemy.[38] In the first case, the commanders stressed that they trusted in God (*in Deo confidentes*) and consequently confessed all of their sins (*de omnibus iniquitatibus nostris confessi*). In their discussion of the value of the Holy Lance, the commanders claimed that they attacked the strongest part of the enemy force (*ubi maior eorum virtus et fortitudo erat*) with the Holy Lance in the lead.[39] From their point of view, religious practice played an important role both in preparing men for battle and in achieving victory during the fighting.

In considering the nature of the religious beliefs and behavior of the crusaders in the period between the capture of Antioch and the defeat of Kherboga's army outside the walls of the city, it would appear that the discovery of the Holy Lance was an exceptionally important event. Even those chroniclers

---

his death (*Etenim cum mane surrexisset, vocavit ad se sacerdotes, et de negligentiis et peccatiis suis confessus, misericordiam a Deo et ab ipsis deprecabatur, denuntians eis imminere sibi vite sue finem*). It would appear that to the very end of his life Anselm retained his faith in the rite of confession as a means of attaining salvation.

[36] Hagenmeyer, *Kreuzzugsbriefe*, p. 160, *aciebus ergo ordinatis, lancea Domini praeeunte et ligno Dominico cum fiducia maxima coeperunt proeliari.*

[37] *Ibid., Deoque iuvante, praedictos principes Turcorum confusos et omnino victos in fugam verterunt. . . .*

[38] *Ibid.*, p. 163. For a more general overview of the use of the Holy Cross in battle by crusaders, see Alan V. Murray, " 'Mighty Against the Enemies of Christ': The Relic of the True Cross in the Armies of the Kingdom of Jerusalem," in *The Crusaders and their Sources: Essays Presented to Bernard Hamilton*, ed. John France and William G. Zajac (Brookfield, 1998), pp. 217–38. There were times, however, when the relic of the True Cross was used in battles in which the crusaders lost. Within the context of explaining the failure of the relic of the cross to save the crusader army at Hattin, Penny J. Cole, "Christian Perceptions of the Battle of Hattin (583/1187)," *Al-Masaq* 6 (1993), pp. 9–39, here p. 13, has correctly observed that the value of the cross for military operations "must belong to considerations of faith." As a result, defeats in battles were ascribed by contemporaries to the sinfulness of Christians rather than to a defect in the cross.

[39] Hagenmeyer, *Kreuzzugsbriefe*, p. 163, *Sed interim, clementissima Dei omnipotentis misericordia nobis subveniente et pro nobis vigilante, lanceam Dominicam, qua salvatoris nostri latus Longini manibus perforatum fuit . . . cuius inventione aliisque multis divinis revelationibus ita confortati et corroborati fuimus, ut qui ante adflicti et timidi fueramus, tunc ad proelandum audacissimi promptissimique alii alios hortabamur . . . certis ordinibus dispositis, ubi maior eorum virtus et fortitudo erat, audacter requisivimus cum lancea Dominica, et a primo belli statione fugere eos coegimus.*

such as Fulcher of Chartres, who considered the lance to have been a fraud, were forced to admit that the great majority of the crusaders understood Peter Bartholomew's vision as a sign from God that they would receive divine support in their time of need. Indeed, belief in the relic gave them strength to fight.

However, despite this manifestation of God's will, the sources also indicate that soldiers and their leaders, including both clerics and military officers, believed that it was necessary to participate in a wide range of religious rites and ceremonies in order to earn continued divine support for the army, and to ensure the individual salvation of the crusaders who fell in battle. This last point is of great importance because, as we have seen, many of the crusaders are reported to have believed that dying in this campaign earned martyrdom for the soldier. Nevertheless, despite the promise of this exceptionally important spiritual reward, the men still recognized that they were sinful and that it was necessary to reconcile themselves to God through the rites of confession and communion, and through a variety of penitential acts including almsgiving, fasting, and processions.

In considering the impact of the religious experiences and behavior of the soldiers upon the conduct of the crusade campaign in the three-week period extending from the capture of the city to the battle against Kherboga, it would seem clear that the discovery of the Holy Lance had a profoundly positive effect on military morale. This enabled the Christian army to maintain its cohesion as a fighting force despite the number of difficulties it faced. In addition, reports from eyewitnesses indicate that the religious behavior of the fighting men, particularly their participation in the rites of confession and communion, as well as their acceptance of the prayers of the clerics serving with the army, helped to motivate them to fight bravely in battle.

Confession and communion

In considering the descriptive sources for the campaign as a whole, it is evident that the ceremonies and religious rites instituted by the crusade commanders following the discovery of the Holy Lance constituted only a fraction of the total religious preparations undertaken by the soldiers and their supporters over the course of the First Crusade. According to both eyewitness reports and secondary narrative accounts, many of the crusaders were eager to prepare themselves for battle throughout the campaign both by confessing their sins and by receiving the host. In a letter written from the siege camp at Antioch, Anselm of Ribemont reported to Archbishop Manasses that before fighting against a Turkish relief army beneath the walls of Nicaea, both the officers and the men participated in the rite of confession and communion. In describing these religious preparations for battle, Anselm recorded that the men felt purified (*mundati*) by the act of confession (*per confessionem*) and fortified through their reception of the body and blood of Christ (*perceptione corporis et sanguinis Dominis nos ipsos munivimus*).[40]

---

[40] *Ibid.*, p. 144, *tam maiores quam minors per confessionem mundati, perceptione corporis et sanguinis Domini nos ipsos munivimus.*

In describing the battle at Dorylaeum (1 July 1097), Fulcher of Chartres similarly emphasized the crucial role that participation in the rite of confession played in preparing soldiers for battle. According to Fulcher, after being trapped in their camp by a Turkish army, the crusaders gave up hope of physical survival. Fearing that they would die in battle (*mori timentes*), many of the troops rushed to Bishop Adhemar, four other bishops and many other priests serving with them (*multi ad eos currebant*) in order to confess their sins (*confiteor eis peccata sua*).[41] In a similar vein, Albert, a canon at Aachen who composed his text c. 1120 after debriefing returning crusaders of all ranks, described a conversation between Duke Godfried of Lotharingia and a high-ranking Muslim prisoner in which the former explained the basic crusader attitude toward religious rituals before battle.[42] The Lotharingian duke is reported to have emphasized that his men were not afraid to fight because, in addition to serving in a holy cause, they had all received Christ's blood during the rite of communion and thus will have eternal life.[43]

The observations of these writers, who either participated in the crusade itself or discussed the events of the campaign with participants, indicate that taking part in the rites of confession and communion played an important role in maintaining the morale of the troops. Anselm of Ribemont's comment that he and his fellow soldiers felt purified by confession and fortified by the reception of Christ's body and blood strongly suggests that these crusaders went into battle with greater confidence because they had done everything in their power to reconcile themselves with God and thereby gain His favor and support. Indeed, as Duke Godfried is reported to have said in a similar context, the crusaders believed that if they died they would have eternal life (*fiduciam habemus vitae eternae*).[44]

---

41 Fulcher of Chartres, *Historia Iherosolymitana*, p. 335, *Jamque nobis nulla spes vitae. Tunc reos nos et peccatores esse fatebamur, misericordiam a Deo devote postulantes aderat ibi episcopus Podiensis, patronus noster, et quatuor alii, aderantque sacerdotes quamplurimi, albis induti vestimentis, qui Dominum misericordiae suae nobis infunderet. Plorando cantabant, cantando plorabant tunc multi ad eos currebant, qui confestim mori timentes confitebantur eis peccata sua.*

42 Albert of Aachen, *Historia Hierosolymitana*, Recueil des Historiens des Croisades: Historiens Occidentaux, 5 vols. (Paris, 1844–95), IV: 492–3. Concerning the date of Albert's *Historia Hierosolymitana*, see Jean Flori, "Faut-il réhabiliter Pierre l'Ermite: une réévaluation des sources de la prémière croisade," *Cahiers de civilisation médiévale* 38 (1995), pp. 35–54, here p. 38; and Peter Knoch, *Studien zu Albert von Aachen. Der erste Kreuzzug in der deutschen Chronistik* (Stuttgart, 1966), p. 148. Claude Cahen, "A propos d'Albert d'Aix et de Richard le Pèlerin," *Le moyen âge* 96 (1990), pp. 31–3, argues that the text of Albert's work may have been written by two different authors, the first of whom wrote at Aachen and the second of whom wrote in the Holy Land. Cahen suggests that the dividing point between the two texts is the end of the First Crusade and the beginning of the Latin kingdom of Jerusalem.

43 Albert of Aachen, *Historia*, pp. 492–3, *Populus hic quem vides et audis in voce exultationis adversus inimicos Domine Ihesu Christi Dei sui committere, scito quia certus est hodie de corona regni coelororum . . . in sanguine Domini nostri Ihesu Christi filii Dei vivi ab omni inquinamento veteris erroris emundati fiduciam habemus vitae aeternae.*

44 *Ibid.*, p. 493.

Army-wide rites

In addition to providing their troops with the opportunity to prepare themselves individually for battle through participation in the rites of confession and communion, the crusade leaders frequently are reported to have organized army-wide religious rites, many of which had a penitential component.[45] For example, in his eulogy for Bishop Adhemar, who died shortly after the victory over Kherboga, the author of the *Gesta Francorum* included a list of attributes for which the legate was particularly well regarded by the army. Among his worthy deeds, the chronicler reported that Adhemar was accustomed to preach to the soldiers (*predicabat et summonebat milites*) insisting they ought to do good works, particularly caring for the poor, so that they would in turn pray to God on behalf of the fighting men (*pro vestris orent delictis*). The bishop insisted that the troops required these prayers for their own salvation because they continually offended God through their sins (*in multis cotidie offenditis*).[46]

Similarly, Raymond of Aguilers reported that during the most difficult period of the siege at Antioch in early January 1098, as thousands of crusaders suffered in the cold Syrian winter, Bishop Adhemar ordered the troops to participate in a three-day fast complemented by prayers and almsgiving. In addition, the papal legate required the priests serving with the army to spend their time celebrating mass and in prayers while the other clerics recited psalms.[47] According to Raymond, the troubles being experienced by the army were understood to be the result of the crusaders' sinfulness, so that penitential ceremonies were the appropriate means to regain God's favor and support.[48] Indeed, the chronicler's emphasis upon *luxuria* and *rapina* as problems in the crusader camp indicates that the penitential rites organized by Adhemar were intended, at least in part, to tighten army discipline.

The rites carried out before the walls of the city can be compared with Raymond of Aguilers' description of the crusaders' behavior at Antioch following the discovery of the Holy Lance. The same Peter Bartholomew, who had seen Saint Andrew the Apostle in his visions, is reported to have announced

---

[45] Bernard McGinn considers some aspects of the crusaders' piety, particularly the perceived need to expiate the sins committed during the course of the First Crusade, in "*Iter sancti sepulchri*: The Piety of the First Crusaders," in *The Walter Prescott Web Memorial Lectures: Essays on Medieval Civilization,* ed. Bede Karl Lackner and Kenneth Roy Philp (Austin, 1978), pp. 33–72, esp. p. 50.

[46] *Gesta Francorum,* p. 74, *predicabat et summonebat milites, dicens quia: 'nemo ex vobis salvari potest nisi honorificet pauperes et reficiat, vosque non potestis salvari sine illis, ipsisque vivere nequeunt sine vobis. Opportet igitur ut ipsi cotidiana supplicatione pro vestris orent delictis Deum, quem in multis cotidie offenditis. Unde vos rogo ut pro Dei amore eos diligatis, et in quantum potestis eos sustentetis'.* Robert of Rheims, *Historia Iherosolymitana,* p. 839, likewise praised Adhemar for his role in preaching to the troops (*pro his operibus et hujusmodi sermonibus carus erat Deo et omni populo*).

[47] Raymond d'Aguilers, *Liber,* p. 54, *Predicavit in eo tempore episcopus triduanum ieiunium, et cum processione orationes et elemosinas ad populum, ad presbiteros autem mandavit ut vacarent missis et orationibus et clerici psalmis.*

[48] *Ibid., Et licet hoc modo exercitum suum Deus flagellaverit, ut lumini quod in tenebris oriebatur intenderemus, tamen ita quorundum mentes cece et precipites erant ut neque a luxuria, vel rapina revocarentur.*

to the crusader army that the troops had offended the Lord and that each man was responsible for giving alms in order to regain God's good will.[49] According to Raymond, the men acted properly by spending the days before the battle marching in processions through the open areas of the city while calling on the aid of God. He described the soldiers weeping and beating their chests (*lacrimantes et pectora percutientes*) as they marched barefoot (*nudis pedibus*) through the city streets.[50]

These army-wide demonstrations of piety were by no means limited to the period during the siege and capture of Antioch. According to the author of the *Gesta Francorum*, during the siege of Jerusalem itself, bishops and priests preached to the men and told them that they ought to march in processions around the walls of the city, pray, fast, and give alms in a faithful manner before launching their attack.[51] Albert of Aachen recorded the similar organization of army-wide rites in the period after the capture of Jerusalem (15 July 1099). According to the chronicler, the Muslim defenders of the walled town of Assur (Arsit) delivered a sharp defeat to the crusader army that was serving under Godfried's command during the late summer of 1099. Consequently, the duke is reported to have addressed his troops in an attempt to explain the soldiers' defeat and to encourage them to keep fighting despite their losses. From Albert's account, it would appear that Godfried chose to rely upon a message of Christian penitential discipline and reconciliation with God in order to achieve these ends.[52]

The Lotharingian duke is reported to have begun his address in negative terms, calling the men miserable and useless (*miseri et inutiles*) and asking why they had volunteered to come to the Holy Land if it were not to offer up their lives for Jesus, to redeem the church, and to free their brothers from captivity.[53] According to Albert, the duke continued in this negative vein, exhorting the men not to become "feminized" and allow Assur to escape capture. In order to overcome the sinful state into which they had fallen, which was understood by Godfried to be responsible for the Muslim victory, the Lotharingian duke is said to have urged that the crusaders do penance (*agite ergo poenitentiam*) for their foul deeds, cleanse themselves of iniquity, and purge themselves through

---

[49] *Ibid.*, p. 77, *Offendistis omnes graviter, et ideo humiliati estis et clamastis ad Dominum et exaudivit vos Dominus, et nunc unusquisque pro suis offensis se Deo convertat, et .v. elemosinas faciat propter .v. plagas Domini.*

[50] *Ibid.*, p. 80, *O quam beatus populus quem Deus elegit! O quam inmutatam faciem huius exercitus a tristicia in alacritate! quippe preteritis diebus ibant per plateas civitatis Dei auxilium appellantes, ad ecclesias principes et nobiles et hi qui erant de populo nudis pedibus lacrimantes et pectora percutientes adeo tristes. . . .*

[51] *Gesta Francorum*, p. 90, *sed antequam invaderemus eam, ordinaverunt episcopi et sacerdotes predicando et commonendo omnes, ut processionem Deo in circuitu Hierusalem celebrarent, et orationes ac elemosinas et ieiunia fideliter facerent.*

[52] Albert of Aachen, *Historia*, p. 509.

[53] *Ibid.*, *Ah! miseri et inutiles, ad quid de terra et cognatione vestra existis, nisi ut animas vestras usque ad mortem pro nomine Ihesu daretis, et redemptione sanctae Ecclesiae et liberatione confratrum vestrorum . . . Videte ne deficiatis a proposito vestro, et tam viliter effeminati, urbem hanc insuperatam relinquatis.*

confession (*venia et confessione delictorum vestrorum purgati*), thereby reconciling themselves to God. The duke ended his exhortation by insisting that without God's aid the crusaders would not be able to accomplish anything.[54]

According to Albert, after Godfried's harangue, the men were then addressed by Arnulf, who was the cellarer of the Church of the Holy Sepulcher. This cleric is reported to have preached a sermon to the troops in which he accused the soldiers of engaging in sinful behavior, which led to the destruction of their siege engines by the Muslim defenders at Assur.[55] After expounding for some time upon their sins, Arnulf is then reported to have urged all of the crusaders to confess (*ad confessionem cohortatus est*) and to correct their sins.[56] Albert, who was working from the eyewitness reports of men who had served on the First Crusade, emphasized that after Arnulf made his appeal, the soldiers were moved to make full and contrite confessions (*ad compunctionem cordis et veniam culparum suarum . . . eriguntur*).[57] Then, they are reported to have returned to the siege, weeping publicly.[58]

Sermons and penitential rites of the types mentioned above were also complemented on occasion by the massed prayers of the soldiers before they went into battle. On 12 August 1099 the crusader army that had just captured Jerusalem the month before, now faced a large Egyptian army camped outside the southern Palestinian city of Ascalon. According to Orderic Vitalis, who had available reports from Anglo-Norman veterans of the campaign, after the Christians had drawn up in battle lines for a surprise assault at dawn on the Egyptians, the soldiers knelt (*genibus in terram defixis*) for a short time with their eyes turned toward heaven (*oculos devote in coelum erexerunt*) and prayed (*oraverunt*).[59] They are reported to have asked for divine aid (*auxilium de coelo*), which they understood often had been available to them in their time of need on previous occasions. Then, according to Orderic, after the soldiers had prayed for a short time, they raised up the banner of the holy cross (*signum salutifere crucis*) and rode into battle with the greatest confidence. The chronicler concluded that the Christian troops attacked the enemy in a brave manner (*viriliter*) in the name of Jesus.[60]

---

54 *Ibid.*, *Agite ergo poenitentiam luxuriae vestrae foedissimae, quam in hac via sancta incesti coluistis, et omnium iniquitatum vestrarum quibus gratiam Dei offendistis; et sic Deum coeli, apud quem non est iniquitas, venia et confessione delictorum vestrorum purgati, facite vobis placabilem, quia sine illo nichil potestis facere.*

55 *Ibid.*, p. 510, *universos magnos et parvos coepit redarguere de perfidia et duritia cordis . . . .*

56 *Ibid.*, *Idcirco omnes de hac impietate cunctorumque foeditate delictorum, ad confessionem et correctionem paterne cohortatus est.*

57 Although Albert did not personally participate in the First Crusade he makes clear in his preface that he based his history of the expedition upon the reports that he received from eyewitnesses. See *ibid.*, p. 271, *. . . temerario ausu decrevi saltem ex his aliqua memoriae commendare quae auditu et relatione nota fierent ab his qui praesentes affuissent. . . .*

58 *Ibid.*, p. 510, *Sic itaque eo adhortante ad compunctionem cordis et veniam culparum suarum, lacrimis profusis in unam eriguntur ac solidantur voluntatem ad urbis obsidionem.*

59 Orderic Vitalis, *Ecclesiastical History* V: 180.

60 *Ibid.*

Religious support from the home front

Thus far, we have considered the actions of those most directly involved in the military operations of the First Crusade: that is, the soldiers who fought and the priests responsible for their spiritual well-being. However, the crusaders also requested and received religious support from their fellow Christians who did not go on campaign, both those in Europe and in the Holy Land itself. One of the earliest surviving requests for such prayers came from Anselm of Ribemont in a letter to Archbishop Manasses of Rheims written from the siege camp at Antioch in November 1097. Anselm asked first that the archbishop, and whomever else received the letter, pray for the souls of those who had died during the siege of Nicaea.[61] Then Anselm requested that the archbishop and all the others reading his letter pray for the crusading army. He followed this by adding a sharp reminder that the archbishop should not be sluggish in having his bishops also authorize such rites.[62]

The commanders of the crusader army also issued public requests for prayers in a circular letter addressed to "all Christian faithful" sent from the camp at Antioch.[63] The leaders of the expedition described their campaign up to that point and claimed losses in excess of 10,000 men at the siege of Antioch alone. They pointed out that all hope for the Holy Land depended upon their victory over the large Muslim forces arrayed against them and therefore asked that a series of religious rites and ceremonies be celebrated on their behalf. The leaders emphasized that these should include fasts (*ieiunia*), almsgiving (*eleemosynae*), and masses (*missae*).[64]

The effect of these requests and others like them can be seen in a letter sent by Archbishop Manasses to his suffragan Bishop Lambert of Arras during the winter of 1099. Manasses noted that although the holy city of Jerusalem had been captured by crusader forces, the Christians in the Levant still required enormous spiritual support from those remaining at home in Europe. The archbishop pointed out that Pope Paschal II (1099–1118), Duke Godfried of Lotharingia, and Patriarch Arnulf of Jerusalem had all sent letters requesting that prayers be said on behalf of the crusading effort. In order to help fill this need, Archbishop Manasses instructed Bishop Lambert to have prayers said on a regular basis in every parish church in his diocese so that God would support the crusaders against their enemies.[65] The archbishop concluded his letter with

---

[61] Hagenmeyer, *Kreuzzugsbriefe*, p. 145, *rogo autem vos et omnes, ad quos haec epistula pervenerit, ut pro nobis et pro defunctis nostris Deum exoretis.* Concerning this letter, see France, *Victory in the East*, pp. 125 and 133.

[62] Hagenmeyer, *Die Kreuzzugsbriefe*, p. 145, *Iterum atque iterum moneo vos, istius epistulae lectores, ut pro nobis oretis, et te, domine archiepiscope, ut id ipsum episcopis tuis insinuare non pigriteris.*

[63] *Ibid.*, p. 153, *Boemundus, filius Rotberti, atque Raimundus, comes S. Aegidii, simulque Godefridus dux, atque Hugo Magnus maioribus et minoribus totius orbis catholicae fidei cultoribus vitam adispisci perpetuam.*

[64] *Ibid.*, p. 155, *Unde vos omnes precamur, ut inde ieiunia ac eleemosynas missasque cum devotione adsidue faciatis.*

[65] *Ibid.*, p. 176, *commoniti igitur, vocati et compulsi, non solum per litteras domini papae Paschalis verum etiam per preces humillimas Godefridi ducis . . . necnon per domini Arnulfi*

instructions for Lambert to pray for those who had fallen during the campaign, including Bishop Adhemar of le Puy and, sadly enough, Anselm of Ribemont, who had similarly requested prayers for his own fallen comrades two years earlier.[66]

In addition to seeking prayers and other intercessory acts from Christians who had remained in Europe, crusade leaders also organized public religious rites among the Christian populations in the Holy Land. The author of the *Gesta Francorum* recorded that in the days before the battle of Ascalon on 12 August 1099, Tancred, co-commander with Eustace of Boulogne of the Christian forces then in the field, sent messengers to Jerusalem to warn Duke Godfried and the patriarch about a dangerous assembly of Muslim troops and to summon reinforcements.[67] As the army prepared to move out of Jerusalem, Peter the Hermit remained in the city in order to organize religious services among both the Greek and Latin clergy on behalf of the crusaders. According to the chronicler, Peter succeeded in convincing both groups of clergy to don their holy vestments and hold processions through the streets of the city to the Church of the Holy Sepulcher where they celebrated mass, and sang prayers so that God would protect the army in the field.[68] Indeed, from the description provided by the author of the *Gesta*, it would appear that the Latin and Orthodox priests acted jointly on behalf of the Christian forces going into battle.

According to participants in the crusade, the rites carried out on their behalf, both by clerics serving with the army and by priests and lay people at home, were intended to secure divine aid for the Christian forces in the field. Requests for aid of this type are consistent, as seen above, with the efforts of military commanders serving in ordinary wars during the eleventh century to enlist God's support. It must be emphasized, however, that this crusade campaign was established as a divinely sanctioned enterprise, organized and led by papal officers. Consequently, the routine efforts of the crusaders to seek prayers, and other intercessory rites on their behalf, might well be understood to indicate that the crusaders themselves, while believing in the holy nature of their cause, were nevertheless also worried that divine support might be withdrawn.

---

supplicationes mellifluas, quem in patriarchum Hierosoloymitanae sedis unanimiter elegit, vobis mandamus caritate consimili, quatenus per singulas parochiarum vestrarum ecclesias cum ieiuniis et eleemosynis indeficienter orare faciatis, ut Rex regum et Dominus dominantium contra hostes Christianorum regi impendat victoriam. . . .

[66] *Ibid.*

[67] *Gesta Francorum*, pp. 93–4.

[68] *Ibid.*, p. 94, *Petrus vero Heremita remansit Hierusalem, ordinando et precipiendo Grecis et Latinis atque clericis, ut fideliter Deo processionem celebrarent, et orationes elemosinasque facerent, ut Deus populo suo victoriam daret. Clerici et presbyteri, induti sacris vestibus ad Templum Domini conduxere processionem, missas et orationes decantantes, ut suum defenderet populum.* Robert of Rheims, *Historia Iherosolymitana*, p. 873, likewise recorded that Peter the Hermit, in conjunction with the patriarch of Jerusalem, organized public masses, prayers, and processions on behalf of the Christian army.

Remission of sins

For many contemporaries of the First Crusade, including those who actually
went to the Holy Land, this extended campaign (1095–1099) was fundamentally
different from other kinds of wars. Indeed, Pope Urban II (1088–1099) had
summoned the fighting men of Europe to serve in a holy cause and granted
them a special spiritual benefit for doing so. In reference to this "crusade,"
Guibert of Nogent recorded that a type of war was now available to Christians in
which soldiers could have the glorious gift of martyrdom and receive a mark of
eternal praise.[69] Bernold of Constance reported in his *Chronicon* that it had
been established that everyone who participated in the campaign to the East
would receive a *remissio peccatorum*.[70] Ekkehard of Aura claimed in his
Chronicon Universale that this remission of sins would be granted to those who
had renounced all that they possessed and went to the aid of their fellow Christians.[71] Baldric of Dol also noted that the pope had offered a remission of sins,
but he emphasized that in order to receive this spiritual benefit, the fighting men
first had to confess all of their sins.[72]

Modern scholars have various disagreements concerning what Pope Urban
meant by this grant of a spiritual benefit. Nevertheless, it would appear that he
was understood by many crusaders to have promised eternal salvation and the
status of martyr to any soldier who died fighting to recapture Jerusalem from the
enemies of Christ.[73] As we saw above, the author of the *Gesta Francorum*
considered his fallen comrades to be martyrs, noting that many of them had
received martyrdom (*receperunt marytrium*). He added that they now were
triumphant in heaven and carried the stole of their martyrdom.[74] According to
Albert of Aachen, Duke Godfried explained to one of his Muslim prisoners that
the Christian troops were eager to go into battle against the "enemies of Christ"
because they were certain of achieving the crown of the kingdom of the heavens
(*certus est hodie de corona regni coelororum*).[75] Godfried is reported to have
added that the soldiers were not afraid of death or the attacks of their enemies
(*non timemus mortem aut inimicorum impetum*) because they were certain (*certi
sumus*) that an eternal reward (*aeterna remuneratio*) awaited them after this

---

[69] Guibert of Nogent, *Gesta Dei per Francos*, p. 138, *Nunc vobis bella proponimus quae in
se habent gloriosum martyrii munus quibus restat praesentis et aeternae laudis titulus.*
[70] Bernold of Constance, *Chronicon*, ed. G.H. Pertz, MG SS 5 (Hanover, 1844), p. 464, *Nam
et in praeteritis sinodis studiosissime omnes de hac expeditione praemonuit, eamque eis in
remissionem peccatorum faciendum firmissime commendavit.*
[71] Ekkehard of Aura, *Chronicon universale*, ed. G. Waitz, MG SS 6 (Hanover, 1844), p. 213,
*remissionem omnium condonat peccatorum, si, renunciatis omnibus quae possidebant,
crucem post Christum unanimiter portantes, periclitantibus conchristianis ferrent auxilium.*
[72] Baldric of Dol, *Historia Jerosolimitana*, Recueil des Historiens des Croisades: Historiens
Occidentaux, 5 vols. (Paris, 1844–95), IV: 15, *Confessis peccatorum suorum ignominiam
securi de Christo celerem paciscimini veniam.* Concerning Pope Urban II's grant of a
remissio peccatorum, see Brundage, *Medieval Canon Law and the Crusader*, pp. 149–50.
[73] On this point, see Brundage, *Medieval Canon Law and the Crusader*, pp. 149–50.
[74] *Gesta Francorum*, p. 17, *multi ex nostris illic receperunt martyrium . . . Qui in caelum
triumphantes portarunt stolam recepti martyrii. . . .*
[75] Albert of Aachen, *Historia*, pp. 492–3.

temporal existence.[76] The important role played by remission of sin in satisfying crusaders' hopes for eternal life was echoed in a popular contemporary song in which it was claimed "whoever goes there and dies will receive the rewards of heaven (*caeli bona receperit*) and remain with the saints."[77] As a consequence, the promise of a remission of sin, as it was interpreted by soldiers, would seem to have had an exceptionally important role in sustaining morale. It was now possible to kill without having to do penance. Furthermore, to die on campaign now meant the promise of eternal salvation.

Perceptions of the crusade

The perception among contemporaries that the campaigning in the Holy Land entailed a special kind of war is also indicated by the emphasis in descriptive sources on two further aspects of the battlefield experiences of the soldiers that were, if not unique to First Crusade, at least present to an unprecedented degree up to that point. These were the appearance of military saints in combat and the descriptions of priests serving with soldiers in the field. The author of the *Gesta Francorum* insisted that during the battle against Kherboga's army, a huge army appeared to come out of the mountains riding white horses and carrying white banners.[78] He claimed that the crusaders understood that these figures were sent

---

[76] *Ibid., Populus hic quem vides et audis in voce exultationis adversus inimicos Domine Ihesu Christi Dei sui committere, scito quia certus est hodie de corona regni coelororum . . . Idcirco non timemus mortem aut inimicorum impetum, quia certi sumus, post temporalem mortem de aeterna illius remuneratione. Hoc vero signum sanctae crucis, quo munimur et sanctificamur, procul dubio spirituale nobis scutum est contra omnia jacula inimicorum et in eodem signo sperantes, tutius adversus cuncta pericula stare audemus. In hoc utique ligno sanctae crucis redempti sumus de manu mortis et inferi ac potestate Angeli nequam. Et in sanguine Domini nostri Ihesu Christi filii Dei vivi ab omni inquinamento veteris erroris emundati fiduciam habemus vitae aeternae.* Albert's emphasis on Duke Godfried, in whose territories Aachen was situated, may suggest that even if the canon did not have a verbatim account of the duke's conversation he was nevertheless reporting views that were current among important people in Lotharingia.

[77] See G.M. Dreves, *Analecta Hymnica* 45B (1904), p. 78, *Illuc quicumque tenderit/Mortuus ibi fuerit/Caeli bona receperit/Et cum sanctis permanserit*. The message of this song has been discussed by Erdmann, *Origins of the Idea of Crusade*, p. 345; and Ernst H. Kantorowicz, "*Pro patriaMori* in Medieval Political Thought," *The American Historical Review* 56 (1951), pp. 472–92, here p. 480.

[78] *Gesta Francorum*, p. 69, *Exibant quoque de montaneis innumerabiles exercitus, habentes equos albos, quorum vexilla omnia erant alba.* The reports that the crusaders saw saints come to their aid at Antioch were received with interest by chroniclers in Europe. Henry of Huntingdon, *Historia Anglorum*, ed. Diana Greenway (Oxford, 1996), p. 438, linked the appearance of Saint George, Saint Mercurius, and Saint Demetrius to the prayers of bishops, priests, and monks, all dressed in white vestments, who were standing on the walls above the gate where the crusaders were marching to battle against Kherboga. William of Malmesbury, *Gesta Regum Anglorum*, I: 638, was skeptical about the actual appearance of these saints and wrote that the crusaders had persuaded themselves that they saw the ancient martyrs (*Persuadebantque sibi videre se antiquos martyres, qui olim milites fuissent*). However, Orderic Vitalis, *Ecclesiastical History*, V: 112, reported that many Christians and Muslims saw the heavenly army and that both sides considered it a sign from heaven (*Hoc multi viderunt Christianorum et sicut putant gentillum . . . Tandem utrique cognoverant signum de caelo factum . . .*). Cowdrey, "Martyrdom and the First Crusade," pp. 52–3, emphasizes the

by God and that the leaders of this force were Saint George, Saint Mercurius, and Saint Demetrius. Moreover, he insisted that "these things must be believed since many of our men saw them."[79] Similarly, the anonymous author of the *Gesta Francorum Expugnantium Iherusalem* reported that certain of the crusaders witnessed two men on white horses pursuing the fleeing Turks after the battle of Dorylaeum. They were identified by participants as Saint George and Saint Demetrius.[80]

The importance with which the crusaders treated the protection offered by Saint George to the army is also indicated by a story told by Raymond of Aguilers about the experiences of a priest with whom he was personally acquainted. According to the chronicler, the priest reported he had been visited by a saint, who turned out to be Saint George. At first the priest did not recognize him and asked who he was. The saint responded by asking "do you not know the name of the standard bearer of this army?" After considering the question for a moment the priest responded "it is said that Saint George is the standard bearer of this army" and in this manner finally recognized his visitor.[81] Raymond's account would appear to suggest that a noteworthy section of the crusader force identified George as a special patron of their army. The respect with which this saint was viewed by the crusaders is further indicated by Orderic Vitalis' observation that veterans from the battle of Antioch thought so highly of Saint George that on the march south from Antioch toward Jerusalem they had their bishop dedicate a church to him just outside of Ramla where he was thought to have been martyred.[82] Robert of Rheims, working with a different group of sources, noted that the soldiers arriving at Ramla gave a tithe of all of their property in order to pay for the construction of this church that was to be dedicated to Saint George.[83]

If intensity of religious feeling was partly responsible for visions of warrior saints among the troops, as most soldiers believed, then the overtly religious justification for this military campaign may explain one of the more striking

importance of warrior saints in indicating the role of martyrdom in the self-conception of the crusaders.

[79] *Gesta Francorum*, p. 69, *Hec verba credenda sunt, quia plures ex nostris viderunt.*

[80] *Gesta Francorum expugnantium Iherusalem*, Recueil des Historiens des Croisades: Historiens Occidentaux, 5 vols. (Paris, 1844–95), III: 496, *Relatum est ergo postea a quibusdam quia duo equites in albis vestibus, super equos albos sedentes, Turcos per triduum persequerentur dicentes unum fuisse Georgium, alterum vero Demetrium, martyres gloriosos.* The main source for the *Gesta Francorum expugnantium Iherusalem* was Fulcher of Chartres' *Historia Iherosolymitana.* See Recueil des Historiens des Croisades: Historiens Occidentaux, III: XXXVI. However, Fulcher did not include this story in his account.

[81] Raymond d'Aguilers, *Liber*, p. 133, *'An ignoras quis sit vexillifer huius exercitus?'* . . . *Et tunc sacerdos ait, 'Domine dicitur de sancto Georgio quod sit vexillifer exercitus huius.'*

[82] Orderic Vitalis, *Ecclesiastical History*, V: 154–6, recorded that the Christian soldiers considered Saint George to be their defender and therefore built a church in order to demonstrate their respect for him (*Hunc quem Christiani viderant in bello Antiocheno preambulum et precursorem et contra gentem erroneam validum propugnatorem volebant etiam promereri semper socium et defensorem. Basilicam eius reverenter honoraverunt et episcopum ut diximus Ramulae constituerunt*).

[83] Robert of Rheims, *Historia Iherosolymitana*, p. 859.

images of priests found throughout narrative accounts of the crusades. As we have already seen, when describing the last-minute religious preparations before the battle against Kherboga at Antioch, the author of the *Gesta Francorum* emphasized that the bishops, priests, clerics, and monks were dressed in their sacred vestments (*sacris vestibus induti*) as they prayed to God on behalf of the soldiers.[84] Similarly, in his account of the siege of the city of Marra, priests praying on behalf of the soldiers are reported to have been dressed in *sacris vestibus*, as were the priests marching in processions on behalf of the crusader army at Ascalon.[85] In his description of the battle of Antioch, Raymond of Aguilers also recorded that priests and monks wore their white stoles while they moved among the troops before the battle against Kherboga.[86] Like his counterparts, Fulcher of Chartres described the priests providing pastoral care to the soldiers at Antioch as dressed in white vestments (*albis indutis vestimentis*).[87] He used the same language to characterize the priests serving with the army at Dorylaeum.[88] Robert the Monk noted that when one of Bohemond's chaplains was explaining a vision of a white clad army, he compared them to priests wearing their whitened stoles (*sacerdotes stolis dealbati*).[89] For his part, Albert of Aachen portrayed the patriarch of Jerusalem dressed in his holy white stole (*stola sancta et candida*) as he prayed for the crusaders attacking the city of Caesarea in 1101.[90]

The image of a priest wearing his vestments in the moments before battle began would appear to have made a powerful impression on both lay and clerical observers. These stoles were meant to separate priests from the lay society in which they functioned, and were, moreover, one of the preeminent symbols of their right to celebrate mass and therefore to intercede with God on behalf of the army.[91] Chroniclers concerned with the crusade as a holy campaign and as a penitential endeavor would appear to have focused more attention on the symbol of a priest's office than was normally the case in narratives describing contemporary secular wars.[92]

---

[84] *Gesta Francorum*, pp. 67–8.

[85] *Ibid.*, pp. 78–9 and 94.

[86] Raymond d'Aguilers, *Liber*, p. 81, *Etenim sacerdotes et multi monachi induti stolis albis ante acies militum nostrorum pergebant Dei adiutorium et sanctorum patrocinia invocando cantantes.*

[87] Fulcher of Chartres, *Historia Hierosolymitana*, p. 348.

[88] *Ibid.*, p. 335.

[89] Robert of Rheims, *Historia Iherosolymitana*, p. 797. The chaplains made these remarks while speaking with an Antiochene guard captain, who is supposed to have had a vision of a white-clad army fighting on behalf of the crusaders. This was the same guard captain whom Bohemond convinced to betray the city, making possible its capture by the Christian army.

[90] Albert of Aachen, *Historia Hierosolymitana*, p. 544.

[91] In order that their peculiar status remain clear to all observers priests were also forbidden by episcopal statute to dress like laymen. For example, the Statutes of Westminster in 1102 insisted that priests wear monochromatic clothing. Concerning this point, see *Councils and Synods* (Oxford, 1981), II: 676.

[92] In an earlier example of this same phenonemon, Bishop Ulrich of Augsburg is reported to have worn his stole during the siege of the city by Hungarians in 955. Gerhard of Augsburg, *Vita S. Oudalrici*, p. 196.

Summary observations

The religious behavior of the participants in the First Crusade demonstrated significant elements of continuity as well as important innovations as compared to the conduct of soldiers in the conventional wars of the later eleventh century. Among the elements carried over from ordinary warfare, we can include the continual emphasis on the importance of the rites of confession and communion, penitential rites, the perceived value of relics on the battlefield, and preaching, as well as intercessory masses and prayers organized both within the army itself and among non-combatant supporters of the soldiers.

The most striking developments in the religion of war would seem to have resulted from soldiers' perception of the crusade as a new type of war that was by nature holy. Thus, there would appear to have been a significant diminution in the concern expressed by contemporaries for the fate of the souls of men who died on campaign. Indeed, participants emphasized that they considered their fallen comrades to be martyrs and of course saved. Although soldiers serving in earlier wars had occasionally received recognition as martyrs, particularly during the second half of the eleventh century, the concentrated emphasis on martyrdom in the context of the First Crusade does mark a noteworthy change in scale if not substance.[93] In addition, the soldiers appear to have perceived a more direct divine intervention in battle than was traditionally the case in secular warfare. Certainly, the invocation of saints and even the appearance of saints was not unprecedented in earlier wars. However, the emphasis placed by chroniclers of the Crusade upon the physical manifestation of George, Demetrius, Mercurius, and their army riding white horses and wielding golden arms, is an innovation. Finally, the repeated emphasis placed by numerous observers on the fact that priests wore gleaming white stoles while carrying out their duties suggests that the sacerdotal office had taken on a new importance in the minds of soldiers and others serving in this campaign. As we have seen in previous chapters, priests regularly accompanied armies into the field. However, it is only in the context of the First Crusade that observers chose to emphasize in such a consistent manner that element of their appearance which marked priests as God's agents on earth.

In considering the impact of religion upon the conduct of the crusade, it would appear that the perceptions of soldiers concerning their participation in a divinely inspired and sanctioned war on behalf of Christ against Muslims had an important role in forging the polyglot contingents from across Europe into a manifestly Christian army, bound together by a strong *esprit de corps*. This unity is indicated by the reactions of the great majority of crusaders following the discovery of the Holy Lance, when they are reported to have rejoiced in this manifestation of God's support for them as Christians. Similar feelings of unity can be observed in the reports of battlefield sermons and harangues delivered to the crusaders in which speakers repeatedly emphasized the duties of the soldiers as Christians to serve God in his holy cause. In this context, it should be noted that none of the surviving *reportationes* dealing with addresses to soldiers contain references to the ethnic or political allegiances of the troops, indicating

---

93 On this point, see Cowdrey, "Martyrdom and the First Crusade," pp. 48–51.

that these differentiated identities had been subsumed within the unifying concept of a Christian army.

In addition to helping to forge army cohesion, religion would also appear to have played in important role in maintaining the morale of the soldiers. In the single most dramatic case, the discovery of the Holy Lance at Antioch is reported by many contemporaries to have inspired the crusaders and convinced them that they could defeat Kherboga's army. Crusade leaders would appear to have maintained the day-to-day morale of the troops by organizing periodic penitential rites such as those instituted by Adhemar of le Puy during the siege of Antioch and by Duke Godfried of Lotharingia during the siege of Arsuf. In addition, as was the case in ordinary wars of the eleventh century, soldiers would appear to have been inspired to fight more bravely in battle by confessing their sins and receiving communion before going into combat. We are told by contemporaries that soldiers saw these rites as the best means of reconciling themselves with God and thereby preparing their places in heaven.

Finally, throughout the First Crusade, military officers and religious leaders would appear to have identified religious observances, particularly penitential rites, with the maintenance of army discipline. Thus, for example, Adhemar of le Puy is reported to have ordered the soldiers besieging Antioch to march in processions, fast, and give alms as a result of their sinful behavior. Similarly, both Duke Godfried of Lotharingia and Arnulf, the cellarer of the Church of the Holy Sepulcher, Jerusalem, insisted that solders at the siege of Arsuf in 1099 give up their sinful behavior and demonstrate their rededication to the crusader cause by confessing their sins. By seeking to combat indiscipline among the crusaders through the imposition of penitential rites, officers and clerics would appear to have concluded that religion was an effective means of maintaining appropriate standards of behavior in the army.

The Religion of War during the Crusades 1100–1215

In general, the source materials available for the study of the religious behavior and beliefs of crusaders are not as rich for the period after 1100 as they are for the First Crusade. The surviving sources that do contain information of value to the study of wartime religion may usefully be divided into four groups, corresponding chronologically to the Second, Third, Fourth, and Albigensian Crusades. In each case, however, the sources that contain material relevant to the religious behavior of the crusaders during these crusades is limited to particular campaigns that were not necessarily the most important or the most interesting from other points of view. Nevertheless, they do indicate the kinds of behaviors that were maintained by participants in those campaigns at least, and in all likelihood these did not differ greatly from what was maintained by their contemporaries in other campaigns of the same crusade.

The Second Crusade: Lisbon Expedition, 1147–1148
In marked contrast to the First Crusade, the Lisbon campaign, which was carried out in the wider context of the Second Crusade, has not received extensive

attention from scholars.[94] Nevertheless, the events of this expedition and the behavior of the soldiers, including their religious behavior, are described in great detail in an account entitled *De expugnatione Lyxbonensi*.[95] The author of the text was almost certainly a Norman-French priest named Raol who had close connections with the Glanville family of East Anglia.[96] The text itself is a narrative of Raol's participation in the campaign and a description of the experiences of the polyglot army composed of contingents from Flanders, Boulogne, the Rhineland, Normandy, and England, under the leadership of six lay commanders. His narrative encompasses the expedition from the time of its departure from Dartmouth, England for Portugal on 23 May 1147 until the capture of Lisbon on 28 June 1148.[97] Raol's account is exceptionally valuable both for its discussion of the links between military religion and parish practice

[94] The standard monographic works concerning the Second Crusade remain B. Kugler, *Studien zur Geschichte des zweiten Kreuzzuges* (Stuttgart, 1866); *Analekten zur Geschichte des zweiten Kreuzzuges* (Tübingen, 1878); and *Neue Analekten* (Tübingen, 1883). There are several specialist studies dealing with particular aspects of the Second Crusade, including Giles Constable, "The Second Crusade as Seen by Contemporaries," *Traditio* 9 (1953), pp. 213–79, repr. with the same pagination in *Religious Life and Thought* (London, 1979); the collection of essays in *The Second Crusade and the Cistercians*, ed. Michael Gervers (New York, 1992); and Alan J. Forey, "The Second Crusade: Scope and Objectives," *Durham University Journal* n.s. 55: 2 (1994), pp. 165–75. Also see the brief discussion by Christopher Tyerman, *England and the Crusades 1095–1588* (Chicago, 1988), pp. 32–5. For a dated but still useful survey of the Second Crusade as a whole, see Virginia G. Berry, "The Second Crusade," in *A History of the Crusades*, ed. Kenneth M. Setton, 6 vols. (Madison, 1969–89), II: 463–512.

[95] *De expugnatione Lyxbonensi*, ed. Charles Wendell David (New York, 1936). As might be expected, the interests of contemporary observers varied greatly over time and consequently there often is little consistency in the matters they chose to record. Thus, for example, Bishop Otto of Freising, who accompanied King Conrad III of Germany on the Second Crusade, reported that after the destruction of the crusader camp at Chörobacchi, the leaders gathered at Duke Frederick of Swabia's (Barbarossa's) tent where they heard mass and sang the *Gaudeamus*. See *Ottonis episcopi Frisingensis et Rahewini gesta Frederici; seu rectius, cronica*, ed. Franz-Josef Schmale, 2nd edn (Darmstadt, 1974), p. 222. However, he had nothing to say about the religious behavior of the German soldiers during the march through Anatolia where Conrad's army was destroyed as a fighting force. Concerning Otto of Freising's reticence on this point, see Constable, "The Second Crusade," p. 220. Similarly, Odo of Deuil, *De profectione Ludovici VII in orientem*, ed. Virginia Gingerick Berry (New York, 1948), discusses the religious behavior of French priests serving with King Louis' crusade army in one case but does not deal with the religious behavior of soldiers or priests in a systematic manner. In this particular case Odo reports that when French clerics celebrated mass along the line of march in Orthodox territories, Greek priests would subsequently purify the altars as if they had been defiled. Odo of Deuil, *De profectione*, p. 54, *nam si nostri sacerdotes missas super eorum altaria celebrabant, quasi essent profanata lustrando et abluendo postea expiabant*. Concerning the importance of Odo's narrative for the history of the French campaign during the Second Crusade, see Constable, "The Second Crusade," p. 217, where he argues that *De profectione* is "without question the most important single work on this campaign and at the same time a remarkable historical document."

[96] Concerning the identity of the author, see Harold Livermore, "The 'Conquest of Lisbon' and its Author," *Portuguese Studies* 6 (1990), pp. 1–16.

[97] Jonathan Phillips, "Ideas of Crusade and Holy War in *De expugnatione Lyxbonensi* (The Conquest of Lisbon)," in *The Holy Land, Holy Lands, and Christian History*, ed. R.N. Swanson (Woodbridge, 2000), pp. 123–41, provides a valuable introduction to this text.

– information not readily available in other contexts – and for his introduction to certain extraordinary religious measures in effect during this campaign, namely weekly confession and reception of communion.

Raol began his narrative by emphasizing that the various contingents of the crusading army, each of which spoke a different language, pledged to maintain peace and concord among themselves. The author then indicates that these pledges of friendship were to be guarantied by a series of regulations, described as very strict laws (*leges severissimae*).[98] These "leges severissimae" included forbidding the display of costly garments, requirements to keep women out of the public eye, and a strict rule providing that all injuries had to be compensated for on a one-to-one basis so that a life had to repaid with a life (*mortuum pro mortuo*).[99]

The leaders of the expedition also included provisions in the "campaign code" that dealt with the religious behavior of the soldiers and the pastoral care that they were to receive. First, each ship in the crusader fleet was required to have a priest aboard.[100] This regulation would appear to indicate that the crusade leaders took very seriously the role played by religion in the conduct of a military campaign. Having a priest aboard each ship required an extensive investment in personnel. Indeed, the sources are in agreement that there were no fewer than 164 ships in the crusader fleet.[101]

The second of the statutes, dealing with religious matters, required soldiers to participate in the same round of weekly religious observances to which they were accustomed from their experiences in their home parishes.[102] The commanders of the expedition would appear to have expected not only that their men had a normal routine of religious behavior at home, but that, in addition, it was a good idea for them as soldiers to maintain this same routine. Unfortunately, the chronicler did not discuss the details of normal parish religious life in this context, probably because this information was so well known that its repetition would have been boring to his audience.

Finally, the statutes included the additional requirements that every soldier confess his sins (*confiteor*) at least once each week and receive communion (*communicare*) every Sunday.[103] These regulations exceeded to a significant

---

[98] *De expugnatione Lyxbonensi*, p. 56, *Inter hos tot linguarum populos firmissima concordie atque amicitie pignora; insuper leges severissimas sanxerunt, ut mortuum pro mortuo, dentem pro dente.*

[99] *Ibid.*

[100] *Ibid.*, . . . *ut singule naves singulos presbyteros haberent.* . . .

[101] Concerning the size of the fleet, see *ibid.*, p. 52; *Annales Sancti Disibodi*, ed. G. Waitz, MG SS 17 (Hanover, 1861), p. 27, *14 kal. Iunii venimus in portum Angliae qui Derthmute dicitur ubi comitem A. de Areschoth cum 200 fere navibus tam Anglorum quam Flandrensium invenimus;* and *Indiculum fundationis monasterii Beati Vincentii*, ed. Alexandre Herculano, in Portugaliae Monumenta Historica Scriptores I (Lisbon, 1856), p. 91. Further information about the size of the army can be gleaned from Sigebert's *Continuatio Praemonstratensis*, ed. G. Pertz, MG SS 6 (Hanover, 1844), p. 453, who put the total Christian force at the siege of Lisbon at 13,000 men.

[102] *De expugnatione Lyxbonensi*, p. 56, . . . *eadem que in parrochiis observari iubentur.*

[103] *Ibid., Ut singuli singulis hebdomadibus confiterentur et die dominico communicarent.*

extent the normal and expected participation by lay people in the rites of confession and communion under more peaceful conditions.[104] Indeed, under normal circumstances even monks were not required generally to confess and receive the host on such a frequent basis.[105] The commanders of the expedition may have believed that the frequent practice of this rite was a means of keeping their men under tight discipline by forcing them to admit all wrongdoing on a regular basis. Indeed, it does not seem unreasonable to suggest that the religious rites normally associated with cleansing oneself of sin and becoming reconciled to God might have been understood by the crusaders as an important means of enforcing the stringent campaign regulations (*leges severissimae*) that they had adopted at Dartmouth.

The desire of the crusade commanders, as indicated by the promulgation of the code of conduct for the campaign, to create a climate of adherence both to familiar religious practice and military discipline was reiterated by Bishop Peter of Oporto, who preached to the crusader army soon after the troops landed in Portugal.[106] In the course of his sermon, Peter stressed that because of their participation in the holy work of the crusade, the soldiers had been reborn through a new baptism of penance.[107] According to the chronicler, the bishop added that the soldiers had been vested with Christ (*Christum induistis*) and received anew an immaculate cloak of innocence (*vestis innocentie*).[108] He then urged the fighting men in his audience to keep themselves pure and resist all temptations, particularly lust, so that their souls and minds would be a temple

---

[104] In the Carolingian period, lay people had been required to confess once, or at most three times a year. On this point, see Avril, "Remarques sur un aspect de la vie religieuse paroissiale," pp. 345–63. As late as 1215 the delegates to the Fourth Lateran Council decided that lay people should only be required to confess their sins once a year. Fourth Lateran Council, c. 21 in *Concilium Oecumenicorum*, p. 221.

[105] Even among fighting orders of monks such as the Teutonic Knights confession was only required seven times a year for the brothers. See *Die Statuten des Deutschen Ordens*, ed. Max Perlbach (Halle, 1890), p. 36. The Templars were supposed to go to confession thirteen times a year. See *The Rule of the Templars*, trans. J.M. Upton Ward (Woodbridge, 1992), p. 98.

[106] The chronicler reported that Bishop Peter of Oporto gave his sermon in Latin so that it could then be translated into the language of each of the individual companies making up this expedition. On this point, see *De expugnatione Lyxbonensi*, p. 70, *Indicto ab omnibus silentio, episcopus sermonem coram omnibus lingua Latina habuit, ut per interpretes cuiusque lingue sermo eius omnibus manifestatur. . . .*

[107] Concerning Bishop Peter's sermon, see Ernst-Dieter Hehl, *Kirche und Krieg im 12. Jahrhundert: Studien zu kanonischem Recht und politischer Wirklichkeit* (Stuttgart, 1980), pp. 259–67, who analyzes its rhetorical structure; and Phillips, "The Ideas of Crusade," pp. 127–33.

[108] *De expugnatione Lyxbonensi*, p. 72, *Ecce filii karissimi, novo penitentie renati baptismate, Christum induistis iterum, vestem innocentie ut immaculatum custodiatis iterum susceptistis.* As early as 1148, Peter Lombard had argued that the sacrament of penance (*poenitentia*), consisting of contrition (*compunctio cordis*), confession (*confessio oris*) and satisfaction (*satisfactio operis*), was the only means of removing the stain of sin from one's soul after baptism, presumably because penance was repeatable while baptism was not. See Peter Lombard, *Sententiae in iv distinctae*, ed. Collegiis Bonaventura ad Claras Aqua (Rome, 1981), Lib. IV Dist. XVI Cap II. and Dist. XIV Cap. II, 1.

for God.[109] According to the chronicler, however, the pure spirit with which the soldiers began the campaign was not treated by the bishop of Oporto as a guarantee against their falling again into sin at a later time. Rather, the prelate urged them to be mindful constantly of the traps, particularly envy, which remained before them, so that they could retain their pure state (*pura sit innocentia mentis*).[110] His arguments in this regard, as they were recorded by Raol, are consistent with the efforts of the military commanders to have their men avoid displaying temporal wealth during the campaign and to engage in weekly confession.

In addition to his discussion of Bishop Peter's sermon, Raol also described an episode during the siege of Lisbon itself when a priest, probably the author himself, preached to the crew of one of the crusaders' siege engines shortly before it was to be put into active service.[111] This sermon was intended to emphasize two points: first, that God and his angels protected good Christians as they went into battle, and second that in order to be good Christians soldiers had to reconcile themselves with God. Raol began his sermon by claiming that one great solace for human weakness is the fact that each person has a guardian angel watching out for him.[112] He also warned, however, that anyone who transgressed and sinned had separated himself from the angel's protection and must reconcile himself to God. This was to be accomplished through penance (*per penitentiam*).[113] Raol emphasized to his audience that the prize of salvation was offered to those who began the crusade as voluntary exiles on behalf of Christ, but that this prize was only given to those who persevered.[114] Once again, he added that it was necessary for the soldiers to trust in God and to reconcile themselves with him. Raol repeated the words preached by Bishop Peter of Oporto, telling the soldiers that they must again vest themselves with Christ so that they could be his immaculate sons.[115] Then he reminded the men that God always shows favor to those who make worthy requests and never denies

---

[109] *De expugnatione Lyxbonensi*, pp. 72–4, *Videte ne iterum post concupiscentias vestras abieritis . . . Animum purgate, id est mentem, in sanctificatum Deo templum.* Although he did not specifically refer to the doctrine of remission of sins, the bishop appears to have been thinking along those lines when discussing rebirth in the baptism of penance. The preacher's emphasis on lust in his sermon to the crusaders going to Lisbon resembles the remarks, noted above, made by Duke Godfried to the Christian soldiers besieging Arsuf in 1099.

[110] *Ibid.*, p. 74.

[111] Concerning Raol's sermon, see Phillips, "Ideas of Crusade," p. 137.

[112] *Ibid.*, p. 146, *Magnum enim fragilitatis humane solatium, unumquemque angelum sibi delegatum custodem habere sui . . . .*

[113] *Ibid.*, p. 148, *Et si ab angeli vestri custodia deviastis, reconciliari studete Domino per penitentiam. . . .*

[114] *Ibid.*, p. 152, *Et vos, fratres karissimi, Christum sequuti, exules spontanei, qui pauperiem voluntariam suscepistis audite et intelligite, qui inchoantibus promittitur se perseverantibus premium donatur.*

[115] *Ibid.*, p. 154, *Reconciliamini iterum Deo et reinduite Christum, ut sitis filii eius immaculati.*

forgiveness to those who confess their sins (*confitentibus numquam veniam negare consuevit*).[116]

The priest concluded his sermon by instructing them to adore Christ their lord who had spread his hands and feet on this wood, which is portrayed in the text as a relic of the true cross, for their salvation, adding that if they did not hesitate under this standard (*vexillum*) they would have victory in battle. The priest promised that whoever was touched by this cross would not really die if he fell in battle but would instead go to a much better place. As a result "to live was to have glory and to die meant riches [eternal salvation]."[117] Finally, he blessed the soldiers and marked each one with the sign of the cross.[118]

Both the regulations for the religious behavior of the soldiers participating in the Lisbon campaign and the reports of sermons delivered to these troops indicate that many of the crusade leaders, and probably the soldiers as well, believed proper religious behavior would have a positive effect on the outcome of the war. However, the chronicler also described an episode from the Lisbon campaign that suggests that not all soldiers were equally religious, and that in some cases the men had to be convinced by the immediacy of danger that they ought to fulfill their ritual obligations. He explained that shortly before reaching Portugal, the crusader fleet was tossed about by an unexpected storm. According to the chronicler, during the worst hours when their ships looked like they might sink, many penitent crusaders came forward to confess their sins all the while pouring out tears and moaning.[119] The chronicler suggested that for some of these men, contrition and penance were not part of their normal activities, noting that the troops participated in the rites "whatever the original [impure] circumstances of their having taken the crusading vow."[120] The chronicler's observation on this point serves as a reminder that even in a holy war individual soldiers could and did have a range of religious beliefs. For some men, it was only the immediate threat of death that made it desirable to participate in the religious rituals organized on their behalf.

The chronicler's description of the organization of religious rites by crusade commanders and the religious behavior of the crusaders indicates that they saw this campaign as a special kind of war requiring a particularly heightened religious awareness from the participants. God was understood to be on their side because they were serving in a Christian cause for holy ends. In this manner, the

---

[116] *Ibid., Non enim ego sed Dominus, qui digne petentibus semper annuit et favet, confitentibusque numquam veniam negare consuevit.*

[117] *De expugnatione Lyxbonensi*, pp. 154–6, *Videbitis auxilium Domini super vos. Adorate Dominum Christum, qui in hoc salutifere crucis ligno manus expandit et pedes in vestram salutem et gloriam. In hoc vexillo, solum non hesitetis, vincetis. Quia si quem hoc insignitum mori contigerit, sibi vitam tolli non credimus, sed in melius mutari non ambigimus. Hic ergo vivere gloria est, et mori lucrum.*

[118] *Ibid.*, p. 158, *Iterumque ad iussum a sacerdotis omnes erecti, venerabili crucis dominice signo in nomine Patris et Filli et Spiritus Sancti consignati sunt.*

[119] *Ibid.*, p. 60, *Quanti illic penitentes, quanti peccata et negligentias cum luctu confitentes et gemitu, peregrinationis sue conversionem utcumque inceptam, inundatione lacrimarum diluentes, in ara cordis contriti Deo sacrificabant.*

[120] *Ibid., . . . peregrinationis sue conversionem utcumque inceptam. . . .*

participants in the Lisbon campaign can be understood to have shared the crusading mentality of their predecessors who served in the First Crusade. However, it is also clear that significant elements of the religious practices required of the crusaders in the Lisbon expedition had no analog in the earlier crusading effort or in ordinary warfare of the eleventh century. In particular, the requirement imposed by the commanders of the expedition, who were laymen, that each of the soldiers confess his sins weekly and receive communion was an extraordinary extension of traditional practice.

Emperor Frederick Barbarossa's Crusade 1189–1190

The Third Crusade as a whole has received extensive attention, largely as a result of the magnetic attraction exerted by King Richard I of England on the modern imagination. Unfortunately, however, contemporary accounts dealing with his crusade as well as with the campaign launched by King Philip II of France have comparatively little to say about the religious lives of English and French crusaders.[121] By contrast, Emperor Frederick Barbarossa's crusade attracted the attention of chroniclers who were interested in emphasizing the important role that religious rites and ceremonies played in the course of the Germans' march through Anatolia. An examination of Barbarossa's campaign has the added benefit to this study of having ended in failure following Frederick's death by drowning in the Saleph river (Gök Su river) on 10 June 1190. It is therefore possible to consider descriptions of the religious behavior of soldiers in a campaign that, by contrast with the First Crusade and the Lisbon expedition, chroniclers writing *post hoc* knew had failed to achieve any noteworthy gains against the Muslims.

When Emperor Frederick I (1153–1190) took his crusading army to war in 1189, he and his military staff had almost four decades of experience maintaining soldiers in the field.[122] As we shall see in the next chapter, they were aware of the crucial role that religious preparations played in maintaining an army as an effective fighting force. It is, therefore, not surprising that in order to

---

[121] As we saw in the previous section, descriptive evidence concerning one or another aspect of the religious behavior of soldiers and their supporters has survived unevenly. In examining the sources dealing with the French and English campaigns under King Philip II and King Richard I in the period 1190–1192, including Ambroise, *L'estoire de la guerre sainte: histoire en vers de la troisième croisade (1190–1192)*, ed. Bruno Paulin Gaston (Paris, 1897); *Itinerarium peregrinorum et gesta regis Ricardi*, ed. William Stubbs in *Chronicles and Memorials of the Reign of Richard I*, 2 vols., Rolls Series 38 (London, 1864); Richard of Devizes, *De rebus gestis Ricardi primi*, ed. Richard Howlett in *Chronicles of the Reigns of Stephen, Henry II, and Richard I*, vol. 3, Rolls Series 82 (London, 1886); and Rigord, *Gesta Philippi Augusti*, ed. H.F. Delaborde in *Oeuvres de Rigord et Guillaume le Breton* (Paris, 1885), I have found no noteworthy evidence for military religious practice. One reason for the lack of attention in these chronicles to the religious behavior of soldiers may be the almost complete absence of major battles involving the French and English armies. The only battle of any size fought by the forces of Richard and Philip during the Third Crusade was the defeat of an ambush at near Arsuf on 6 September 1192.

[122] The most recent and thorough account of Frederick I's crusade is Edgar N. Johnson, "The Crusades of Frederick Barbarossa and Henry VI," in *The History of the Crusades II*, ed. Peter Lee Wolf and Harry W. Hazard (Madison, 1969), pp. 87–122.

provide a sufficiently large cadre of priests to lead the religious exercises required by his troops, Frederick recruited at least nine prelates – including the bishops of Liège, Würzburg, Passau, Regensburg, Basel, Meissen, Osnabrück, Toul, and Tarentaise – to serve on this campaign, along with their episcopal *familiae*.[123] Imperial bishops had long played an important role in providing chaplains for service in Barbarossa's Italian campaigns, and the emperor now made use of their support for the largest military undertaking of his reign.[124] Complementing the personnel available in the episcopal entourages were priests who served in the military household of the emperor himself, as well as in the *familiae* of his secular officers, counts, and dukes.[125]

One of the best surviving sources for the religious conduct of the soldiers in the imperial crusading army is the *Historia de expeditione Friderici Imperatoris* (HEF) whose still-anonymous author has been identified by scholars as an inti-mate of the emperor.[126] This chronicler periodically interrupted his description of the army's progress through Anatolia in order to describe the range of reli-gious activities in which the German troops participated. As we saw in the context of the First Crusade, it was not unusual for military commanders to impose fasts upon their troops in the hope that this act would make them worthy of God's support. Consequently, it is not surprising that the author of HEF recorded that Barbarossa's army also participated in this penitential rite when battle against the Turks seemed imminent. On one occasion, the author described a fast undertaken by the troops on the vigil of Pentecost (12 May 1190). He stressed that the men, including himself, worked all night long "starving" and surrounded on all sides by Turkish forces.[127] According to the

---

123 *Ibid.*, p. 92.

124 Siegfried Haider, *Das bischöfliche Kapellanat von den Anfängen bis in das 13. Jahrhundert* (Vienna, 1977), pp. 193–4, argues that chaplains serving in episcopal entourages had an important role to play in Barbarossa's military campaigns in Italy as well as during the Third Crusade.

125 The basic work on the history of the German royal chapel is Josef Fleckenstein, *Die Hofkapelle der deutschen Könige*, 2 vols. (Stuttgart, 1959–66). Barbarossa's royal chapel routinely employed priests who held prebends in cathedral chapters. For example, late in Barbarossa's reign, John, the provost of St Germanus in Speyer, served in the royal chapel from May 1182 until November 1189. Concerning the service of John, see *Die Urkunden der Deutschen Könige und Kaiser*, 10.4, ed. Heinrich Appelt (Hanover, 1990), passim.

126 Two writers have been identified by scholars as the authors of this text. Ansbert, a cleric believed to have served as a chaplain in the emperor's household, wrote the first part of the chronicle corresponding to the period before the Third Crusade. The second, anonymous author, is considered by scholars to have been an intimate of the emperor and a member of his household during the course of the crusade because of his access to certain letters that originated with Frederick and were only known subsequently through references in narrative sources. Concerning the identity of the author and the value of the *Historia de expeditione Friderici Imperatoris* as a source, see Anton Chroust, *Tageno, Ansbert, und die Historia Peregrinorum: Drei kritische Untersuchungen zur Geschichte des Kreuzzuges Friedrichs I* (Graz, 1892), pp. 48–80.

127 *Historia de expeditione Friderici Imperatoris* in *Quellen zur Geschichte des Kreuzzuges Kaiser Friedrich I*, ed. Anton Chroust, MGH SRG n.s. 5 (Berlin, 1928), p. 80, *IV. idus maii scilicet in vigilia pentecostes inter condensissimas Turcorum acies usque in noctem ieiunando famelici laboravimus . . .* (my emphasis).

chronicler, the German advance the next morning against the Turks was successful because God had protected them from the attack of their enemies (*qua die pepercit nobis dominus ab incursionibus malorum Turcorum*).[128] In this context, it should be emphasized that the soldiers not only fasted the night before but also participated in the celebration of mass (*auditis misarum solemniis*) early on the morning of 13 May.[129]

From the chronicler's account, it would appear that in addition to their participation in fasts and intercessory masses, those German soldiers also shared with their crusading predecessors the practice of holding prayer services in order to invoke supernatural support on their behalf. Shortly after the hungry vigil of Pentecost, the German army again faced an imminent battle with the Turkish forces dogging their flanks and impeding their march. According to the author of the HEF, Barbarossa's bishops recognized that the morale of the troops was low (*coepimus valde contristari et mesti esse*) and consequently organized camp-wide religious rites in order to energize the men.[130] The bishops ordered their attendant priests to celebrate special votive masses designed to bring divine support. Everyone else was required to participate in public prayers focusing on Saint George as their special object of devotion. According to the chronicler, the soldiers were instructed to invoke this saint because he always appeared when the crusaders were in their time of greatest need.[131]

Indeed, the chronicler recorded that a few days before Pentecost, some sentries guarding the crusader camp reported that they saw an army dressed all in white flying over the emperor's tent. Only a few days later, a soldier named Ludwig of Helfenstein was reported to have seen a white-clad warrior riding a white horse attacking the Turks. Ludwig is reported to have identified him as Saint George.[132] These reported sightings, which the chronicler gives no indication that anyone doubted, and the special prayers directed towards the saint by the crusaders suggest a belief among the troops in the reality of divine aid on the battlefield – aid that could be brought to bear for Christ's army through participation in appropriate Christian rituals.[133]

As had been common practice during the First Crusade, Frederick also sought to complement these army-wide prayer services and penitential rites with reli-

---

[128] *Ibid.*

[129] *Ibid.*

[130] *Ibid.*, p. 83.

[131] *Ibid.*, *quod paterna et salutari commonitione populum ad implorandum divinum auxilium excitaverunt et nomen sancti Georgii martyris . . . qui in anxietatibus nostris aliquotiens viris religiosis apparuit, laudibus ymnis ieiuniorum votis pro posse suo extulerunt. . . .* In considering the penetration of crusading ideology into contemporary culture, it should be noted that the German soldiers are reported to have been accustomed to call on Saint George because this was common for Christians everywhere (*quod celebre quidem habetur in tota ecclesia catholica*).

[132] *Ibid.*, pp. 80–1.

[133] Cf. *Cronica Fratris Salimbene de Adam Ordinis Minorum*, ed. Oswald Holder-Egger, MG SS 32 (Hanover, 1913), p. 12, *Gothfredus Herbipolensis* [Würzburg] *episcopus asseverens se vidisse beatum Georgum contra hostes pro christianis fortiter propugnantem, indicta penitentia et carnium edendarum data licentia, processerunt ad bellum.*

gious support from the home front. In a letter sent in November 1189 from Philippopolis, Barbarossa included a detailed list of orders to his son Henry VI concerning action to be taken on behalf of the crusade. So, after recapitulating the progress of the campaign up to this point, Frederick stressed that despite having a force of superb soldiers, it was necessary for him to place his hope in prayers for divine assistance because, "a king is saved by the grace of the eternal King, which exceeds the merit of any individual, rather than by his own strength."[134] Frederick therefore ordered Henry to summon the most devoted clerics of the empire to pour out copious prayers to God on behalf of the army.[135] Henry also was instructed to pursue wrongdoers in the empire with great zeal in order to earn God's grace and the favor of the people.[136]

In addition to organizing general intercessory rites on behalf of the army, including the invocation of divine and saintly support in the field and on the home front, Barbarossa and his officers also sought to assure the spiritual well-being of the individual soldiers. According to the author of the *HEF*, on the evening before battle against the Turks (13 May 1190), the emperor ordered all of his troops, who were going into battle on the next day, to confess their sins and accept penances.[137] The author of the *Historia de expeditione Friderici Imperatoris* emphasized that on the morning of the battle a multitude of soldiers received communion after hearing mass.[138] He recorded that this process went very slowly (*valde paulatim*) because the sick and wounded also wanted to participate in the sacred rite, although they would not be in the battle that day.[139] The last detail is significant, as it suggests that the ordinary soldiers truly valued the rites in question, and did not take part in them either because of coercion or mere habitual obedience.

An interesting alternate version of this account is to be found in the *Historia peregrinorum* written by an anonymous contemporary shortly after the end of the Third Crusade. The author of this text had access to the HEF, and used it as the basis for his own work.[140] However, in his account of the pre-battle religious preparations made by the soldiers, the author of the *Historia peregrinorum* added a very significant detail and described the eucharist received by the troops as a *viaticum* rather than a *hostia*.[141] The author's substitution of the

---

[134] *Die Urkunden der deutschen Könige und Kaiser*, 10.4, p. 305, *Quamvis autem electissimorum militum in obsequio vivifice crucis habeamus copiam, tamen orationum instantia ad divinum recurrendum est subsidium, quia rex non salvatur per multam virtutem, sed per eterni regis gratiam singulorum merita excedentem.*

[135] *Ibid.,* . . . *apud religiosas imperii nostri personas summe devotionis studio obtineas, ut iugi vigilanti copiosas pro nobis deum fundant orationes.*

[136] *Ibid., ut iudicium arripiat manus regia et in malefactores regie dignitatis zelus exardescat, profecto quia per hoc gratiam consequeris dei et favorem populi.* . . .

[137] *Gesta Federici Imperatoris*, ed. G.H. Pertz, MG SS 18 (Hanover, 1863), p. 380, *praecepit tunc imperator, ut omnes acciperent poenitentiam qui in mane proeliaturi.*

[138] *Historia de expeditione Friderici Imperatoris*, p. 84, *Mane vero facto XVI kal. iunii auditis missarum sollempniis et accepta sacrosancta communione in nomine domini.* . . .

[139] *Ibid., ita quod etiam multi debiles et infirmi sustinerent.* . . .

[140] See Anton Chroust, *Tageno, Ansbert und die Historia Peregrinorum*, p. 81.

[141] *Historia peregrinorum* in *Quellen zur Geschichte des Kreuzzuges Kaiser Friedrich I*, ed. Anton Chroust, MGH SRG n.s. 5 (Berlin, 1928), p. 164.

former word for the latter indicates that the soldiers from whom he heard the story saw the eucharist not as the normal rite but rather as a means of preparing for death. As we have already seen, the *viaticum* had long been associated with death and grave illness. It might also have been the case that he used the expression because of its popularization as the technical term for the reception of communion by soldiers, which is exemplified by its use in this manner by both Burchard of Worms and Ivo of Chartres in their canonical collections written during the previous century.[142]

During the course of the Germans' battle against the Turks on 14 May, the priests, who had already heard the confessions of the German soldiers and given them communion, now took a more active role. The author of the HEF reported that while the fighting was going on, the bishops and priests at the risk of injury or even death went among the troops dressed in their vestments thereby making themselves obvious targets for the Muslims. According to the chronicler, they placed their white stoles around their shoulders intending that this would be a clear mark of their offices (*in argumentum officii sui*).[143] He argued that the clerics were offering themselves up as if they were living hosts (*hostia viva*), and claimed that they were to be compared with the soldiers of the Theban legion who wished to pour out their blood on behalf of Christ.[144] Because it was so obvious, the chronicler did not call attention to the fact that the clerics also were there to give last rites to the dying and to inspire the living by their conspicuous presence and by their obvious personal bravery in the face of mortal danger.

The evidence from the descriptive sources dealing with the religiosity of Barbarossa's troops suggests that the developments in the religious practices and beliefs of soldiers brought about by the First Crusade had become a normal part of crusading warfare during the course of the twelfth century. Thus, for example, Saint George was now seen as the normal defender of crusaders against their enemies and even as the standard bearer of their army. Observers also emphasized the appearance of priests, particularly the fact that they wore white stoles as a mark of their office, while they served on the battlefield with the troops. These continuities are mirrored by the enduring importance of religion to the maintenance of army morale. Both the emperor himself and his bishops are reported to have ordered the organization of religious rites, including confessions, intercessory masses, and prayers, in order to prepare their men for battle. In addition, the sources note that soldiers were eager to participate in traditional wartime rites because they understood that these were the means by which they could enlist divine and saintly support.

---

[142] See Burchard, *Decretum*, 1.119, PL 140: 612–13; and Ivo of Chartres, *Decretum*, 5.333, PL 161: 424.
[143] *Historia de expeditione Friderici*, p. 85, *Nam episcopi et plurimi sacerdotes . . . in argumentum officii sui stolas collis suis circumdederunt desiderantes. . . .*
[144] *Ibid.*, . . . *offerentes se hostiam vivam . . . sancta legio etiam electissimorum militum, in omnibus conparanda legioni Thebeorum martyrum, pari voto unaque voluntate sanguinem suum cupientes pro Christo fundere. . . .*

The Fourth Crusade 1202–1204

As is well known, the Fourth Crusade was exceptionally controversial in its own time, and continues to excite historical controversy today.[145] This section does not seek to resolve the question of the crusade's legitimacy or settle any of the historiographical disputes arising from the sack of Constantinople in 1204 in which the expedition culminated. However, the fact that these crusaders fought against fellow Christians and the fact that the crusade itself was condemned in its own time offer an important opportunity to identify the specific religious behaviors of crusaders, and to consider the role played by religion in the conduct of a campaign that was more than a little unusual even by the standards of crusading warfare.

The three most detailed and reliable sources for this expedition – Robert of Clari's *La conquête de Constantinople*, Geoffroi de Villehardouin's work by the same name, and Henry of Valenciennes' *Histoire de l'Empereur Henri de Constantinople* – were all written by participants in the crusade.[146] Robert of Clari was a low-ranking officer in the crusader army whose account is generally accepted by scholars as an accurate reflection of the hopes and fears among the non-noble elements of the crusader force.[147] Geoffroi de Villehardouin, a noble of very distinguished lineage, was one of six legates sent by Count Theobald of Champagne, Count Louis of Blois, and Count Baldwin of Flanders to Venice in order to organize the transportation of the crusader army in which he led a large contingent as well. Villehardouin's chronicle is understood by scholars to reflect his interest in the overall state of the army and the efforts necessary to maintain it as a cohesive fighting force.[148] Henry of Valenciennes was a cleric in the service of Henry, the brother of Count Baldwin of Flanders and his successor as Latin emperor of Constantinople. Consequently, he was in a position to observe the religious behavior of the crusaders from the point of view of one responsible for their pastoral care.[149] Together, therefore, these three authors present an unusually well-rounded view of the behavior of soldiers on crusade.

The first important test of the unity of the crusading force came in the wake of the military leaders' decision to attack the Dalmatian city of Zara in the fall of

---

[145] The basic work on the Fourth Crusade is Donald E. Queller and Thomas F. Madden, *The Fourth Crusade: The Conquest of Constantinople 1201–1204*, 2nd rev. edn (Philadelphia, 1997).

[146] Robert of Clari, *La conquête de Constantinople*, ed. Philippe Lauer (Paris, 1924); Geoffroi de Villehardouin, *La conquête de Constantinople*, 2 vols., ed. Edmond Faral (Paris, 1938–9), and Henri de Valenciennes, *Histoire de l'Empereur Henri de Constantinople*, ed. Jean Longnon (Paris, 1948).

[147] Concerning the value of this work as a historical source, see C.P. Bagley, "Robert of Clari's *La conquête de Constantinople*," *Medium Aevum* 40 (1971), pp. 109–15, and Raymond H. Schmandt, "The Fourth Crusade and the Just War Theory," *Catholic Historical Review* 61 (1975), pp. 191–221, here p. 215.

[148] Concerning Villehardouin's perspective and reliability, see Edmond Faral, "Geoffroi de Villehardouin: La question de sa sincérité," *Revue historique* 176 (1936), pp. 530–82; and Jeanette M.A. Beer, *Villehardouin: Epic Historian* (Geneva, 1968), pp. 2–3.

[149] Concerning his service with the comital family of Flanders, see Henri de Valenciennes, *Histoire de l'Empereur Henri de Constantinople*, pp. 7–8.

1202.[150] Both Villehardouin and Robert of Clari noted in their accounts of the campaign that the decision to attack Zara before proceeding to the Holy Land caused an uproar among the crusaders, many of whom had no wish to fight against fellow Christians.[151] A substantial contingent of the crusaders thought that it was wrong for them to attack a Christian city under any circumstances. Guy, the Cistercian abbot of Vaulx-de-Cernay, is reported to have shared this view and attempted to persuade the army against attacking Zara by reading publicly a letter from Pope Innocent III that specifically forbade an attack on the city under pain of excommunication.[152] In the wake of this incident many soldiers left the crusader army.[153]

It would appear that Pope Innocent III's letter and the public position taken by Abbot Guy sapped the will of the army to fight. Even among those crusaders who remained at Zara there was considerable worry about their cause and about the subsequent decision to go to Constantinople in support of Alexius, the legitimate heir to the Byzantine throne. According to Villehardouin, it should have been no surprise that the simple fighting men were confused about what was right because the Cistercian monks themselves were divided on the issue.[154] In order to restore the faith of the army in its mission and in the decision of the commanders to participate in the assault on Zara, the bishops and abbots who remained in camp were enlisted to convince the crusaders of the justice of their actions.[155] Villehardouin recorded that Simon, the Cistercian Abbot of Loos, in conjunction with those clerics who agreed with him, preached (*preçoeint*) to the men, calling on them to keep the army together and go to Constantinople because this offered the best chance to recover the Holy Land.[156] That they were successful in persuading the crusaders to continue is an important indication of the great influence exercised by clergy during this military campaign. Fortunately for the crusader army, Pope Innocent III never followed through on his threat to excommunicate the French troops who participated in the attack on Zara, thereby avoiding the enormous morale problem of fighting under the threat of imminent damnation.[157]

The next stage of the crusade took place at Constantinople where the

---

[150] The Venetians had offered to give the crusaders an extension on the payment of their debt if they would attack this former Venetian protectorate. On this point, see Queller, *The Fourth Crusade*, pp. 55–60.

[151] Villehardouin, *La conquête de Constantinople*, I: 97–9, and Robert of Clari, *La conquête de Constantinople*, p. 14.

[152] On this point, see Schmandt, "Just War Theory," p. 205.

[153] Concerning Innocent's negative impact upon the campaign, see Queller, *The Fourth Crusade*, pp. 63–75. Concerning the decision by some crusaders to abandon the army at Zara, see *ibid.*, pp. 76–8.

[154] Villehardouin, *La conquête de Constantinople*, I: 97, *Ensi ere en discorde l'oz, et ne vos mer veilliez mie se la haie genz ere en discorde, que le blanc moine de l'ordre de Cistiaus erent altresi en discorde en l'ost.*

[155] Schmandt, "Just War Theory," pp. 206–8, convincingly demonstrates that the bishops serving in the crusader force used just war theory to support military action against Zara.

[156] Villehardouin, *La conquête de Constantinople*, I: 109.

[157] Concerning Pope Innocent III's reaction to the attack on Zara, see Queller, *Fourth Crusade*, pp. 88–90.

crusaders attempted to capture the city on behalf of Alexius, the son of the deposed emperor Isaac. It was in the context of this siege that Count Hugh IV of St Pol (1174–1205) wrote to his friend, Duke Henry I of Louvain (1190–1235), from the crusaders' camp and recounted a recent Byzantine assault against his men. As we have seen on numerous occasions, the rite of confession generally was treated by both priests and laymen as one of the crucial preparations a soldier should make before going into battle. Count Hugh neatly summed up his agreement with this view by explaining to his friend that before going into combat he and his men rushed to confess their sins because they entrusted their safety to God's mercy.[158] The count's letter is particularly valuable because it allows a glimpse into the thinking of one of the participants in battle whom we would only otherwise know from a chronicler's description of the behavior of the army as a whole.

The short battle described by Count Hugh was only one of many occasions during which the crusaders found themselves in danger before the general assault on the walls of Constantinople (5 July 1203), and serves to highlight the continuing stress and risk to life and limb under which the Latin troops operated.[159] It is therefore not surprising that in his account of the crusaders' preparations for the attack on the city, Villehardouin emphasized the sermons by bishops and priests in which they stressed how important it was that each man confess his sins before going into combat. According to Villehardouin, while explaining the summons to participate in this rite, the clerics pointed out that no one knew God's plans for him, and that it was better to be prepared for one's end.[160] Villehardouin himself shared Count Hugh's belief in the importance of confession, and, furthermore, believed that the bishops and priests were successful in communicating their message to the soldiers. He reported that the entire army participated in the sacrament eagerly (*mult volentiers*) and with great devotion (*mult pitosement*).[161]

The observations by Count Hugh and Villehardouin indicate that it was normal for soldiers to confess their sins before going into battle, even when there was little time to prepare. According to Hugh, the men believed that God would help those who trusted in Him and wanted to obtain this divine support. Villehardouin emphasized that it simply made sense for soldiers to reconcile themselves with God before putting their lives in danger.[162] From a military point of view, men who thought that God would help them can be understood to have had higher morale. What is striking about the case of the Fourth Crusade is that soldiers held these views despite the fact that their campaign was seen by

---

[158] This text is a letter embedded within the *Annales Coloniensis maximi*, ed. K. Pertz, MG SS 17 (Hanover, 1861), p. 813, *quod videntes ad peccatorum nostrorum cucurrimus confessionem, in Dei solum misericordia confidentes.*

[159] Concerning the period before the first general assault against the city, see Queller, *Fourth Crusade*, pp. 111–14.

[160] Villehardouin, *La conquête de Constantinople*, I: 152, *Lors parelerent li evesque et li clergiés al pueple, et lor monstrerent que il fussent confés et feïst cascuns sa devise, que il ne savoient quant Diex feroit son commandement d'els.*

[161] *Ibid., Et il si firent mult volentiers par tote l'ost et mult pitosement.*

[162] *Ibid.*

many of the participants as a perversion of crusading ideals, and was recognized as such by many of their contemporaries, including the pope.

The narrative sources indicate that religion continued to play an important role in the lives of the crusaders even after the collapse of their position at Constantinople in the wake of their betrayal by the westerners' erstwhile protégé Alexius late in 1203.[163] Indeed, rather than giving up hope in face of the grim necessity to besiege and then assault the enormous city yet again, the morale of the army remained high, in part because of the energetic efforts of the priests serving with the troops. For example, Henry of Valenciennes noted that on the night of 8 April 1204, after the military commanders had decided upon a major assault to capture the city for a second time, the army was assembled to hear a sermon that was meant to encourage them for the next day's action. A chaplain named Philip was chosen by the officers to lead the army in prayer and to exhort them to participate in the proper religious preparations before battle. Philip, speaking in French to his French audience, stressed that the soldiers depended upon God's aid in the upcoming battle because they had no refuge and nowhere to run. But, he reassured them that they would be worthy of this aid because they would make true confessions of their sins.[164] Indeed, Philip even ordered them to participate in this rite.[165]

The next day saw the celebration of the full array of rites and ceremonies that we can recognize as appropriate for a medieval army going into battle. At the break of dawn, the chaplains (*li chapelain*) celebrated mass and prayed that God would grant the Latin soldiers honor and victory over their enemies. According to Henry of Valenciennes, the soldiers confessed (*se confiessierent li preudome*), and received the body of the Lord (*rechurent corpus domini*).[166] Then, after the crusaders had formed their battle lines, Philip is reported to have addressed the army again. On this occasion, he stressed that the troops had confessed and were therefore washed clean of all their sins.[167] Finally, he told them that they were to attack their enemy as a form of penance.[168]

---

[163] Concerning the collapse of the Latin position at Constantinople following Alexius' defection and murder, see Queller, *Fourth Crusade*, pp. 148–71.

[164] Henri de Valenciennes, *Histoire de l'Empereur Henri de Constantinople*, pp. 37–8, *Biau segnor, vous qui estes assamblé por le service nostre Segnor, por Diu gardés que la paine ne li travail ke vos avés eu ne soient pierdu, vos estes ichi assamblé en estrange contree, ne n'i avés castiel ne recet u vos aiiés esperance de garant avoir, fors les escus et les espees et les chevaus, et l'aide de Diu premierement, la quele vos serra prestee, pruec que vous soiés confiés a vo pooir. Car confiesions o vraie conpunction de cuer si est eslavement de toz visses.*

[165] *Ibid., Et por chou commandons nous a toz que cascuns confiés selon son pooir.*

[166] *Ibid.,* p. 38, *Et li chapelain qui estoient en l'ost ont celebré le siervice nostre Segneur en l'ounour dou Saint Esprit, pour chou que Dex lor donnast hounour et victoire contre leur anemis. Apriès che se confiessierent li preudome par l'ost, et puis rechurent corpus Domini, cascuns endroit soi, au plus devotement qu'il pot.*

[167] *Ibid.,* p. 44, *Et vous qui boin Crestien iestes et tout preudome, se Diu plaist . . . vous iestes tout confiessés et mondé de toz pechiés et de toutes ordures de vilenie.*

[168] *Ibid., Je vous commanc a toz, en non de penitence, que vous poigniés econtre les anemis Jhesu Crist.* Cf. *La chanson de Roland,* 2 vols., ed. Cesare Segre (Geneva, 1989), I: 150, where Archbishop Turpin orders his men to kill the enemy as a penance, *d'altre part est li*

Henry's report of Philip's two sermons would appear to indicate that this priest and the officers who chose him to preach wanted the crusaders to know that divine aid was available to them and that this aid would be forthcoming if the soldiers carried out their religious obligations, particularly confessing their sins before battle. In this, the soldiers serving in the Fourth Crusade would seem to have followed the same pattern of military religious observances common in earlier crusades, despite the fact that their campaign betrayed the goals of the crusading movement and had been condemned at one point by the pope himself. In addition, the accounts of this crusade indicate that the personal religious rites of soldiers were complemented by intercessory masses and prayers carried out by chaplains (*li chapelain*) serving with the army. In this too, the participants in the Fourth Crusade followed the norms of religious behavior traditional in crusading warfare. These observations suggest that whatever the circumstances of the campaign in which they fought, the religious practices identified here formed an invariable element in the lives of crusading soldiers.

The Albigensian Crusade: The Muret campaign of 1213

The final group of sources we will consider deals with the prosecution of the Albigensian crusade. Particular emphasis is given to the battle of Muret (12 September 1213) between the forces of Simon de Montfort and King Peter of Aragon.[169] This battle is of great interest in the context of crusading warfare because the leaders on both sides were important Christian leaders. Indeed, both men had won significant victories in their careers over the enemies of the church. King Peter had been a leading force behind the Christian victory over the Muslims at the battle of Las Navas de Tolosa in 1212, and Simon de Montfort was the commander of the Catholic forces of northern France that had undertaken to extirpate the Cathar or Albigensian heresy that had taken root among the Christians of southern France.[170] Although at Muret King Peter and his men were acting against the immediate interests of the papacy, there was never any claim that either the Aragonese or Peter's vassals in southern France were heretics.[171] Thus, even more so than the war against the Orthodox Christians of Constantinople, the battle of Muret marks the breakdown of the traditional notion of the crusade as a war against the enemies of the faith.

There are two basic sources for this encounter that discuss in detail the religious preparations made by Simon de Montfort's army. The earlier of the two accounts was written by Peter of Vaulx-Cernay, who was a participant in the Albigensian Crusade. Although not present at the battle of Muret, he did have

---

arcevesque Turpin/ . . . Franceis apelet, un sermon lur ad dit/Pur nostre rei devum nus ben murir/Chrestïentét aidez a sustenir/Bataille avrez, vos en estes tuz fiz/Kar a voz oilz veez les Sarrazins/Clamez vos culpes, si preiez Deu mercit/A soldrai vos pur vos anmes guarir/ . . . Par penitence les cumandet a ferir (my emphasis).

169 Concerning the organization and development of the military campaigns in southern France, see Joseph R. Strayer, *The Albigensian Crusades*, 2nd edn (Ann Arbor, 1992).

170 The war between these two famous crusaders developed out of King Peter's efforts to defend his loyal subordinates to the north of the Pyrenees. On this point, see *ibid.*, pp. 88–94.

171 *Ibid.*, pp. 89–93.

access to many eyewitness reports during his subsequent stay in southern France through the spring of 1214.[172] According to Peter, before the battle outside Muret began, Simon's troops gathered in the courtyard of the fortress around Bishop Fulk of Toulouse, one of the army's leading clerics, in order to hear him speak.[173] As he prepared to address the soldiers, Bishop Fulk brought forth a relic that, the author claimed, was a piece of the true cross. However, at that moment Bishop Garsias of Comminges, who decided that there could be no delay in adoring the relic, seized it from Bishop Fulk's hand, and climbed onto a high point to gain everyone's attention and signaled that he wanted to speak to the soldiers.[174]

According to the chronicler, Garsias delivered a sermon to the troops in which he dealt with a wide range of religious injunctions and promises of spiritual support. The bishop of Comminges began by calling upon the men to go forth to fight in the name of Jesus Christ. He promised them that he would stand as a witness for anyone who died in battle so that the dead would receive their eternal prize and a martyr's glory.[175] In this context, standing as a witness probably indicates that the bishop would pray to God on behalf of the soldiers. Bishop Garsias then added that the men should either have confessed and felt contrition already, or that they should make a firm commitment to confess their sins to a priest as soon as the battle was over.[176] From the context of the bishop's remarks, it is clear that the fighting was about to begin, and that soldiers who had thus far failed to confess no longer had the time to do so, at least in the traditional complete form. Thus, it would appear that Bishop Garsias was offering a provisional exception to the general rule that soldiers confess before battle by asserting that for the moment the intention to confess later on was sufficient.

One further element of the sermon that might indicate a new development in contemporary thinking about the spiritual benefits that accrued to crusaders is Bishop Garsias' promise that anyone who died in this battle would go to heaven immediately without any punishment in purgatory.[177] It is not clear from the context of Peter's account whether Bishop Garsias saw purgatory as a

---

172　Peter of Vaulx-Cernay, *Hystoria Albigensis*, 3 vols., ed. Pascal Guébin and Ernest Lyon (Paris, 1926–39), III: viii–ix.

173　*Ibid.*, II: 151.

174　*Ibid.*, p. 152, *Episcopus autem Convenarum, vir mire sanctitatis videns quod in ista adoratione crucis a singulis nimia fieret mora, arripiens de manu Tolosani episcopi lignum crucis ascendensque in locum eminentiorem signavit omnes, dicens. . . .*

175　*Ibid., Ite in nomine Jhesu Christi! Et ego vobis testis sum et in die Judicii fidejussor existo quod quicumque in isto glorioso occuberit bello absque ulla purgatorii pena statim eterna premia et martyrii gloria consequetur. . . .*

176　*Ibid., dummodo contritus sit et confessus vel saltem firmum habeat propositum quod, statim peracto bello, super peccatis de quibus nondum fecit confessionem ostendet se sacerdoti.*

177　This is the first instance that I have found of purgatory being mentioned in the context of spiritual benefits for crusaders. I am also unaware of any cases in which purgatory was mentioned with respect to soldiers fighting in ordinary wars before 1213. The basic work on purgatory remains Jacques le Goff, *La Naissance du Purgatoire* (Paris, 1981), translated into English by Arthur Goldhammer, *The Birth of Purgatory* (Chicago, 1984). Le Goff does not appear to deal with this text.

normal fate for soldiers, or even what he meant by purgatory other than as a place of suffering. Nevertheless, Garsias' comments might be illuminated by J.A. Brundage's observation concerning the difference between remission of sins and the remission of temporal punishment required by God in satisfaction for a sin.[178] In the first case, the penitent was to serve in a crusade in lieu of the penances due for the sins he had confessed. However, no penitent could know with absolute certainty whether these penances were sufficient to account for his entire burden of sin. This meant that even after receiving a remission of sins and fulfilling his penitential obligation by going on crusade, the soldier might still owe additional satisfaction when he died. By contrast, a remission of temporal punishment meant that the entire burden of sin was now accounted for without question. Garsias' promise that the soldiers would spend no time in purgatory may indicate that he was offering a remission of temporal punishment, which would have been a novelty.[179] As we have seen, however, in many instances the highly nuanced distinction between remission of sins and remission of temporal punishment would not seem to have been of great importance to soldiers who simply thought of their dead comrades as martyrs.[180]

In addition to describing Bishop Garsias' sermon, including his promise of spiritual benefits, the chronicler also recorded the subsequent religious preparations made by Simon de Montfort's troops as well as their feelings before battle. According to Peter of Vaulx-Cernay, the soldiers demanded that Garsias' promise be repeated many times and that the other bishops confirm that the men were, in fact, eligible to receive the spiritual benefits described by the bishop of Comminges.[181] While Peter did not explicitly say so, the soldiers' concern about the validity of Bishop Garsias' promise may have arisen from the fact that they were fighting against fellow Christians, many of whom were themselves crusade heroes who had recently won a great victory over the Muslims at the battle of Las Navas de Tolosa.

Nevertheless, whatever the cause of their initial skepticism, Peter recorded that after the soldiers had finally been convinced that they were to receive spiritual rewards, they quickly purified themselves of sin through the contrition of their hearts (*cordis contricio*) and oral confessions (*oris confessio*).[182] According to the chronicler, the soldiers' religious preparations helped to eliminate their fear of the enemy whom they approached "intrepidi." It would appear that from Peter's point of view that the combination of religious rites and preaching, including the bishops' confirmation of Garsias' promises, served to raise the morale of the fighting men before they went into battle.

---

[178] Concerning this distinction, see Brundage, *Medieval Canon Law and the Crusader*, p. 146.

[179] Brundage, *ibid.*, p. 148, notes that an official grant of remission of temporal punishment by the papal government did not predate the First Council of Lyon in 1245.

[180] On this point, see *ibid.*, pp. 149–50.

[181] Peter of Vaulx-Cernay, *Hystoria Albigensis*, II: 152, *qua promissione ad instantiam militum nostrorum repetita sepius et multociens ab episcopis confirmata....*

[182] *Ibid., statim nostri, per cordis contricionem et oris confessionem mundati a peccatis....*

In the meantime, according to this chronicler, following their efforts to convince the soldiers that a martyr's prize awaited them if they fell in battle, the bishops retired to the fortress along with their attendant clerics. Once there, all of the bishops and priests continued to support their men throughout the battle by praying to God on behalf of his servants (*deprecaturi Dominum pro servis suis*), who were risking their lives for Him. Indeed, Peter reported that the bishops prayed with such emotion that it sounded as if they were engaged in ululations rather than in prayer.[183] As was true of the soldiers' personal religious preparations for battle, the bishops' prayers would appear to have had an important role to play in preparing the men for combat. Peter concluded that as a consequence of the prelates' efforts, Simon's men went into battle joyfully (*gaudentes ad locum certaminis*).[184] The chronicler's observation regarding the soldiers' responses to the prayers of the bishops permits the inference that they knew that these prayers were being said on their behalf.

The basic outline of Peter de Vaulx-Cernay's account is confirmed by William of Puylaurens in his *Chronica*, which was written three decades after the battle of Muret, but was based upon the author's personal experiences during the Albigensian campaigns in southern France.[185] According to William, the troops at Muret prepared for battle by confessing their sins, hearing mass, and receiving communion. Indeed, in describing these religious rites, the chronicler claimed that the soldiers acted in their customary manner (*ex more*).[186] William also pointed out that these rites had the effect of comforting (*confortati*) the soldiers before facing the enemy.[187]

The one major difference between the two accounts is William's claim that Simon chose to attack the superior forces outside Muret because of his own belief that God would support his men against a force of excommunicates.[188] According to William, Simon chose to attack on the eve of the feast of the exaltation of the Holy Cross (13 September 1213) in order to emphasize the moral superiority of his forces over against Peter of Aragon's army.[189] This decision was important because, as was noted above, Peter of Aragon was a Christian hero who had played a leading role just one year before at the battle of Las

---

[183] *Ibid.*, *Episcopi autem et clerici intraverunt ecclesiam, deprecaturi Dominum pro servis Suis, qui se pro Ejus nomine morti exponebant inminenti; qui, orantes et clamantes in celum, tantum pro inminenti angustia mugitum emittebant quod 'ululantes' dici deberent pocius quam orantes.*

[184] *Ibid.*

[185] William of Puylaurens, *Chronica*, ed. Jean Duvernoy (Paris, 1976), pp. 1–9.

[186] *Ibid.*, p. 82, *et factis confessionibus peccatorum et audito ex more divino officio, ciboque salutari altaris refecti et prandio sobrio confortati, arma sumunt. . . .*

[187] *Ibid.*

[188] *Ibid.*, p. 80, *considerans causam Dei et fidei prosequebatur, ceteris in contrarium currentibus vinculo exommunicationis astrictis, satius duxit una die periculum experiri, quam languida prolixitate adversariorum audaciam adaugere.* It is not clear that Peter and his men had, in fact, been excommunicated by Pope Innocent III, although the bishops serving with Simon de Montfort may have undertaken this action on their own authority.

[189] *Ibid.*, pp. 80–2.

Navas de Tolosa. Thus, in order to assure his own men that they were really on the side of God, it was important to associate their attack more firmly with the preeminent symbol of Christian devotion, namely the cross.

Conclusion

The most important element in the emerging conception of crusade campaigns as holy wars would appear to be the belief, shared by participants and outside observers alike, that soldiers who died fighting for God would receive the prize of martyrdom and eternal redemption. Although there were cases in earlier wars in which Christian soldiers were understood to have earned a martyr's reward, the campaign leading to the capture of Jerusalem saw an unprecedented emphasis on this idea. The importance of martyrdom was subsequently emphasized by participants and other contemporaries dealing with the crusades over the course of the twelfth and early thirteenth centuries. Indeed, it would appear that the emphasis upon the spiritual benefits enjoyed by crusaders marks a clear break with eleventh-century conceptions of ordinary wars, even including just wars fought on behalf of Christians against the enemies of the church.

This conception of the peculiar interpenetration of religion and war in the crusade would also appear to have been responsible, at least in part, for the frequent references in descriptive sources to the dress of priests serving with crusader armies, and to the appearance of warrior saints on the battlefield. Chroniclers writing in the tenth and eleventh centuries had occasionally noted the white stoles of priests and the physical manifestation of saints in battle. The novel phenomenon of an army of penitent pilgrims fighting as literal *milites Christi* against the enemies of God might well have called forth the idea of a parallel spiritual army composed of Christian martyrs and led by soldier-saints. And even the invisible presence of such an army or its leaders would surely have served to convince a large number of soldiers of the essential righteousness of their cause and the security of their spiritual condition.

In addition to these noteworthy areas of change in the religious behavior and beliefs of crusading soldiers and their supporters as compared with their counterparts in the ordinary wars of the eleventh century, it must be emphasized that there were also exceptionally important elements of continuity. Thus, for example, crusaders can be seen to have received communion on a regular basis before going into battle. According to many observers, participation in this rite was intended to fortify (*munire*) the men before they fought. As we have seen, this seems to have been a regular element in the preparation of soldiers fighting in ordinary wars since at least the mid-tenth century. Similarly, sermons and battlefield harangues emphasizing the importance of religious preparation before battle played a regular part in the religious lives of crusaders. Once again, we have seen in previous chapters that sermons and battlefield addresses of this type had been employed in a routine manner in ordinary wars no later than the eighth century.

The element of continuity that is most striking is the almost universal emphasis in descriptive sources on confession, intercessory prayers, and masses. The authors of our sources almost all mention these as pre-battle rites either for individual soldiers or for crusading armies as a whole. Clearly, the crusaders were understood by many and perhaps most contemporaries to be potential martyrs, who had received a remission of their sins for their service in a divinely sanctioned campaign. The fact that soldiers felt the need to unburden their souls on a regular basis indicates, however, that remissions of sin were not understood to include all of the sins committed over the course of the soldier's actual service. Moreover, the desire of the soldiers themselves to confess their sins, as is reported by several contemporary observers, suggests that these fighting men thought of themselves as sinful even while they suffered in God's service. Similarly, the desire of many fighting men, as well as their officers, and their clerical supporters to ask for intercessory prayers, suggests a general concern that crusade campaigns would not necessarily receive divine or saintly assistance. Rather, it would appear that there was at least some unease among crusaders concerning their own relationships to God, and the concomitant status of their campaign as a whole.

When the actual role of religion in the conduct of the crusades as military campaigns is examined carefully, therefore, it would appear that the fears of soldiers, officers, and clerics about the state of their souls and the status of their crusade as a divinely supported venture had an enormous impact on morale. In this context, it is certainly of great importance that the sources – including those composed by lay participants in the events described – regularly emphasized soldiers' feelings of being cleansed and strengthened for battle after they had confessed their sins and received communion. The employment of relics on the battlefield can also be seen to have played a significant role in giving courage to the troops. In addition, the invocation of divine and saintly support through intercessory prayers and masses, both within the army and by supporters on the home front, is reported in many circumstances to have given confidence to soldiers that God and the saints would aid them in battle. Indeed, many soldiers are reported to have seen George, Demetrius, and their white-clad hosts on the battlefield.

As was true in ordinary wars from the eighth through the late eleventh centuries, religion also played a crucial role in maintaining both *esprit de corps* and discipline in crusader armies. On a number of occasions, the manifestly Christian nature of the crusading effort can be seen to have helped forge disparate contingents of fighting men, recruited from a wide variety of ethnic and linguistic backgrounds, into cohesive fighting forces. Evidence for the feeling of unity among the crusaders appears in numerous crusade sermons that stressed the common bonds of the soldiers as Christians while ignoring their ethnic and political allegiances.

These sermons also provide important evidence for the role played by religion in maintaining army discipline. *Reportationes* in descriptive sources frequently stress that soldiers had to abjure sinful behaviors, including envy, greed, and lust in order to make themselves worthy of divine support. The repeated use of sermons to define both proper and improper behavior indicates that officers and clerics thought that these addresses could have a beneficial impact on the discipline of their men. However, rather than relying on exhortations alone, crusade commanders can also be seen to have employed other forms of religious observance to stem indiscipline among their troops. In particular, officers and clerics are reported to have organized penitential rites, particularly confessions, processions, almsgiving, and fasting, both to encourage proper behavior and to punish men who had failed to meet the standards of behavior enunciated by their leaders.

The relationship between continuity and change in the religious behavior and beliefs of crusaders, as compared with those of their counterparts in ordinary wars, sheds light on the fundamental paradox of holy war within the Christian tradition. Many Christian fighting men were convinced that they fought in divinely sanctioned wars with the prospect of attaining eternal redemption, and yet they frequently worried both about the state of their souls, and about God's willingness to aid them in battle. As a consequence, rather than disappearing as a superfluous factor in the conduct of crusade campaigns, religion continued to play a significant role in maintaining army morale, cohesion, and discipline.

5

Religion of Secular War c. 1095–c. 1215

Introduction

This chapter considers the period c. 1095–c. 1215 from the perspective of Christians fighting against other Christians in ordinary wars as contrasted to the crusades. In particular, this chapter will be concerned with elements of continuity and change in the religious behavior and beliefs of these fighting men as compared both with their predecessors in ordinary wars of the eleventh century, and with their contemporaries fighting in crusades, including questions of remissions of sins, and penitential rites such as fasting and almsgiving. A substantially larger number of narrative sources dealing with one or another aspect of battlefield religious practice survive from the twelfth and early thirteenth centuries than for the earlier periods dealt with in this study. It is therefore possible to consider regional differences in religious practice in greater detail than was possible for the tenth or even the eleventh century. However, as was true of writers in earlier periods, the interests of individual authors in the twelfth and early thirteenth centuries varied greatly over time and geographic location. For example, chroniclers and other historical writers working in the Anglo-Norman tradition demonstrated a more consistent concern for the religious behavior and beliefs of soldiers than did their contemporaries living in other regions of the Latin West.[1]

In previous chapters dealing with ordinary wars, the nature and extent of the evidence made it necessary to organize the various individual elements of religious behavior comprising military religion generically. Thus, for example, the personal religious behaviors of soldiers in the French kingdom are grouped together with those from Germany and Italy. By contrast, the substantially larger body of evidence in the twelfth and early thirteenth centuries makes it possible to consider as a unit the entire range of religious rites celebrated by soldiers and their supporters in the context of a single campaign. As is clear from the discussion of the crusade campaigns in the previous chapter, this approach has the benefit of providing a specific context for each element of the soldiers' religious

---

[1] In this regard, see Emily Albu (Hanawalt), *The Normans in their Histories: Propaganda, Myth, and Subversion* (Woodbridge, 2001); Leah Shopkow, *History and Community: Norman Historical Writing in the Eleventh and Twelfth Centuries* (Washington, D.C., 1997); and Cassandra W. Potts, "*Atque unum ex diversis gentibus populum effecit*: Historical Tradition and the Norman Identity," *Anglo-Norman Studies* 18 (1996), pp. 139–52, who examine the historical self-consciousness of Norman writers as Normans.

preparation within a particular time and place. In order to highlight elements of change as well as continuity in religious practice across the Latin West, this chapter is organized geographically, considering first the Anglo-Norman state, the German empire, and finally the kingdom of France.

Religion of War in the Anglo-Norman State

Anglo-Norman historians of the twelfth century tended to highlight the religiosity of Norman soldiers serving in the eleventh century, even to the extent of denying to their enemies any sense of legitimate religious conviction. A clear example of this practice can be seen in William of Malmesbury's account of the battle of Hastings, where he contrasted the drunken behavior of Harold's men with the desire of William the Conqueror's soldiers to confess their sins.[2] Wace similarly emphasized the religiosity of Duke William's troops and even suggested that when there were an insufficient number of priests to hear every man's confession, the soldiers confessed to each other in order to reconcile themselves with God.[3] The importance to William the Conqueror's soldiers of the reconciling themselves with God was also addressed by the author of the Battle Abbey chronicle, who was a contemporary of Wace and wrote his account over the course of the seventh and eighth decades of the twelfth century.[4] He added a story to the standard account of the battle at Hastings in which he emphasized the importance of divine aid to the Norman troops. Duke William is reported to have promised to build an abbey on the site of the battle if he were victorious in order to assure the salvation of all those who had died in the fighting. According to the chronicler, the men were all heartened to hear this (*his animosiores effecti pugnam constanter ineunt*).[5]

The emphasis placed by these twelfth-century writers on the religious behavior of Norman soldiers in the eleventh century suggests that these aspects of military life were important to their audiences. William of Malmesbury had an audience that included not only his fellow monks but also important secular officials, including Robert of Gloucester, Henry I's bastard son.[6] In Wace's case, the audience almost certainly included King Henry II of England, who had commissioned him to write *Le Roman de Rou*.[7] The author of the Battle Abbey Chronicle intended his work serve as a part of a legal defense of the monastery's property holdings. Consequently, his intended audience included not only the

---

2 William of Malmesbury, *Gesta regum Anglorum*, I: 454.

3 Wace, *Roman de Rou*, II: 157, *e qui nen out proveires pres a son veisin se fist confés*.

4 The *Chronicle of Battle Abbey*, p. 66.

5 Concerning the date and authorship of the Battle Abbey chronicle, see Gransden, *Historical Writing in England*, I: 272.

6 On this point, see *Gesta regum Anglorum*, II: xli.

7 Concerning King Henry II's patronage of Wace's work, see Karen M. Broadhurst, "Henry II of England and Eleanor of Aquitaine: Patrons of Literature in French?" *Viator* 27 (1996), pp. 53–84, esp. pp. 56–9.

brothers at Battle Abbey but also contemporary lawyers and judges, perhaps even the king, concerned with the house's property claims.[8]

The emphasis placed on religion by twelfth-century historians dealing with William's invasion of England can also be seen in the works of Anglo-Norman writers dealing with the events of their own day. Clearly, no single event in Anglo-Norman history of the twelfth century could match in importance Duke William's victory at Hastings and his conquest of England. This had obvious consequences for the historiographical tradition. Nevertheless, military campaigns, particularly during the first half of the twelfth century, did attract the attention of historians concerned with religious as well as with military matters, so we are reasonably well supplied with material directly relevant to this study.

For example, two contemporary texts treating the Battle of the Standard fought between the English and Scots in 1138 describe in great detail the program of religious preparations undertaken on behalf of the Anglo-Norman army as well as the religious behavior of the soldiers themselves.[9] Richard, first a canon and then prior at Hexham in Northumbria, wrote his history of King Stephen's reign and the Battle of the Standard shortly after 1139.[10] He had access to many eyewitness reports both because his canonry was included in the area from which Anglo-Norman soldiers were mobilized to serve in the war, and because Hexham itself was attacked by the Scots. As a result, Richard had ample opportunity to interrogate eyewitnesses to the battle. Aelred of Rievaulx also lived through the Battle of the Standard, and later served as abbot of Rievaulx from 1147 to 1167.[11] Aelred composed his text about seventeen years after the battle (between 1155–57) and is likely to have had available Richard of Hexham's account of the conflict.[12] However, the abbot also had access to sources of information that were unavailable to Richard of Hexham. In particular, Aelred was a close friend of Walter of Espec, one of the leading lay commanders on the English side.[13]

Preparations for the campaign began in late July or early August when news arrived at York that the Scots, under the command of King David, had invaded England.[14] King Stephen was thoroughly engaged in the south of the kingdom,

---

[8] *Chronicle of Battle Abbey*, pp. 9–11.

[9] Richard of Hexham, *De gestis Regis Stephani et de bello standardii*, Rolls Series 82, 4 vols., ed. Richard Howlett (London, 1884–9), III: 139–78, and Ailred of Rievaulx, *Relatio Venerabilis Aelredi Abbatis Rievallensis de Standardo*, Rolls Series 82, 4 vols., ed. Richard Howlett (London, 1886), III: 181–99.

[10] The best modern treatment of Richard of Hexham's historical work is Antonia Gransden, *Historical Writing in England c. 550 to c. 1307*, 2 vols. (Ithaca, 1974), I: 216–18. The house at Hexham was attacked by the Scots during their invasion and three of the canons were killed. See *Councils and Synods with Other Documents Relating to the English Church A.D. 871–1204*, 2 vols., ed. D. Whitelock, M. Brett, and C.N.L. Brooke (Oxford, 1981), II: 767–8.

[11] See Gransden, *Historical Writing*, I: 212–16.

[12] *Ibid.*, p. 213.

[13] Concerning Aelred's relationship with Walter Espec, see *ibid.*, pp. 214–15; and Derek Baker, "Ailred of Rievaulx and Walter Espec," *Haskins Society Journal* 1 (1989), pp. 91–8.

[14] For an overview of the Battle of the Standard and its political context, see David Crouch, *The Reign of King Stephen, 1135–1154* (Harlow, 2000), pp. 72–83.

and the defense of the northern marches devolved upon the leading secular and ecclesiastical magnates. In response to the Scottish invasion, the northern barons gathered at York to discuss matters with Archbishop Thurstan. According to Richard of Hexham, the barons' mood was very pessimistic. They feared that with the main field army engaged in the south under Stephen, they would be unable to face the Scottish king in battle. But the archbishop, who had been given overall command of the north by Stephen, successfully raised the barons' spirits with a rousing sermon. He promised the barons that if they and their men placed all of their trust in God, and reconciled themselves to the Lord through a true rite of penance (*per veram poenitentiam Deo reconciliati*), they would be victorious against their enemies.[15] Commenting on the archbishop's actions, Richard of Hexham added that Thurstan had spoken appropriately because the English were fighting for a just and most pious cause. Their enemies were the enemies of the church and of God, and the English were putting themselves in harm's way for "the sake of the holy church and for the defense of their homeland."[16]

In addition to attempting to raise their spirits, Archbishop Thurstan also promised to provide the barons with practical, military aid. He would mobilize the rural militias in the archdiocese in support of the baronial troops.[17] Thurstan also committed himself to sending parish priests into the field with their communities. In Richard of Hexham's account, these parish priests were to bring crosses into the field.[18] Abbot Aelred noted that the priests were ordered to bring relics and banners in addition to their crosses.[19]

Following their meeting with Archbishop Thurstan, the northern barons returned home to mobilize their troops. Richard noted that after a short time, the barons returned to York with their contingents and began a process of religious preparation for war. The first rite was carried out within each of the contingents as the soldiers made their individual confessions and received what Richard described as private penance (*privata poenitentia*).[20] After individual ritual preparations had been undertaken by the men, Archbishop Thurstan organized religious ceremonies that involved all of the soldiers in the army as well as the people of York. In order to help the soldiers fulfill their penitential obligations,

---

[15] Richard of Hexham, *De gestis Regis Stephani*, p. 160, *sed potius cuncti pariter cum suis per veram poenitentiam Deo reconciliati, et ad eum toto corde conversi . . . Quod si devote facerent, de misericordia Dei presumans, eos victores fore praenunciabat.*

[16] *Ibid.*, *Ipsorum vero causa justa ac piissima erat, quippe pro sanctae ecclesiae ac suae patriae defensione periculo se objiciebant.*

[17] C. Warren Hollister, *The Military Organization of Norman England* (Oxford, 1965), pp. 229–30, discusses the important role played by the rural levies in this campaign.

[18] Richard of Hexham, *De gestis Regis Stephani*, p. 161.

[19] Ailred of Rievaulx, *Relatio de Standardo*, p. 182, *sed et Thurstinus Eboracensis archiepiscopus per totam diocesim suam edictum episcopale proposuit ut, de singulis parochiis suis presbyteris cum cruce et vexillis reliquiisque sanctorum praeuntibus, omnes qui possent ad bella procedere, ad proceres properarent, ecclesiam Christi contra barbaros defensuri.*

[20] Richard of Hexham, *De gestis Regis Stephani*, p. 161, *post acceptam privatam poenitentiam.*

the archbishop imposed a three-day fast on the entire non-combatant population. This was to be complemented by almsgiving.[21] Then, following the three-day fast, Thurstan granted absolution to all of the men and offered them his blessing.[22]

At a broader level, the public religious ceremonies carried out by the people of York on behalf of the army were given great support by the regular prayers of monks, canons, and other religious both in England and in Normandy for the well-being of the Anglo-Norman domain. King Stephen followed in the tradition of his continental and Anglo-Norman predecessors by making donations and confirming gifts to religious foundations in return for prayers *pro pace et stabilitate regni*.[23] In February 1136, for example, Stephen confirmed gifts made by Archbishop Thurstan of York to the Cistercian house of Fountains "out of love for God, for the salvation of my soul and the souls of my relatives, and for the state of my kingdom."[24] Similarly, in 1137 Stephen confirmed all of the donations made to Mortemer Abbey *pro salute mea et incolumitate regni mei Anglie et ducatus Normannie*.[25]

At his first meeting with the barons before their troops had mobilized at York, Archbishop Thurstan promised that he would travel with the army and provide spiritual support during the course of the campaign. However, Richard of Hexham recorded that when the army began its departure from York, the barons begged Thurstan to remain behind because they were worried about his health. They requested that, rather than risking his life to no purpose, he remain at York and support the soldiers with prayers, vigils, fasts, and "everything else that pertained to God."[26] Thurstan acceded to their wishes, but insisted that, in addition to taking along some of his clerics, the army commanders also take into the field his personal cross and a banner of St. Peter (*sancti Petri vexillum*).[27]

After the army left York, some of the barons, including Robert the Brus and Bernard of Baliol, went to King David of Scotland to try to make peace before the two armies met in battle. This effort ended in failure. However, in the meantime, Archbishop Thurstan kept his promise to mobilize the rural militias and parish priests (*presbyteri cum parochianis suis*) for service with the baronial

---

[21] *Ibid.*, *illis* [those who had accepted private penance] *pariter et omni populo archipraesul triduanum cum eleemosinis indixit jejunium.*

[22] *Ibid.*, *ac deinde absolutionem, et benedictionem Dei et suam eis sollempniter tribuit.* Concerning the immediate grant of absolution to soldiers on campaign, see Vogel, *Le pécheur et la pénitence au moyen âge*, pp. 20–1.

[23] King Henry I of England made regular donations to religious houses in return for prayers. *Regesta Regum Anglo-Normannorum 1066–1154*, vol. 2, ed. C. Johnson and H.A. Cronne (Oxford, 1956), #160, p. 340; #248, p. 372; #252, p. 373; and #270, p. 378.

[24] *Regesta Regum Anglo-Normannorum 1066–1154*, vol. 3, ed. H.A. Cronne and R.H.C. Davis (Oxford, 1968), #335, p. 126.

[25] *Ibid.*, #598, p. 220. For similar grants made in return for prayers, see *ibid.*, #189, p. 69; #327, p. 123; #681, p. 252; #798, p. 294; #938, p. 344; #945, p. 348; #946, p. 349; and #947, p. 350.

[26] *Ibid.*, *at illi ipsum remanere fecerunt, obsecrantes ut in orationibus et eleemosinis, vigiliis et jejuniis, et in ceteris, quae ad Deum pertinent, pro eis intercedere satageret.*

[27] *Ibid.*

army.[28] In addition, he sent Bishop Ralph of Orkney in his place, along with one of his archdeacons and a substantial company of priests for the expressed purpose of assigning penances (*poenitentiam injungere*) and granting absolution (*absolutionem dare*) to the militiamen who were then pouring into the English camp at Northallerton.[29]

The stage for the battle was set on 21 August 1138. The Scots were ensconced a bare two miles from the English encampment, and everyone expected the fighting to begin the next morning. The professional soldiers serving in the baronial contingents had performed their ritual obligations, accepted their penances, and had received absolution from Archbishop Thurstan while still at York. The rural levies had received penances either from their parish priests or from the clergy brought by Bishop Ralph of Orkney, and also had received absolution for their sins from the bishop or from the priests on his staff. But as we shall see, these religious behaviors formed only the first sequence in the religious preparation of the army.

According to Robert of Hexham, as the troops prepared for battle on the morning of 22 August, the commanders raised a ship's mast from the middle of a battle wagon.[30] On this mast were hung sacred banners bearing the images of St Peter the Apostle and of two Northumbrian saints, Bishop John of Beverley and Bishop Wilfrid of Ripon, both of whom were renowned as confessors. The base of the standard bore a placard onto which was written "the task of soldiers either is to conquer or die."[31] On the very top of the wooden pole the commanders placed a silver pyx containing a consecrated host, which Richard of Hexham pointedly identified as the body of Christ.[32]

In Richard's view, the military commanders were attempting to bring Christ directly on to the battlefield through the presence of his body, so that he would act as their commander (*dux belli*) during the battle. The saints were to be summoned by invoking their presence through the sacred banners dedicated to them. Richard noted that the Anglo-Norman troops hoped the saints would be motivated to defend their particular churches (*pro eius ecclesia ac sua patria defendenda susceperunt*) from the onslaught of the Scots.[33] In his account of the

---

[28] As was noted earlier, by the end of the eleventh century, French bishops expected parish priests to go to war with their parishioners carrying *vexilla* with them. Orderic Vitalis, *Ecclesiastical History*, VI: 156.

[29] *Ibid.*, p. 162, *Eodem tempore misit archiepiscopus eis Radulfum cognomento Novellum, Orcadensium episcopum, cum quodam de archidiaconibus suis et aliis clericis, qui populis cotidie ad eos undique catervatim confluentibus, vice sua et poenitentiam injungaret, et absolutionem daret. Misit quoque eis presbyteros cum parochianis suis, sicut eis promiserat.*

[30] We have already seen that as early as 1039 the Milanese had used a similar battle wagon, which they called a *carroccio*.

[31] Richard of Hexham, *De gestis Regis Stephani*, pp. 163–4, *mox autem aliqui eorum in medio cujusdam machinae, quam ibi adduxerunt, unius navis malum erexerunt, quod Standard appellaverunt. Unde Hugo Sotevagina, Eboracensis archidiaconus, 'dicitur a stando Standardum, quod stetit illic militiae probitas, vincere sive mori'* . . . *et sanctorum Petri Apostoli, et Johannis Beverlacensis et Wilfridi Ripensis confessorum ac pontificum, vexilla suspenderunt.*

[32] *Ibid.*

[33] *Ibid.*, p. 163, *hoc autem ideo fecerant, ut Jesus Christus Dominus noster per praesentiam*

battle, Abbot Aelred focused his attention on Walter Espec, his close friend and the founder of the monastery at Rievaulx.[34] Aelred recorded that the baron mounted the wagon at the base of the standard and delivered a harangue to the troops. Walter touched on many issues in his battlefield oration, including the good record of the English and Norman troops under difficult circumstances, the need to defend their wives and children from the bestial enemy, and the anti-Christian acts of the Scottish army. However, Walter saved his best material for last and focused on the divine support available to the Anglo-Norman army, and the spiritual preparations that would ensure their victory.[35]

According to Abbot Aelred, Walter encouraged the men to go into battle by claiming that there would be divine aid on their side, and that all of the heavens would fight alongside them.[36] Michael would be there with the angels in order to take vengeance upon those who shed human blood in his churches. Peter the Apostle would fight for the English against those who had transformed his churches into stables and brothels. The holy martyrs would go before their battle line against enemies who had filled their sacred places with corpses.[37] Walter then added that the holy virgins would be fighting for the army with prayers (*oratione pugnare*), and that Jesus Christ, himself, would take up arms and a shield and come to their aid.[38] Finally, Walter drew three pointed contrasts between the enemy and the English army. First, the Scots came to the battle filled with arrogance, whereas the English proceeded with humility. Second, the enemy soldiers spent their time belching after having eaten stolen meat, whereas the English troops had been nourished by the blood and body of Christ after completing a sacred fast. Finally, the northerners had nothing but actors and dancers to accompany them into battle, whereas the defenders were proceeded into combat by Christ's cross and the relics of the saints.[39]

---

sui corporis eis dux belli esset, quod pro ejus ecclesia ac sua patria defendenda susceperant. Richard also noted that the standard could be used as a rallying point for the army.

[34] Concerning Walter Espec's relationship to the monastery, see Aelred, *Relatio de Standardo*, pp. 184–5. Concerning the battlefield orations by the English commanders, see John Bliese, "Aelred of Rievaulx's Rhetoric and Morale at the Battle of the Standard 1138," *Albion* 20 (1988), pp. 543–56, and "The Battle Rhetoric of Aelred of Rievaulx," *The Haskins Society Journal* 1 (1989), pp. 99–107.

[35] Henry of Huntingdon, *Historia Anglorum*, pp. 714–16, put a very similar speech in the mouth of Bishop Ralph of Orkney. On this point, see Gransden, *Historical Writing*, p. 215.

[36] Aelred, *Relatio de Standardo*, p. 188, *secure igitur congrediamur, cum nobis sit causa justior, manus fortior . . . quibus divinum auxilium praesto est, cum quibus tota coelestis curia dimicabit.*

[37] *Ibid.*, pp. 188–9, *aderit Michael cum angelis suam ulturus injuriam, cujus ecclesiam humano sanguine foedaverunt . . . Petrus cum Apostolis pugnabit pro nobis, quorum basilicas nunc in stabulum, nunc in prostibulum converterunt. Sancti martyres nostra praecedant agmina quorum incenderunt memorias, quorum atria caedibus impleverunt.*

[38] *Ibid.*, p. 189, *virgines sanctae licet pugnae dubitent interesse, pro nobis tamen oratione pugnabunt. Amplius dico, ipse Christus apprehendet arma et scutum, et exurget in adjutorium nobis.*

[39] *Ibid., Ipsi enim veniunt ad nos in superbia; nos cum humilitate procedimus, illi carnes raptas quas voraverunt eructant; nos post sacra jejunia Christi carne et sanguine saginamur. Illos histriones, saltatores et saltatrices, nos crux Christi et reliquiae Sanctorum antecedunt.*

It would appear that this harangue was intended to raise the morale of the Anglo-Norman troops by emphasizing their advantages and by stressing the evil nature of their adversaries. Thus, for example, Walter Espec is reported to have stressed that Normans had always fought well against long odds.[40] Consequently, the fact that Walter emphasized the participation of the Anglo-Norman troops in a ritual fast, and their subsequent reception of Christ's body and blood, suggests that these rites were understood by both the officers and men to be advantageous to soldiers going into battle.

But even this harangue was not the last stage in the religious preparation of the soldiers for combat. As the troops were drawn up for battle, standing shoulder to shoulder and shield to shield, they held aloft their banners and spears so that they would catch the morning light.[41] The priests, dressed in their white habits, are then reported to have walked among the soldiers carrying crosses and saints' relics. According to Aelred, they were there to strengthen (*roborare*) the men with comforting words and prayers (*sermo simul et oratio*).[42]

After the battle began, Bishop Ralph and the other priests are reported to have climbed onto a high point behind the lines. Aelred emphasized that the bishop granted a final remission of sins (*remissio peccatorum*) to those who were fighting. Then, he and his fellow priests raised their arms to heaven and prayed to God to give aid to the army. Finally, Aelred recorded that Ralph gave the soldiers his blessing and the priests responded in chorus saying "amen amen."[43]

The depiction of priests dressed in their white stoles while giving spiritual support to troops going into battle, and the promise of remission of sins to soldiers, played an important role in contemporary narrative accounts of the crusades, including those written by Anglo-Norman writers such as Orderic Vitalis and Henry of Huntingdon. Aelred's discussion of these events might indicate only that he had read contemporary accounts of the crusades, and wished to incorporate some elements of the rhetorical iconography of crusading warfare into his description of a battle fought to protect his monastery. This is possible but hardly proven. Indeed, even if Aelred had been inspired to discuss white vestments and remissions of sin by his reading of crusade narratives, this does not mean that his description of the events at the Battle of the Standard is inaccurate. In fact, the influence of crusade narratives may well have played a role in encouraging a genuine *imitatio* in the army and not only in the writing of history.

---

[40] *Ibid.*, p. 186.

[41] *Ibid.*, p. 192. It is possible that these banners were the same as those brought into the field by the parish priests. For French practice, see Orderic Vitalis, *Ecclesiastical History*, VI: 156.

[42] *Ibid.*, p. 192, *sacerdotes sacris vestibus candidati, cum crucibus et reliquiis Sanctorum exercitum ambiebant, et sermone simul et oratione populum decentissme roborabant.*

[43] *Ibid.*, pp. 195–6, *interea episcopus Orchadensis, quem illo miserat archiepiscopus, stans in eminentiori loco, cum populo proeliandi necessitatem in remissionem peccatorum indixisset, tundentes pectora, erectis manibus divinum auxilium precabantur; factaque super eos absolutione, episcopus benedictonem sollempni voce adjecit, cunctis alta voce respondentibus amen amen.*

In his description of the aftermath of the battle, Abbot Aelred once more turned his focus to Walter Espec. Aelred claimed that the soldiers crowded around the baron and revered him as the architect of the victory. But it is important to note as well that the soldiers also are reported to have given thanks to God for giving them victory over the Scots.[44] Finally, Richard of Hexham recorded that after the battle was over, the army dispersed, each man going to his own home. But he emphasized that the soldiers returned the banners (*vexilla*) to the churches of the saints from which they had originally received them.[45]

The religious preparations undertaken by the English army as these were described by Richard of Hexham and Aelred of Rievaulx can be divided into three distinct phases: first, the initial organization of rites at the commencement of the campaign, which continued until the day of the battle had arrived, second, those performed on the morning of the battle, and finally, the rites undertaken during the battle itself. Each element of the military campaign required complicated planning and a distinct set of ritual practices designed both to prepare the individual soldiers for battle and to prepare the army as a whole in order to obtain victory.

According to Richard of Hexham, Archbishop Thurstan promised the barons that reconciliation with God through the act of penance would assure victory against their enemies. Thurstan's emphasis on the connection between appropriate religious preparation and divine aid, culminating in victory, has clear antecedents both in ordinary wars of the eleventh century and in contemporary accounts of the crusades. In addition, the benefits for military morale that accompanied belief in the likelihood of divine assistance would also appear to have had the same importance in 1138 as they did in earlier periods.[46]

By the morning of 22 August, all of the soldiers in the English army, who so desired, had able to confess their sins, receive penance and absolution, and were able to draw strength and spiritual comfort from the presence of wide variety of sacred objects including relics, holy banners, and crosses. As the time for battle drew near, the men further strengthened themselves for the approaching conflict by engaging in one final fast and then receiving communion, that is the body and blood of Christ (*Christi carno et sanguis*). We have seen in numerous other contexts that soldiers considered the reception of the eucharist to be an effective

---

[44] *Ibid.*, pp. 198–9, *Sane Anglorum duces omnes sani incolumesque reversi et circa Walterum Espec, quem ducis et patris loco venerabantur, conglobati, immensas gratias Deo Omnipotenti pro insperata victoria retulerunt.*

[45] Richard of Hexham, *De gestis Regis Stephani*, p. 165, *vexilla quae acceperant cum gaudio et gratiarum actione ecclesiis sanctorum reconsignant.*

[46] Concerning the importance of saints in English warfare before the Norman conquest, see Kent G. Hare, "Apparitions and War in Anglo-Saxon England," in *The Circle of War in the Middle Ages: Essays on Medieval Military and Naval History*, ed. Donald J. Kagay and L.J. Andrew Villalon (Woodbridge, 1999), pp. 75–86. Christopher Holdsworth, " 'An Airier Aristocracy': The Saints at War," *Transactions of the Royal Historical Society*, 6th ser. 6 (1996), pp. 103–22, provides an insightful tour of the appearance of military saints in a variety of literary genres up through the early twelfth century. It is clear from Holdsworth's trove of examples that although soldier saints were commonly the object of prayer, they rarely appeared on the battlefields of pre-crusade Europe.

means of gaining both inner spiritual peace and outward strength, and this would appear to have been a common view among the Anglo-Norman troops gathered at Northallerton.[47]

After the reception of the eucharist, the Anglo-Norman army moved into position where Aelred recorded that Walter Espec gave his rousing harangue, discussed above. This was not in itself a religious act. There were no rites or ceremonies involved. However, Walter did remind the soldiers of their previous participation in important religious rites, and encouraged them to rely on God and the saints in the approaching battle. The entire speech can be understood as a type of gloss on the series of religious practices in which the soldiers had participated that were intended to comfort them before the battle began. According to Aelred, following Walter's address, priests moved among the troops dressed in their white vestments, thereby clearly marking themselves as agents of God. They carried with them holy relics and crosses, and began to give last-minute blessings and words of encouragement to the troops. Aelred claimed that some of the priests delivered sermons, and one can imagine that they reminded the soldiers to have faith in God and his saints and to trust in the power of the holy relics to deliver them in battle. And as this was going on, high above the soldiers' heads where everyone could see, the banners of Saint Peter, Saint John, and Saint Wilfrid waved in the breeze, topped only by a silver pyx containing Christ's body. The final series of events before the battle would appear to have been designed both to invoke God's aid and that of his saints on behalf of the army, and to convince the soldiers that this help certainly was forthcoming.

Finally, as the battle began, Bishop Ralph and his fellow priests began a last series of prayers and blessings on behalf of the soldiers. At this point, there were no soldiers in position to observe closely what the priests were doing, and Aelred does not give the impression that the soldiers could actually hear what prayers were being said on their behalf. However, Aelred's description of the events indicates that the men could see a crowd of priests standing on elevated ground reaching their arms towards heaven. As a result, while the priests on the hill directed their efforts toward God, the men in the field benefited from the knowledge that everything possible was being done on their behalf.

Just before the priests began their massed prayers, Ralph was described by Aelred as granting a remission of sins (*remissio peccatorum*) to the entire Anglo-Norman army.[48] It is not clear from the context why the bishop should have done so, given the earlier grants of absolution to the English soldiers both by Archbishop Thurstan at York, and by Bishop Ralph himself at Northallerton. As was noted above, however, *remissio peccatorum* was the standard phrase used by crusade preachers to describe the benefits enjoyed by those men who went on crusade. It may therefore have been the case that Aelred imported the concept of remission of sins into his text for the purpose of emphasizing the

---

[47] The reception of the host was regularly described as a rite that strengthened (*munire*) men for battle both in crusade narratives and in accounts dealing with secular wars.

[48] Aelred, *Relatio de Standardo*, p. 196.

justice of the Anglo-Norman side and the anti-Christian nature of the enemy Scots, thereby further underlining the contribution of religious authorities and sacred power to their victory. However, the possibility cannot be excluded that Bishop Ralph of Orkney actually granted this spiritual benefit to the soldiers following the model provided to him by crusade preachers.

Parish priests played a crucial role in providing pastoral care to the members of the levies of militia troops serving in the Anglo-Norman army at the Battle of the Standard. However, these parish priests and militiamen formed only part of the Anglo-Norman military establishment. During the course of their daily lives, the vast majority of militiamen were simple farmers or craftsmen, while parish priests had a series of obligations to all of their parishioners at home. There were, however, men present at the Battle of the Standard who served as career soldiers. Most of the members of the baronial contingents may be considered in this category. For men such as these, it was important to have available priests who were familiar with the pastoral needs of professional soldiers. Unfortunately, very little evidence survives that sheds light on the provision of pastoral care to the particular units serving under the command of any of the particular northern barons who participated in the Battle of the Standard. However, anecdotal evidence about the pastoral care afforded to professional troops in the Anglo-Norman realm can be gleaned from sources that discuss the military households of King Henry I of England (1100–1135) before his accession, the military household of Hugh of Avranches, earl of Chester, and of William Clito, the son of Duke Robert Curthose of Normandy and Henry I's nephew.[49]

The best surviving account of Henry's military household, before his royal accession, comes from the pen of William of Newburgh (1135–1198), who wrote his history at the request of Abbot Ernald of Rievaulx – himself a student of Abbot Aelred.[50] William's treatment of the pastoral care available to Henry's military household is contained in an account detailing one of the prince's campaigns in Normandy. According to William, when Henry stopped to hear mass in a church along his line of march, he requested that the incumbent priest finish the service quickly. William reported that the cleric was so successful that he pleased all of the future king's military household. The soldiers are reported to have been very positively impressed by the speed with which the priest was able to complete the service and called out "one could not find a better chaplain for soldiers."[51] Henry hired him on the spot.

---

[49] The basic works on the Anglo-Norman military household are Marjorie M. Chibnall, "Mercenaries and the *familia regis* under Henry I," *Proceedings of the Society for Antiquaries of Scotland* 62 (1977), pp. 15–23; and John O. Prestwich, "The Military Household of the Norman Kings," *English Historical Review* 96 (1981), pp. 1–35.

[50] William is accounted one of the more careful historians of his period and was one of the few to attack Geoffrey of Monmouth for producing fiction rather than true accounts of the past. See Gransden, *Historical Writing*, pp. 263–8.

[51] William of Newburgh, *Historia rerum Anglicarum*, 4 vols., ed. Richard Howlett, Rolls Series 82 (London, 1884–9) I: 36, *eodem tempore Henricus junior fratri regi militans, casu ex itinere cum comitibus divertit ad ecclesiam in qua ille (Roger) ministrabat, petiit sibi celebrari sacra. Sacerdos vero petitione suscepta, ad incipiendum promptus et ad finiendum*

William of Newburgh's account gives the impression that at least some Anglo-Norman professional soldiers wanted nothing more than a quick mass and communion before combat. Indeed, a slow priest might leave some soldiers unprepared for battle. However, this story is told by William Newburgh in order to cast aspersions on the reputation of Bishop Roger of Salisbury whom the chronicler identified as the priest in the story. William described Roger as a poorly educated man and notes that recruiting this incompetent as a military chaplain was tantamount to having the blind lead the blind.[52] Nevertheless, it is likely that William's description of the reaction of the soldiers towards a priest who said mass quickly was valid for at least some of the men under Henry's command, who appreciated the need to have all of the troops provided with care before battle.

It was not always the case, however, that military commanders sought out priests whose best quality was an ability to say mass quickly. Orderic Vitalis notes that Earl Hugh of Chester catered to the deeper religious concerns felt by some of his soldiers by recruiting priests who were well respected for their religious lives. Gerold, the son of a Norman magnate, who served in Hugh's household, earned a reputation as a pious man who was strict with the soldiers under his care.[53] Orderic Vitalis notes that Gerold was particularly vexed by the sexual promiscuity of the soldiers and by their neglect of the proper rites of the church. Gerold included both the high-ranking officers (*barones*) and the simple fighting men (*modesti milites*) in his criticisms, and was known for lecturing them about the proper behavior of soldiers. Orderic reports that Gerold never tired of repeating to them the *vitae* of famous military saints including George and Demetrius whose moral example he felt Henry's soldiers should follow.[54]

The provision of pastoral care to the military households of Henry I and Hugh of Avranches can be compared with the efforts of William Clito during his campaign to conquer Flanders following the murder of Count Charles the Good (1127). Galbert, a notary from Bruges, took pains in his discussion of the war of succession in Flanders between William Clito and Thierry of Alsace to emphasize the important role that confession played in raising the fighting spirit of

---

succinctus, in utroque militibus sic placuit, ut dicerent tam aptum militibus reperiri non posse capellanum.

[52] *Ibid., factusque illi et ejus militibus capellanus ad libitum, caecus praestabat caecis ducatum. Et cum esset fere illiteratus, innata tamen astutia ita callebat, ut domino suo in brevi carus exsisteret, et secretoria ejus negotia procuraret.*

[53] Orderic Vitalis, *The Ecclesiastical History of Orderic Vitalis*, III: 216, *in capella eius serviebat Abrincatensis clericus nomine Geroldus religone et honestate peritiaque litterarum praeditus.*

[54] *Ibid., praecipuis baronibus et modestis militibus puerisque nobilibus salutares monitus promebat et de veteri testamento novisque Christianorum gestis imitanda sactorum militum tirocinia ubertim coacervabat. Luculenter enim enarrabat conflictus Demetrii et Georgii, Teodori et Sebastiani Mauricii ducis et Thebeae legionis, et Eustachii precelsi magistri militum cum sociis suis qui per martirium coronari meruerunt in coelis.* It is likely that Gerold wished the soldiers to imitate the good lives of these Christian heros if not their martyrdoms. Gerold's service with Hugh is discussed by Holdsworth, ' "An Airier Aristocracy," ' pp. 103–4.

soldiers.[55] Galbert recorded that on 21 June 1128, William Clito prepared for battle by confessing his sins to Abbot Harnulf of Oudenburg, and then receiving penance from him. William was followed by all of his soldiers, who marked their penitential status by cutting their hair short, and by putting aside their finery and replacing these garments with linen shirts and mail coats.[56] According to Galbert, after pledging their faithfulness to God, William's troops went into battle with great zeal, convinced that they had achieved the reconciliation with Christ necessary for their salvation.[57] Abbot Harnulf was not a military chaplain of the type exemplified by either Roger of Salisbury or Gerold. However, it would appear that he knew how to care for soldiers in an effective manner. Indeed, William and his troops are reported to have appreciated the abbot's response, including his imposition of haircuts and change of clothing, to such an extent that they were well motivated before going into battle.

In the aftermath of Thierry of Alsace's defeat, the townspeople of Bruges, who had supported him in his effort to gain control of Flanders, learned that William Clito and his troops had demonstrated their penitence and submission to God by cutting their hair and shedding their fine clothing. According to Galbert, the Brugeois decided that since the ostentatious displays of penitence had worked for their enemies they too would undertake these penitential actions.[58] In addition, the priests of Bruges also called upon the local people, presumably including the town militiamen, to confess their sins and accept penance following, as Galbert pointed out, the example set by their enemies.[59]

These three accounts dealing with the provision of pastoral care to fighting men are important anecdotal evidence for the religious needs of professional soldiers. The incidental nature of the first two stories within the context of narratives concerned with other matters also indicates that the behavior ascribed to professional soldiers and their chaplains was more common than might be

---

[55] In his discussion of the murder of Charles and the count's supporters, Galbert, *De multro, traditione, et occisione gloriosi Karoli comitis Flandriarum*, ed. Jeffrey Rider, Corpus Christianorum 131 (Turnholt, 1994), p. 37, stressed that the Castellan of Bourbourg was able to prepare himself for death by confessing his sins and receiving communion "according to Christian custom" (*hic tamen castellanus confessionem peccatorum suorum presbyteris ecclesiae ipsius confessus, corpori et sanguini Christi communicatus more christiano*).

[56] Galbert, *De multro*, p. 159, *In Oldenburg ab abbate illius loci, religioso et prudenti viro, penitentiam suorum peccatorum devotus suscepit et vovit Deo ut deinceps pauperum foret advocatus et ecclesiam Dei. Similiter omnes strenui milites eius voverunt, circumcisisque crinibus et rejectis vulgaribus indumentis, camisia et lorica.*

[57] *Ibid., humili voto apud Deum et fortissimo zelo progredientes ad bellum.*

[58] *Ibid., tandem audientes nostrates quod Willelmus comes ante ingressum belli se Deo humiliter subiecisset penitentiae remedium insumpsisset, crines et superfluas vestes ipse et omnes sui truncassent post belli infortunia sua, cives nostri simul cum consule Theoderico crines et vestes circumciderunt.*

[59] *Ibid., et ipsi quoque presbyteri nostri ad exemplum inimicorum tandem penitentiam preadicaverunt*. The failure of the local priests to hear confessions of the people of Bruges before the battle likely resulted from the fact that Archbishop Radulf of Rheims supported William Clito and had placed Bruges under interdict. According to Galbert, even after the battle the archbishop was under the impression that no religious services were being held in the city. It was only following the devastating battle that the local clergy felt compelled to exercise their sacerdotal offices in spite of their superior's action. See *ibid.*, p. 161.

suggested by the relatively small corpus of evidence dealing with the topic. In addition, the accounts of Orderic Vitalis and William of Newburgh provide a useful reminder that medieval soldiers could have complex feelings about the role of religion in warfare. Even those soldiers who were regarded by contemporaries as lax in the observance of their religious duties are reported to have thought it worthwhile at least to hear mass while on campaign. On the other end of the spectrum, pious priests such as Gerold could find employment as military chaplains and maintain very strict codes of conduct for the men for whose spiritual well-being they were responsible. Soldiers would appear to have expressed a range of religious concerns, and these concerns may very well have varied over the course of their careers and as they found themselves in new situations. Whatever their normal circumstances, however, the evidence suggests that many officers and soldiers, even if they did not normally behave in a religious manner, "got religion" before going into battle.

Religion of War in the German Empire

In thinking about the religious behavior of German soldiers it is important to differentiate between those who participated in local campaigns and those who served in campaigns sanctioned, organized, and led by the emperor himself. In this section, we will first consider a regional war between the archbishop of Trier and the count palatine of the lower Rhine. We will then turn to one of Emperor Frederick Barbarossa's campaigns against the city of Milan.

Balderic, who served as the *magister scholarum* at the Cathedral of Trier from 1147 to 1158, emphasized the vital role played by religious rites, including confession, in motivating men for battle while discussing a campaign carried out by Archbishop Albero of Trier (1131–1152) against Count Palatine Hermann in 1148.[60] Balderic, who may have been an eyewitness to the events he described, and who certainly had access to many first-hand accounts, recorded that the archiepiscopal army laid siege to the fortress of Treis in September of 1148. The count palatine subsequently marched to relieve the siege, and the two armies faced each other for three days.[61] Finally, Archbishop Albero decided to end the stalemate and launch an attack against Hermann's army.

Balderic stressed that before sending his troops into battle, the archbishop preached to the entire army, all the while holding the archiepiscopal cross in his hands. Albero's sermon was divided into four parts each of which would appear to have been intended to motivate the troops to fight well in the battle. The archbishop began his sermon by calling his soldiers, "you friends of Saint Peter, you defenders of the holy Church, who place your mortal bodies in danger against the swords of your enemies on behalf of God and justice."[62] By identifying the soldiers as the agents of justice acting on behalf of their patron saint and the

---

[60] See *Gesta Alberonis archiepiscopi*, ed. Georg Waitz, MG SS 8 (Hanover, 1848), p. 235.

[61] *Ibid.*, pp. 255–6.

[62] *Ibid.*, p. 256, *O vos amici beati Petri! O sanctae defensores ecclesiae!, qui hodie pro Deo atque pro iusticia mortalia corpora vestra hostili gladio opposuistis. . . .*

church, the archbishop clearly hoped to eliminate any qualms they might have had about the justness of their cause in fighting their fellow Christian Rhinelanders.[63] Albero also may be seen to have tried to reinforce the *esprit de corps* among his men by emphasizing their common bond as "friends of Saint Peter," the patron of their city. Finally, the archbishop's comments would appear to have had important implications for the discipline on the battlefield of the city's troops. By couching his exhortation in such a manner that the men were encouraged to be prepared to die on behalf of the saint, Albero gave religious sanction to fighting bravely, even at the cost of their own lives. This type of behavior was fundamental to the maintenance of discipline and the well-recognized needs of an army in battle.

The second element of Albero's sermon dealt with the supernatural aid available to his soldiers if they maintained their faith. He encouraged his men to let Saint Peter come into their minds because they were serving as his soldiers on this day (*cuius milites hodie existitis*).[64] The archbishop told his men that they should believe Peter alongside a great host of saints fighting with invisible shields would protect them in the battle. If they did so, they could be sure of victory.[65] It may be significant that the archbishop is reported to have described his men as Peter's soldiers specifically on this day rather than making only a general acknowledgment of their service to the saint. The implication of the archbishop's statement would appear to be that as long as the men fought for Albero and their city they were under the protection of heaven. One might infer from this that service in other contexts might not so obviously earn saintly support.

In the third section of his sermon, Archbishop Albero strove to portray the enemy soldiers in as negative a light as possible. Clearly, Count Palatine Hermann and his men were Christians. However, the archbishop attempted to show that they were bad Christians against whom it was proper for true sons of the church to fight. Albero held up his archiepiscopal cross and brandished it while crying out, "look at this cross, this I say is a terrifying symbol to the enemies of Christ."[66] He then added that this was the very cross upon which Hermann had sworn his oaths of fidelity to the church of Trier and sworn to protect it as its advocate. The cross was therefore a symbol of strength for the troops of Trier and a mark of shame to the soldiers serving under the count palatine. Albero concluded this part of his sermon by promising to carry the cross to Count Palatine Hermann, and show him the evil of having violated of his oath.[67]

In the final section of his sermon, Archbishop Albero called upon his men to

---

[63] As we shall see below, it was particularly important in this case for the archbishop to identify the soldiers as agents of justice because they were fighting against their former allies in the army of Count Palatine Hermann, the advocate of the archbishopric.

[64] *Gesta Alberonis*, p. 256, *nunc veniat vobis in mentem beatus Petrus, cuius milites hodie existitis.*

[65] *Ibid.*, *credatis eum cum magna sanctorum caterva invisibilibus clipeis hodie vos protegere; certe estote de victoria.*

[66] *Ibid.*, *Respicite hoc signum crucis, hoc, inquam, signum terribile adversariis Ihesu Christi.*

[67] *Ibid.*

prepare themselves for battle by reconciling themselves to God through the rites that, as we have seen, are traditionally associated with military religion. He called out "but now, O faithful supporters of Jesus Christ, who offer your lives and your blood for the defense of his church, prepare your hearts for God and wash your consciences clean."[68] The archbishop then explicitly noted that there was insufficient time for each man to make an individual and private confession of his sins and therefore ordered, "make a general confession of your sins to me as your pastor." He then added, "by the power granted to us by God I will grant you an indulgence and remission of all of your sins through our office, so that if anyone should be summoned today from this temporal and uncertain life he will pass to a better, namely an eternal life."[69]

It would appear from the *reportatio* of Albero's sermon that, despite the general confession made by the soldiers on that day, there was an expectation and perhaps a strong personal desire among the men that they would make individual and private confessions before battle. This is indicated by the fact that the archbishop felt the need to justify the general confession and to explain its implications. Indeed, he pointed out explicitly that there was insufficient time for the men to make individual confessions (*quia non vacat ut singillatim faciatis*). It is obvious that Albero mentioned individual confessions because they were a normal, that is, an institutional element in the soldiers' pre-battle preparations, which could only be bypassed under extreme circumstances.

However, it is also necessary to recognize that even if individual confessions to priests were not available, the archbishop's soldiers still wanted to confess before battle. As was noted above, the content of sermons delivered by preachers familiar with their audiences can offer insights into the thinking of the latter, because it was in the interest of the speaker to employ concepts and arguments that were meaningful to his listeners. It is important for our understanding of the religious behavior and beliefs of soldiers that their desire to confess before battle could be satisfied only partly in the fashion noted in his sermon, namely through a communal recognition of fault. Nevertheless, it would appear that for these Rhinelanders in the mid-twelfth century, communal confession of sins was a suitable temporary replacement for individual confessions. Indeed, Balderic makes clear in his account that the men did participate in the rite, noting it was only after the soldiers had confessed and received absolution that the archbishop continued his religious preparation of the army for battle.[70] Of course, as one might suspect in a situation where soldiers made a

---

68 *Ibid.*, p. 256, *Sed nunc, o fideles Ihesu Christi, qui vitam et sanguinem vestrum pro defensione ecclesiae suae offertis, preparate corda vestra Domino, mundate conscientias vestras. . . .*

69 *Ibid., et quia non vacat ut singillatim faciatis confessiones, generalem michi pastori vestro facite peccatorum vestrorum confessionem; et ego, potestate a Deo nobis tradita, faciam vobis per officium nostrum indulgentiam et remissionem omnium delictorum vestrorum, ut, si quis hodie ex hac temporali et incerta vita evocatur, transeat ad meliorem vitam, scilicet aeternam.*

70 *Ibid., Tunc cum accepisset omnium communem confessionem, indulgentia facta absolutione, benedictionem super eos faciens, ita omnes animavit, quod nec in uno signum timidatis apparuit.*

communal confession of their sins, there could be no question of assigning individual penances to the men. Thus, in contrast to the Anglo-Norman soldiers at York who received private penances, there is no indication that any of the men of Trier received any penances at all before Albero granted them a general absolution of their sins.

The second important point to be drawn from this last portion of the archbishop's sermon is that the crusading notions of indulgences and remission of sin, or at least notions that first gained wide popularity during the crusades, had penetrated ordinary warfare in Germany by the mid-twelfth century. We saw above that Bishop Ralph of Orkney had promised a remission of sins to the Anglo-Norman troops at the Battle of the Standard. Ten years later, the archbishop of Trier, clearly employing a crusading vocabulary, also promised a remission of sins (*remissio omnium delictorum vestrorum*) as well as an indulgence (*indulgentia*) on the basis of his own authority, which he stressed, had been granted to him by God. It is not clear from the context of his sermon what the archbishop intended to convey by offering both a remission of sins and an indulgence. It is likely that these terms were used as synonyms, because a general legal definition of an indulgence as something different from a remission of sins would not be available in canon law for at least another century.[71]

As important as the evidence of the sermon is for evaluating Archbishop Albero's estimation of his soldiers' religious concerns and needs, Balderic provides even clearer evidence of the role played by religion in maintaining the morale of the men before battle. After finishing his recapitulation of the archbishop's address, the chronicler noted that, following the communal or general confession and grant of indulgences, Albero blessed his troops. According to Balderic, this blessing, when combined with the previous rites, so motivated the men that there was not the slightest hint of fear in any of the soldiers.[72] Quite clearly, Balderic, who was in a position to know, considered the religious preparations to be a crucial factor in motivating the troops to fight bravely in battle.

Balderic's account of Archbishop Albero's campaign against Count Palatine Hermann dealt with the provision of religious support to soldiers serving in one of the continuous internal struggles carried out among the empire's office holders.[73] While these small wars were the most common kind of conflict within the German empire of the twelfth century, the participants lacked one significant pillar of moral support, namely the justification provided by service in a royal campaign commanded by the German king in person or by his legally appointed deputy. In order to understand the nuances inherent in military reli-

[71] On this point, see Brundage, *Medieval Canon Law and the Crusader*, pp. 145–8.

[72] *Gesta Alberonis*, p. 56, . . . *ita omnes animavit, quod nec in uno signum timidatis apparuit* (my emphasis).

[73] The German empire of the twelfth century was riven with internal disputes at all levels of the political hierarchy, including the struggle between Archbishop Albero of Trier and Count Palatine Hermann. Benjamin Arnold, *Count and Bishop in Medieval Germany: A Study in Regional Power 1100–1350* (Philadelphia, 1991), investigates the struggle for dominance between powerful local office-holders in southern Germany, particularly in Bavaria. Concerning studies for regional dominance in northern Germany during Barbarossa's reign, see Karl Jordan, *Heinrich der Löwe: Eine Biographie* (Munich, 1979).

gion it is necessary to consider the organization of military religion in this latter type of war.

First is it crucial to note that the German kings of the twelfth century followed closely in the path of their eleventh-century predecessors by expending considerable resources to secure intercessory prayers, masses, and other rites for the safety of the kingdom generally, as well as for individual campaigns. Lothar III (1125–1137), Conrad III (1137–1151), and Frederick I Barbarossa (1152–1190) regularly gave gifts or confirmed earlier donations to religious houses *pro stabilitate regni nostri, pro statu totius imperii, ob regni nostri firmam stabilitatem*, and *pro statu rei publice*.[74] Thus, for example, as he marched to Rome in 1137, Lothar granted an immunity to the monastery of St Columba at Chiaravalle so that the brothers would be free *pro imperio Romano orare*.[75] In 1139, Conrad granted all of the tolls from a bridge over the Meuse river to the house of St Servatius at Maastricht in return for which the monks were to pray *pro regni etiam nostri quieta et statu pacifico*.[76]

As we saw in the previous chapter, Conrad's successor Frederick Barbarossa considered it exceptionally important to secure prayers for his army during the Third Crusade. Frederick's request for prayers in 1189 was simply a continuation of his long-standing effort to assure the provision of prayers and intercessory masses on behalf of his army and realm.[77] In 1157, for example, Frederick sent a letter to Abbot Wibald of Stablo informing him that negotiations with the Polish emissaries sent to the imperial court had collapsed and that therefore Frederick had dispatched his military forces on 4 August.[78] Paraphrasing Proverbs 21.1, Frederick emphasized that he placed all of his hope in God's mercy and therefore asked the abbot to pray to God on behalf of the German forces in the field.[79]

After a lightning campaign into Poland during which he overwhelmed Polish resistance, captured a large number of fortresses, and imposed a heavy tribute on the Poles, Frederick wrote again to Wibald to describe his success and to invite the abbot to an assembly at Würzburg. In composing this letter, Frederick was careful to ascribe victory over the Poles to divine piety (*divina pietas*),

---

[74] The charters of King Henry V (1106–1125) have not yet been edited.

[75] *Die Urkunden der deutschen Könige und Kaiser*, vol. 8, ed. Emil von Ottenthal and Hans Hirsch (Berlin, 1927), p. 176. Cf. *ibid*., pp. 22, 25, 58, 76, 118, 145, 179, and 191.

[76] *Die Urkunden der deutschen Könige und Kaiser*, vol. 9, ed. Friedrich Hausmann (Vienna, 1969), pp. 49–50. Cf. *ibid*., pp. 4, 27, 40, 91, 128, 142, 145, 151, 175, 177, 213, 232, 280, 281, 403, 459, 477, and 504.

[77] In this regard, see *Die Urkunden der deutschen Könige und Kaiser*, vol. 10.1, ed. Heinrich Appelt, MGH (Hanover, 1975), pp. 18, 26, 128, 180, 209, 291, 324, and 360; *Die Urkunden der deutschen Könige und Kaiser*, vol. 10.2, ed. Heinrich Appelt, MGH (Hanover, 1979), pp. 24, 140, 193, 263, and 285; and *Die Urkunden der deutschen Könige und Kaiser*, vol. 10.3, ed. Heinrich Appelt, MGH (Hanover, 1985), pp. 209, 213, 233, 267, 307, 358, and 371.

[78] *Die Urkunden der deutschen Könige und Kaiser*, vol. 10.1, p. 303.

[79] *Ibid., Inde nos in misericordia Dei, in cuius manu cor regis est, omnem fiduciam nostram ponens II non. Augusti movimus expeditionem rogantes quam intime dilectionem tuam, ut apud divinam pietatem prosperos successus et felicem reditum indefessis precibus nobis optineas.*

which granted its grace to the German forces and exalted the Roman empire in glory and honor.[80] Barbarossa explained that Poland posed great difficulties to invaders because it was heavily protected by both natural and man-made fortifications. However, the emperor emphasized "by the *virtus* of God which visibly proceeded us," the German army was able to cross the Oder river and penetrate the deep forests to defeat the Poles.[81]

Rahewin, who succeeded Bishop Otto of Freising as Frederick I's biographer, offers further insights into the nature of military religion on imperial campaigns in the context of recording Barbarossa's planned invasion of Lombardy in 1158. In the course of discussing the approaching military operations, Rahewin noted that Frederick summoned his religious advisors in order to consider the impending campaign against the city of Milan. Rahewin emphasized that, as had been true of the campaign against Poland in the previous year, Barbarossa placed his primary hope for victory in God and, as a result, he hoped to use these, "learned men proven in the holiness of their lives" as a kind of divine oracle (*divinum oraculum*).[82]

Rahewin described, in particular, Frederick's discussion with Bishop Hartmann of Brixen, whom the chronicler characterized as the man to whom the emperor entrusted his own personal salvation.[83] Rahewin recorded that after baring his soul, Frederick submitted himself devotedly to the counsel of the bishop.[84] Rahewin emphasized that by doing so, Frederick exercised the office of a Christian ruler by arming himself first with spiritual weapons (*arma spirituales*), and by considering his soul before his temporal body.[85] By acting in this manner, Barbarossa also demonstrated publicly to his supporters that all appropriate measures were being taken to assure God's aid for the imperial army.

In addition to his personal religious preparations, which might be considered here as a kind of synecdoche for the religious preparations of the German army

---

[80] *Ibid.*, p. 304, *Quantam in expeditione Polonica, quam nuper gloriose peregimus, divina pietas gratiam nobis contulerit quantava gloria et honore Romanum imperium exaltaverit.*

[81] *Ibid.*, . . . *in virtute Dei, que visibiliter nos precessit.*

[82] Rahewin, *Gesta Frederici sue rectius Cronica*, ed. Franz-Josef Schmale (Darmstadt, 1974), p. 428, *Instabat iam tempus, quo reges ad bella proficisci solent, ipseque in proximo ad Transalpina exercitum ducturus, primo omnium in Deo spem suam responens, adscitis religiosis et probatis sanctitate viris tamquam divinum eos oraculum consultabat. . . .*

[83] *Ibid.*, p. 428, *Quibus in negotiis specialem habebat preceptorem et salutis anime sue fidelem secretarium Hartemannum Brixinorensem episcopum, virum qui tunc inter Germanie episcopos singularis sanctitatis opinione et austerioris vite conversatione preminebat.* The conversation between the emperor and Bishop Hartmann, as described by Rahewin, would appear to have been private. It is therefore not clear how Rahewin came to be informed of the details he provided in his narrative. However, whether this conversation actually happened or not in the exact form described by the chronicler, the discussion of preparations to be taken by soldiers going off to war can still be understood to reflect ideas current at Frederick's court.

[84] *Ibid.*, pp. 428–30, *Hoc ad se adscito, de secretis suis pii se pontificis submisit devote consiliis religiosi. . . .*

[85] *Ibid.*, p. 430, *ac Christianissimi principis officium exercens, quatenus iturus ad bellum spiritualibus armis ante muniret animam quam corpus, ante celestibus se disciplinis prestrueret, quam ad pugnam iturum militem militaribus instruere preceptis curaret.*

as a whole, Frederick also discussed with Bishop Hartmann whether this campaign constituted a just war. Not unexpectedly, Rahewin recorded that Hartmann and the other clergy serving with the imperial army recognized that the war was in fact just. In the view of the clergy, it was fitting for the German soldiers to be eager in their efforts against the rebels, as they characterized the citizens of the Lombard city, because by disturbing the peace of the empire the Milanese had also injured the peace and tranquility of the church.[86] As a consequence, it was made clear to the German troops that they were fighting in a just war. Indeed, in order to reinforce publicly his claim to be acting in defense of the church Barbarossa made large gifts to the churches of the bishops whom he had summoned to advise him and serve with the army.[87]

Milan

In turning from the German to the northern Italian region of the empire, Barbarossa's (and, by extension, his soldiers') personal preparations for war can be compared with the efforts taken by their Milanese enemies to secure God's aid for themselves, and to assure themselves of salvation should they fall in battle. In 1160, the emperor once again launched an invasion of Milanese territory with the intention of breaking the power of the Lombard city. The most thorough account of the campaign that deals with aspects of military religious practice comes from the *Gesta Federici Imperatoris. De rebus gestis in Lonbardia*, whose author portrayed the defenders of the city in a positive light because he intended his work to be read as a catalogue of the sufferings that the people of Lombardy had suffered at the hands of waves of invaders including the Germans.[88]

As was true of many communes in northern Italy, the Milanese were particularly conscious of the important role that pastoral care played in maintaining the fighting spirit of their urban militia. As a rule, they brought into battle a *carroccio*, or banner wagon, adorned with religious symbols, and often accompanied by priests who provided pastoral care to soldiers in the field.[89] The Milanese traditionally raised a large flag of Ambrose, their patron saint, on a mast set in the center of the *carroccio*.[90] So it was a routine matter in early

---

[86] *Ibid.*, *Causas autem belli exponens, dum eas iustas tam memoratus antistes quam reliqui sacerdotes cognovissent, ne dignitas imperialis ab indignis imminueretur et sic pax et tranquillitatis ecclesiarum turbaretur salutaribus mandatis premonitum et premunitum ad proficiscendum contra rebelles animarunt.*

[87] *Ibid.*, p. 428, *atque illorum persuasionibus ecclesiis Dei multa donaria imperiali largitate dispergebat.*

[88] On this point, see *Gesta Federici Imperatoris. De rebus gestis in Lonbardia*, ed. G.H. Pertz. MG SS 18 (Hanover, 1863), p. 360.

[89] For other examples of the use of the *carroccio*, particularly by Genoese forces, see Ogerius Panis, *Annales*, ed. G.H. Pertz, MG SS 18 (Hanover, 1863), pp. 116–17; and Bartholomaeo the Scribe, *Annales*, ed. G.H. Pertz, MG SS 18 (Hanover, 1863), pp. 196 and 223.

[90] On this point, see Erdmann, *Idea of Crusade*, pp. 53–6; and Peter Munz, *Frederick Barbarossa: A Study in Medieval Politics* (Ithaca, 1969), p. 182. Concerning the earliest recorded use of a *carroccio* by Milanese forces, noted above, see Cowdrey, "Archbishop Aribert II of Milan," pp. 12–13.

August 1160 for the city government to send a *carroccio* with the army as the militia attempted to block the Germans' approach to Milan.[91] Indeed, in a letter sent to Count Ivo of Soissons in 1162, Barbarossa noted that during the surrender ceremony following the capitulation of Milan, the citizens brought forward the banner of Saint Ambrose (*vexillum Sancti Ambrosii*), which they customarily transported on their "karrotio," along with all of the other banners they were accustomed to carry into battle.[92]

When the army went into the field, it was accompanied by Archbishop Obert of Milan along with his archiepiscopal *familia* and many other priests (*multi alii clerici*). According to the chronicler, the clerics spent their time speaking with the soldiers and encouraging them in the face of the approaching battle. They are reported to have said that the soldiers should go into the fight with confidence, because God and Saint Ambrose were on their side. In fact, the chronicler emphasized that the clerics spoke to the men in order to motivate them to fight with more confidence in battle (*ut confidenter ad bellum procederent*).[93]

Mass was then celebrated by the archbishop, and the attendant priests organized a public ritual of confession and penance in which the entire army participated. According to the chronicler, the soldiers stood in a public assembly where they made a confession of their sins and then accepted penances for their transgressions.[94] From the description provided by the chronicler, it would appear that we are not dealing here with individual confessions. It is therefore not clear how soldiers could have been assigned penances for their individual sins. For how could any priest know what each soldier had done after hearing a wave of sound from the crowd? It may be that the Milanese soldiers were simply promising to participate in a fuller rite of confession when time permitted.

The events described by the chronicler suggest important parallels to other pre-battle preparations that we have seen in Germany and England, particularly in the important role played by confession and absolution in preparing the men for battle and the invocation of the support of their patron saint. The communal battle wagon, festooned with flags and topped by a banner of Saint Ambrose looking down upon the men, gave the Milanese soldiers a visual reminder of the special protection offered to the city by its holy patron. Archbishop Obert and his fellow priests repeatedly stressed the saint's power, and explicitly called upon the troops to maintain their faith in Ambrose as they went into battle.

However, despite the broad similarity of the Milanese religious preparations to other accounts we have seen, certain elements of their ceremony appear to have been influenced by local needs. The *carroccio* was a peculiarly Italian

---

[91] *Gesta Federici Iimperatoris. De rebus gestis in Lonbardia*, p. 370. During the course of the battle the Milanese troops used the *carroccio* as a rallying point.

[92] *Die Urkunden der deutschen Königer und Kaiser*, vol. 10.2, p. 193.

[93] *Ibid.*, p. 369, *dominus Obertus Mediolanensis archiepiscopus, et Milus archipresbiter, Gaudinus archidiaconus atque Algisius cimiliarcha, et multi alii clerici qui in exercitu aderant, praeceperunt populo ex parte Dei omnipotentis et beati Ambroxii in publica concione et militibus omnibus ut confidenter ad bellum procederent.*

[94] *Ibid.*, *Celebrato itaque divino offitio, et confessione in publica concione facta et penitentia de delictis eorum accepta.*

phenomenon during the middle years of the twelfth century.[95] Its use by the Milanese militia forces marks a difference of style from their German enemies and other northern contemporaries. The second element of the religious preparations that appears to have differed from the cases studied above was the public nature of the rite of penance. William the Conqueror's men confessed their sins individually to priests, and in cases of emergency to their fellow soldiers. The accounts of Anglo-Norman practice in the twelfth century emphasized the important role that priests played in hearing the confessions of individual soldiers. The men of Trier would appear to have expected to confess individually and only participated in communal confession as a result of time constraints. By contrast, the Milanese seem to have been content to confess their sins in public before a crowd of their fellow soldiers, although the sources do not indicate that they lacked the time necessary to make individual confessions. Within this context, it should be noted that unlike Balderic of Trier, the anonymous author of the *Gesta Federici imperatoris* did not record whether each soldier recited a catalogue of his own sins or simply admitted in public that he was a sinner. The latter explanation seems more likely, particularly given the archbishop's immediate assignment to the men of a blanket penance whose contents were not recorded. In either case, however, the chronicler's account makes clear that whatever the manner in which they confessed, Milanese militiamen, like their contemporaries elsewhere in Europe, considered confession to have a crucial role in preparing them for combat.[96]

Liège

In order to gain an even fuller appreciation of regional variations in pre-battle religious practice in the empire, we can compare the program of religious rites and ceremonies set in motion by German and Milanese commanders with those organized by Liégeois leaders from the mid-twelfth through the early thirteenth centuries. In late August of 1141, Bishop Albero II of Liège ordered the city militia to mobilize in order to support his siege efforts at the fortress of Bouillon, which had been seized and was being held illegally by Count Rainald of Bar.[97] However, the townsmen refused to go off to war unless they were

---

[95] The only other example I have found of a banner wagon being used in combat outside of Italy during the course of the twelfth century was deployed by the Anglo-Norman forces in 1138 during the Battle of the Standard. On the use of the *carroccio* by Italian cities, see Webb, "The Cities of God," pp. 111–27.

[96] It is worthy of note that civic militiamen in the Iberian peninsula were equally concerned to provide themselves access to priests while they served on campaign. These townsmen frequently included provisions in their town charters (*fueros*) setting aside resources to pay for the service of chaplains during their frequent military actions. In many cases priests who volunteered to serve in the host would receive a portion of the booty that was captured. See, for example, *Fuero de Bejar*, ed. Juan Gutierrez Cuadrado (Salamanca, 1975), p. 161, *De Soldada de Capellan e del Escriuano. Al capellan de conçeio den un moro e al escriuano otros si den un moriello, si fueren en la hueste: cassi non hy fueren, non les den nada.* Concerning the widespread recruitment of chaplains to serve with the city militias, see James F. Powers, *A Society Organized for War: Iberian Municipal Militias in the Central Middle Ages, 1000–1284* (Berkeley, 1988), pp. 50, 52, and 178.

[97] Concerning this conflict, see *Triumphus Sancti Lamberti de castro Bullono*, ed. W. Arndt,

preceded into battle by Saint Lambert, the patron saint of their city.[98] At first, the cathedral provost, who had been given the responsibility of mobilizing the town militia, was opposed to removing the relics of the saint from their resting place because he feared that they might be damaged. Finally, pressed by the bishop's urgent need for troops, the provost acquiesced to the demands of the townsmen.[99]

On 27 August, the body of Saint Lambert was removed from its crypt and placed in the church where, it is reported, the walls resonated with *laudes* sung to God and to the saint by townsmen and women packed into the cathedral.[100] For the next two days, the entire population of the city participated in a series of religious celebrations intended to summon the aid of their patron saint for the militiamen going off to war. On the 28th, the saint's body was carried in a procession to Publemont on the Meuse river, led by priests carrying crosses and candles. At the very head of the procession was a priest who bore a piece of wood said to be a "portion of the life-giving wood" (*portio ligni vivificae crucis*), which the anonymous author of the chronicle described as an object of such power that it would bring victory. Indeed, he stressed that it was capable of defeating as great an enemy as the devil himself. The chronicler added that this piece of the true cross provided an "altar of salvation" to all those who were pious believers.[101] The line of the procession was crowded by young and old, who were there to pray for the safety and victory of their sons, husbands, and fathers going off to war.[102] That night, the relics of Saint Lambert were placed in the church at Freyr where the townspeople kept a vigil all night long with bright burning candles.[103]

This series of rites and ceremonies in which soldiers, their families, and their fellow townspeople participated would appear to have had important implications both for the morale of the troops and for their *esprit de corps*.[104] Not only

---

MG SS 20 (Hanover, 1868), pp. 497–511. Claude Gaier, "Le rôle militaire des reliques et de l'étendard de Saint Lambert dans la principauté de Liège," *Le moyen âge* 72 (1966), pp. 235–49, here pp. 236–40, offers helpful commentary concerning the value of relics for maintaining military morale. However, Gaier would like to see the Liégois experience as unique.

[98] *Triumphus Sancti Lamberti*, p. 505, *responderunt se non ituros nec opem aliquam nisi praecederet eos beatus martyr.*

[99] *Ibid.*

[100] *Ibid., resonabat ecclesia laudes Deo pro memoria beati martyris omnisque sexus et ordo.*
. . .

[101] *Ibid.*, p. 506, *Antecebat quoque beatum martyrem portio ligni vivificae crucis quae cum magna veneratione apud nos servatur, quam portabat sacerdos quidam nomine Iohannes, lignum per quod diabolus est victus, in quo signum victoriae portusque et ara salutis datur omnibus pie credentibus.*

[102] *Ibid., Plena erat via matronis et pueris imprecantibus prospera maritis et filiis et patribus et se luctuose sacris reliquiis effundentibus, ut laetificaret iocundo reditu, quos contristabat tam lacrimoso discessu.*

[103] *Ibid., Nocte illa ad Ufey in ecclesiam delatae sunt reliquae, ubicum cereis et luminaribus devotio fidelium pernoctavit oppido guadens pro tanto hospite.*

[104] The veneration of Lambert's relics should not be confused with the ritual humiliation of relics at Liège identified by Little, *Benedictine Maleditions*, pp. 141 and 149.

were the men being supported by a full mobilization of the religious resources of their city, they were repeatedly reminded of their common bond as the *fideles* of Saint Lambert, whose relics would accompany them on campaign. This allegiance to the saint can be understood, in some respects, to have had political overtones. However, it would appear that the townspeople did not separate completely the religious from the political components of the ceremonies carried out on behalf of the troops.

According to the chronicler, on the night of the 29th, a report reached the archdeacon of the cathedral that Count Rainald was approaching with a force of 2,000 men and would reach Bishop Albero's army at the fortress of Bouillon on the next day. So early on the 30th, the militia forces marched out of the city carrying banners with the images of the saint (*cum pignoribus beati martyris*). Even more importantly, they were also accompanied by the saint, himself, whose bier was being carried in a wagon.[105] When the army stopped at the end of the first day's march, the priests serving with the militia forces joined together around the wagon bearing the saint's bier and began to sing *laudes* to God.[106] The soldiers are reported to have joined in with voices of "exultation and confession."[107] In the meantime many of the soldiers (*milites*) prostrated themselves before Saint Lambert's relics and commended themselves to the saint, perhaps praying that he give them protection in the approaching battle.[108] This report of the soldiers' behavior would seem to indicate that they believed in the power of Saint Lambert to aid them in battle.

When the militia forces joined the bishop's army at the siege of Bouillon, Albero ordered that Saint Lambert's bier containing his relics be placed in a small tent in the camp. He also directed that three times each day, in the morning, noon, and at vespers, the priests serving with the army were to gather around the tent and sing *laudes*. The explicit purpose of these ceremonies, as noted by the author of the *Triumphus Sancti Lamberti*, was to plead their cause to God.[109]

Three days after the militia forces arrived at Bouillon, Albero ordered a general assault on the walls of the fortress. The chronicler reported that in preparation for the attack, the bishop celebrated mass and then preached a sermon. Following these public rites, the soldiers confessed their sins and received absolution.[110] The laconic nature of the chronicler's report makes it impossible to determine whether the soldiers confessed their sins individually to priests or

---

[105] *Triumphus Sancti Lamberti*, p. 506.
[106] *Ibid.*, *Cantabant clerici Deo laudes imposita antiphona: O crux splendior cunctis astris, et ad laudem sancti patroni sui conclamantes: Fortis in adversis.*
[107] *Ibid.*, *in voce exultationis et confessionis.*
[108] *Ibid.*, *milites vero nostri ut erant hac expectatione loricati occurrerunt beati martyris reliquiis humique prostrati salubribus lacrimis eius se devotioni commendaverunt et humeris gestantes. . . .*
[109] *Ibid.*, p. 508, *Illic in parvo artoque satis posuerunt feretrum tentoriolo, deputatis in circuitu suis in tuguriis cum domno Iohanne archidiacono clericis, qui vespere, et mane et meridie narrarent et annuntiarent laudes Domini, ut in tempore opportuno exaudiret Deus voces eorum.*
[110] *Ibid.*, pp. 508–9, *Tertio vero die postquam illuc novus venerat exercitus, ut sua moenia*

communally. What we do know is that the close religious support given to the Liégeois troops was continued throughout the battle. This is made clear by the wounds that were reported to have been suffered by a priest named Gerard who was struck in the head by a spear during the assault on the fortress. This presumably occurred while he was giving aid to one of the many soldiers who were wounded in the attack.[111]

Unfortunately for the Liégeois forces, the assault failed, and the siege of Bouillon lasted for another three weeks until the sons of Count Rainald, who commanded the fortress, finally agreed to surrender. After the enemy troops were ejected from Bouillon, the relics of Saint Lambert were carried in through the main gates and brought into the church, where the Liégeois army gathered to sing *laudes* in praise of God.[112] The next day, the martyr's bier was placed onto a wagon and carried to the town of Dinant, accompanied by great celebration because, according to the chronicler, the victory and capture of Bouillon were ascribed to the saint.[113]

The religious rites and ceremonies performed during the campaign to capture the fortress at Bouillon permit some insight into the varying expectations and needs of both professional and militia soldiers. Bishop Albero's original force, as contrasted to the town levy, was made up of professional soldiers, very likely from the bishop's own extended military *familia*. While we are not informed about their religious practices before the civic forces joined them, it is quite clear that they were comfortable going off to war without the aid of the relics of Saint Lambert. Indeed, they could not have had them available because the saint's bier was still at Liège when the militia troops were ordered to mobilize. The townsmen, on the other hand, flatly refused to go to war unless the saint's relics accompanied them into battle. Moreover, they would appear to have insisted upon a whole series of religious celebrations intended to "activate" Saint Lambert on their behalf, including special rites in the cathedral as well as extramural liturgical processions. While these religious rites were led by the cathedral clergy, it is equally clear from the chronicler's report that the townspeople, both men and women, participated in large numbers. It would appear that they were there because they thought that by praying to the saint, he would

---

solveret hostibus, post missarum sollempnia post ammonitionem verbi Dei et confessionem absolutionemque peccaminum . . . vi assiliunt.

[111] *Ibid.*, p. 509, *Contingit autem eo die . . . pluribus vulneratis, inter quos et Gerardus sacerdos iaculo ictus caput. . . .* There is no reason to believe that Gerard was actually participating in the fighting. This is a positive account of the battle with a pro-Liégois bias. Gerard was a priest from Liège and his wound is mentioned in the context of a battle carried out with all of the appropriate religious preparations. Priests were explicitly prohibited from participating in combat, and it is exceptionally unlikely that Gerard would have been mentioned if he had been acting in a criminal manner.

[112] *Ibid.*, p. 511, *Sic eiectis de castro adversariis intromittuntur reliquiae beati martyris et locantur in medio ecclesiae, omnibus commune Deo laudes canentibus.*

[113] *Ibid.*, *Mane post missarum sollempnia cum exultatione et laetitia inclitus triumphator castro elatus est, cuius sacrum feretrum super carrum impositum usque Dionantum oppidum evectum est.*

be persuaded to bring back their husbands, sons, and fathers from the war, not only alive but victorious.

After the militia forces had joined the bishop's professional soldiers at Bouillon, the chronicler does not mention distinctions among the various kinds of troops regarding their participation in the practices of military religion. All of the men heard mass, listened to Albero's sermon, confessed their sins, and received absolution. They all purportedly benefited from the thrice daily singing of *laudes* in camp and from the presence of Saint Lambert's relics. It would appear that once the bishop's agents had overcome the original hurdle of raising the morale of militia troops, it was sufficient for them to adopt the normal mixture of religious rites and practices traditionally associated with warfare.

In considering the entire range of religious observances in which Bishop Albero's men participated, it seems that the soldiers of Liège enjoyed access to religious care of a level equal to or greater than that of their contemporaries in England, Germany, and northern Italy. In particular, we can see the massive participation of the Liégeois in a series of public religious celebrations matching those performed at York in 1138. By contrast, the men of Trier, Milan, and the soldiers serving with William Clito in Flanders appear to have done without such elaborate rites. A second and not inconsiderable element of Liégeois military religion was the desire to mobilize saints' relics on behalf of the troops. By contrast, the Anglo-Normans and Milanese were content to bring banners of their patron saints with them into the field while the soldiers of Trier had only the word of their archbishop that Saint Peter would come to their aid. In still other cases, including Barbarossa's invasion of Italy and William Clito's war in Flanders, there is no mention in the sources of the role of holy relics on the battlefield.

In evaluating the nature of the religious rites celebrated by and for the Liégeois army, we are fortunate to have evidence from more than one period. In addition to the revealing reports dealing with the war of 1141 valuable sources also survive that discuss the continuing participation of city military forces in religious rites into the early thirteenth century. The Battle of the Steppes (13 October 1213), as the conflict between the Liégeois and Duke Henry of Brabant has come to be called, benefited from two detailed descriptions of the events written by churchmen from the city of Liège. The *Annales* were composed by a priest named Reinerus, who was born in 1157 and served in Liège for more than thirty-five years. He lived through the events that he described, and consequently his text offers a vivid account of the war that devastated the territory of the diocese of Liège.[114] His narrative is complemented by the anonymous author of *De triumpho S. Lamberti in Steppes*, who served as a canon at the cathedral of Liège about a generation after the events described in his history.[115]

---

114 Reinerus, *Annales*, ed. G.H. Pertz, MG SS 16 (Hanover, 1859), pp. 651, 659, and 673.
115 *Vitae Odiliae liber iii: de triumpho S. Lamberti in Steppes*, ed. I. Heller, MG SS 25 (Hanover, 1880), pp. 171–2.

Both Reinerus and the Anonymous agreed that Bishop Hugh II (1200–1229) was forced to mobilize his forces quickly in response to an invasion by Duke Henry of Brabant. Reinerus recorded that the bishop's main ally, Count Louis of Loos, rode up to the gates of episcopal palace, stormed into Hugh's chamber on the night of 11 October 1213, roughly wakened him, and accused the still somnolent figure of neglecting his duties to protect his people.[116] The Anonymous portrayed Bishop Hugh riding through the night, rousing the nearby communities, and calling upon them to hurry with their arms to the staging area near Liège.[117] The speed with which the campaign got under way had important repercussions for the pastoral care of the soldiers involved in the fighting. There was simply no time for men to make individual confessions to their local priests, or for the bishop to organize large-scale ceremonies at the cathedral. As we shall see below, Hugh solved these problems on the field of battle.

The soldiers under the bishop's command spent a difficult night on 12 October, as they were forced to march for hours before finally making a rough camp where they waited for the reinforcements promised by Count Louis. The anonymous chronicler reported that in an effort to lift the spirits of his men the bishop appeared before his entire force, and gave them a general blessing. According to the chronicler, Hugh hoped that this would inspire them to fight well and keep disciplined formations (*ordinibus congregatis*) on the next day.[118]

In the course of describing these events, the anonymous chronicler emphasized that Hugh also hoped his blessing would cause the Liégeois to follow the banner (*vexillum*) bearing the image of Saint Lambert, the patron saint of the cathedral at Liège, into battle.[119] Of course, he had a very strong foundation for believing that the banner could have this effect. In 1141, the Liégeois had brought banners bearing images of Saint Lambert into the field in order to lift the morale of the troops and incorporated these flags into ceremonies designed to invoke the martyr's aid on behalf of their army. Furthermore, the banner mentioned in the context of the Battle of the Steppes is almost certainly the same *vexillum* that had been carried to battle by the Liégeois in May 1212 and then returned to the altar of the Holy Trinity in the cathedral of Liège where it normally rested.[120] This fact is of great importance, because it demonstrates that the *vexillum* continued to be perceived by the soldiers as more than a piece of cloth – it was a blessed object associated directly with the saint and success in war.

Indeed, the author of *De triumpho S. Lamberti* emphasized that both Bishop Hugh and his soldiers understood these banners to have value in summoning the

---

116 Reinerus, *Annales*, p. 668.
117 *De triumpho S. Lamberti*, pp. 181–2.
118 *Ibid.*, p. 183, *in prima igitur noctis vigilia presul misit precones per totum exercitum, ut universi surgerent et procidentes vexillum sequerentur beati martyris, ordinibus congregatis.*
119 See Gaier, "Le rôle militaire des reliques," p. 247.
120 *De triumpho S. Lamberti*, p. 175, *Econtra vero suum episcopus vocavit exercitum et Rasoni militi portandum mandavit banneriam. . . . Proxima ergo tercia feria ante ascensionem Domini dictus Raso in medio maioris ecclesie, ut est moris, armatus est, et vexillum accipiens, cum civitatis populo urbem egreditur. . . . Regrediens itaque primo mane vigilie ascensionis Domini, vexillum reportavit, unde illud sumpserat, sancte Trinitatis ipsum recollocans in altari.*

aid of the saint. The saint's standard helped to focus the minds of the troops on their duty to him, and on his corresponding obligation to aid his supporters. Thus, on the morning of the battle, Bishop Hugh drew his soldiers up into formation and ordered them to bend their knees in prayer and beg Saint Lambert and the Virgin Mary to save them from danger. At that very moment the banners of these saints were cracking in the breeze above their heads.[121]

In addition, many of the Liégeois believed that Lambert would actually manifest himself on the battlefield, and give them material support during the fighting. It is in this context that the author of *De triumpho S. Lamberti* reported visions of the saint before the battle. During the bishop's battlefield oration, a woman was reported to have looked up from her devotions, at the very moment when Bishop Hugh was exhorting his men to fight for their city and saint, and to have seen Lambert passing by, bearing shining golden arms (including a spear and a shield) and riding a glowing white horse.[122] This description bears a remarkable similarity to crusade accounts of Saint George appearing on the battlefield at Antioch during the First Crusade as well as in later campaigns, including Barbarossa's march through Anatolia. In a second case, one of the townsmen, who was serving in the army at the Battle of the Steppes, is also reported to have had a vision of the saint.[123]

As well as relying upon supernatural support from their patron saint, the Liégeois soldiers who fought in the Battle of the Steppes also participated in a series of more personal religious rites. First, the men were asked to pray to Lambert and Mary to protect them during the battle. Then, according to Reinerus, Bishop Hugh approached his troops and informed them that the moment had come both to confess their sins (*confiteor*) and to enunciate all of their faults (*culpas suas dicere*). When they had finished, he granted them a blanket absolution.[124] The grant of such an absolution is confirmed by the author of *De triumpho S. Lamberti*.[125]

---

[121] *Ibid.*, p. 183, *suas quoque episcopus allocutus acies, precepit genuflectere, gloriosam virginem et beatum martyrem devocius exorare, ut ab instanti eos periculo eripere dignarentur.* Given the great value attached to these banners by the Liégeois, the question remains why they did not also bring the actual relics of Lambert into the field, as their grandfathers had done sixty years earlier. Although the two chroniclers do not address this question, it would be reasonable to conjecture that the very speed with which the bishop's forces were mobilized left no time for the extensive religious ceremonies tied to disinterring Lambert's remains.

[122] This report bears a close resemblance to accounts of saints appearing in crusade battles.

[123] *De triumpho S. Lamberti*, p. 183, *Ipsa quoque devota mulier, que virum Dei genuerat, dum intentius vacaret in vigiliarum precibus, vidit in aeris medio gloriosum martyrem armis fulgentem aureis, clipeum in humeris gestare clarissimum, hastam quoque vibrare auream et equo candidissimo insidentem . . . civis quoque quidam in acie ipsum euntem martyrem confessus est veraciter se vidisse.* The appearance of Saint Lambert on the battlefield may be the result of the transplantation of crusading ideology back to Europe by returning veterans of the crusades.

[124] Reinerus, *Annales*, p. 668, *interim episcopus ad eos venit, et ut peccata sua confiterentur et culpas suas dicerent monuit, et sic eos absolvit.*"

[125] *De triumpho S. Lamberti*, p. 183, *Absolutosque a peccatis omnibus verbis huiusmodi animabat. . . .*

Reinerus did not record in his account whether the Liégeois troops confessed their sins individually to priests or as a group to the bishop. His remark that Bishop Hugh absolved them (*absolvere*) may be understood to indicate that the men engaged in a general confession of sin in a manner similar to the Milanese militiamen noted above. However, unlike the author of the *Gesta Federici imperatoris*, Reinerus does not describe the men actually confessing *en masse*. In fact, it would appear that he used the redundant expression "peccata sua confiterentur et culpas suas dicerent" to indicate that each man confessed his own sins. If this is, in fact, what happened there are two likely possibilities for the manner in which this rite was carried out. First, the soldiers, surrounded on all sides by their friends and neighbors, may have confessed their sins all at once to the bishop. The second possibility is that the men made individual confessions to priests. As we saw in the case of the Battle of the Standard, it certainly was not impossible for priests to move among soldiers in their battle line and speak to men individually. Consequently, the fact that Bishop Hugh made one general grant of absolution to the Liégeois troops is not in itself demonstrative of a general confession of sins.

Whatever the particular form of the rite of confession, after absolving his troops, Bishop Hugh preached to the men and attempted to inspire them for the approaching battle. According to the author of *De triumpho S. Lamberti*, Hugh began by pointing out that fighting had become unavoidable. The enemy was directly before them and offered no way forward and no way back. Then Hugh added, "I enjoin battle upon you in place of penance."[126] At this point, the bishop is reported to have promised that whoever died during the fighting would be joined to the holy martyr (Saint Lambert), and would enjoy paradise for eternity.[127] As a result, the soldiers were instructed that they should be brave during the fighting, and keep in mind all of the evils that the Brabanters had committed against their homes, their families, and their city. Finally, Hugh called upon the soldiers to keep their faith in Christ, who would be willing and able to save them from their present dangers because of the intercession of his holy mother and Saint Lambert.[128]

Hugh's address would appear to have important implications both for the morale of his men and for the cohesion of his army. In the first instance, Hugh's promise to the troops of supernatural aid and eternal salvation offered the hope to the Liégeois soldiers that they would have victory in this world and paradise in the next. Secondly, Hugh's emphasis upon their efforts in the service of Saint Lambert would seem to have been intended to reinforce the common ties of the men already bound to one another by their residence in the same city. Indeed, in this case it is difficult, if not impossible, to disentangle the political and religious implications of Saint Lambert's status as the patron of Liège. And it is

---

126 *Ibid.*, *video, karissimi, quod absque certamine transire non possumus, sed securus loco penitentie instans vobis iniungo prelium.*

127 *Ibid.*, p. 183, *quisquis hic ruerit beato coniuctus martyri, paradisi gaudio perhenniter potietur.*

128 *Ibid.*, *habeamus ergo fiduciam in eo, qui sue matris meritis et nostri prece martyris a presenti periculo nos potens est liberare.*

highly unlikely that the militiamen of Liège had any inclination to make such a distinction.

Bishop Hugh's incorporation of imagery of Saint Lambert, including a banner of the saint, into his hastily organized program of religious rites has some important parallels to the programs of military religion discussed above, particularly at York and Milan. Similarly, the sermon recorded by the anonymous author of *De triumpho S. Lamberti* touches on many of the same points stressed by battlefield commanders in other regions of the Latin West. These themes include the need to trust in God for strength, and the importance of relying on the saints to intercede on the soldiers' behalf. Indeed, the protection offered by saints to their faithful supporters would seem to be an exceptionally important element of twelfth- and early thirteenth-century military religion generally. This emphasis upon support and even the manifestation of saints on the battlefield would also seem to mark a significant development in the practices of military religion in ordinary warfare from the eleventh century. As was noted in the context of the Battle of the Standard, the origins of this development may be sought in the crusading campaigns from the late eleventh to the early thirteenth centuries.

The intrusion of crusading ideas into ordinary warfare would also appear to be indicated by Bishop Hugh's promise of eternal salvation to soldiers who fell in battle against the Brabanters. Clearly, the campaign against the duke of Brabant was neither a crusade nor a holy war. It was, however, manifestly a just war – at least from the Liégeois point of view. Bishop Hugh, although apparently not as comfortable as either Bishop Ralph of Orkney or Archbishop Albero of Trier in promising a crusade-type indulgence on the basis of his own episcopal authority, wanted a similar kind of morale-boosting incentive for his troops. Given the just nature of a war conducted to defend one's homeland, the bishop would appear to have found a compromise solution by promising eternal salvation to those who fell in battle, and anchoring this promise on Saint Lambert's *virtus* rather than on any power of his own as bishop. Consequently, the battlefield sermon would seem to be further evidence of the continuing penetration of crusading practices into secular warfare, even if not in the fully developed form noted earlier in the context of Archbishop Albero's battlefield sermon in 1148.

One final point to be considered in our treatment of the Battle of the Steppes is the description found in the accounts of both Reinerus and the Anonymous concerning the Brabantine reaction to the prayers carried out by the Liégeois forces. Reinerus recorded that while the men of Liège were receiving the episcopal blessing, soldiers from Brabant, who could look down upon the Liégeois from their hilltop positions, made cat-calls at them and said, "see, they are looking for mercy and are kneeling before us in order to beg."[129] The Anonymous also noted that the Brabanters laughed saying, "they adore us out of

---

[129] Reinerus, *Annales*, p. 668, *ecce misericordiam petunt, et ut eis misereamur nobis inclinant.*

fear."[130] It is unlikely that the Brabantine soldiers were unfamiliar with the celebration of Christian rituals before battle. Indeed, given the routine participation of soldiers in confession, and their reception of communion, it is almost certainly the case that the men from Brabant had fulfilled their own religious obligations earlier in the morning. The description of the behavior of the Brabanters by the two pro-Liégeois chroniclers might, therefore, be explained as an attempt to characterize them as anti-Christian. We have already seen this technique used with some success by William of Malmesbury in his comparative description of the Norman and Anglo-Saxon armies before the battle of Hastings.

Religion of War in France

For the greater part of the twelfth century, the territories directly subject to the king of France clustered around Paris and the Île de France. As a consequence, the French kings were very rarely involved in major military actions that were subject to the comment of chroniclers. However, by the beginning of the thirteenth century, King Philip II (1179–1222) embarked on a particularly successful period of territorial expansion that gained for him most of the territories previously controlled by King John of England, including Normandy, Anjou, Touraine, and northern Maine. Two cases will be dealt with in this section. The first concerns the religious behavior of soldiers during Louis VI's (1108–1137) mobilization of the resources of the French kingdom in order to ward off a threatened invasion by King Lothar of Germany (1124). The second deals with King Philip II Augustus' successful defense of his conquests against King Otto IV of Germany (1209–1218) and King John of England (1199–1216) at the battle of Bouvines (1214).

In 1124, King Louis VI rallied the military resources of his kingdom in order to prepare for an invasion by Lothar of Supplingenburg, the newly elected king of Germany. This was to prove the largest single military undertaking during the king's three-decade reign. Abbot Suger (1080–1151), the king's biographer and advisor, gave some attention to the extensive military preparations that undergirded this campaign. In this context, he emphasized, above all else, Louis' efforts to mobilize the sacred strength of his kingdom. While the French royal army was assembling, King Louis made a very public visit to the monastery of St Denis, where he engaged in a series of ceremonies designed to bring his army and kingdom under the protection of the saint. According to Suger, it was commonly known and understood that if the forces of another kingdom attacked France, Saint Denis and his fellow saints were to be placed upon their altars and would then offer devoted protection to the kingdom.[131] In order to bring Denis

---

130 *De triumpho S. Lamberti*, p. 183, *pro eo quod tercio nostri flexissent genua, deridebant eos adversarii et dicebant: 'isti pre timore nos adorant.'*
131 Suger, *Vita Ludovici Grossi regis*, ed. Henri Waquet (Paris, 1929), p. 220, *et quoniam beatum Dionisium specialem patronum et singularem post Deum regni protectorem et multorum relatione et crebro cognoverat experimento ad eum festinans . . . si regnum aliud*

into the conflict on the side of the French, to provide the king with personal protection, and to defeat the enemies of France, *in the customary manner,* Louis VI is reported to have offered public prayers to the saint and brought gifts to the monastery.[132] Then, Louis took a banner from the altar to bring with him into the field. In Suger's view, this act marked the king's personal subjugation to the will of the saint.[133]

The public ceremony during which King Louis prayed to Saint Denis, gave gifts to the monastery, venerated the relics of Saint Denis and the other saints, and finally took a consecrated banner from the church, formed only the first phase of the program intended to obtain divine *virtus* on behalf of the French army. Suger recorded that during the entire course of the campaign against the Germans, the relics of the saints remained on the altars, providing enduring spiritual power to the French troops. In addition, the monks at St Denis offered perpetual prayers on behalf of the soldiers in the field. They were joined in these prayers by nuns, as well as by pious lay people.[134] Finally, after the German army had been driven back, King Louis returned to St Denis to give his thanks to the saints and to the monks. Suger recorded that the king personally carried the relics, which are described as his lords and masters (*domini et patroni*), back to their own places all the while shedding tears in the manner of a small boy. Then he gave extensive gifts and lands to the monastery in order to repay the great services that the saint had provided to the kingdom.[135]

Suger's portrayal of the organization of religious rites on behalf of the army bears some striking similarities to the accounts treating the Battle of the Standard, Barbarossa's invasion of Italy, and especially Liégeois ceremonies involving Saint Lambert. The first point that must be emphasized is the public quality of King Louis' actions. As we have seen in the narrative accounts of Anglo-Norman, German, and Liégeois practice, the invocation of saints,

regnum Francorum invadere audeat, ipse beatus et admirabilis defensor cum sociis suis tanquam ad defendendum altari suo superponatur, eo presente fit tam glorioso quam devote.

[132] *Ibid., tam precibus quam benefitiis precordaliter pulsat ut regnum defendat, personam conservet, hostibus* more solito *resistat* (my emphasis).

[133] *Ibid., Rex autem, vexillum ab altari suscipiens quod de comitatu Vilcassini (Vexin), quo ad ecclesiam feodatus est, spectat, votive tanquam a domino suo suscipiens.* The basic work on French royal standards is Anne Lombard-Jourdain, *Fleure de lis et oriflamme: signes célests du royaume de France* (Paris, 1991). The use of Saint Denis' relics by the kings of France has been addressed by Gabrielle M. Spiegel, "The Cult of Saint Denis and Capetian Kingship," *Journal of Medieval History* 1 (1975), pp. 43–70, here pp. 59–60; and Richard Hamann-Maclean, "Die Reimser Denkmale des französischen Königtums in 12. Jahrhundert. Saint Remi als Grabkirche im frühen und hohen Mittelalter," in *Beiträge zur Bildung der französischen Nation im Früh-und Hochmittelalter,* ed. Helmut Beumann (Sigmaringen, 1983), pp. 93–260, here pp. 222–3.

[134] Suger, *Vita Ludovici Grossi regis,* p. 228, *sacras etiam venerabiles sacratissimorum corporum lecticas argenteas que altari principali superposite toto spacio bellici conventus extiterant, ubi continuo celeberrimo diei et noctis offitio fratrum colebantur, multa devotissimi populi et religiosarum mulierum ad suffragandum exercitui frequentabuntur multiplici oratione.*

[135] *Ibid., rex ipse proprio collo dominos et patronos suos cum lacrimarum affluentia filialiter loco suo reportavit multisque, tam terre quam aliarum commoditatum donariis, pro his et aliis impensis benefitiis remuneravit.*

requests for divine support, and the organization of intercessory prayers were intended to appeal to divine power on behalf the soldiers with the hope that this would end in victory on the field. This was a strategic goal. However, it was also important for the soldiers to know that a series of ceremonies was being performed on their behalf. This knowledge had the potential to provide an extra layer of comfort to the men by assuring them that everything that could be done was being done to assure their victory. In order to make his supporters aware of his efforts to invoke the aid of Saint Denis, in early August 1124, King Louis sent out a circular letter to the archbishops, bishops, dukes, counts, and all other royal officials notifying them of the ceremonies that had taken place at the monastery.[136] Louis stressed, in particular, that he had venerated these patrons of France "pro regni defensione."[137] This action was, furthermore, part of a consistent effort by King Louis to seek divine aid on behalf of his kingdom. These efforts are exemplified by a grant of immunity to the college of canons at Notre Dame de Puiseaux made in 1112.[138] According to the royal charter, in return for the king's favor, the canons were expected to pray to God to show mercy to his soul and to protect his kingdom.[139]

Suger did not record the actual prayers said by the participants in the processions carried out on behalf of the French royal army in 1124. However, an early thirteenth-century ordinal from the cathedral chapter at Chartres, which itself was based on a twelfth-century ordinal, contains instructions for a fast, prayers, and processions in time of war that may shed light on this question.[140] According to this text, the day of the ceremony was to begin in the normal manner with the standard hymns, antiphons, readings, and prayers. However, at terce, the cathedral bell was to be sounded (*sonatur cum grandi signo*) in order to signal the beginning of the special liturgy. After the signal had been given, the members of the cathedral chapter were to begin chanting the "vii psalmi," (probably the seven penitential psalms), followed by the other psalms that were required by the customary usages of the chapter (*cetera sicut mos est*).[141]

Then, at sext, the chapter was required to hold a special intercessory mass based almost entirely on the Friday mass celebrated during the third week of Lent.[142] The opening prayer of this mass (Ps. 85.17, "make of me a token for the

[136] *Recueil des actes de Louis VI, roi de France*, 2 vols., ed. Jean Dufour (Paris, 1992), I: 465.

[137] *Ibid.*

[138] *Ibid.*, p. 134.

[139] *Ibid.*, *qui videlicet tam pro nobis quam pro salute regni nostri Dei misericordiam implorarent*. For further grants of this type, see *ibid.*, pp. 157, 167, 178, and 486; and *Recueil des actes de Louis VI roi de France*, ed. Jean Dufour (Paris, 1992), II: 19, 105, and 399.

[140] *L'Ordinaire chartrain du XIIIe siècle*, ed. Yves Delaporte (Chartres, 1953), pp. 195–6. Concerning the twelfth-century origin of this ordinal and the presence of a prayer in time of war in the older work, see *ibid.*, p. 16.

[141] *Ibid.*, p. 195. The seven penitential psalms are 6, 31, 37, 50, 101, 129, and 142. Concerning the origin of the grouping of these seven psalms and their particular penitential nature, see Michael S. Driscoll, "The Seven Penitential Psalms: Their Designation and Usages from the Middle Ages Onwards," *Ecclesia orans* 17 (2000), pp. 153–201.

[142] The introit of this mass is *Fac mecum* and the text of this mass can be found in *Missale*

good so that those who hate me might see me and be confounded since you, O Lord, have aided me and comforted me") would appear to have been of value in time of war.[143] Following this standard introit, the celebrant was then to add an additional prayer at the *oratio* that has been identified by scholars as a prayer to be said *in tempore belli*.[144] This prayer clearly invokes God's aid to protect his people (*tibi subditum protege principatum*). In addition, the prayer specifies that this aid is required so that those who trust in God's power (*in tua virtute fidentes*) might excel above all other kingdoms (*super omnia regna praecellant*). The final benediction *super populo* of the standard Friday mass for the third week of Lent was similarly an appropriate prayer for time of war. The celebrant was to say, "we ask O omnipotent God, that you stand before us, we who trust in your protection, so that with your aid we might conquer all those who oppose us."[145]

At each hour following mass, the chapter was to chant Psalm 119, a triple *Kyrie* and *Christe eleison*, and a series of prayers concluding with the prayer "O Lord, we beg that you crush the arrogance of our enemies and strike them down by the strength of your right hand."[146] This prayer can be traced back to the eighth-century Gelasian sacramentary, where it appeared as the *post communio* in the "*missa in profectionem hostium euntibus in proelium*," noted above in Chapter 2, in the context of Carolingian battlefield liturgies.

Immediately following mass, the cathedral chapter was to hold a procession (*fit processio*) to whichever church had been chosen (*ad ecclesiam quam voluerint*).[147] Along the way, the members of the chapter were to chant Psalm 1, followed by the psalms in their correct order until they reached the church toward which they were marching. Then, at the entrance of the church, the chapter was to sing the antiphon of the saint to whom the church was dedicated, followed by a triple *Kyrie, Christe*, and *Kyrie Eleison*, and a *Pater Noster.* Finally, after the canon who was serving as the weekday minister (*sacerdos septimanarius*) said the prayer *Et ne nos*, the entire chapter was to say the customary prayers (*consuetis orationibus*), and then one additional prayer for the particular war (*una de illo bello*). The ceremony ended with the canons

---

ad usum ecclesie Westmonasteriensis, 3 vols., ed. John Wickham Legg (London, 1891–7), I: 169–74.

[143] *Biblia sacra vulgata*, p. 879, *Fac mecum signum in bono et videant qui oderunt me et confundantur quoniam tu Domine adiuvasti me et consolatus me.*

[144] On this point, see *Corpus orationum*, CCSL 160A, ed. Eugenius Moeller, Johannes Maria Clément, and Bertrand Coppieters't Wallant (Turnholt, 1993), p. 155. For the text of this prayer, see *ibid.*, *Deus cuius regnum, regnum est omnium saeculorum, supplicationes nostras clementer exaudi et romanorum regum tibi subditum protege principatum, ut in tua virtute fidentes et tibi placeant et super omnia regna praecellant.*

[145] *Missale ad usum ecclesie Westmonasteriensis*, I: 170, *Presta quesumus omnipotens deus ut qui in tua proteccione confidimus cuncta nobis adversancia te adiuvante vincamus.*

[146] For the text of this prayer, see *Corpus orationum*, CCSL 160C, ed. Eugenius Moeller, Johannes Maria Clément, and Bertrand Coppieters't Wallant (Turnholt, 1994), p. 313.

[147] *L'Ordinaire chartrain du XIIIe siècle*, p. 196.

chanting the psalms on their way back to the cathedral where they said the antiphon for Saint Mary and a Marian prayer.[148]

Bouvines

The second case for which the sources provide a sufficient corpus of information to consider the religious care provided to soldiers in the French royal army is the battle of Bouvines (1214) fought by the army of King Philip II against Emperor Otto IV and his allies. This battle received enormous attention and is mentioned in more than ninety contemporary and near-contemporary chronicles and histories.[149] We are fortunate that one of the fullest accounts of the battle was written by William the Breton, who not only was an eyewitness but actually served as King Philip's chaplain during the fighting.[150]

According to William, before the battle began, King Philip went alone into a church dedicated to Saint Peter near the site of the battle and prayed to God for victory. When he came out, dressed for battle, the banner of Saint Denis was brought forward. William emphasized that this was fitting because the banner ought always to proceed the troops into battle.[151] William then used the image of Saint Denis to draw a contrast between the French king, steeped in the religious power of the patron saint of France, and the German king who stood among his troops under the symbol of a gilded eagle hovering over a dragon.[152] Given the chronicler's juxtaposition of them with the banner of Saint Denis, these symbols would appear to have had pagan overtones.

After having the banner of Saint Denis brought out of the church, King Philip is reported to have addressed his soldiers. According to William, the king urged his men to place all of their faith in God. He denounced King Otto and his army as excommunicates and despoilers of the church, while lauding the French army as a Christian force enjoying communion and peace with the holy church. Philip continued by stressing that although the Frenchmen, including himself, were sinners, they were in accord with the church, and could expect God to show them mercy and grant them victory over their enemies. At the end of the oration, the French soldiers are reported to have begged the king for his blessing. In response Philip reportedly raised his hands to heaven and pleaded with God to bless the army.[153] The French king's prayers to God were also emphasized by

---

[148] *Ibid.*

[149] Concerning the historical treatment of the battle at Bouvines, see Georges Duby, *The Legend of Bouvines: War, Religion, and Culture in the Middle Ages*, trans. Catherine Tihanyi (Berkeley, 1990). For the number of chronicles treating the battle, see p. 143.

[150] William the Breton, *Gesta Philipi Augusti*, ed. François Delaborde (Paris, 1882), pp. 270–4.

[151] *Ibid.*, p. 271, *revocatur vexillum beati Dionysii quod omnes precedere in bella debebat.* . . .

[152] *Ibid.*, p. 272, *ab opposita parte stabat Otho in medio agminis concertissimi qui sibi pro vexillo erexerat aquilam deauratam super draconem.* . . .

[153] *Ibid.*, pp. 272–3, *Rex autem antequam congrederetur, hac brevi et humili oratione suos fuit milites allocutus, 'in Deo tota spes et fiducia nostra est posita; rex Otho et exercitus suus a domino papa excommunicati sunt, qui sunt inimici et destructores rerum sancte ecclesie, et pecunia qua eis stipendia ministrantur, de lacrymis pauperum et de rapina ecclesiarum Dei et clericorum acquisita est. Nos autem christiani sumus et communione et pace sancte*

Richer, a monk from Sens who composed his text in the mid-thirteenth century.[154] Richer's account differs somewhat from that of William the Breton's, perhaps because he was relying on a different eyewitness source. According to the later chronicler, Philip encouraged his men by telling them that Saint Denis stood with his most holy companions (*sanctissimi sodales*), and would intercede with God on behalf of the kingdom (*pro statu regni*) and for the army (*pro nobis*).[155]

These two accounts of King Philip's behavior before the battle at Bouvines clearly indicate the importance to the French ruler of establishing the just nature of his cause in a public manner for his troops. Philip is reported to have stressed in his harangue that his men were fighting on behalf of the church while their enemies, although baptized Christians, were excluded from the church as a result of the ban of excommunication. The king is reported to have added that his men would receive the aid of Saint Denis and God because they were serving in a noble cause. It will be recalled that King Louis VI, Philip's grandfather, reportedly used this same imagery when attempting to inspire his own troops against German invaders almost a century before.

According to William the Breton, after the initial ceremony was completed and the battle had begun, he and another priest stood near the king and began to chant psalms, particularly Psalms 143, 67, and 20. All three of these psalms can be described as having a military character. Psalm 143 begins with the lines "blessed is the Lord who teaches my hands to be strong in war and prepares my fingers for battle."[156] Psalms 67 and 20 also contain military themes. In particular, Psalm 20 includes the verses "you give him glory and victory . . . because he trusted in the Lord he found your hand raised against his enemies (Ps. 20.6–9)." After reciting these warlike psalms, the priests praised King Philip to God because he had granted freedom to the church, and then castigated Otto and his ally King John of England for their unjustified attack on the French kingdom.[157]

William the Breton's account is exceptionally valuable because it allows insight into the mind of a priest who served on the field as a chaplain familiar

---

ecclesie fruimur, et quamvis peccatores simus, tamen ecclesie Dei consentimus et cleri pro posse nostro defendimus libertates. Unde presumere fiducialiter debemus de Dei misericordia qui nobis licet peccatoribus, dabit de suis et de nostris hostibus triumphare.' *His dictis, petierunt milites a rege benedictionem, qui manu elevata, oravit eis a Domino benedictionem.*

154 *Gesta Senoniensis ecclesiae*, ed. G. Waitz, MG SS 25 (Hanover, 1880), p. 251.

155 *Ibid.*, p. 294, *Scito etenim et vere scio, quia contra adversarium dispositionem beatissimus ac semper reminiscendus patronus noster Dyonisius hodie cum suis sanctissimis sodalibus pro nobis et pro statu regni nostri misericordissimum Filium Dei gemitibus inenarrabilibus interpellat.*

156 *Ibid.*, p. 273. See *Biblia Sacra Vulgata*, p. 947, *benedictus Dominus fortis meus qui docet manus meas ad proelium digitos ad bellum.*

157 William, *Gesta Philipi Augusti*, p. 274, *et cum pura devotione coram Deo reducebant ad memoriam honorem et libertatem qua Dei ecclesia gauderet in potestate regis Philippi, et dedecus et opprobria que patitur et passa est per Othonem et per regem Johannem, cujus muneribus omnes illi hostes provocati contra regem in regno suo et contra dominum suum presumebant pugnare.*

with the religious needs of soldiers and of his king. When praying on behalf of the French troops, William chose those psalms that seemed to him the most appropriate for soldiers fighting in a just cause. All three of these psalms deal with the intervention of God against the enemies of those who are faithful to Him. In addition, William portrayed King Philip making exactly this connection in his battlefield oration promising that God would intervene on the side of the French because they were Christians and placed their hope in Him. The second element of William's prayers, as he remembered them, concerned King Philip's good treatment of the church and the correspondingly evil deeds committed by King Otto and King John. This dichotomy also appeared in Philip's address to the soldiers where Otto and his men were dismissed as excommunicates while the French king prayed in church and called down God's blessings on his men. We are, in fact, presented with a sustained effort to demonstrate the moral superiority of the French army and the concomitant expectation that God and the saints would as a result aid the French soldiers in battle.

Conclusion

The surviving sources indicate that military religion in the ordinary wars of the twelfth and early thirteenth centuries was marked by important developments in religious practice when compared with the patterns of religious behavior in the eleventh century. The most striking change in practice was the increasing tendency of bishops to grant remissions of sins to soldiers fighting against other Christians. Bishop Anselm II of Lucca had offered this spiritual benefit to the militiamen of his city for fighting against the enemies of the pope as early as 1085, so it cannot be argued that remissions of sin of the type identified at the Battle of the Standard, and in later campaigns, were an entirely new phenomenon in the twelfth century, or the direct result of the crusading movement. However, it does appear that there was a tendency to employ this spiritual benefit in a wider range of contexts in the later period. When Anselm promised a *remissio peccatorum* to his troops, they were engaged in a war on behalf of Pope Gregory VII against the excommunicated followers of King Henry IV of Germany. By contrast, Bishop Ralph of Orkney's grant of a remission of sins to Anglo-Norman troops in 1138 came in the context of a war against fellow Christians in good standing with their own church, serving under their own king. Similarly, there is no evidence that Archbishop Albero of Trier's war against Count Palatine Hermann or Bishop Hugh of Liège's war against the duke of Brabant were anything other than ordinary wars fought for straightforward political objectives. When considering the factors that may have contributed to the spread of this spiritual benefit into ordinary warfare, it would appear that the grant of remissions of sins to crusaders may have provided a model to bishops seeking additional means of raising the morale, that is, strengthening the resolve of their troops.

The initially distinctive ideology and phenomena of crusading warfare may also have been responsible for the increased emphasis in narrative accounts from the twelfth and early thirteenth centuries on the role of the saints in the conduct of military campaigns. Soldiers from across the Latin West were promised that the particular saintly patrons of their cities and regions would protect them in battle. In addition, soldiers were also told both by priests and army officers that saints would actually appear on the field of battle in order to protect them during the fighting. The widespread reports of saints participating on the side of Christians in the First Crusade and in later campaigns may have influenced contemporaries in Europe to look toward the aid of supernatural patrons.

In addition to these changes in practice as compared with military religion during the eleventh century, the larger corpus of source materials available for the twelfth and early thirteenth centuries makes it possible to identify regional variations in the religious behavior of soldiers. For example, although it would appear to have been an almost invariable element of pre-battle preparations for soldiers to have confessed their sins, the actual performance of the rite took different forms in different regions. In some instances soldiers either confessed individually to priests or expected to do so. However, contemporary evidence indicates that at least on occasion Milanese soldiers made a communal confession of their sins before battle. In a similar manner, despite the apparent consensus among observers that soldiers in this period believed in and hoped for the aid of saints, the efforts of soldiers and their supporters to obtain supernatural intervention are reported to have differed dramatically in extent and nature from region to region. At Trier, the archbishop's men went into battle with promises of support from Saint Peter without any indication in the sources that the soldiers had participated in special intercessory rites. At the other end of the spectrum, the people of Liège engaged in a three-day series of litanies and processions, which included removing Saint Lambert's relics from their resting place and parading them outside the walls of the city. The range of religious responses to the perceived need to obtain saintly support for soldiers going into battle is an important indication that, while certain general aspects of religious doctrine were common to Christians across the Latin West, the manifestation of these beliefs in practice depended heavily upon local traditions and conditions.

Alongside these important developments in practice, however, we can also see extensive continuities in ordinary warfare from the end of the eleventh through the beginning of the thirteenth century. Rulers in much of the West continued to support religious institutions in order to secure divine aid both for the safety and well-being of their territories and in order to assure success in war. Moreover, Christian rulers publicized these donations of property, grants of immunities, and confirmations of older privileges in order to show that their wars aims were in accord with the will of heaven and to assure their supporters that divine assistance could be expected. These factors were, of course, crucial to soldiers' perceptions of themselves as combatants in a just cause and for their expectations of victory in battle.

Furthermore, army-wide rites and personal religious preparations by soldiers for combat continued to play a vital role in maintaining morale, *esprit de corps*, and discipline. Eyewitnesses routinely observed that soldiers went into battle with more spirit after confessing their sins, receiving absolution, and being promised eternal salvation. In addition, the frequent declaration by preachers that soldiers were bound together by their common ties to their patron saint would appear to have had important implications for the *esprit de corps* of armies. Indeed, as Frederick Barbarossa observed regarding the Milanese, it was Saint Ambrose who led them into battle, and it was therefore the banner of Saint Ambrose that led them in surrender. Finally, the discipline of soldiers went hand in hand with their expectations for divine aid. In the view of their contemporaries, when soldiers were convinced of the justness of their cause and of the support of God and the saints, they fought more bravely and followed the orders of their commanders even when facing a difficult battle. Similarly, the behavior of the soldiers along the line of march was conditioned by the knowledge that divine aid was only available to those who were worthy of it.

Conclusion

Supplication of the gods or God, that is, the effort to obtain heavenly intervention in human affairs, played a crucial role in the conduct of Western warfare throughout Late Antiquity and the Middle Ages down through the early thirteenth century. Religious rites and ceremonies served to build a sense of *esprit de corps* among soldiers on campaign and bound them more closely to the communities on whose behalf they were fighting. Religious ideology and sanctions were intrinsic elements in the creation of military codes of conduct, both on the battlefield and on the march, and these consequently were crucial to the development and maintenance of military discipline. Perhaps most importantly, religious ideals and practices played a fundamental role in sustaining morale among soldiers and among their supporters on the home front.

In the West, the classical world of Greece and Rome, like the Hebrews, set great store by the power of divine forces to bring military victory or defeat. The army religion of the Roman Empire encompassed all aspects of military life beginning with soldiers' oaths of induction and continuing through their burial. At the time of his accession to the *imperium* in 306, Constantine I inherited an army whose religious traditions had been forged through centuries of struggle. Even had he wished to do so – and there is very little evidence to suggest that he did – Constantine could not replace wholesale traditional army religion with his new-found Christianity. Not only were his troops wedded to their practices, the pacifist Christian cult was manifestly unsuited to a role as the *ancilla imperii*. What we see during the fourth, fifth, and even sixth century is the gradual fusion of traditional pagan Roman and Christian practices. Over time, the soldiers in the Christian Roman army and its successors states followed crosses rather than legionary eagles into battle, prayed to the Christian triune God rather than to the pagan pantheon and the genius of Rome, and participated in the celebration of mass rather than in auguries and divinations. The greatest challenge faced during Late Antiquity and the early Middle Ages by both secular and ecclesiastical leaders in Christianizing warfare was the continuing insistence in Christian doctrine that homicide of any kind, including homicide committed in a just war, was a sin that removed a sinner from the community of the faithful. It was only the evolution of a more nuanced view of homicide coupled with a dramatic development in Christian penitential practice – the introduction of repeatable confession – that finally permitted the soldier to find a comfortable place in Christian religious life.

Thus, by the Carolingian period, the mobilization of religious resources among the general population on behalf of the army, and the celebration of religious rites by soldiers and clerics serving in the field, had had a long history stretching back to the late Roman Empire and continuing on in its Christian successors states in the West. As had been true of their predecessors, during the course of the eighth and ninth centuries, the rulers of the *regnum Francorum* authorized and organized a wide range of religious rites in an effort to assure divine support for Frankish soldiers and armies in the field. These included intercessory masses celebrated by priests and bishops, processions in which both lay people and clergy participated, both public and private prayers, almsgiving at all levels of the society, and fasts that were undertaken by all adults, including both men and women, clerics and lay people. These efforts on the home front were mirrored by the army's participation in religious rites in the field, which were similarly intended to obtain divine aid in battle. Thus, soldiers in the armies of the *regnum Francorum* regularly prayed to God before battle, fasted, gave alms, and participated in liturgical processions while clerics serving in the field celebrated intercessory masses, chanted psalms, and prayed to God for victory.

During the course of the eighth century, these wide-scale and public religious rites, which were intended to invoke divine aid for the Carolingian kingdom and army, were augmented by more private rites that were intended to reconcile individual Christian soldiers with God. The *Concilium Germanicum*, held in 742 under the direction of Charlemagne's uncle Carloman, highlights the important new trajectories in contemporary Christian doctrine and in the organization of pastoral care for soldiers. The rulers of the *regnum Francorum*, cognizant of the emerging trend in Christian penitential doctrine toward repeatable private confession, authorized in the second canon of this council that the commander of each military unit in the army was to have a priest on his staff who was capable of hearing confessions and assigning penances. The important role assigned by the secular and ecclesiastical leadership to these field chaplains marks an important shift in emphasis in army religion toward the responsibility of each individual Christian soldier to assure on a regular basis his own reconciliation with God. From the perspective of the soldier himself, it was now possible to go into battle confident that he had done everything in his power to obtain eternal salvation should he die in combat.

The collapse of Carolingian power in the later ninth century and the subsequent decline and reestablishment of local and regional secular authority in the Latin West, in the period c. 900–c. 1095, had important consequences for the organization and conduct of wartime religion. It was now the case that Christian armies in the field faced each other in battle to an extent unknown in either the Carolingian or late antique periods. As a consequence, both ecclesiastical and secular leaders were forced to adapt military-religious practices to these potentially troubling new situations. It is in this context that we observe an increasing tendency among rulers to demonstrate publicly the justness of their causes and the concomitant perfidy of their foes. A related aspect of military religion in this period was the expenditure of considerable human and financial resources to secure prayers and other intercessory rites for the souls of soldiers who had been killed in battle. The most dramatic examples of these efforts were enshrined at memorial "battle abbeys" such as Fulk Nerra of Anjou's foundation at *Belli Locus* and William the Conqueror's monastic foundation on the site of his victory over Harold Godwinson at Hastings – Battle Abbey.

In addition to these developments at the public level, the tenth and eleventh centuries also witnessed significant developments in the religious practices of soldiers and their supporters at home. Confession, penance, the deployment of relics and sacred banners on the battlefield, as well as preaching, remained exceptionally important elements of military religion in preparing individual soldiers for battle, as had been the case during the Carolingian era. However, soldiers added to these rites the regular reception of the eucharist before battle, a practice that was not a regular part of the normal preparations of soldiers in the Carolingian period.

A further significant development in religious doctrine, which was to have exceptionally important consequences for Christian soldiers, was the radical transformation of the traditional understanding of the sinfulness of homicide. Ecclesiastical leaders, including Pope Alexander II (1061–1073) and Bishop Anselm II of Lucca (1073–1086), argued that under some circumstances killing was not only removed from the realm of sin, but that it became a positive good that could be carried out in lieu of penances required to expiate previous sins. The concept of granting a remission of sin to a soldier for killing marked an important shift in a Christian doctrine that had been maintained from the eighth until the middle decades of the eleventh century. For more than three centuries, it had been established that even when fighting against non-Christian enemies of the church in a just war, soldiers sinned when they killed in battle and owed penance in order to cleanse their souls. Indeed, as late as 1066, the soldiers in the army of William the Conqueror had been required to do penance for their actions at the battle of Hastings – a battle fought with the approval of Pope Alexander II and under the protection of a papal banner. Although no definitive explanation for this change in doctrine is now available, it would appear to have been occasioned, at least in part, by the gradual expansion of Christian military operations against the Muslim powers in Iberia, southern Italy, and North Africa during the second half of the eleventh century. In addition, Pope Gregory VII's efforts to extend papal authority, particularly in his conflict with King Henry IV of Germany, carried out from 1076 until the pontiff's death in 1085, likely also played a role in this process.

The crusading movements of the late eleventh, twelfth, and early thirteenth centuries had a dramatic effect in shaping a new Christian mentality toward war while at the same time confirming the importance of traditional religious rites in the lives of individual soldiers and their non-combatant supporters. The efforts of church leaders to establish a new paradigm for understanding the sinfulness of killing in war helped to lay the foundation for the routine grant of remissions of sin to crusaders fighting against Muslims, and then later against the Christian enemies of the papacy. The crusades were instrumental in popularizing the view that under some circumstances killing itself could constitute an act of penance and therefore serve as a positive good.

The crusades were further distinguished from ordinary wars of the eleventh century by an increased emphasis on the part of observers both in regard to the intervention of heavenly forces on the side of the crusaders, and to the important role played by priests in preparing soldiers for battle. In particular, contemporary writers stressed the appearance of clerics on the battlefield who were easily identifiable by their white stoles, which served as a particular insignia of their sacerdotal office. Observers in the tenth and eleventh centuries occasionally observed these elements in wars fought by Christians against non-Christian enemies. However, the exceptional emphasis by contemporaries of the early crusades on the appearance of warrior saints on the battlefield and on the service of white-clad clerics with the troops does not appear to have an earlier analog.

Nevertheless, alongside the radical shift in Christian doctrine encompassed within the concept of remission of sin for killing the enemy and the novel emphasis on direct divine intervention on the field of battle, many of the actual religious practices carried out by crusaders and their non-combatant supporters on the home front demonstrate remarkable continuity with those of soldiers and their supporters in ordinary or non-crusade campaigns. Preaching, confession, penance, reception of the eucharist, and the deployment of relics and banners on the battlefield all continued to play a very important role in maintaining the morale, discipline, and *esprit de corps* of crusaders serving in the eastern Mediterranean, Anatolia, North Africa, southern France, and Iberia. In addition, the general population of Europe as well as Christians in the Holy Land frequently were called on to support their troops in a traditional manner through prayers, fasting, almsgiving, processions, and intercessory masses.

Over the course of the twelfth and early thirteenth centuries, the religious experiences of hundreds of thousands of crusade veterans and their even more numerous supporters, who lived throughout Europe, would appear to have influenced in a significant manner the behavior of soldiers and priests serving in the ordinary, non-crusading wars of this period. These effects manifested themselves both in the manner that contemporaries portrayed ordinary warfare from c. 1100 to c. 1215, and in the grants to ordinary soldiers of spiritual benefits originally associated with crusaders. Chroniclers of the twelfth and early thirteenth centuries, more so than their predecessors in earlier periods, emphasized the crucial part played by patron saints in protecting soldiers as they went into battle. Indeed, in some cases such as Liège in 1213, observers noted not only the religious rites undertaken by fighting men and their supporters to invoke supernatural aid, but even reported the actual appearance of the saint on the battlefield, using language strongly reminiscent of crusade narratives. Even more importantly, bishops serving with or commanding troops in battle against other Latin Christians promised remissions of sin to their men. This spiritual benefit had been completely alien to ordinary warfare until the final decades of the eleventh century when Bishop Anselm II of Lucca offered a remission of sin to his city militia for fighting against the enemies of Pope Gregory VII. However, by the middle decades of the twelfth century, the promise of remission of sin had become a useful additional tool in the hands of military commanders, such as Archbishop Albero of Trier (1131–1152), who sought to raise the morale of their men before battle in ordinary wars against other Christians.

Despite the introduction of important aspects of crusading practice, however, ordinary warfare during the twelfth and early thirteenth centuries demonstrated exceptionally important continuities with the wartime religion of pre-crusade Europe. Thus, confession and the reception of the eucharist remained essential pre-battle rites for individual soldiers, even if the form taken by these rites differed from region to region. Similarly, the deployment of sacred battle flags, relics, pre-battle sermons, and prayers served to prepare soldiers for combat. At the broadest level, the rulers of twelfth- and thirteenth-century Europe continued to expend considerable resources to assure the provision of intercessory prayers and masses through donations to religious houses. As a consequence, post-crusade warfare within Europe was marked by considerable continuity with traditional Christian wartime practice.

Religion and the Conduct of War c. 300–1215 is a work of both military and religious history. In considering the first strand, there can no longer be any doubt that military leaders in Late Antiquity and in the Middle Ages saw in religion a crucial element in the conduct of war, an element essential to such fundamental elements of military life as morale, discipline, and *esprit de corps*. Furthermore, given the surviving corpus of information regarding the celebration of religious rites by soldiers and by their supporters on the home front, it is clear that the expectations of both military officers and religious leaders very frequently were fulfilled. When considered from the point of view of religious history, this study has explored a number of rites and ceremonies practiced by soldiers and their supporters in time of war, considered the belief system that underlay these elements of religious life, and identified the development of practices and belief over time.

Wartime religion, however, formed only one element of an exceptionally rich mosaic of late antique and medieval religious life. Consequently, the evidence developed in this study suggests several avenues for future research into the more general problem of lay religiosity in the period before the Fourth Lateran Council (1215), an era about which we seem to be particularly uninformed with regard to ordinary lay religious practice. Did, for example, the regular participation by part-time soldiers and militia troops in rites such as confession, penance, and communion reflect the behavior of these men when they were back at home pursuing their normal occupations as farmers, craftsmen, and merchants? Did the routine participation of non-combatants on the home front in intercessory rites such as masses, prayers, almsgiving, and fasting in order to secure the victory of their fighting men in battle have analogs in peacetime, when these same people were threatened by drought, disease, or other natural disasters? One might also ask whether developments in military-religious practice, such as the introduction of the reception of the eucharist as a routine pre-battle rite in the tenth century, came about as a result of a widespread increase in the popularity of this rite among lay people in general. In the future, I hope to address these questions in an effort to further the integration of military and religious history and to understand the complex and multivalent lives of medieval people.

Bibliography

Published Sources

Aelred of Rievaulx. *Relatio Venerabilis Aelredi Abbatis Rievallensis de Standardo*, Rolls Series 82, 4 vols., ed. Richard Howlett (London, 1886), III: 181–99.

Albert of Aachen. *Historia Hierosolymitana*, Recueil des Historiens des Croisades: Historiens Occidentaux, 5 vols. (Paris, 1844–95), IV: 265–713.

Alcuin. *De virtutibus et vitiis liber*, PL 101: 613–38.

Amatus. *Storia de Normanni*, ed. Vincenzo de Bartholomaeis (Rome, 1935).

Ambroise. *L'estoire de la guerre sainte: histoire en vers de la troisième croisade (1190–1192)*, ed. Bruno Palin Gaston (Paris, 1897).

Ambrose. *De fide*, CSEL 78 part 3, ed. Otto Faller (Vienna, 1962).

Andrieu, Michel. *Les ordines Romani du haut moyen âge: Les manuscripts* (Louvain, 1931).

Annales Coloniensis maximi, ed. K. Pertz, MG SS 17 (Hanover, 1861).

Annales Fuldenses, ed. F. Kurze, MGH SRG 7 (Hanover, 1891).

Annales regni Francorum, ed. G.H. Pertz and F. Kurze, MGH SRG 6 (Hanover, 1895).

Annales Sancti Disibodi, ed. G. Waitz, MG SS 17 (Hanover, 1861).

Annalista Saxo, ed. D.G. Waitz, MG SS 6 (Hanover, 1844).

Anselmi episcopi Lucensis collectio canonum, ed. Friedrich Thaner (Vienna, 1906–15).

Arnulf of Milan. *Gesta archiepiscopum Mediolanensium*, ed. L.C. Bethmann and W. Wattenbach, MG SS 8 (Hanover, 1848).

Astronomer. *Vita Hludowici imperatoris*, ed. E. Tremp, MGH SRG separatim editi 64 (Hanover, 1995).

Baldric of Dol. *Historia Jerosolimitana*, Recueil des Historiens des Croisades: Historiens Occidentaux, 5 vols. (Paris, 1844–95), IV: 1–111.

Bartholomaeo the Scribe. *Annales*, ed. G.H. Pertz, MG SS 18 (Hanover, 1863).

Bede's Ecclesiastical History of the English People, ed. Bertram Colgrave and R.A.B. Mynors (Oxford, 1969).

Bernold of Constance. *Chronicon*, ed. G.H. Pertz, MG SS 5 (Hanover, 1844).

Biblia Sacra iuxta Vulgatam Versionem, ed. Boniface Fischer (Stuttgart, 1994).

Bruno. *Saxonicum bellum*, in *Quellen zur Geschichte Kaiser Heinrichs IV*, ed. Franz Josef Schmale (Berlin, 1963).

Burchard of Worms. *Decretum Libri XX*, PL: 140.

Die Bußbücher und die Bußdisciplin der Kirche, 2 vols., ed. H.J. Schmitz (1898, repr. Graz, 1958).

Die Bußordnungen der abendländischen Kirche, ed. F.W.H. Wasserschleben (1851, repr. Graz, 1958).

Caesarius of Arles. *Sermones*, 2 vols., ed. D.G. Marin, CCSL 103 (Turnholt, 1953).

Capitularia regum Francorum 1, ed. A. Boretius, MGH (Hanover, 1883).

Capitularia Spuria, ed. G.H. Pertz, in MGH Legum I.2 pars altera (Hanover, 1837).

Cartulaire noire de la cathédrale d'Angers, ed. Ch. Urseau (Paris, 1908).

La chanson de Roland, 2 vols., ed. Cesare Segre (Geneva, 1989).

The Chronicle of Battle Abbey, ed. Eleanor Searle (Oxford, 1980).

Chronicon Laurissense breve, ed. H. Schnor von Carolsfeld, in *Neues Archiv* 36 (1911), pp. 15–39.

Concilia aevi Karolini 2.1, ed. A. Werminghoff, MGH Concilia (Hanover, 1906).

Conciliorum Oecumenicorum Decreta, 3rd edn, ed. Instituto per le Scienze Religiose (Bologna, 1973).

Concilium Aurelianense, ed. F. Maassen, MGH Concilia 1 (Hanover, 1893).

Concilium Clippiancense, ed. F. Maassen, MGH Concilia 1 (Hanover, 1893).

Concilium Epaonense, ed. F. Maassen, MGH Concilia 1 (Hanover, 1893).

Concilium Remense, ed. J. P. Mansi in *Sacrorum Conciliorum nova et amplissima collectio* 18A (Venice, 1772), col. 345–6.

Concilium Turonicum, ed. J.P. Mansi in *Sacrorum Conciliorum nova et amplissima collectio* 7 (Florence, 1762), col. 946.

Concilium Veneticum, ed. J.P. Mansi in *Sacrorum Conciliorum nova et amplissima collectio* 7 (Florence, 1762), col. 953.

Constance of Lyon. *Vie de Saint Germain d'Auxerre*, ed. René Borius (Paris, 1965).

Constitutiones et Acta Imperatorum et Regum 1, ed. Ludwig Weiland, MGH (Hanover, 1893)

Corpus orationum, CCSL 160A and 160C, ed. Eugenius Moeller, Johannes Maria Clément, and Bertrand Coppieters't Wallant (Turnholt, 1993).

Councils and Synods with Other Documents Relating to the English Church 1205–1313, 2 vols., ed. F.M. Powicke and C.R. Cheney (Oxford, 1964).

Councils and Synods with Other Documents Relating to the English Church A.D. 871–1204, 2 vols., ed. D. Whitelock, M Brett, and C.N.L. Brooke (Oxford, 1981).

Cronica Fratris Salimbene de Adam Ordinis Minorum, ed. Oswald Holder-Egger, MG SS 32 (Hanover, 1913).

De expugnatione Lyxbonensi, ed. Charles Wendell David (New York, 1936).

Dhuoda. *Manuel pour mon fils*, ed. Pierre Riché, Sources chrétiennes 225 (Paris, 1975).

Dreves, G.M. *Analecta hymnica* 45B (1904).

Dudo of St Quentin. *De moribus et actis primorum Normannie ducum*, ed. Jules Lair (Caen, 1865).

Dudo of St. Quentin: History of the Normans, trans. Eric Christiansen (Woodbridge, 1998).

Ekkehard of Aura. *Chronicon universale*, ed. G. Waitz, MG SS 6 (Hanover, 1844).

Epistolae Merovingici et Karolini aevi, 8 vols., MGH (1892–1939).

Epistolae pontificum romanorum ineditae, ed. S. Loewenfeld (1885, repr. Graz, 1959).

Epistolae saeculi XIII e regestis pontificum romanorum, 3 vols., ed. Charles Rodenberg, MGH (1883–94).

Eusebius. *Über das Leben des Kaisers Konstantin*, 2nd edn, ed. F. Winkelmann (Berlin, 1991)

Ex continuatione gestorum episcoporum Autissiodorensium, ed. G. Waitz, MG SS 26 (Hanover, 1882).

Flavii Cresconii Corippi Iohannidos seu de bellis Lybycis libri viii, ed. Jacob Diggle and F.R.D. Goodyear (Cambridge, 1970).

Flodoard. *Les annals de Flodoard*, ed. P. Lauer (Paris, 1906).

Formulae Merkelianae Salicae, ed. K. Zeumer, MGH Formulae (Hanover, 1882).

The Fourth Book of the Chronicle of Fredegar with its Continuations, ed. J.M. Wallace-Hadrill (London, 1960).

Fuero de Bejar, ed. Juan Gutierrez Cuadrado (Salamanca, 1975).

Fulbert of Chartres. *Epistolae*, PL 141: 185–278.

Fulcher of Chartres. *Historia Iherosolymitana*, Recueil des Historiens des Croisades: Historiens Occidentaux, 5 vols. (1844–95), III: 311–485.

Galbert. *De multro, traditione, et occisione gloriosi Karoli comitis Flandriarum*, ed. Jeffrey Rider, Corpus Christianorum 131 (Turnholt, 1994).

Geoffroi de Villehardouin. *La conquête de Constantinople*, 2 vols., ed. Edmond Faral (Paris, 1938–9).

Gerhard of Augsburg. *Vita S. Oudalrici Episcopi Augustani*, ed. Walter Berschin and Angelika Häse (Heidelberg, 1993).

Gesta Alberonis archiepiscopi, ed. G. Waitz, MG SS 8 (Hanover, 1848).

Gesta episcoporum Cameracensium, ed. L.C. Bethmann, MG SS 7 (Hanover, 1840).

Gesta Federici Imperatoris, De rebus gestis in Lonbardia, ed. G.H. Pertz, MG SS 18 (Hanover, 1863).

Gesta Francorum et aliorum Hierosolomitanorum, ed. Rosalind Hill (London, 1962).

Gesta Francorum expugnantium Iherusalem, Recueil Des Historiens des Croisades: Historiens Occidentaux, 5 vols. (Paris, 1844–95), III: 491–543.

Gesta Senoniensis ecclesiae, ed. G. Waitz, MG SS 25 (Hanover, 1880).

Gratian. *Corpus iuris canonici*, ed. A. Friedberg (Leipzig, 1879).

Gregory of Tours. *Historia Francorum*, ed. W. Arndt and B. Krusch, MGH SRM 1 (Hanover, 1884).

Guibert of Nogent. *Gesta Dei per Francos*, Recueil des Historiens des Croisades: Historiens Occidentaux, 5 vols. (1844–95), IV: 113–263.

Hagenmeyer, Heinrich. *Die Kreuzzugsbriefe aus den Jahren 1088–1100* (repr. Hildesheim, 1973).

Halphen, Louis. *Le Comté d'Anjou au Xe siècle* (repr. Geneva, 1974).

Henri de Valenciennes. *Histoire de l'Empereur Henri de Constantinople*, ed. Jean Longnon (Paris, 1948).

Henry of Huntingdon. *Historia Anglorum*, ed. Diana Greenway (Oxford, 1996).

Historia de expeditione Friderici Imperatoris in *Quellen zur Geschichte des Kreuzzuges Kaiser Friedrich I*, ed. Anton Chroust, MGH SRG n.s. 5 (Berlin, 1928).

Historia peregrinorum in *Quellen zur Geschichte des Kreuzzuges Kaiser Friedrich I*, ed. Anton Chroust, MGH SRG n.s. 5 (Berlin, 1928).

Historia Wambae regis, ed. B. Krusch and W. Levison, MGH SRM 5 (Hanover, 1910).

Indiculum fundationis monasterii Beati Vincentii, ed. Alexander Herculano in Portugaliae Monumenta Historica Scriptores I (Lisbon, 1856).

Isidore of Seville. *Isidore Hispalensis episcopi etymologiorum sive originum*, 2 vols., ed. W.M. Lindsay (Oxford, 1990).

Itinerarium peregrinorum et gesta regis Ricardi, ed. William Stubbs in *Chronicles of the Reigns of Stephen, Henry II, and Richard I*, vol. 3, Rolls Ser. 82 (London, 1886).

Ivo of Chartres. *Decretum*, PL 161.

Pope John VIII. *Epistolae et decreta*, PL 126: 631–966.

Jordanes, *De origine actibusque Getorum*, ed. Francesco Giunta and Antonino Grillone (Rome, 1991).

Die Konzilen der karolingischen Teilreiche 843–859, ed. Wilfired Hartmann, MGH Concilia (Hanover, 1984)

Lactantius. *De Mortibus Persecutorum*, ed. J.L. Creed (Oxford, 1984).

Lambert of Ardres. *Historia comitatum Ghisnensium*, ed. J. Heller, MGH SS 24 (Hanover, 1879).

Pope Leo I. *Epistolae*, PL 54: 551–1506.

Pope Leo IV. *Epistolae et decreta*, PL 115: 655–74.

The Letters and Poems of Fulbert of Chartres, ed. Frederick Behrends (Oxford, 1976).

Le liber ordinum en usage dans l'église wisigothique et mozarabe d'Espagne du cinquième siècle, ed. Marius Férotin, *Monumenta ecclesia liturgica* 5 (Paris, 1996).

Liber sacramentorum Engolismansis, ed. Patrick Saint-Roch, CCSL 159C (Turnholt, 1987).

Liudprand of Cremona. *Antapodosis*, ed. P. Chiesa, Corpus Christianorum 156 (Turnholt, 1998).

Livy. *Ab condita urbe libri xxi–xxv*, ed. Thomas Alan Dorey (Leipzig, 1971–6).

Ludwigslied, in *Die kleinen althochdeutschen Sprachdenkmäler*, ed. E. von Steinmeyer (Berlin, 1916).

Mauricius (Maurice). *Strategikon*, ed. G.T. Dennis, CFHB 17 (Vienna, 1981).

Maximus of Turin. *Collectionem sermonum antiquam nonnullis sermonibus extra vagantibus adjectis*, ed. Almut Mutzenbecher, CCSL 23 (Turnholt, 1962).

The Missal of Robert of Jumièges, ed. H.A. Wilson (London, 1846).

Missale ad usum ecclesie Westmonasteriensis, 3 vols., ed. John Wickham Legg (London, 1891–7).

Nithard. *Historiae*, ed. Reinhold Rau (Darmstadt, 1968).

Notker the Stammerer. *Gesta Karoli Magni Imperatoris*, MGH SRG n.s. 12 (Munich, 1980).

Odo of Cluny. *De vita Sancti Geraldi*, PL 133: 709–52.

Odo of Deuil. *De profectione Ludovici VII in orientem*, ed. Virginia Gingerick Berry (New York, 1948).

Ogerius Panis. *Annales*, ed. G.H. Pertz, MG SS 18 (Hanover, 1863).

Onasander. *Strategikos,* ed. B.G. Teubner (Leipzig, 1860).

Orderic Vitalis. *The Ecclesiastical History of Orderic Vitalis*, 6 vols., ed. Marjorie Chibnall (Oxford, 1969–80).

L'Ordinaire chartraine du XIIIe siècle, ed. Yves Delaporte (Chartres, 1953).

Orosius. *Histoires contre le païens*, 3 vols., ed. and trans. Marie-Pierre Arnaud-Lindet (Paris, 1990–1).

Ottonis episcopi Frisingensis et Rahewini gesta Frederici, seu rectius, cronica, ed. Franz-Josef Schmale, 2nd edn (Darmstadt, 1974).

Paenitentiale Oxoniensis II, in *Paenitentialia minor Franciae et Italiae saeculi VIII–IX*, ed. Raymond Kottje, CCSL 156 (Turnholt, 1994).

Paenitentialia minor Franciae et Italiae saeculi VIII–IX, ed. Raymond Kottje (Turnholt, 1994).

Pásztor, Edith. "Lotta per le investiture e 'ius belli': La posizione di Anselmo di Lucca," in *Sant'Anselmo, Mantova e la lotta per le investiture*, ed. Paolo Golinelli (Bologna, 1987), pp. 375–421 [pp. 405–21].

Paulinus of Aquileia. *Liber exhortationis*, PL 99: 197–282.

Peter Lombard. *Sententiae in iv distinctae*, ed. Collegiis Bonaventura ad Claras Aqua (Rome, 1981).

Peter of Vaulx-Cernay. *Hystoria Albigensis*, 3 vols., ed. Pascal Guébin and Ernest Lyon (Paris, 1926–39).

Poenitentiale Cummeani, in *Die Bußbücher und die Bußdisciplin der Kirche*, 2 vols., ed. H.J. Schmitz (1898, repr. Graz, 1958).

Poenitentiale Valicellanum II, in *Die Bußbücher und die Bußdisciplin der Kirche*, 2 vols., ed. H.J. Schmitz (1898, repr. Graz, 1958).

Le pontifical romano-germanique du dixième siècle, ed. Cyrille Vogel and Reinhard Elze (Vatican, 1963).

Procopius Caesariensis Opera Omnia: De bellis libri I–IV, 2 vols., ed. Jakob Haury (Leipzig, 2001).

Prosper of Aquitaine. *Chronicon*, ed. T. Mommsen, MGH AA (Berlin, 1892).

The Pseudo-Turpin, ed. H.M. Smyser (Cambridge, 1937).

Quellen zur Geschichte Kaiser Heinrichs IV, ed. Franz-Josef Schmale (Berlin, 1963).

Rabanus Maurus. *Poenitentiale*, PL 110: 467–94.

Rahewin. *Gesta Frederici seu rectius cronica*, ed. Franz-Joseph Schmale (Darmstadt, 1974).

Raymond d'Aguilers. *Liber*, ed. John Hugh and Laurita L. Hill (Paris, 1969).

Recueil des actes de Charles II le Chauve, roi de France, vol. 2, ed. A. Giry, M. Prou, and G. Tessier (Paris, 1963).

Recueil des actes de Charles III le Simple, roi de France (893–923), ed. Philippe Lauer (Paris, 1940).

Recueil des actes des ducs Normands d'Italie (1046–1127), ed. Léon-Robert Ménager (Bari, 1980).

Recueil des actes de Louis VI, roi de France, 2 vols., ed. Jean Dufour (Paris, 1992).

Recueil des actes de Philippe Ier roi de France (1059–1108), ed. M. Prou (Paris, 1908).

Regesta pontificum Romanorum, 2nd rev. edn, ed. S. Löwenfeld, F. Kaltenbrunner and P. Ewald (Leipzig, 1885).

Regesta Regum Anglo-Normannorum: The Acta of William I (1066–1087), ed. David Bates (Oxford, 1998).

Regesta Regum Anglo-Normannorum 1066–1154, vol. 2, ed. C. Johnson and H.A. Cronne (Oxford, 1956).

Regesta Regum Anglo-Normannorum 1066–1154, vol. 3, ed. H.A. Cronne and R.H.C. Davis (Oxford, 1968).

Regino of Prüm. *De synodalibus causis et disciplinis ecclesiasticis*, ed. F.G.A. Wasserschleben (repr. Graz, 1964).

La règle du temple, ed. Henri de Curzon, Société de l'Histoire de France 228 (Paris, 1886).

Reinerus. *Annales*, ed. G.H. Pertz, MG SS 16 (Hanover, 1859).

Richard of Devizes. *De rebus gestis Ricardi primi*, ed. Richard Howlett in *Chronicles of the Reigns of Stephen, Henry II, and Richard I*, vol. 3, Rolls Series 82 (London, 1886).

Richard of Hexham. *De gestis Regis Stephani et de bello standardii*, ed. Richard Howlett, Roll Series 82.3 (London, 1886), pp. 139–78.

Richer. *Histoire de France (888–995)*, 2nd edn, ed. and trans. R. Latouche, 2 vols., (Paris, 1969).

Rigord. *Gesta Philippi Augusti*, ed. H.F. Delaborde in *Oeuvres de Rigord et Guillaume le Breton* (Paris, 1895).

Robert of Clari. *La conquête de Constantinople*, ed. Philippe Lauer (Paris, 1924).

Robert of Rheims. *Historia Iherosolymitana*, Recueil des Historiens des Croisades: Historiens Occidentaux, 5 vols. (1844–95), III: 717–882.

Rodulfus Glaber. *Historiarum libri quinque*, ed. Neithard Bulst, trans. John France and Paul Reynolds (Oxford, 1989).

Das Rolandslied des Pfaffen Konrad, ed. Horst Richter (Darmstadt, 1981).

Rufinus. *Historiae ecclesiasticae* in *Eusebius Werke 2.2: Die Kirchengeschichte*, ed. E. Schwartz and T. Mommsen (Leipzig, 1908), repr. in an unrevised form in *Eusebius Werke 2.2: Die Kirchengeschichte*, ed. Friedhelm Winkelmann (Berlin, 1999).

The Rule of the Templars, trans. J.M. Upton-Ward (Woodbridge, 1992).

Ruotger. *Vita Brunonis archiepiscopi Coloniensis*, ed. Irene Ott, MGH SRG n.s. 10 (Weimar, 1951).

Le sacramentaire gélasien d'Angoulême, ed. P. Cagin (Angoulême, 1919).

Sacramentarum gellonense, ed. A. Dumas, Corpus Christianorum 159 (Turnholt, 1981).

Salvian of Marseilles. *De gubernatione Dei*, ed. F. Pauly, CSEL 8 (Vienna, 1883).

Salvian of Marseilles. *Oeuvres*, ed. Georges Lagarrigue, Sources Chrétiennes 176 (Paris, 1971).

Schmitz, Wilhelm. *Miscellanea tironiana* (Leipzig, 1896).

———— "Tironische Miszellen," *Neues Archiv* 15 (1890).

Shopkow, Leah. *The History of the Counts of Guines and Lords of Ardres* (Philadelphia, 2001).

Sigebert. *Continuatio Praemonstratensis*, ed. G. Waitz, MG SS 6 (Hanover, 1844).

Die Statuten des Deutschen Ordens, ed. Max Perlbach (Halle, 1890).

Suger. *Vita Ludovici Grossi regis*, ed. Henri Waquet (Paris, 1929).

Suger. *The Deeds of Louis the Fat*, trans. Richard Cusimano and John Moorhead (Washington, D.C., 1992).

Tellenbach, Gerd. "Mass prayers from the sacramentary of Gellone," in *Sitzungsbericht der heidelberger Akademie der Wissenschaft* 24 (1934), pp. 67–70.

Theodulf of Orlèans. *Opus Carolini regis contra synodum (Libri Carolini)*, ed. Anne Freeman, MGH Concilia 2 suppl. 1 (Hanover, 1998).

————. *Capitula ad presbyteros parochiae suae*, PL 105: 191–224.

Thietmar of Merseburg. *Chronicon*, ed. Werner Trillmich based on the original edition by R. Holtzmann (Darmstadt, 1985).

Die Totenbücher von Merseburg, Magdeburg, und Lüneburg, ed. G. Althoff and J. Wollasch, MGH Libri Memoriales et Necrologia n.s. 2 (Hanover, 1983).

Triumphus sancti Lamberti de castro Bullonio, ed. W. Arndt, MG SS 20 (Hanover, 1868).

Die Urkunden Friedrich I, 4 vols., ed. Heinrich Appelt, MGH UKK 10 (Hanover, 1975–90).

Die Urkunden Heinrichs II und Arduin, ed. H. Bresslau, MGH UKK 4 (Hanover, 1903).

Die Urkunden Heinrichs III, ed. H. Bresslau and P. Kehr, MGH UKK 5 (Berlin, 1931).

Die Urkunden Heinrichs IV, 3 vols., ed. D. von Gladiss and A. Gawlik, MGH UKK 6 (Hanover, 1941–78)

Die Urkunden Konrad I. Heinrich I. und Otto I. ed. T. Sickel, MGH UKK 1 (Hanover, 1884).

Die Urkunden Konrads II, ed. H. Wibel and A. Hessel, MGH UKK 4 (Hanover, 1909).

Die Urkunden Konrads III, ed. F. Hausmann, MGH UKK 9 (Vienna, 1969).

Die Urkunden Lothar III und der Kaiserin Richenz, ed. E. von Ottenthal and H. Hirsch, MGH UKK 8 (Berlin, 1923).

Die Urkunden Otto des II, MGH UKK 2 (Hanover, 1888).

Die Urkunden Otto des III, MGH UKK 3 (Hanover, 1893).

Vegetius. *Epitoma Rei Militari*, ed. Alf Önnerfors (Stuttgart, 1995).

Vegetius. *Epitome of Military Science*, 2nd edn, trans. N.P. Milner (Liverpool, 1996).

Vita Anselmi episcopi Lucensis, ed. Roger Wilmans, MG SS 12 (Hanover, 1856).

Vitae Odiliae liber iii: de triumpho S. Lamberti in Steppes, ed. I. Heller, MG SS 25 (Hanover, 1880).

Wace. *Le Roman de Rou*, 2 vols., ed. A.J. Holden (Paris, 1971).

Waltarius, ed. K. Strecker (Berlin, 1947).

Widukind of Corvey. *Rerum gestarum Saxonicum*, ed. Paul Hirsch, MGH SRG 60 (Hanover, 1935).

William of Apulia. *La geste de Robert Guiscard par Guillaume de Pouille*, ed. Marguerite Mathieu (Palermo, 1961).

William the Breton. *Gesta Philipi Augusti*, ed. François Delaborde (Paris, 1882).

William of Malmesbury. *Gesta regum Anglorum*, 2 vols., ed. R.A.B. Mynors, R.M. Thomson, and M. Winterbottom (Oxford, 1999).

William of Newburgh. *Historia rerum Anglicarum*, ed. Richard Howlett, Rolls Series 82 (London, 1884).

William of Poitiers. *Gesta Guillelmi*, ed. R.H.C. Davis and Marjorie Chibnall (Oxford, 1998).

William of Puylaurens. *Chronica*, ed. Jean Duvernay (Paris, 1976).

Zosimus. *Historia Nova*, rev. edn, ed. François Paschoud (Paris, 2000).

Secondary Literature

Abels, Richard P. *Lordship and Military Obligation in Anglo-Saxon England* (Berkeley, 1988).

Adelson, Howard L. "The Holy Lance and the Hereditary German Monarchy," *The Art Bulletin* 48 (1996), pp. 177–91.

Aho, James. *Religious Mythology and the Art of War: Comparative Religious Symbolisms of Military Violence* (Westport, 1981).

Airlie, Stuart. "True Teachers and Pious Kings: Salzburg, Louis the German, and the Christian Order," in *Belief and Culture in the Middle Ages*, ed. Richard Gameson and Henrietta Leyser (Oxford, 2001), pp. 89–105.

Albu (Hanawalt), Emily. *The Normans and their Histories: Propaganda, Myth, and Subversion* (Woodbridge, 2001).

———. "Dudo of Saint-Quentin: The Heroic Past Imagined," *The Haskins Society Journal* 6 (1994), pp. 111–18.

Alfödy, Géza. *Römische Heeresgeschichte Beiträge 1962–1985* (Amsterdam, 1987).

Alphandéry, Paul. *La chrétienté et l'idée de croisade* (Paris, 1954).

Althoff, Gerd. "Widukind von Corvery, Kronzeuge und Herausforderung," *Frühmittelalterliche Studien* 27 (1993), pp. 253–72.

——— and Coué, Stephanie. "Pragmatische Geschichtsschreibung und Krisen. I. Zur Funktion von Brunos Buch vom Sachsenkrieg. II. Der Mord an Karl dem Gutem (1127) und die Werke Galberts vom Brügge und Walters von Thérouanne," in *Pragmatische Schriftlichkeit im Mittelalter: Erscheinungsformen und Entwicklungsstufen*, ed. Hagen Keller, Klaus Grubmüller, and Nikolaus Staubach (Munich, 1992), pp. 95–129.

Arnst, Ludwig. "Der Feldaltar in Vergangenheit und Gegenwart," *Zeitschrift für christliche Kunst* 28 (1915), pp. 89–105.

———. "Mittelalterliche Feldzeichen: Eine kunstgeschichtliche Studie," *Zeitschrift für christliche Kunst* 28 (1915), pp. 164–80.

Auer, Leopold. "Der Kriegsdienst des Klerus unter den sächsischen Käiser," *MIÖG* 79 (1971), pp. 316–407 and *MIÖG* 80 (1972), pp. 48–70.

Avril, Joseph. "Remarques sur un aspect de la vie religieuse paroissiale: la pratique de la confession et de la communion du Xe au XIVe siècle," in *L'Encadrement religieux des fidèles au moyen âge et jusqu'au concile de Trente* (Paris, 1985), pp. 345–63.

Bachrach, Bernard S. *Early Carolingian Warfare: Prelude to Empire* (Philadelphia, 2001).

———. "Early Medieval Military Demography: Some Observations on the Methods of Hans Delbrück," in *The Circle of War in the Middle Ages: Essays on Medieval Military and Naval History*, ed. Donald J. Kagay and L.J. Andrew Villalon (Woodbridge, 1999), pp. 3–20.

———. "Medieval Military Historiography," in *Companion to Historiography*, ed. Michael Bentley (London, 1997), pp. 203–20.

———. *Fulk Nerra, the Neo-Roman Consul, 987–1040: A Political Biography of the Angevin Count* (Berkeley, 1993).

————. "The Combat Sculptures at Fulk Nerra's 'Battle Abbey,'" *Haskins Society Journal* 3 (1991), pp. 63–80.

————. "The Northern Origins of the Peace Movement of Le Puy in 975," *Historical Reflections/Réflexions historique* 14 (1987), pp. 405–21.

————. "Pope Sergius IV and the Foundation of the Monastery of Beaulieu-lès-Loches," *Revue bénédictine* 95 (1985), pp. 240–65.

————. "Some Observations on the Military Administration of the Norman Conquest," *Anglo-Norman Studies* 7 (1985), pp. 1–26.

————. "Toward a Reappraisal of William the Great, Duke of Aquitaine (995–1030)," *Journal of Medieval History* 5 (1979), pp. 11–21.

Bachrach, David S. "Confession in the 'Regnum Francorum' (742–900): The Sources Revisited," *Journal of Ecclesiastical History* (forthcoming 2003).

Bagley, C.P. "Robert of Clari's *La Conquête de Constantinople*," *Medium Aevum* 40 (1971), pp. 109–15.

Bainton, Roland H. *Christian Attitudes toward War and Peace* (New York, 1960).

Baker, Derek. "Ailred of Rievaulx and Walter Espec," *Haskins Society Journal* 1 (1989), pp. 91–8.

Banniard, Michel. *Vive voce: communication ècrite et communication orale du Ie au IXe siècle en occident latin* (Paris, 1992).

Bataillon, Louis-Jacques. "Sermons rédigés, sermons réportés (XIIIe siècle)," *Medioevo e rinascimento* 3 (1989), pp. 69–86.

Beer, Jeanette M.A. *Villehardouin: Epic Historian* (Geneva, 1968).

Bennett, Matthew. "The *Roman de Rou* of Wace as a Source for the Norman Conquest," *Anglo-Norman Studies* 5 (1982), pp. 21–39.

Berry, Virginia G. "The Second Crusade," in *A History of the Crusades*, ed. Kenneth M. Setton, 6 vols. (Madison, 1969–89), II: 463–512.

Birely, Eric. "Religion of the Roman Army: 1885–1977," *Aufstieg und Niedergang der Römischen Welt II Principat 16.2* (Berlin, 1978), pp. 1506–41.

Blake, E.O. "The Formation of the 'Crusading Idea,'" *The Journal of Ecclesiastical History* 21 (1970), pp. 11–31.

Bliese, John R.E. "The Just War Concept and Motive in the Central Middle Ages," *Medievalia et Humanistica* n.s. 17 (1991), pp. 1–26.

————. "Rhetoric and Morale: A Study of Battle Orations from the Central Middle Ages," *Journal of Medieval History* 15 (1989), pp. 201–26.

————. "The Battle Rhetoric of Aelred of Rievaulx," *The Haskins Society Journal* 1 (1989), pp. 99–107.

————. "Aelred of Rievaulx's Rhetoric and Morale at the Battle of the Standard 1138," *Albion* 20 (1988), pp. 543–56.

Blumenthal, Uta-Renate. *The Investiture Controversy: Church and Monarchy from the Ninth to the Twelfth Century* (Philadelphia, 1988).

Bonnassie, Pierre. *La Catalogne du milieu du Xe à la fin du XIe siècle: Croissance et mutations d'une société*, 2 vols. (Toulouse, 1975–6).

Boreau, Alain. "Droit et théologie au XIIIe siècle," *Annales: histoire, sciences sociales* 46: 6 (1992), pp. 1113–25.

Bouët, Pierre. "Orderic Vital lecteur critique de Guillaume de Poitiers," in *Mediaevalia christiana, XIe–XIIIe siècles: homage à Raymonde Foreville de ses amis, ses collègues et ses anciens élèlves*, ed. Coloman Etienne Viola (Paris, 1989), pp. 25–50.

Bowman, Jeffrey A. "Do Neo-Romans Curse?: Law, Land, and Ritual in the Midi (900–1100)," *Viator* 28 (1997), pp. 1–32.

Braun, Joseph. *Der Christliche Altar in seiner geschichtlichen Entwicklung*, 2 vols. (Munich, 1924).

Broadhurst, Karen M. "Henry II of England and Eleanor of Aquitaine: Patrons of Literature in French?" *Viator* 27 (1996), pp. 53–84.

Brown, Peter. *The Making of Late Antiquity* (Cambridge, 1978).

———. *The World of Late Antiquity AD 150–750* (New York, 1971).

Brundage, James A. "The Hierarchy of Violence in Twelfth- and Thirteenth-Century Canonists," *The International History Review* 17 (1995), pp. 671–92.

———. "The Rise of the Professional Canonists and the Development of the *ius commune*," *ZRG kan.* 112: 125 (1995), pp. 26–63.

———. *The Crusades, Holy War, and Canon Law* (Brookfield, 1991).

———. *Medieval Canon Law and the Crusader* (Madison, 1969).

Bull, Marcus. *Knightly Piety and the Lay Response to the First Crusade: The Limousin and Gascony, c. 970–c. 1130* (Oxford, 1993).

Bünemann, Richard. *Robert Guiskard, 1015–1085: Ein Normane erobert Süditalien* (Cologne, 1997).

Cadoux, John C. *The Early Christian Attitude to War: A Contribution to the History of Christian Ethics* (New York, 1982).

Cahan, Claude. "A propos d'Albert d'Aix et de Richard le Pèlerin," *Le moyen âge* 96 (1990), pp. 31–3.

Callahan, Daniel F. "The Cult of the Saints in Aquitaine," in *The Peace of God: Social Violence and Religious Response in France around the Year 1000*, ed. Thomas Head and Richard Landes (Ithaca, 1992), pp. 165–83.

Cameron, Averil and Hall, Stuart G. eds. *Eusebius: Life of Constantine* (Oxford, 1999).

Campbell, Brian. *The Roman Army, 31 BC–AD 337: A Sourcebook* (London, 1994).

Carroll, Robert. "War in the Hebrew Bible," in *War and Society in the Greek World*, ed. John Rich and Graham Shipley (London, 1993), pp. 25–44.

Chélini, Jean. *L'Aube du moyen âge: naissance de la chrétienité occidentale* (Picard, 1991).

Chibnall, Marjorie. *The World of Orderic Vitalis* (Oxford, 1984).

———. "Mercenaries and the *familia regis* under Henry I," *Proceedings of the Society for Antiquaries of Scotland* 62 (1977), pp. 15–23.

Chroust, Anton. *Tageno, Ansbert, und die Historia Peregrinorum: Drei kritische Untersuchungen zur Geschichte des Kreuzzuges Friedrichs I* (Graz, 1892).

Cole, Penny J. "Christian Perceptions of the Battle of Hattin (583/1187)," *Al-Masaq* 6 (1993), pp. 9–39.

Constable, Giles. *The Reformation of the Twelfth Century* (Cambridge, 1996).

———. "The Language of Preaching in the Twelfth Century," *Viator* 25 (1994), pp. 131–52.

———. "The Second Crusade as Seen by Contemporaries," *Traditio* 9 (1953), pp. 213–29, and with the same pagination in Constable, *Religious Life and Thought* (London, 1974).

Contamine, Philippe. *War in the Middle Ages*, trans. Michael Jones (Oxford, 1984).

———. *La guerre au moyen âge*, 4th edn (Paris, 1994).

Cowdrey, H.E.J. *Pope Gregory VII 1073–1085* (Oxford, 1998).

———. "Martyrdom and the First Crusade," in *Crusade and Settlement*, ed. P.W. Edbury (Cardiff, 1985), and repr. with the same pagination in Cowdrey, *The Crusades and Latin Monasticism, 11th and 12th Centuries* (Brookfield, 1999).

———. "The Mahdia Campaign of 1087," *English Historical Review* 92 (1977), pp. 1–29.

———. "Pope Gregory VII and the Anglo-Norman Church and Kingdom," *Studi Gregoriani* 9 (1972), pp. 78–114.

————. "Bishop Ermenfrid of Sion and the Penitential Ordinance following the Battle of Hastings," *Journal of Ecclesiastical History* 20 (1969), pp. 225–42.

————. "Archbishop Aribert of Milan," *History* 51 (1966), pp. 1–15.

Cramer, Peter. *Baptism and Change in the Early Middle Ages c. 200–c. 1400* (Cambridge, 1993).

Cronin, James E. "And the Reapers are Angels: A Study of Crusade Motivation as Described in the *Historia Iherosolimitana* of Robert of Rheims" (New York University, 1973), unpublished dissertation.

Cross, J. E. "The Ethic of War in Old English," in *England before the Conquest: Studies in the Primary Sources Presented to Dorothy Whitelock*, ed. Peter Clemoes and Kathleen Hughes (Cambridge, 1971), pp. 269–82.

Crouch, David. *The Reign of King Stephen, 1135–1154* (Harlow, 2000).

Dawson, Doyne. *The Origins of Western Warfare: Militarism and Morality in the Ancient World* (Boulder, 1996).

Delaruelle, Etienne. "Charlemagne et l'Église," *Revue d'histoire de l'église de France* 133 (1953), pp. 165–99.

————. *L'idée de croisade au moyen âge* (Turin, 1980); originally published in *Bulletin de littérature ecclésiastique* 42 (1942), pp. 24–45 and 86–103; 45 (1944), pp. 13–46 and 73–90; 54 (1953), pp. 226–39; and 55 (1954), pp. 50–63.

Domaszewski, Alfred. "Die Religion des römischen Heeres," *Westdeutsche Zeitschrift für Geschichte und Kunst* 14 (1895), pp. 1–128 [Repr. *Aufsätze zur römischen Heeresgeschichte* (Darmstadt, 1972)].

Drew, Katherine Fischer. "The Carolingian Military Frontier in Italy," *Traditio* 20 (1964), pp. 434–47.

Driscoll, Michael S. "The Seven Penitential Psalms: Their Designation and Usages from the Middle Ages Onwards," *Ecclesia orans* 17 (2000), pp. 153–201.

————. "*Ad Pueros Sancti Martini*: A Critical Edition, English Translation, and Study of the Manuscript Transmission," *Traditio* 53 (1998), pp. 37–61.

————. "Penance in Transition: Popular Piety and Practice," in *Medieval Liturgy: A Book of Essays*, ed. Lizette Larson Miller (New York, 1997), pp. 121–63.

Duby, Georges. *The Legend of Bouvines: War, Religon, and Culture in the Middle Ages*, trans. Catherine Tihanyi (Berkeley, 1990).

Duggan, Charles. "Papal Judges Delegate and the Making of the 'New Law' in the Twelfth Century," in *Cultures of Power: Lordship, Status, and Process in Twelfth-Century Europe*, ed. Thomas N. Bisson (Philadelphia, 1995), pp. 172–179.

Erdmann, Carl. "Kaiserliche und päpstliche Fahnen im hohen Mittelalter," *Quellen und Forschungen aus italienischen Archiven und Bibliotheken* 25 (1933), pp. 1–48.

————. *The Origin of the Idea of Crusade*, trans. Marshall W. Baldwin and Walter Goffart (Princeton, 1977).

Ewig, Eugen. *Handbook of Church History III*, trans. Anselm Biggs (New York, 1969).

Faral, Edmond. "Geoffroi de Villehardouin: La question de sa sincérité," *Revue historique* 176 (1936), pp. 530–82.

Fleckenstein, Josef. *Die Kofkapelle der deutschen Könige*, 2 vols. (Stuttgart, 1959–66).

Flori, Jean. "Faut il réhabiliter Pierre l'Ermite: une réévaluation des sources de la première croisade," *Cahiers de civilisation médiévale* 38 (1995), pp. 35–54.

————. "Pur eschalchier sainte crestiënté: croisade, guerre saint et guerre just dans les anciennes chansons de geste française," *Le moyen âge* 5th series 5 (1991), pp. 171–87.

Forey, Alan J. "The Second Crusade: Scope and Objectives," *Durham University Journal* n.s. 55: 2 (1994), pp. 165–75.

Fournier, Paul. "Études critiques sur le décret de Burchard de Worms," *Nouvelle revue historique de droit français et étranger* 34 (1910), pp. 41–112, 213–21, 289–331, and 564–84 [repr. *Mélanges de droit canonique I* (Darmstadt, 1983)].

France, John. *Victory in the East: A Military History of the First Crusade* (Cambridge, 1994).

———. "The Occasion of the Coming of the Normans to Southern Italy," *Journal of Medieval History* 17 (1991), pp. 185–205.

Frantzen, Allen J. "The Significance of the Frankish Penitentials," *The Journal of Ecclesiastical History* 30 (1979), pp. 409–21.

Frolow, A. *Les reliquaires de la vrai croix* (Paris, 1965).

Gaier, Claude. "Le rôle militaire des reliques et de l'éntard de Saint Lambert dans la principauté de Liège," *Le moyen âge* 72 (1966), pp. 235–49.

Ganshof, F.L. L'église et le pouvoir royal dans la monarchie franque sous Pèpin III et Charlemagne," in *Le chiese nei regni dell' Europa occidentale ei loro rapporti con Roma sino all'800: Settimane di Studio del Centro Italiano di Studi sull'Alto Medioevo* 7 (1960), pp. 95–141, trans. as "The Church and Royal Power under Pippin III and Charlemagne," in *The Carolingians and the Frankish Monarchy*, trans. Janet Sondheimer (London, 1971), pp. 205–39.

———. *Recherches sur les capitulaires* (Paris, 1958).

———. "Charlemagne et le serment," *Mélanges Halphen* (Paris, 1951), pp. 261–67.

Geary, Patrick. "Humiliation of Saints," in *Saints and their Cults: Studies in Religious Sociology, Folklore, and History*, ed. Stephen Wilson (Cambridge, 1983), pp. 123–40.

Giese, Wolfgang. "Die *Lancea Domini* von Antiocha (1098/1099)," in *Fälschungen im Mittelalter: Internationaler Kongress der Monumenta Germaniae Historica*, 5 vols. (Hanover, 1988), V: 485–504.

Goetz, Hans-Werner. "Protection of the Church, Defense of the Law, and Reform: On the Purpose and Character of the Peace of God, 989–1038," in *The Peace of God: Social Violence and Religious Response in France around the Year 1000*, ed. Thomas Head and Richard Landes (Ithaca, 1992), pp. 259–79.

Goffart, Walter. "The *Historia Ecclesiastica*: Bede's Agenda and Ours," *Haskins Society Journal* 2 (1990), pp. 29–45.

———. *The Narrators of Barbarian History (A.D. 550–800): Jordanes, Gregory of Tours, Bede, and Paul the Deacon* (Princeton, 1988).

———. "The Date and Purpose of Vegetius' *De Re Militari*," in *Rome's Fall and After* (London, 1985); originally published in *Traditio* 33 (1977), pp. 65–100.

Goldberg, Eric J. " 'More Devoted to the Equipment of Battle than the Splendor of Banquets': Frontier Kingship, Martial Ritual, and Early Knighthood at the Court of Louis the German," *Viator* 30 (1999), pp. 41–78.

Goubert, Paul. "Religion et superstitions dans l'armée byzantine à la fin du VIe siècle," in *Orientalia christiana periodica: miscellanea Guillaume de Jerphanion* 13 (1947), pp. 495–500.

Gransden, Antonia. *Historical Writing in England c. 550 to c. 1307*, 2 vols. (Ithaca, 1974).

Haider, Siegfried. *Das bischöfliche Kapellanat von den Anfängen bis in das 13. Jahrhundert* (Vienna, 1977).

Hamann-Maclean, Richard. "Die Reimser Denkmale des französischen Königtums in 12. Jahrhundert. Saint Remi als Grabkirche im frühen und hohen Mittelalter," in *Beiträge zur Bildung der französischen Nation im Früh-und Hochmittelalter*, ed. Helmut Beumann (Sigmaringen, 1983), pp. 93–260.

Hamilton, Sarah. *The Practice of Penance 900–1050* (London, 2001).

Hare, Kent G. "Apparitions and War in Anglo-Saxon England," in *The Circle of War in the Middle Ages: Essays on Medieval Military and Naval History*, ed. Donald J. Kagay and L.J. Andrew Villalon (Woodbridge, 1999), pp. 75–86.

Hartmann, Wilfried. *Die Synoden der Karolingerzeit im Frankreich und in Italien* (Paderborn, 1989).

Heer, Joseph Michael. *Ein karolingischer Missionskatechismus* (Freiburg, 1911).

Hehl, Ernst-Dieter. *Kirche und Krieg im 12. Jahrhundert: Studien zu kanonischem Recht und politischer Wirklichkeit* (Stuttgart, 1980).

Heisenberg, A. "Kriegsgottesdienst in Byzanz," *Aufsätze zur Kultur-und Sprachgeschichte vornehmlich des Orients* (Munich, 1916), pp. 244–57.

Helgeland, John. "Roman Army Religion," *Aufstieg und Niedergang der Römischen Welt II Principat 16.2* (Berlin, 1978), pp. 1470–1505.

Hoffmann, Hartmut. *Gottesfriede und Treuga Dei* (Stuttgart, 1964).

———— and Pokorny, Rudolf. *Das Dekret des Bischofs Burchard von Worms* (Munich, 1991).

Holdsworth, Christopher. " 'An Airier Aristocracy': The Saints at War," *Transactions of the Royal Historical Society*, 6th ser. 6 (1996), pp. 103–22.

Hollister, C. Warren. *The Military Organization of Norman England* (Oxford, 1965).

————. *Anglo-Saxon Military Institutions on the Eve of the Norman Conquest* (Oxford, 1962).

Jameson, Michael H. "Sacrifice Before Battle," in *Hoplites: The Classical Greek Battle Experience*, ed. Victor Davis Hanson (London, 1991), pp. 197–227.

Johnson, Edgar N. "The Crusades of Frederick Barbarossa and Henry VI," in *The History of the Crusades II*, ed. Peter Lee Wolf and Harry W. Hazard (Madison, 1969), pp. 87–122.

Jones, A.H.M. "Military Chaplains in the Roman Army," *Harvard Theological Review* 46 (1953), pp. 239–40.

Jones, Michael E. "The Historicity of the Alleluja Victory," *Albion* 18 (1986), pp. 363–73.

Joranson, Einor. "The Inception and the Career of the Normans in Italy – Legend and History," *Speculum* 23 (1948), pp. 353–96.

Kantorowicz, Ernst H. "*Pro patria mori* in Medieval Political Thought," *The American Historical Review* 56 (1951), pp. 472–92.

————. *Laudes Regiae: A Study in Liturgical Acclamations and Medieval Ruler Worship* (Berkeley, 1946).

Karpf, Ernst. "Von Widukind's *Sachsengeschichte* bis zu Thietmar's *Chronicon*: Zu den literarischen Folgen des politischen Aufschwungs im ottonischen Sachsen," *Angli e Sassoni al di quà e al di là del mare: Settimane di Studi del Centro Italiano di Studi sull'Alto Medieoevo* 33 (Spoleto, 1986), pp. 547–80.

Keller, Hagen. "Widukinds Bericht über die Aachener Wahl und Krönung Ottos I," *Frühmittelalterliche Studien* 29 (1995), pp. 390–453.

Kellner, Wendelin. *Libertas und Christogram: Motivesgeschichtliche Untersuchungen zur Münzprägung des Kaisers Magnentius (350–353)* (Karlsruhe, 1968).

Knoch, Peter. *Studien zu Albert von Aachen. Der erste Kreuzzug in den deutschen Chronistik* (Stuttgart, 1966).

Koeniger, Albert Michael. *Die Militärseelsorge der Karolingerzeit: Ihr Recht und ihre Praxis* (Munich, 1918).

Kottje, Raymond. "Die Tötung im Kriege: Ein moralisches und rechtliches Problem im frühen Mittelalter," *Beiträge zur Friedensethik* 11 (1991), pp. 1–21.

Koziol, Geoffrey. *Begging Pardon and Favor: Ritual and Political Order in Early Medieval France* (Ithaca, 1992).

Kugler, B. *Neue Analekten* (Tübingen, 1883).

————. *Analekten zur Geschichte des zweiten Kreuzzuges* (Tübingen, 1878).

————. *Studien zur Geschichte des zweiten Kreuzzuges* (Stuttgart, 1866).

Landes, Richard. "Popular Participation in the Limousin Peace of God," in *The Peace of God: Social Violence and Religious Response in France around the Year 1000*, ed. Thomas Head and Richard Landes (Ithaca, 1992), pp. 184–219.

Le Goff, Jacques. *Naissance du Purgatoire* (Paris, 1981), trans. Arthur Goldhammer as *The Birth of Purgatory* (Chicago, 1984).

Levison, Wilhelm. *England and the Continent in the Eighth Century* (Oxford, 1946).

Leyser, Karl. "Early Medieval Warfare," in *Communications and Power in Medieval Europe: The Carolingian and Ottonian Centuries*, ed. Timothy Reuter (London, 1994), pp. 29–50.

————. "Ritual, Ceremony, and Gesture: Ottonian Germany," in *Communications and Power in Medieval Europe: The Carolingian and Ottonian Centuries*, ed. Timothy Reuter (London, 1994), pp. 189–213.

Little, Lester K. *Benedictine Maledictions: Liturgical Cursing in Romanesque France* (Ithaca, 1993).

Livermore, Harold. "The 'Conquest of Lisbon' and its Author," *Portuguese Studies* 6 (1990), pp. 1–16.

Lot, Ferdinand. *L'Art militaire et les armées au moyen âge en Europe et dans le proche orient*, 2 vols. (Paris, 1946).

Lutterbach, H. "Die Bußordines in den iro-fränkischen Paenitentialen: Schlüssel zur Theologie und Verwendung der mittelalterlichen Bußbücher," *Frühmittelalterliche Studien* 30 (1996), pp. 150–72.

Macmullen, Ramsay. *Christianizing the Roman Empire A.D. 100–400* (Yale, 1984).

————. *Soldier and Civilian in the Later Roman Empire* (Cambridge, 1967).

Magnou-Nortier, Elisabeth. *La société laïque dans la province ecclésiastique de Narbonne* (Toulouse, 1974).

Maier, Christoph T. "Crisis, Liturgy, and the Crusade in the Twelfth and Thirteenth Centuries," *Journal of Ecclesiastical History* 48 (1997), pp. 628–57.

Mathisen, Ralph W. "Barbarian Bishops and the Churches 'in barbaricis gentibus' during Late Antiquity," *Speculum* 72 (1997), pp. 664–97.

Mayer, Hans Eberhard. *The Crusades*, trans. John Gillingham (Oxford, 1972).

McCormick, Michael. "Liturgie et Guerre des Carolingiens à la première Croisade," in *'Militia Christi' e Crociata nei secoli XI–XIII: miscellanea del centro di studi medioevali* 13 (1992), pp. 209–40.

————. "A New Ninth-Century Witness to the Carolingian Mass Against the Pagans," *Revue bénédictine* 97 (1987), pp. 68–86.

————. *Eternal Victory: Triumphal Rulership in Late Antiquity, Byzantium, and the Early Medieval West* (Cambridge, 1986).

————. "The Liturgy of War in the Early Middle Ages: Crisis, Litanies, and the Carolingian Monarchy," *Viator* 15 (1984), pp. 1–24.

McGinn, Bernard. "*Iter sancti sepulchri*: The Piety of the First Crusaders," in *The Walter Prescott Web Memorial Lectures: Essays on Medieval Civilization*, ed. Bede Karl Lackner and Kenneth Roy Philp (Austin, 1978), pp. 33–72.

McKitterick, Rosamond. *The Carolingians and the Written Word* (Cambridge, 1989).

————. *The Frankish Kingdoms under the Carolingians, 751–987* (London, 1983).

————. *The Frankish Church and the Carolingian Reforms 789–895* (London, 1977).

Meens, Rob. "The Frequency and Nature of Early Medieval Penance," in *Handling Sin in the Middle Ages*, ed. Peter Biller and A.J. Minnis (York, 1998), pp. 35–63.

Meyer, Otto. "Überlieferung und Verbreitung des Dekrets des Bischofs Burchard von Worms," *ZRG kan.* 24 (1935), pp. 141–83.

Mordeck, Hubert. *Bibliotheca Capitularum regum Francorum manuscripta: Überlieferung und Traditionszussamenhang der fränkischen Herrschererlasse* (Munich, 1995).

———. "Handschriftforschungen in Italien: Zur Überlieferung des Dekrets Bischof Burchards von Worms," *Quellen und Forschungen aus italienischen Archiven und Bibliotechen* 51 (1971).

Moreton, Bernard. *The Eighth-Century Gelasian Sacramentary: A Study in Tradition* (Oxford, 1976).

Morris, Colin. "Policy and Visions. The Case of the Holy Lance at Antioch," in *War and Government: Essays in Honour of J.O. Prestwich*, ed. John Gillingham and J.C. Holt (Woodbridge, 1984), pp. 33–45.

———. "Propaganda for War: The Dissemination of the Crusading Ideal in the Twelfth Century," in *The Church at War: Studies in Church History* 20 (1983), pp. 79–102.

Morton, Catherine. "Pope Alexander and the Norman Conquest," *Latomus* 34 (1975), pp. 362–82.

Munz, Peter. *Frederick Barbarossa: A Study in Medieval Politics* (Ithaca, 1969).

Murray, Alan V. " 'Mighty Against the Enemies of Christ': The Relic of the True Cross in the Armies of the Kingdom of Jerusalem," in *The Crusaders and their Sources: Essays Presented to Bernard Hamilton*, ed. John France and William G. Zajac (Brookfield, 1998), pp. 217–38.

Murray, Alexander. "Confession before 1215," *Transactions of the Royal Historical Society*, 6th series 3 (1993), pp. 51–81.

———. "Religion Among the Poor in Thirteenth-Century France: The Testimony of Humbert of Romans," *Traditio* 30 (1974), pp. 285–324.

———. "Piety and Impiety in Thirteenth Century Italy," in *Popular Beliefs and Practice: Studies in Church History* 8 (1972), pp. 83–106.

Naß, Klaus. *Die Reichschronik des Annalista Saxo und die sächsische Geschichtsschreibung im 12. Jahrhundert* (Hanover, 1996).

Nelson, Janet L. "Public Histories and Private History in the Work of Nithard," in *Politics and Ritual in Early Medieval Europe* (London, 1986) [originally published in *Speculum* 60 (1985), pp. 251–93].

Noble, Thomas F.X. "Introduction," to *The Letters of Saint Boniface* (New York, 2000).

———. *The Republic of St. Peter: The Birth of the Papal State, 680–825* (Philadelphia, 1984).

Ohler, Norbert. *Krieg und Frieden im Mittelalter* (Munich, 1997).

Önnerfors, Alf. *Die Verfasserschaft des Waltharius-Epos aus sprachlicher Sicht* (Düsseldorf, 1978).

Paxton, Frederick S. *Christianizing Death: The Creation of a Ritual Process in Early Medieval Europe* (Ithaca, 1990).

The Peace of God: Social Violence and Religious Response in France around the Year 1000, ed. Thomas Head and Richard Landes (Ithaca, 1992).

Phillips, Jonathan. "Ideas of Crusade and Holy War in *De expugnatione Lyxbonensi* (The Conquest of Lisbon)," in *The Holy Land, Holy Lands, and Christian History*, ed. R.N. Swanson (Woodbridge, 2000), pp. 123–41.

Pierce, Rosamond (McKitterick), "The 'Frankish' Penitentials," *Studies in Church History*, ed. Derek Baker 11 (1975), pp. 31–9.

Poschmann, Bernard. *Penance and the Annointing of the Sick*, trans. and rev. by Francis Courtney (New York, 1968).

———. *Buße und letzte Ölung* (Freiburg, 1951).

———. *Die abendländische Kirchenbuße im frühen Mittelalter* (Breslau, 1930).

Potts, Cassandra W. "*Atque unum ex diversis gentibus populum effecit*: Historical Tradition and Norman Identity," *Anglo-Norman Studies* 18 (1996), pp. 139–52.

Powell, James M. "Myth, Legend, Propaganda, History: The First Crusade, 1140–c. 1300," in *Autour de la première croisade: actes du colloque de la Society for the Study of the Crusade and the Latin East*, ed. Michael Balard (Paris, 1996), pp. 127–41.

Powers, James F. *A Society Organized for War: Iberian Municipal Militias in the Central Middle Ages, 1000–1284* (Berkeley, 1988).

Prestwich, J.O. "The Military Household of the Norman Kings," in *Anglo-Norman Warfare*, ed. Matthew Strickland (Woodbridge, 1992), pp. 93–128.

Prinz, Friedrich. *Klerus und Krieg im früheren Mittelalter* (Stuttgart, 1971).

Pritchett, W. Kendrick. *The Greek State at War*, 5 vols. (Berkeley, 1971–91).

Queller, Donald E. and Madden, Thomas F. *The Fourth Crusade: The Conquest of Constantinople 1201–1204*, 2nd rev. edn (Philadelphia, 1997).

Ray, Roger D. "Orderic Vitalis and William of Poitiers: A Monastic Reinterpretation of William the Conqueror," *Revue belge de philologie et d'histoire* 50 (1972), pp. 1116–27.

Regout, Robert H.W. *La doctrine de la guerre juste de Saint Augustin à nos jours* (1934, repr. Aalen, 1974).

Reuter, Timothy. " 'Kirchenreform' und 'Kirchenpolitik' im Zeitalter Karl Martells: Begriffe und Wirklichkeit," in *Karl Martell in seiner Zeit*, ed. Jörg Jarnut, Ulrich Nonn, and Michael Richter (Sigmaringen, 1994), pp. 35–9.

———. "Saint Boniface and Europe," in *The Greatest Englishman: Essays on St. Boniface and the Church at Crediton*, ed. Timothy Reuter (Exeter, 1980), pp. 69–94.

Reynolds, Susan. *Kingdoms and Communities in Western Europe, 900–1300* (Oxford, 1984).

Riley-Smith, Jonathan. *The First Crusaders, 1095–1131* (Cambridge, 1997).

Rosenwein, Barbara H. *Rhinoceros Bound: Cluny in the Tenth Century* (Philadelphia, 1982).

Ross, James Bruce. "Two Neglected Paladins of Charlemagne: Eric of Friuli and Gerold of Bavaria," *Speculum* 20 (1945), pp. 212–35.

Rouillard, Philippe. *Histoire de la pénitence des origins à nos jours* (Paris, 1996).

Runciman, Steven. "The Holy Lance Found at Antioch," *Analecta Bollandiana* 68 (1950), pp. 197–209.

Russell, Frederick H. *The Just War in the Middle Ages* (Cambridge, 1975).

Schieffer, Rudolf. *Die Entstehung des päpstlichen Investiturverbots für den deutschen König* (Stuttgart, 1981).

Schieffer, Theodor. *Angelsachsen und Franken: Zwei Studien zur Kirchengeschichte des 8. Jahrhunderts* (Wiesbaden, 1950).

Schmandt, Raymond H. "The Fourth Crusade and Just War Theory," *The Catholic Historical Review* 61 (1975), pp. 191–221.

Schmitz, Gerhard. "Die Waffe der Fälschung zum Schutz der Bedrängten? Bemerkungen zu gefälschten Konzils-und Kapitilarientexten," in *Fälschungen im Mittelalter: Internationaler Kongress der Monumenta Germaniae Historica*, 5 vols. (Hanover, 1988), II: 79–110.

The Second Crusade and the Cistercians, ed. Michael Gervers (New York, 1992).

Semmler, Joseph. "Bonifatius, die Karolinger, und die Franken," in *Mönchtum-Kirche-Herrschaft, 750–1000*, ed. Dieter R. Bauer, Rudolf Hiestand, Brigitte Kasten, and Sönke Lorenz (Sigmaringen, 1998), pp. 3–49.

Shopkow, Leah. *History and Community: Norman Historical Writing in the Eleventh and Twelfth Centuries* (Washington, D.C., 1997).

Somerville, Robert. "The Council of Clermont and the First Crusade," *Studia Gratiana* 20 (1976), pp. 323–37.

Southern, Richard W. "Aspects of the European Tradition of Historical Writing: 1. The Classical Tradition from Einhard to Geoffrey of Monmouth," *Transactions of the Royal Historical Society*, 5th ser. 20 (1970), pp. 173–96.

Speidel, Michael P. *The Religion of Iuppiter Dolichenus in the Roman Army* (Leiden, 1978).

Spiegel, Gabrielle M. "The Cult of Saint Denis and Capetian Kingship," *Journal of Medieval History* I (1975), pp. 43–70.

Sprandel, Rolf. *Ivo von Chartres und seine Stellung in der Kirchengeschichte* (Stuttgart, 1962).

Stelzer, Winfrid. "Die Rezeption des gelehrten Rechts nördlich der Alpen," in *Kommunikation und Mobilität im Mittelalter: Begegnungen zwischen dem Süden und der Mitte Europas (11.–14. Jahrhundert)*, ed. Siegfried de Rachewitz and Joseph Riedmann (Sigmaringen, 1995), pp. 231–47.

Strayer, Joseph R. *The Albigensian Crusades*, 2nd edn (Ann Arbor, 1992).

Strickland, Matthew. *War and Chivalry: The Conduct and Perception of War in England and Normandy 1066–1217* (Cambridge, 1996).

Tyerman, Christopher. *England and the Crusades 1095–1588* (Chicago, 1988).

Van Houts, Elisabeth. "The Memory of 1066 in Written and Oral Traditions," *Anglo-Norman Studies* 19 (1996), pp. 167–80.

———. "The Norman Conquest Through European Eyes," *English Historical Review* 110 (1995), pp. 832–53.

Vauchez, André. *Les laïcs au moyen âge: pratiques et expériences religieuses* (Paris, 1987).

———. "Présentation," in *Faire croire, modalités de la diffusion et de la réception des messages religieux du XIIIe au XVe siècle* (Rome, 1981).

Vaughn, Pamela. "The Identification and Retrieval of the Hoplite Battle-Dead," *Hoplites: The Classical Greek Battle Experience*, ed. Victor Davis Hanson (London, 1991), pp. 38–62.

Verbruggen, J.F. *The Art of Warfare in Western Europe During the Middle Ages from the Eighth Century to 1340*, 2nd edn, trans. Sumner Ward and Mrs R.W. Southern (Woodbridge, 1997).

Vieillefond, J.-R. "Les pratiques religieuses dans l'armée byzantine d'après les traités militaires," *Revue des études anciennes* 37 (1935), pp. 322–30.

Vodola, Elisabeth. "Sovereignty and Tabu: Evolution of the Sanction against Communication with Excommunicates. Part 1: Gregory VII," in *The Church and Sovereignty c. 500–1918: Essays in Honour of Michael Wilks*, ed. Diana Wood (London, 1991), pp. 35–55.

Vogel, Cyrille. "Les rituals de la pénitence tarifée," in *Liturgica opera divina e umana, studi offerti à S.E. Mons A. Bugnini: Bibliotheca 'ephemerides liturgicae' subsidia* 26 (Rome, 1982), pp. 419–27.

———. *Le pécheur et la pénitence au moyen âge* (Paris, 1969).

———. *La discipline pénitentielle en Gaule: des origines à fin du VIIe siècle* (Paris, 1952).

Von Haehling, Raban. *Die Religionszugehörigkeit der hohen Amtsträger des Römischen Reiches seit Constantins I.: Alleinherrschaft bis zum Ende der Theodosianischen Dynastie* (Bonn, 1978).

Wallach, Liutpold. "Alcuin on Virtues and Vices: A Manual for a Carolingian Soldier," *The Harvard Theological Review* 48 (1955), pp. 75–95.

Watson, G.R. *The Roman Soldier* (Ithaca, 1969).

Webb, Diana M. "The Cities of God: The Italian Communes at War," *Studies in Church History* 20: *The Church and War*, ed. W.J. Sheils (1983), pp. 111–27.

Webster, Graham. *The Roman Imperial Army of the First and Second Centuries A.D.*, 3rd edn (Totowa, 1985).

Weinrich, L. "Laurentius-Vehrehrung in ottonischer Zeit," *Jahrbuch für die Geschichte Mittel-und Ostdeutschlands* 21 (1972), pp. 45–66.

Werner, Karl Ferdinand. "Hludovicus Augustus: gouverner l'empire chrétien – idées et réalitès," in *Charlemagne's Heir: New Perspectives on the Reign of Louis the Pious (814–840)*, ed. Peter Godman and Roger Collins (Oxford, 1990), pp. 3–123.

————. "Heeresorganization und Kriegführung im deutschen Königreich des 10. und 11. Jahrhunderts, "*Ordinamenti Militari in Occidente nell'Alto Medioevo: Settimane di Studio del Centro Italiano di Studi sull'Alto Medioevo* 15 (Spoleto, 1968), pp. 791–843.

Whitelock, Dorothy. "After Bede: Jarrow Lecture 1960" (Jarrow, 1960).

Wolf, Kenneth Baxter. *Making History: The Normans and their Historians in Eleventh-Century Italy* (Philadelphia, 1995).

Wright, Roger. Review of *Vive voce: communication ècrite et communication orale du IVe au IXe siècle en occident latin* in *The Journal of Medieval Latin* 3 (1993), pp. 78–94.

Index

Warfare in History

The Battle of Hastings: Sources and Interpretations
edited and introduced by Stephen Morillo

Infantry Warfare in the Early Fourteenth Century:
Discipline, Tactics, and Technology
Kelly DeVries

The Art of Warfare in Western Europe during
the Middle Ages, from the Eighth Century to 1340 (second edition)
J.F. Verbruggen

Knights and Peasants:
The Hundred Years War in the French Countryside
Nicholas Wright

Society at War:
The Experience of England and France during the Hundred Years War
edited by Christopher Allmand

The Circle of War in the Middle Ages:
Essays on Medieval Military and Naval History
edited by Donald J. Kagay and L. J. Andrew Villalon

The Anglo-Scots Wars, 1513–1550: A Military History
Gervase Phillips

The Norwegian Invasion of England in 1066
Kelly DeVries

The Wars of Edward III: Sources and Interpretations
edited and introduced by Clifford J. Rogers

The Battle of Agincourt: Sources and Interpretations
Anne Curry

War Cruel and Sharp:
English Strategy under Edward III, 1327–1360
Clifford J. Rogers

The Normans and their Adversaries at War:
Essays in Memory of C. Warren Hollister
edited by Richard P. Abels and Bernard S. Bachrach

The Battle of the Golden Spurs (Courtrai, 11 July 1302)
A Contribution to the History of Flanders' War of Liberation
J.F. Verbruggen

War at Sea in the Middle Ages and Renaissance
edited by John B. Hattendorf and Richard W. Unger

Swein Forkbeard's Invasions and the Danish Conquest of England, 991–1017
Ian Howard